# INFLECTIONAL PARADIGMS

Sometimes dismissed as linguistically epiphenomenal, inflectional paradigms are, in reality, the interface of a language's morphology with its syntax and semantics. Drawing on abundant evidence from a wide range of languages (French, Hua, Hungarian, Kashmiri, Latin, Nepali, Noon, Old Norse, Sanskrit, Turkish, Twi, and others), Stump examines a variety of mismatches between words' content and form, including morphomic patterns, defectiveness, overabundance, syncretism, suppletion, deponency, and polyfunctionality. He demonstrates that such mismatches motivate a new grammatical architecture in which two kinds of paradigms are distinguished: *content paradigms*, which determine word forms' syntactic distribution and semantic interpretation, and *form paradigms*, which determine their inflectional realization. In this framework, the often nontrivial linkage between a lexeme's content paradigm and its stems' form paradigm is the nexus at which incongruities of content and form are resolved. Stump presents clear and precise analyses of a range of morphological phenomena in support of this theoretical innovation.

GREGORY STUMP is a Professor of linguistics at the University of Kentucky. His principal research area is the theory and typology of complex systems of inflectional morphology.

## In this series

Earlier issues not listed are also available

# CAMBRIDGE STUDIES IN LINGUISTICS

*Inflectional Paradigms*

# INFLECTIONAL PARADIGMS

## CONTENT AND FORM AT THE SYNTAX–MORPHOLOGY INTERFACE

GREGORY STUMP

*University of Kentucky*

## CAMBRIDGE
### UNIVERSITY PRESS

Shaftesbury Road, Cambridge CB2 8EA, United Kingdom

One Liberty Plaza, 20th Floor, New York, NY 10006, USA

477 Williamstown Road, Port Melbourne, VIC 3207, Australia

314–321, 3rd Floor, Plot 3, Splendor Forum, Jasola District Centre, New Delhi – 110025, India

103 Penang Road, #05–06/07, Visioncrest Commercial, Singapore 238467

Cambridge University Press is part of Cambridge University Press & Assessment, a department of the University of Cambridge.

We share the University's mission to contribute to society through the pursuit of education, learning and research at the highest international levels of excellence.

www.cambridge.org
Information on this title: www.cambridge.org/9781107460850

First published 2016

*A catalogue record for this publication is available from the British Library*

ISBN    978-1-107-08883-2    Hardback
ISBN    978-1-107-46085-0    Paperback

For Marcia and Jorie

# Contents

# *Figures*

# Tables

# *Acknowledgements*

---

I must thank a number of people for their invaluable contributions to the realization of this book. I wish to thank the Laboratoire de Linguistique Formelle at the Université Paris–Diderot for inviting me to present much of this material there in early 2013; my progress on this book benefited from the discussions afforded by this exceptional opportunity. I particularly thank Olivier Bonami, Berthold Crysmann, Bernard Fradin, Philip Miller, Jana Strnadová and Géraldine Walther for their valuable perspectives.

I likewise wish to thank the members of the Surrey Morphology Group for extremely fruitful discussions on a number of different occasions. In developing the ideas in this book, I have especially profited from the comments and criticisms offered by Greville Corbett, Matthew Baerman, Dunstan Brown and Marina Chumakina.

A number of colleagues at other institutions have been similarly helpful in helping me (or forcing me) to sharpen the theoretical outlook advocated here. I especially thank Farrell Ackerman, Jim Blevins, Gilles Boyé, Alice Harris, Brian Joseph, Ana Luís, Rob Malouf, Erich Round, Andrea Sims, Andrew Spencer, Pavol Štekauer, Tom Stewart and Delphine Tribout.

Colleagues at the University of Kentucky have contributed in all kinds of ways to the realization of this research. I am sincerely indebted to Raphael Finkel, Fabiola Henri and Andrew Hippisley.

I must thank a number of students at the University of Kentucky for discussing a variety of issues under consideration here; I am specially grateful to Anfal Ali, Noor Bueasa, Eleanor Feltner, Nathan Hardymon, Amelia Holloway, Razia Husain, Ben Jones, Jo Mackby, Sedigheh Moradi and Joseph Rhyne.

I wish to thank the researchers on whose work I have depended in developing the ideas presented here. I have already mentioned a number of them above. The remainder are simply too numerous to list encyclopedically, but among them, I must at least single out Stephen Anderson, Mark Aronoff, Gerald Gazdar, Peter Matthews, Richard Montague and Arnold Zwicky for their foundational contributions to understanding the architecture of natural language.

Finally, I thank Andrew Winnard, Bethany Gaunt, Robert Judkins, Damian Love and their colleagues at Cambridge University Press for their help and advice.

# Abbreviations

| | |
|---|---|
| 1 | first person |
| 2 | second person |
| 3 | third person |
| Ā | *ātmanepada*, Sanskrit middle voice |
| Ab, abl | ablative |
| **AbG** | ablative/genitive morphome (Sanskrit) |
| Ac, acc | accusative |
| act | active |
| aff | affirmative |
| AGR | agreement |
| aor | aorist |
| APP | applicative |
| ART | article |
| ASP | aspect |
| BEN | benefactive |
| CAUS | causative |
| CL | class |
| CLF | classifier |
| COL | column |
| CONC | concord |
| cond | conditional |
| COP | copula |
| copsbj | copula subject |
| COS | change of state |
| CTRL | controller |
| D, dat | dative |
| **DAb** | dative/ablative morphome (Sanskrit) |
| def | definite |
| dem | demonstrative |
| dobj | dative object |
| du | dual |

| | |
|---|---|
| excl | exclusive |
| exclam | exclamatory |
| f., fem | feminine |
| FCD | Function Composition Default |
| fut | future |
| FV | final vowel |
| G, gen | genitive |
| GEND | gender |
| **GL** | genitive/locative morphome (Sanskrit) |
| hab | habitual |
| HON | honorific |
| **IDAb** | instrumental/dative/ablative morphome (Sanskrit) |
| IFD | Identity Function Default |
| imp | imperative |
| impf | imperfect |
| incl | inclusive |
| ind | indicative |
| inf | infinitive |
| INFL | inflection |
| ins | instrumental |
| intrg | interrogative |
| iobj | indirect object |
| ipfv | imperfective |
| ki/vi | Swahili gender (Meinhof 7/8) |
| L, loc | locative, location |
| m., masc | masculine |
| m/wa | Swahili gender (Meinhof 1/2) |
| masc | masculine |
| mid | middle |
| n., neut | neuter |
| N, nom | nominative |
| narr | narrative |
| neg | negative |
| NMLZ | nominalizer |
| nonpret | nonpreterite |
| NUM | number |
| **NV** | nominative/vocative morphome (Sanskrit) |
| **NVA** | nominative/vocative/accusative morphome (Sanskrit) |
| OBJ | object agreement |

| | |
|---|---|
| opt | optative |
| P | *parasmaipada*, Sanskrit active voice |
| pass | passive |
| PCL | particle |
| PER | person |
| perf | perfect |
| pfv | perfective |
| pl | plural |
| POSS | possessor |
| pret | preterite |
| PROG | progressive |
| prs | present |
| pst | past |
| ptcp | participle |
| punct | punctual |
| rel | relational |
| SBJ | subject agreement |
| sbjv | subjunctive |
| sg | singular |
| TNS | tense |
| TRANS | transitivizing suffix |
| VCE | voice |
| voc | vocative |

# Symbols and operators

| | |
|---|---|
| $m \geq n$ | $m$ is greater than or equal to $n$ |
| $\sigma:\{x\}$ | metalinguistic variable over property sets of which $\{x\}$ is a subset |
| $\neg p$ | not $p$ |
| $p \wedge q$ | $p$ and $q$ |
| $p = q$ | $p$ equals $q$ |
| $p \supset q$ | $p$ implies $q$ |
| $p \equiv q$ | $p$ is logically equivalent to $q$ |
| $p \neq q$ | $p$ is not equal to $q$ |
| $p \vee q$ | $p$ or $q$ |
| $\sigma \cap \tau$ | the intersection of $\sigma$ and $\tau$ |
| $\sigma[x/y]$ | the set that results from substituting $y$ for $x$ in $\sigma$ |
| $\sigma \backslash \tau$ | the set $\{x \mid x \in \sigma$ but $x \notin \tau\}$ |
| $\sigma \sqcup \tau$ | the unification of $\sigma$ and $\tau$ |
| $\sigma \cup \tau$ | the union of $\sigma$ and $\tau$ |
| $x \in \sigma$ | $x$ is a member of $\sigma$ |
| $x \notin \sigma$ | $x$ is not a member of $\sigma$ |
| $\tau \sqsubseteq \sigma$ | $\sigma$ is an extension of $\tau$ |
| $\tau \subseteq \sigma$ | $\tau$ is a subset of $\sigma$ |

# *Introduction*

In recent years, a growing number of linguists have arrived at the conviction that inflectional paradigms play an essential role in the definition of a language's grammar and lexicon. Research on the properties and significance of inflectional paradigms is now being conducted in many subdisciplines of linguistics, including grammatical theory (e.g. Stump 2001, Blevins 2006, Ackerman, Blevins and Malouf 2009, Round 2013, O'Neill 2014, and the contributions to Plank 1990), language typology (Carstairs 1987, Baerman et al. 2005, 2007, 2010, Chumakina and Corbett 2013, Stump and Finkel 2013), historical linguistics (Fuß 2005, Maiden et al. 2011, Cruschina et al. 2013, Gardani 2013, Fertig 2013), psycholinguistics (Baayen and Schreuder 2003, Bittner et al. 2003, Milin et al. 2009) and computational linguistics (Beesley and Karttunen 2003, Brown and Hippisley 2012).

My purpose here is to examine the theoretical indispensability of inflectional paradigms, and in particular, their role as a grammatical interface. Thus, at the most general level, I am concerned with asserting two hypotheses about inflectional paradigms: (i) the *irreducibility hypothesis*, according to which some morphological regularities are, irreducibly, regularities in paradigm structure; and (ii) the *interface hypothesis*, according to which a language's paradigms are the interface of its inflectional morphology with its syntax and semantics. At a more concrete level, I will propose and justify a formal theory of inflectional morphology that is compatible with the irreducibility and interface hypotheses. This theory, the *paradigm-linkage theory*, was first proposed by Stump 2002, and was subsequently elaborated on by Ackerman and Stump 2004, Ackerman, Stump and Webelhuth 2011, Spencer and Stump 2013, Stewart and Stump 2007, Stump 2006, 2010, 2012, 2014a, 2015, Stump: to appear A, Stump: to appear B. O'Neill 2011, 2013 and Round 2013 have also advanced proposals that are closely akin to the paradigm-linkage theory, and the analysis of Nepali verb inflection proposed by Bonami and Boyé (2008, 2010) has important similarities as well.[1]

The gist of the paradigm-linkage theory is that the definition of a language's inflectional morphology is based on three interlocking kinds of paradigms. A lexeme L's **content paradigm** identifies the range of morphosyntactic property sets with which L is associated in syntax and which determine L's semantic interpretation in accordance with its syntactic context; a stem X's **form paradigm** identifies the range of property sets for which the various word forms arising from X are inflected; and a lexeme L's **realized paradigm** associates each of L's fully inflected word forms with the content that it expresses. Canonically, a lexeme's content paradigm is isomorphic to the form paradigm of its stem and to its realized paradigm; but this isomorphic relationship is often disrupted by a variety of disparate morphological phenomena, including defectiveness, overabundance, syncretism, suppletion, heteroclisis, homomorphy, deponency, polyfunctionality and morphomically conditioned inflection.

This new conception of inflectional paradigms affords new explanations for synchronic mismatches between a word's content and its morphological form. It is a novel but natural extension of the inferential-realizational theories of inflection proposed by Matthews 1972, Anderson 1992 and Stump 2001. Like them, it entails that morphology is an autonomous domain of linguistic structure; but it is set apart by its premise that the definition of a language's inflectional morphology must account not only for patterns of inflectional exponence, but for the sometimes complex linkage between content and form that these patterns entail.

The book can be seen as comprising two parts. The first part (Chapters 1–6) lays the book's conceptual groundwork; the second (Chapters 7–14) proposes and motivates the paradigm-linkage theory.

**Chapter 1** ("What are inflectional paradigms?") introduces the notion of an inflectional paradigm and its relevance to morphology, syntax and semantics. Current theories of grammar are in stark disagreement over the significance of inflectional paradigms; some hold that paradigms are merely an epiphenomenon of principles of morpheme combination and therefore have no role in the definition of a language's inflectional morphology; others maintain that the definition of a language's inflectional morphology makes essential reference to the structure of paradigms. I discuss the numerous shortcomings of a morpheme-based conception of inflectional morphology and present two hypotheses that assume a paradigm-based approach.

---

1 I discuss these similarities in Chapter 8.

Drawing on the principles of canonical typology (Corbett 2005, 2009, Brown et al. 2013), **Chapter 2** ("Canonical inflectional paradigms") develops the notion of a canonical inflectional paradigm: a typological idealization relative to which the inflectional paradigms of natural languages may be compared. A morpheme-based approach to inflection would suffice if inflectional paradigms were always canonical; but as I demonstrate at length in this book, actual inflectional paradigms deviate from the canonical ideal in a variety of ways, and each such deviation engenders a different kind of problem for morpheme-based inflection. Even so, the notion of a canonical inflectional paradigm provides a crucial point of reference for the discussion of such phenomena.

The inflectional paradigm of a lexeme may be seen as a set of cells, each cell being the pairing of a word's lexical and morphosyntactic content with its morphological form. In order to develop and refine this preliminary conception of inflectional paradigms, it is essential to understand its fundamental components. Chapters 3–6 accordingly present a detailed explanation of four basic notions: morphosyntactic properties, lexemes, stems and inflection classes.

**Chapter 3** ("Morphosyntactic properties") is a detailed examination of the nature of morphosyntactic properties (or "features," Corbett 2012). Morphosyntactic properties are part of the shared vocabulary of morphology, syntax and semantics. They serve in syntax to determine a word form's distribution with respect to other constituents and to regulate its relations with other parts of a sentence; in morphology, they determine the inflectional exponents involved in a word form's phonological expression; and at least some morphosyntactic properties are associated with specific semantic content. In order to understand the structure of inflectional paradigms, it is essential to be precise about the characteristics of morphosyntactic properties – their association with syntactic categories, the ways in which they may be associated with word forms, the ways in which they combine, the logical relations that may exist between different sets of morphosyntactic properties, property constraints and their satisfaction, and the nature of morphosyntactic properties' exponence.

**Chapter 4** ("Lexemes") presents a detailed discussion of the notion "lexeme," a lexical abstraction allowing distinct word forms to be classified according to their shared lexical content and contrasting morphosyntactic content. Lexemes are central to understanding the organization of a language's lexicon, but cannot simply be identified with lexical entries. A language's lexemes are intuitively regarded as differing from one another in both content and form, but this, too, is an oversimplification.

**Chapter 5** ("Stems") is a detailed account of the role of stems in the definition of inflectional paradigms. In the simplest cases, the same stem serves as the basis for every word form in a lexeme's paradigm. But a lexeme's inflection often depends on more than one stem. Stem alternations within a lexeme's inflectional paradigm are of various kinds. Sandhi alternations are purely an effect of automatic phonology. Among nonautomatic alternations, some are phonologically conditioned and others grammatically conditioned; crosscutting this distinction is a distinction between **class-determined** alternations (alternations that follow from membership in a particular inflection class) and **class-independent** alternations (alternations that are not simply an effect of membership in a particular inflection class); and grammatically conditioned stem alternations may themselves be morphosyntactically conditioned (in which each alternant is invariably associated with a particular morphosyntactic property set) or **morphomic** (Aronoff 1994), following a distributional pattern whose significance is purely morphological, with no invariant phonological, syntactic or semantic correlate.

Languages with rich inflectional systems frequently exhibit contrasting inflection classes, each of which is associated with its own particular inventory of inflectional markings; examples are the Latin declension classes and conjugation classes. In **Chapter 6** ("Inflection classes"), I discuss the properties of such classes, distinguishing between global inflection classes (which determine full paradigms) and segregated inflection classes (which determine specific subparadigms). I address the important question of what inflection classes are classes of; as I show, the standard assumption that they are classes of lexemes is difficult to reconcile with the phenomenon of heteroclisis (Stump 2006), which instead favors the assumption that they are classes of stems. While inflection classes are often distinguished by different inventories of affixes, they are very frequently distinguished by their patterns of stem formation and stem alternation.

If all inflectional paradigms conformed to the canonical ideal described in Chapter 2, there would be no reason to attribute any theoretical significance to them, since each of a lexeme's word forms could be seen as arising through a simple "spelling out" of its associated morphosyntactic properties. But inflectional paradigms rarely conform to the canonical ideal; on the contrary, there are numerous ways in which content and form may be misaligned in a lexeme's inflectional realization; such misalignments invariably involve patterns defined not over individual word forms but over inflectional paradigms. The second part of the book comprises detailed examinations of the different kinds of misalignment observed in the world's languages and the development of a theory of inflectional morphology that is compatible with the full range of observed misalignments.

As a preliminary to this presentation, **Chapter 7** ("A conception of the relation of content to form in inflectional paradigms") distinguishes three ways of conceiving of inflectional paradigms (Stump 2002, 2006, Stewart and Stump 2007).

- A lexeme L's content paradigm enumerates the morphosyntactic property sets with which L may be associated in syntax and semantics. The cells in this paradigm ("content cells") are therefore pairings of the lexeme L with each relevant morphosyntactic property set σ: ⟨L, σ⟩.
- A stem X's form paradigm specifies the range of property sets that may be realized through the inflection of X. The cells in this paradigm ("form cells") are therefore pairings of the stem X with each relevant property set τ: ⟨X, τ⟩.
- The realized paradigm of a stem X is the smallest set R such that for each pairing ⟨X, τ⟩ in X's form paradigm, ⟨*w*, τ⟩ belongs to R if and only if *w* realizes X and τ.

In general, each content cell is realized by being linked to a form cell whose realization it shares; this form cell is the content cell's **form correspondent**. In the canonical case, a lexeme L has a single stem X such that each content cell ⟨L, σ⟩ in L's content paradigm has ⟨X, σ⟩ as its form correspondent, so that ⟨L, σ⟩ and ⟨X, σ⟩ share a realization ⟨w, σ⟩. In noncanonical cases, however, the correspondence between content cells and form cells is more complex; each such case involves one or another kind of mismatch between content and form.

Mismatches can be observed at different levels of granularity. Some can be observed within a single paradigm (Chapters 8–11). Others can only be seen by comparing distinct paradigms belonging to the same category (Chapter 12) or to different categories (Chapter 13). In **Chapter 8** ("Morphomic properties"), I discuss several noncanonical systems of inflection in which the grammatical distinctions relevant for a lexeme's syntax are neither identical nor isomorphic to those relevant for its inflectional realization; these include the systems of subject–verb agreement in Hua and Nepali, the system of tenses in Twi, and the system of verb inflection in Noon. I show that in these systems, a lexeme's inflected forms are not directly determined by the morphosyntactic property sets relevant to their syntax, but instead involve the realization of **morphomic** properties (Aronoff 1994) – properties whose sole motivation is morphological. Thus, these systems involve a mismatch between the property sets distinguishing the cells of a lexeme's content paradigm and the property sets distinguishing the cells of its stem's form paradigm.

**Chapter 9** ("Too many cells, too few cells") examines cases in which a content cell fails to correspond to any form cell (and hence lacks a realization) as well as cases in which a lexeme has more realizations than expected. Instances of this latter sort include cases of overabundance, in which a lexeme has more than one realization for the same morphosyntactic property set (as with English *dreamed* and *dreamt*); cases of overdifferentiation, in which a lexeme's inflection expresses more morphosyntactic distinctions than are normal for members of its syntactic category (as with English *am* and *are*); and cases of shape alternation, in which synonymous word forms are restricted to complementary phonological or syntactic contexts (as with English *my* and *mine*).

**Chapter 10** ("Syncretism") examines the very widespread phenomenon of syncretism: the realization of distinct cells in a paradigm by the same word form. In general, syncretism involves two or more content cells sharing a single form correspondent, but such instances arise in more than one way. Natural-class syncretisms arise only because no rule of inflectional realization is sensitive to the morphosyntactic distinction between the syncretized cells; other syncretisms are directly stipulated by rules of morphology. These stipulated syncretisms include directional syncretisms (which arise when the realization of one property set systematically patterns after that of some distinct property set) and morphomic syncretisms (which arise when two property sets that do not form a natural class are nevertheless alike in their realization and neither set is associated with that realization independently of the other set).

**Chapter 11** ("Suppletion and heteroclisis") focuses on the related phenomena of suppletion (the replacement of one stem by a morphophonologically unrelated stem in a lexeme's inflectional paradigm) and heteroclisis (suppletion of stems belonging to distinct inflection classes). Suppletion and heteroclisis reflect two dimensions of variation among class-independent stems: they may differ in form in a way that is not predicted by their inflection-class membership (and may, in that case, still be members of the same inflection class); instead or in addition, they may differ in their inflection-class membership (and may, in that case, still be alike in form). Though suppletion is seen as a kind of irregularity, it does exhibit certain cross-linguistic regularities.

Another well-documented phenomenon involving a mismatch of content and form is that of deponency. In **Chapter 12** ("Deponency and metaconjugation"), I discuss deponent paradigms, in which morphology that ordinarily serves to realize one class of morphosyntactic property sets is instead used to realize a contrasting class of property sets. In Latin, for example, deponent verbs possess the morphology usual for passives but exhibit the syntax and semantics of active verbs. Deponency involving morphosyntactic properties other than properties of voice are observable in a number of languages. I distinguish deponency from metaconjugation, the realization of content-level morphosyntactic contrasts as form-level distinctions in inflection-class membership.

In **Chapter 13** ("Polyfunctionality"), I discuss a final phenomenon in which a difference of content between two paradigm cells coincides with a similarity in form. This is the phenomenon of polyfunctionality, the systematic use of the same morphology for different purposes. Instances of polyfunctionality vary widely in their characteristics. In some cases, the same morphology has more than one use in the inflection of the same class of lexemes. In other instances, the same morphology expresses one kind of content in the inflection of one category of lexemes and a distinct kind of content in the inflection of a distinct category of lexemes. Examples of these sorts show that languages often put the same morphology to more than one use in expressing the inventory of grammatical contrasts relevant to syntax; that is, content cells that are different may nevertheless have form correspondents and realized cells that are alike.

**Chapter 14** ("A theoretical synopsis and two further issues") presents a summary of the formalization proposed for the paradigm-linkage theory over the course of Chapters 7–13, then addresses two issues pertinent to its formalization and application. The first of these concerns the possibility of paring down the paradigm-linkage theory by adopting a purely abstractive approach to inflectional exponence (Blevins 2006); adopting such an approach would seem to open the possibility of eliminating form paradigms from the paradigm-linkage architecture, but as I show, there are good reasons not to pursue this strategy. The second issue relates to the relevance of paradigm linkage to morphological change; as I show, the proposed theoretical architecture sheds important light on the sometimes conflicting pressures that affect the evolution of inflectional systems.

The evidence presented here shows that inflectional paradigms constitute a theoretically indispensable grammatical interface; this evidence motivates the development of a theory of inflectional morphology with the essential characteristics of the paradigm-linkage theory.

# 1 *What are inflectional paradigms?*

In this chapter, I examine the defining characteristics of inflectional paradigms (Section 1.1). A central issue in morphological theory is whether inflectional paradigms have theoretical significance. According to paradigm-based theories of inflection (e.g. those of Stump 2001, Blevins 2006, Ackerman, Blevins and Malouf 2009, Brown and Hippisley 2012), the definition of a language's inflectional morphology makes essential reference to the structure of paradigms; but according to morpheme-based theories (e.g. those of Halle and Marantz 1993, Bobaljik 2002, Müller 2002), paradigms are instead merely an epiphenomenal effect of principles of morpheme combination, having no essential role in the definition of a language's inflectional morphology. I compare the morpheme-based perspective (Section 1.2) with the paradigm-based approach (Section 1.3); of these, only the latter is compatible with two central hypotheses for which I argue in this book: the irreducibility hypothesis and the interface hypothesis.

## 1.1    *What is an inflectional paradigm?*

In a language with inflectional morphology, **morphosyntactic properties** are grammatical properties to which the language's syntax and morphology are both sensitive. In French, for example, the gender properties "feminine" and "masculine" and the number properties "singular" and "plural" are morphosyntactic properties. On one hand, syntactic agreement relations are sensitive to contrasts in gender and number; thus, the noun phrase in (1) is grammatical because its constituents agree in gender and number, and the noun phrase in (2) is ungrammatical because its constituents fail to agree in this way. At the same time, rules of inflectional morphology are likewise sensitive to contrasts in gender and number; thus, the French adjective NATIONAL has distinct feminine and masculine forms in the plural (feminine plural *nationales* /nasjɔnal/, masculine plural *nationaux* /nasjɔno/), while in the singular, the feminine and masculine forms of NATIONAL are distinguished orthographically though not phonologically (feminine singular *nationale*, masculine singular *national*, both /nasjɔnal/).

(1)     *les*     *musées*        *nationaux*
        the.PL  museum.MASC.PL  national.MASC.PL
        the  national museums'

(2)     *\*le*         *musées*        *nationales*
        the.MASC.SG  museum.MASC.PL  national.FEM.PL

Some morphosyntactic properties have specific semantic correlates; thus, noun phrases with singular reference tend to be headed by nouns in their singular form. But morphosyntactic properties may also lack any obvious semantic correlate; thus, while noun phrases with female reference may tend to be headed by feminine nouns, some feminine nouns (e.g. *recrue* 'recruit,' *sentinelle* 'sentinel') ordinarily have male reference and others – in fact, the large majority – fail to refer specifically to either sex (*souris* 'mouse,' *table* 'table,' *invention* 'invention,' and so on). Even so, a French noun's gender may be seen as part of its content, if content is assumed to encompass properties whose significance is either semantic or primarily grammatical.

The **inflectional categories** ("features")[1] of gender and number crosscut each other in the inflection of French adjectives: "feminine" and "masculine" combine with "singular" and "plural" to define a matrix of up to four (orthographic) word forms for each adjective, as in (3). Each gender/number combination is a combination of morphosyntactic properties arising in syntax, and each adjectival word form expresses one or more such combinations.

(3)                    Feminine   Masculine
        Singular  *nationale*   *national*
        Plural    *nationales*  *nationaux*

In order to understand the structure of such matrices, it pays to be precise about a number of conceptual distinctions. First, the semantico-grammatical content shared by the word forms in such a matrix constitutes the **lexeme** realized by those word forms; thus, the content shared by the word forms in (3) is the

---

1 I favor the term "inflectional category" over "feature"; the latter term tends to be used imprecisely, sometimes referring to true inflectional categories (e.g. tense) and sometimes to specific morphosyntactic properties (e.g. past tense).

French adjectival lexeme NATIONAL. Because a lexeme is composed of elements of semantic and grammatical content, it is not a linguistic form; rather, it is expressed by linguistic forms. One cannot equate a lexeme with the stem common to all the linguistic forms that express it, since for some lexemes, there is no such stem; in French, for example, the lexeme ALLER ģo' is realized by *vais* /vɛ/ I go,' *allons* /alɔ̃/ ẁ e go,' and *iras* /iʁa/ ẏou (sg) will go' (among other word forms), which share no part of their form. I follow the convention of representing lexemes in SMALL CAPITAL letters; but such representations are to be understood as referring to an abstract combination of semantic and grammatical properties.[2]

Each of a lexeme's word forms expresses one or more of its cells, where a lexeme L's **cells** are form–content pairings. The content of each such pairing includes L and a complete and coherent morphosyntactic property set $\sigma$ compatible with L; the pairing's form is the inflected word form $w$ that realizes both L and $\sigma$. Thus, a cell pairing the lexical content of L and the morphosyntactic content of $\sigma$ with the word form $w$ may be represented as $\langle L, \sigma : w \rangle$. A lexeme's complete set of such cells is its **paradigm**. For example, the paradigm of French NATIONAL is the set of cells in (4).

(4)      The paradigm of French NATIONAL

   { ⟨NATIONAL, {e m sg} *nationale*⟩,   ⟨NATIONAL, {masc sg} : *national*⟩,
     ⟨NATIONAL, {e m pl} : *nationales*⟩,   ⟨NATIONAL, {masc pl} : *nationaux*⟩ }

In a cell $\langle L, \sigma : w \rangle$, the word form $w$ **realizes** (is the **realization** of)

- the lexeme L,
- the property set $\sigma$,
- the combined content of L and $\sigma$, and
- the cell itself.

In cases of gross irregularity, the word form $w$ in a cell $\langle L, \sigma : w \rangle$ is stipulated lexically; but more often, $w$ is deducible from L and $\sigma$. In particular, it is a language's inflectional morphology that ordinarily determines the form $w$ from the lexeme L and the property set $\sigma$ in a cell $\langle L, \sigma : w \rangle$.

Both within and across languages, lexemes' paradigms vary widely in shape and size. If a lexeme's realization is sensitive to a large number of crosscutting morphosyntactic properties, its paradigm comprises a correspondingly large number of word forms. This correspondence is complicated by the fact that

---

2 In Chapter 4, I examine the defining properties of lexemes in systematic detail.

the morphosyntactic properties belonging to a lexeme's inflectional categories don't always combine freely; in French, for example, the future tense is not distinguished from other tenses in any mood other than the indicative. Thus, the shape and size of a lexeme's paradigm depends on both (a) the inventory of crosscutting inflectional categories available to it and (b) the restrictions defining permissible combinations of the morphosyntactic properties constituting those categories.

In traditional grammatical descriptions, paradigms are customarily represented as tables; for example, the paradigm of French ALLER ġo' is typically represented as in Table 1.1. This mode of representation is both compact and precise, and will be employed throughout this book. But care should be taken not to misinterpret such tables.

The rows and columns in a table such as Table 1.1 are inevitably ordered: where two columns (or rows) appear together in a table, one must precede the other, given the graphic constraints imposed by all existing writing systems. But it is not clear that this ordering has any importance.[3] A paradigm is, again, a set of cells, and sets are unordered. The fact that first-person forms precede their second-person counterparts in Table 1.1 is purely a matter of convention; one could just as well represent the paradigm of ALLER with a table in which second-person forms preceded their first-person counterparts. (Indeed, the order of representation in traditional Sanskrit grammar has third person before second, followed by first person.)

Because of the order that it must arbitrarily impose, a two-dimensional table tends to obscure the multidimensional network of relations among the cells in a paradigm. For instance, the cell of *irai* (I will go') in Table 1.1 adjoins that of *iras* (ẏou (sg) will go') but is rather distant from that of *vais* (I go'). Even so, the morphosyntactic properties of *irai* differ from those of *iras* and *vais* to exactly the same extent: *irai* differs from *iras* only with respect to person and from *vais* only with respect to tense.

Despite these potentially misleading characteristics, tables are redeemed by the fact that every table is mechanically reducible to a single set of cells (= to a single paradigm); for example, Table 1.1 reduces to the unordered set of cells in (5). Moreover, tables give a more vivid visual impression of the crosscutting inflectional categories that form the basis for a lexeme's inflection.

---

3 Nevertheless, it has sometimes been argued that paradigms exhibit regularities that imply that their cells are ordered in some fashion; see Jakobson 1984 [1958], McCreight and Chvany 1991 and Nesset and Janda 2010.

Table 1.1 *The inflection of French* ALLER *'go'*

| | | Finite forms | | | | | | | | Non-finite forms | |
| --- | --- | --- | --- | --- | --- | --- | --- | --- | --- | --- | --- |
| | | Present | | Imperfect | | | | | | | |
| | | Indicative | Subjunctive | Indicative | Subjunctive | Preterite | Future | Conditional | Imperative | | |
| 1sg | | vais | aille | allais | allasse | allai | irai | irais | | Infinitive | aller |
| 2sg | | vas | ailles | allais | allasses | allas | iras | irais | va | Present participle | allant |
| 3sg | | va | aille | allait | allât | alla | ira | irait | | Past participle | allé |
| 1pl | | allons | allions | allions | allassions | allâmes | irons | irions | allons | | |
| 2pl | | allez | alliez | alliez | allassiez | allâtes | irez | iriez | allez | | |
| 3pl | | vont | aillent | allaient | allassent | allèrent | iront | iraient | | | |

(5)     Paradigm of French ALLER 'go'

{   ⟨ALLER, {1sg prs ind} : *vais*⟩                  ⟨ALLER, {1sg prs sbjv} : *aille*⟩
    ⟨ALLER, {2sg prs ind} : *vas*⟩                   ⟨ALLER, {2sg prs sbjv} : *ailles*⟩
    ⟨ALLER, {3sg prs ind} : *va*⟩                    ⟨ALLER, {3sg prs sbjv} : *aille*⟩
    ⟨ALLER, {1pl prs ind} : *allons*⟩                ⟨ALLER, {1pl prs sbjv} : *allions*⟩
    ⟨ALLER, {2pl prs ind} : *allez*⟩                 ⟨ALLER, {2pl prs sbjv} : *alliez*⟩
    ⟨ALLER, {3pl prs ind} : *vont*⟩                  ⟨ALLER, {3pl prs sbjv} : *aillent*⟩
    ⟨ALLER, {1sg pst ind} : *allai*⟩                 ⟨ALLER, {1sg fut ind} : *irai*⟩
    ⟨ALLER, {2sg pst ind} : *allas*⟩                 ⟨ALLER, {2sg fut ind} : *iras*⟩
    ⟨ALLER, {3sg pst ind} : *alla*⟩                  ⟨ALLER, {3sg fut ind} : *ira*⟩
    ⟨ALLER, {1pl pst ind} : *allâmes*⟩               ⟨ALLER, {1pl fut ind} : *irons*⟩
    ⟨ALLER, {2pl pst ind} : *allâtes*⟩               ⟨ALLER, {2pl fut ind} : *irez*⟩
    ⟨ALLER, {3pl pst ind} : *allèrent*⟩              ⟨ALLER, {3pl fut ind} : *iront*⟩
    ⟨ALLER, {1sg ipfv ind} : *allais*⟩               ⟨ALLER, {1sg ipfv sbjv} : *allasse*⟩
    ⟨ALLER, {2sg ipfv ind} : *allais*⟩               ⟨ALLER, {2sg ipfv sbjv} : *allasses*⟩
    ⟨ALLER, {3sg ipfv ind} : *allait*⟩               ⟨ALLER, {3sg ipfv sbjv} : *allât*⟩
    ⟨ALLER, {1pl ipfv ind} : *allions*⟩              ⟨ALLER, {1pl ipfv sbjv} : *allassions*⟩
    ⟨ALLER, {2pl ipfv ind} : *alliez*⟩               ⟨ALLER, {2pl ipfv sbjv} : *allassiez*⟩
    ⟨ALLER, {3pl ipfv ind} : *allaient*⟩             ⟨ALLER, {3pl ipfv sbjv} : *allassent*⟩
    ⟨ALLER, {1sg cond} : *irais*⟩                    ⟨ALLER, {2sg imp} : *va*⟩
    ⟨ALLER, {2sg cond} : *irais*⟩                    ⟨ALLER, {1pl imp} : *allons*⟩
    ⟨ALLER, {3sg cond} : *irait*⟩                    ⟨ALLER, {2pl imp} : *allez*⟩
    ⟨ALLER, {1pl cond} : *irions*⟩                   ⟨ALLER, {inf} : *aller*⟩
    ⟨ALLER, {2pl cond} : *iriez*⟩                    ⟨ALLER, {prs ptcp} : *allant*⟩
    ⟨ALLER, {3pl cond} : *iraient*⟩                  ⟨ALLER, {pst ptcp} : *allé*⟩}

Linguists disagree about whether inflectional paradigms are indispensable for the definition of a language's morphology. The view that they are dispensable – that they are nothing more than an epiphenomenal effect of the definition of a language's morphology – is one legacy of morpheme-based morphology, whose leading ideas include the representational determinism hypothesis (6).[4] I therefore distinguish morpheme-based theories of inflection (in which the RD hypothesis is seen as rendering any reference to paradigms unnecessary) from paradigm-based theories (according to which the definition of a language's inflectional morphology makes essential reference to the structure of paradigms).

(6)     The representational determinism (RD) hypothesis:
        The grammatical and semantic content of an inflected word form is fully
        determined by its representation as a combination of morphemes.

---

4  In modern linguistics, the term "morpheme" has been used (not always consistently) in two distinct ways. In the Bloomfieldian sense, a morpheme is a minimal meaningful string, e.g. the *-s* in *dogs* (Bloomfield 1933). In the later usage of Harris (1942) and Hockett (1947), a morpheme is a minimal unit of abstract grammatical factorization, e.g. the factor "plural" shared by *dogs*, *oxen* and *geese*. In this latter sense, it is not morphemes that are segmentable, but rather the morphs that realize them.

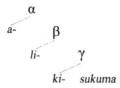

Figure 1.1 *The hierarchical structure of Swahili* alikisukuma *'s/he pushed it' under the RD hypothesis*

As a concrete illustration of the difference between morpheme-based and paradigm-based accounts of inflection, consider the Swahili sentence in (7). The verb in this sentence exhibits inflection for subject concord, tense, and object concord. The nouns MGENI 'stranger' and KIKAPU 'basket' belong to the *m/wa* and *ki/vi* genders, respectively; accordingly, the verb form *alikisukuma* 'pushed' exhibits the subject concord *a-* for singular nouns belonging to the *m/wa* gender and the object concord *ki-* for singular nouns belonging to the *ki/vi* gender.[5]

(7)    *m-geni*            *a-li-ki-sukuma*                 *ki-kapu.*
       GEND.NUM-stranger  SBJ.CONC-TNS-OBJ.CONC-push      GEND.NUM-basket
       The stranger pushed the basket.

In a morpheme-based analysis, the word form *alikisukuma* might be assigned the structure in Figure 1.1, in which α, β and γ represent syntactic categories associated with morphosyntactic property sets.

There are two ways in which the content of α, β and γ might be understood in a morpheme-based analysis. On one approach (that of e.g. Selkirk 1982, Lieber 1992), each of the prefixal morphemes *a-*, *li-* and *ki-* carries a morphosyntactic property set (as in (8)) and each joins with a verb stem X to produce a verb form [prefix X]. By convention, the morphosyntactic property set of a prefixed verb form [prefix X] is the union of that of the prefix with that of X. In this way, the structure of *alikisukuma* is as in Figure 1.2; in accordance with the RD hypothesis, this representation determines the morphosyntactic property set associated with the form *alikisukuma*. This is an **incremental**[6] approach to the elucidation of the structure in

---

5 Often, the concordial prefix by which a verb inflects for agreement with a noun belonging to a particular noun class is identical to the noun-class prefix by which that noun inflects for number; thus, in (7), the *ki-* in *alikisukuma* matches the *ki-* in *kikapu*. Not all concordial prefixes exhibit this sort of identity; thus, the *a-* in *alikisukuma* fails to match the *m-* in *mgeni*. See Ashton 1944: 12.

6 This terminology is taken from the taxonomy of theoretical approaches to inflection presented by Stump (2001: Ch.1). In this taxonomy, **incremental** theories are contrasted with **realizational** theories: in the former, exponents introduce morphosyntactic properties, while in the latter, morphosyntactic properties license the introduction of their exponents.

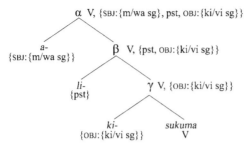

Figure 1.2 *The hierarchical structure of Swahili* alikisukuma *'s/he pushed it' under the RD hypothesis (incremental approach)*

Figure 1.1, whose morphosyntactic property set is assembled in increments as an effect of affix insertion.

(8)       *a-* :  {SBJ:{m/w a sg}
          *li-* :  {ps t}
          *ki-* :  {OBJ:{ki/vi  sg}

Another way in which a morpheme-based analysis might account for the content of α, β and γ in Figure 1.1 is to assume that the morphosyntactic property set of node α is determined by the syntax of Swahili – that the structure in Figure 1.1 arises through the successive application of head movement into three functional projections (which encode properties of subject agreement, tense and object agreement); in the resulting structure, Figure 1.3, branching nodes acquire the union of the morphosyntactic property sets of their daughter nodes. Each of the prefixal morphemes in (8) is then inserted into the nonbranching node of Figure 1.3 whose property set it matches. This is a **realizational** approach to the structure in Figure 1.1, since the prefixal morphemes serve to realize property sets that are independently specified in syntactic structure prior to affix insertion (cf. Halle and Marantz 1993, Noyer 1992, Harley and Noyer 1999).

In both of these morpheme-based analyses, a word form's representation uniquely determines its morphosyntactic content, in accordance with the RD hypothesis. Consider, on the other hand, a paradigm-based account, in which the verb form *alikisukuma* š /he pushed it' forms part of the cell

⟨SUKUMA, {SBJ:{m/w a sg} OBJ:{ki/vi s g} ps t}: *alikisukuma*⟩.

In this account, the morphosyntactic content of *alikisukuma* is determined not by the representation of the verb form itself, but by the cell that this representation occupies. In paradigm-based approaches to inflection, it is

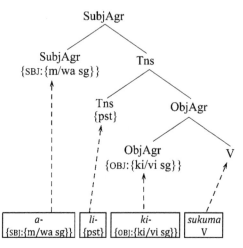

Figure 1.3 *The hierarchical structure of Swahili* alikisukuma *'s/he pushed it' under the RD hypothesis (realizational approach)*

customary to assume that the morphology of a word form *w* appearing in a cell $\langle$L, $\sigma$ : *w*$\rangle$ is deduced from L and $\sigma$ by means of **rules of exponence** realizing particular subsets of $\sigma$ (Zwicky 1985, Anderson 1992, Stump 2001). Thus, the word form *alikisukuma* is (contrary to the RD hypothesis) not represented as a combination of morphemes, nor is the morphosyntactic content of *alikisukuma* determined by its morphology. Indeed, the reverse is true: it is the property set

{SBJ:{m/w a sg} OBJ:{ki/vi s g}ps t}

together with the characteristics of the lexeme SUKUMA 'push' that determines the morphology of *alikisukuma*.

In the following sections, I compare the adequacy of morpheme-based theories of inflection with that of paradigm-based theories.

## 1.2    *Morpheme-based theories of inflection*

Proponents of morpheme-based approaches to inflectional morphology argue that paradigms are epiphenomenal because they play no essential role in analyses such as those sketched in Figures 1.2 and 1.3. But these analyses are ultimately not at all probative, because *alikisukuma* is so obviously amenable to a morpheme-based analysis. Its form–content relations are very simple: its morphology is purely agglutinative, every part of its content receives overt

Table 1.2 *The finite inflection of Bulgarian* KRAD *'steal'*

|          |   | Present      | Imperfect       | Aorist           |
|----------|---|--------------|-----------------|------------------|
| Singular | 1 | *krad-ɔ́*     | *krad-'á-x*     | *krád-o-x*       |
|          | 2 | *krad-é-š*   | *krad-é-š-e*    | *krád-e*         |
|          | 3 | *krad-é*     | *krad-é-š-e*    | *krád-e*         |
| Plural   | 1 | *krad-é-m*   | *krad-'á-x-me*  | *krád-o-x-me*    |
|          | 2 | *krad-é-te*  | *krad-'á-x-te*  | *krád-o-x-te*    |
|          | 3 | *krad-ɔ́t*    | *krad-'á-x-a*   | *krád-o-x-a*     |

expression, it exhibits neither extended nor overlapping exponence,[7] and its meaning is compositionally computable from its form. In short, *alikisukuma* behaves as an instance of canonical inflection (Corbett 2009).[8] But not all inflection is canonical; indeed, most inflection is noncanonical in one or more ways, and once one begins examining form–content relations in such noncanonical patterns, the weaknesses of morpheme-based approaches to inflection become evident. Consider six noncanonical patterns of this sort.

## *1.2.1 Underdetermination*
In many paradigms, the word form realizing a particular morphosyntactic property set does not contain exponents of all of the properties in that set. This is most obviously the case in instances of syncretism; the fact that the English word form *cut* may be infinitive (*I will cut the rope*), present indicative (*I always cut the rope or untie it*), past indicative (*I always cut the rope or untied it*), imperative (*Cut the rope!*), participial (*I have cut the rope*), subjunctive (*They will require that he cut the rope*), or irrealis (*If he cut the rope, the balloon would float away*) is nowhere reflected in its morphology. But even nonsyncretic forms may exhibit underdetermination. In Bulgarian, for example, the verb form *krádox* 'I stole' in Table 1.2 has three inflectional exponents (initial stress and the suffixes *-o* and *-x*), none of which expresses the first person singular; nor can one say that

---

7 An **exponent** of a set of morphosyntactic properties is any kind of morphological marking that expresses that set of properties; thus, the *-s* in *dogs* and the vowel change in *goose* → *geese* are both exponents of the property set ⟨plura 1⟩ I follow Matthews (1972: 67, 82, 93) in distinguishing **extended exponence** (a word form exhibits more than one morphological marking expressing the same morphosyntactic property), **cumulative exponence** (two or more inflectional categories are invariably expressed together, so that every exponent of one is an exponent of the other(s)), and **overlapping exponence** (a morphological marking serves to express two or more morphosyntactic properties whose inflectional categories are not invariably expressed together).
8 We return to the matter of canonical inflection in Chapter 2.

Table 1.3 *The imperfective indicative inflection of two Latin verbs*

| | | MONĒRE 'warn' | | | VERĒRĪ 'fear' | | |
|---|---|---|---|---|---|---|---|
| | | Present | Imperfect | Future | Present | Imperfect | Future |
| Active | 1sg | *moneō* | *monēbam* | *monēbō* | *vereor* | *verēbar* | *verēbor* |
| | 2sg | *monēs* | *monēbās* | *monēbis* | *verēris* | *verēbāris* | *verēberis* |
| | 3sg | *monet* | *monēbat* | *monēbit* | *verētur* | *verēbātur* | *verēbitur* |
| | 1pl | *monēmus* | *monēbāmus* | *monēbimus* | *verēmur* | *verēbāmur* | *verēbimur* |
| | 2pl | *monētis* | *monēbātis* | *monēbitis* | *verēminī* | *verēbāminī* | *verēbiminī* |
| | 3pl | *monent* | *monēbant* | *monēbunt* | *verentur* | *verēbantur* | *verēbuntur* |
| Passive | 1sg | *moneor* | *monēbar* | *monēbor* | | | |
| | 2sg | *monēris* | *monēbāris* | *monēberis* | | | |
| | 3sg | *monētur* | *monēbātur* | *monēbitur* | | | |
| | 1pl | *monēmur* | *monēbāmur* | *monēbimur* | | | |
| | 2pl | *monēminī* | *monēbāminī* | *monēbiminī* | | | |
| | 3pl | *monentur* | *monēbantur* | *monēbuntur* | | | |

the properties "first person singular" are assigned to *krádox* by default, since "third person singular" is the default person/number combination in Bulgarian (as *kradé* 's/he steals' shows). Morpheme-based approaches of the incremental type are not compatible with this phenomenon of underdetermination, since they provide no means of explaining how a word form might possess nondefault properties without possessing exponents of those properties; in such approaches, the fact that *krádox* is unambiguously a first-person singular form is puzzling because its content cannot be deduced from its inflectional exponents, but instead seems to follow from its paradigmatic opposition to forms expressing other person/number combinations. Thus, underdetermination is one kind of evidence that the RD hypothesis is not viable in incremental approaches to inflection.[9]

### 1.2.2    Overt form–content conflict

Phenomena such as Latin deponency are another kind of evidence against the RD hypothesis. Latin deponent verbs have two distinguishing features: (i) they lack finite passive forms but (ii) their finite active forms have the morphology that is usual for passives; compare the inflection of the deponent verb VERĒRĪ fe ar' with that of the nondeponent MONĒRE ẃ arn' in Table 1.3.

---

9 The postulation of zero affixes (Harris 1942, Bloch 1947, Hockett 1947) is a familiar but uncon-
   vincing strategy for challenging this conclusion (Matthews 1972: 57ff).

Facts of this sort demonstrate that a word's form and content are sometimes in conflict. Neither incremental nor realizational approaches to morpheme-based inflection are easily reconciled with such conflicts. In such approaches, the RD hypothesis entails that word forms with parallel representations express parallel content – yet, while the morphology of *vereor* I fear' is that of *moneor* I am warned' and not that of *moneō* I warn,' the content of *vereor* parallels that of *moneō* and not that of *moneor*. Squaring this mismatch with the assumptions of morpheme-based inflection would seemingly necessitate either the massive postulation of systematically homophonous morphemes (missing the generalization that the inflectional morphology of active deponents is exactly that of passive nondeponents) or the postulation of property-changing operations that transform the active morphemes in a deponent verb's paradigm into passive morphemes.

Although the focus here is on inflection, it should be noted that mismatches between a word form's morphology and its semantics can also be found in the derivational domain. Thus, Hyman (2003) observes that in Chichewa (Niger-Congo, Malawi), a derived verb's derivational affixes often adhere to a templatic ordering that is at odds with the verb's semantic composition; for example, the morphology of applicativized causative derivatives is indistinguishable from that of causativized applicative derivatives. In the examples in (9), the suffix sequence *-its-il* (-CAUSATIVE-APPLICATIVE) represents both the applicativization of a causative verb and the causativization of an applicative verb. Evidence of this kind is not obviously reconcilable with the view that a word form's semantic structure is isomorphic to its morphological structure. (See Gerner 2014 for additional evidence of the noncompositionality of morphological form.)

(9)     a. **Applicativized causative:**
           *alenjé    a-ku-líl-íts-il-a*              *mwaná   ndodo*
           hunters   3PL-PROG-cry-CAUS-APP-FV   child      sticks
           the  hunters are [making the child cry] with sticks'

        b. **Causativized applicative:**
           *alenjé    a-ku-tákás-its-il-a*          *mkází   mthíko*
           hunters   3PL-PROG-stir-CAUS-APP-FV   woman   spoon
           the  hunters are making the woman [stir with a spoon]'
                                                        (Hyman 2003:248)

*1.2.3   Extended exponence*

In morpheme-based approaches of the incremental type, affixes supply word forms with the morphosyntactic properties necessary for their syntax and semantics. But not all inflectional affixes can be "justified" in this way. Inflectional affixes can't

Table 1.4 *The inflection of the Noon adjective* YAK *'big'*

| | | | | Indefinite | Definite | | |
|---|---|---|---|---|---|---|---|
| | | | | | Proximal | Medial | Distal |
| Nondiminutive | Inanimate | **sg** | 1 | *wi-yak* | *wi-yak-w-ii* | *wi-yak-w-um* | *wi-yak-w-aa* |
| | | | 2 | *fi-yak* | *fi-yak-f-ii* | *fi-yak-f-um* | *fi-yak-f-aa* |
| | | | 3 | *mi-yak* | *mi-yak-m-ii* | *mi-yak-m-um* | *mi-yak-m-aa* |
| | | | 4 | *ki-yak* | *ki-yak-k-ii* | *ki-yak-k-um* | *ki-yak-k-aa* |
| | | | 5 | *pi-yak* | *pi-yak-p-ii* | *pi-yak-p-um* | *pi-yak-p-aa* |
| | | | 6 | *ji-yak* | *ji-yak-j-ii* | *ji-yak-j-um* | *ji-yak-j-aa* |
| | | pl | 1–3 | *ci-yak* | *ci-yak-c-ii* | *ci-yak-c-um* | *ci-yak-c-aa* |
| | | | 4–6 | *ti-yak* | *ti-yak-t-ii* | *ti-yak-t-um* | *ti-yak-t-aa* |
| | Animate | sg | | *yi-yak* | *yi-yak-y-ii* | *yi-yak-y-um* | *yi-yak-y-aa* |
| | | pl | | *ɓi-yak* | *ɓi-yak-ɓ-ii* | *ɓi-yak-ɓ-um* | *ɓi-yak-ɓ-aa* |
| Diminutive | | sg | | *ji-yak* | *ji-yak-j-ii* | *ji-yak-j-um* | *ji-yak-j-aa* |
| | | pl | | *ti-yak* | *ti-yak-t-ii* | *ti-yak-t-um* | *ti-yak-t-aa* |

*Source:* Soukka 2000

always be seen as supplying necessary properties, since they sometimes express properties that receive expression elsewhere in a word form's morphology. Consider, for example, the inflection of adjectives in Noon (Niger-Congo; Senegal). In Noon, adjectives agree with nouns

- in number (singular, plural),
- in definiteness (indefinite, definite),
- in spatial deixis (for definite nouns only: proximal, medial, distal), and
- in noun class (diminutive, nondiminutive animate, and six nondiminutive inanimate classes).

The inflection of the adjective YAK big' in Table 1.4 illustrates. Number and noun class are expressed cumulatively; in definite forms, an adjective's combination of number and noun class is expressed twice, prefixally and suffixally. That is, every definite form has a redundant affix, one which simply duplicates the content of another affix in the word form. Clearly the appearance of an affix is not simply motivated by a word form's need for morphosyntactic properties.

This phenomenon of extended exponence is similarly problematic for morpheme-based approaches of the realizational type, which must postulate, without independent motivation, "enrichment" rules (Müller 2007) for the duplication of functional heads to accommodate multiple exponents of the same content.

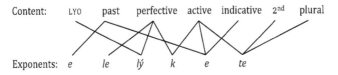

Figure 1.4 *Exponence relations in Ancient Greek* elelḱ ete *'you had unfastened' (Matthews 1991: 171ff)*

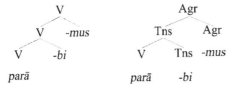

Figure 1.5 *Alternative morpheme-based analyses of Latin* parābimus *'we will prepare'*

### 1.2.4   Overlapping exponence

A key premise of morpheme-based approaches of the realizational type is that inflectional affixes are inserted into functional head nodes in syntax (see again Figure 1.3). This implies that inflectional affixes should tend to participate in very simple exponence relations: their content should generally be that of a single functional head. Sometimes this is so; but very often, an inflectional affix serves as the exponent of a heterogeneous set of properties that cannot be plausibly seen as originating at the same functional head node; moreover, a word's affixes often exhibit a partial overlap in their exponence relations, so that it is unclear which affix belongs with which functional head node. A striking example discussed by Matthews (1991: 171ff) is that of Ancient Greek *ele-lýkete* 'you had unfastened,' whose exponence relations may be diagrammed as in Figure 1.4. Proponents of morpheme-based approaches of the realizational type (Halle and Marantz 1993, Harley and Noyer 1999) have argued that the exponence relations in such cases reflect the operation of syntactically unmotivated rules of "fusion" and "fission" that copy morphosyntactic properties from one functional head node to another; but the phenomena that such rules are used to repair are prima facie evidence against equating a word form's inflectional affixes with functional heads in the first place.

### 1.2.5   Amorphousness

In morpheme-based theories of inflection, it is usual to portray word forms as having an internal constituent structure similar to that of a multiword phrase; so portrayed, the Latin verb form *parābimus* 'we will prepare' has a structure similar to those in Figure 1.5.

Table 1.5 *Diverse morphological processes expressing number*

|                | Singular | Plural |  |
|----------------|----------|--------|--|
| English | *dog* | *dog-s* | |
| Gikuyu | *mũ-rũũthi* | *mĩ-rũũthi* | 'lion' |
| Oaxaca Chontal | *kwepoʔ* | *kwe-ł-poʔ* | 'lizard' |
| Tohono Oʼodham | *bana* | *baabana* | 'coyote' |
| | *kuna* | *kuukuna* | 'husband' |
| Indonesian | *babi* | *babibabi* | 'pig' |
| English | *woman* | *women* | |
| Fulfulde | *yiite* | *giite* | 'fire' |
| Russian | *oknó* | *ókna* | 'window (nom)' |
| Somali | *èy* (falling tone) | *éy* (high tone) | 'dog' |

Although this sort of structure is like the structure attributed to phrases in syntax, there is, in fact, a clear difference between word structure and phrase structure: Whereas grammatical principles such as those that govern movement, binding, ellipsis and parenthesis are demonstrably sensitive to the internal structure of a complex syntactic expression, such principles are insensitive to the internal morphological structure of a complex morphological expression. Thus, even if a complex word form such as *parābimus* is defined in successive stages (*parā-* → *parābi-* → *parābimus*), there is no compelling reason to assume that the resulting verb form *parābimus* itself has any internal hierarchical structure other than its internal prosodic or phonological structure. This is the content of the **amorphousness hypothesis** (10), most extensively justified by Anderson 1992. Morpheme-based approaches to inflection, which define word structure through the insertion of stems and affixes into hierarchically organized nodes, are incompatible with this hypothesis, which is fundamentally at odds with the RD hypothesis.

(10)    **Amorphousness.** Noncompound word forms have no internal hierarchical structure other than their prosodic or phonological structure.

### 1.2.6    Nonconcatenative morphology

Morpheme-based approaches to inflection are often predicated on the idea that word forms possess the same kind of hierarchical structure as phrases do in syntax, but this idea is dubious even if one questions the amorphousness hypothesis. Branching tree diagrams such as those in Figure 1.5 are possible only because they involve affixal inflection. But affixation is only one kind of morphological marking, and there is no convincing evidence that affixes have a privileged status among inflectional exponents. The number inflections in Table 1.5 involve exponents of various kinds, few of which lend themselves to representations such as those in Figure 1.5. Nonconcatenative modes of inflection cast serious doubt on the claimed similarity of morphological structure to syntactic structure: The plausibility of the assumption that word forms may have a syntax-like structure is seriously diminished by the fact that not all can.[10]

The phenomena exemplified in Sections 1.2.1–1.2.6 raise serious doubts about the viability of the assumptions underlying morpheme-based approaches to inflection; they show that an inflected word's content and form fail to exhibit the sort of isomorphism that the morpheme concept predicts. Consider now the alternative to morpheme-based inflection.

## 1.3    Paradigm-based theories of inflection

The facts discussed in the preceding section are incompatible with the view that paradigms are simply epiphenomenal – that they exist only as a post hoc device for the classification of word forms that are independently defined by a language's principles of morpheme combination. In this section, I present two hypotheses that underlie the approach to inflection described in this book – hypotheses that are both clearly motivated by empirical evidence. These are:

- **The irreducibility hypothesis**: Some morphological regularities are, irreducibly, regularities in paradigm structure.
- **The interface hypothesis**: Paradigms are the interfaces of inflectional morphology with syntax and semantics.

Consider the fundamental content of these hypotheses.

### 1.3.1    The irreducibility hypothesis

In classical morphemics, a language's morphology is assumed to allow the form and content of complex words to be analyzed in parallel through a factoriza-

---

10 Claims such as (i) and (ii) (Trommer 2012: 2) should be weighed against bibliographic observation.

  (i)   "The position that non-concatenative morphology is the result of genuinely morphological processes .ha   s generally been given up in the practice of current research."
  (ii)   "[P]aradigmatic approaches to morphology have silently abandoned this domain [that of non-concatenative exponence] as an area of research."

In the chapters that follow, I present analyses of nonconcatenative phenomena in Old English (Section 5.5.1), Sanskrit (Sections 5.5.2, 8.1), Hua (Section 8.3) and Twi (Section 8.5).

tion into morphemes (Matthews 1972: 41–55). For example, Latin *parābimus* 'we will prepare' can be analyzed into three morphemes, which jointly account both for its form and for its content: *parā-* 'prepare' + *-bi* FUTURE + *-mus* 1PL. The feasibility of morphemic factorization in such cases has led many linguists to assume that a language's morphology is fundamentally a system of syntagmatic relations among morphemes below the word level. It is clear, however, that morphology is not just a system of syntagmatic relations, but also includes systematic relations in the paradigmatic dimension. That is, an adequate account of a language's morphology must do more than account for word-internal morphotactics; it must also account for a variety of systematic relations among distinct cells in the same paradigm as well as among cells in distinct paradigms.

The cells in the paradigm of a lexeme L are, again, specifications of the form–content correspondences exhibited by L's realizations; we are (for the moment) assuming that such specifications take the form $\langle$L, $\sigma : w\rangle$, where $w$ is the realization of L's lexical content and the morphosyntactic property set $\sigma$. Thus, relations in the paradigmatic dimension are irreducible relations between $\langle$L, $\sigma_1 : w_1\rangle$ and $\langle$L, $\sigma_2 : w_2\rangle$ (distinct members of L's paradigm) or between $\langle$L$_1$, $\sigma_1 : w_1\rangle$ and $\langle$L$_2$, $\sigma_2 : w_2\rangle$ (members of distinct paradigms).

Many patterns in a language's inflectional morphology are observable in more than one cell of a lexeme's paradigm, but that alone doesn't entail that these patterns serve primarily to express paradigmatic relations among cells. Consider again the paradigm of French ALLER 'go' in Table 1.1. Although the suffix *-ons* /ʒ/ appears in seven different cells, the suffixation of *-ons* does not serve primarily to express a relation among these cells. Instead, it is the default realization of the first person plural, a property combination that happens to appear in eight different cells of a verb's paradigm: even if it is relevant for the inflection of all but one of these cells, the generalization that the first person plural has *-ons* as its default realization is fundamentally a generalization about exponence rather than about the organization of a paradigm's cells.

On the other hand, consider the declensional paradigms of the twelve Latin nouns in Table 1.6. In the paradigm of AQUA 'water,' that of DOMINUS 'master' and that of DŌNUM 'gift,' the dative plural form and the ablative plural form are identical (*aquīs, dominīs, dōnīs*). This identity cannot be plausibly attributed to the coexistence of a dative plural suffix *-īs* and a distinct but homophonous ablative plural suffix, since precisely the same pattern of syncretism is embodied by different morphology in the inflection of the nine remaining nouns. It is likewise implausible to portray this identity as a consequence of the purported fact that the dative and the ablative form a natural class, since in the singular of AQUA, RĒS 'thing' and DIĒS 'day,' the dative is

Table 1.6 *The declension of twelve Latin nouns*

| | | 1st declension | 2nd declension | | 3rd declension | | | 3rd (*i*-stem) declension | | 4th declension | | 5th declension | |
|---|---|---|---|---|---|---|---|---|---|---|---|---|---|---|
| | | AQUA f. 'water' | DOMINUS m. 'master' | DŌNUM n. 'gift' | RĒX m. 'king' | HOMŌ m. 'man' | CORPUS n. 'body' | CĪVIS m. 'citizen' | MARE n. 'sea' | FRŪCTUS f. 'fruit' | CORNŪ n. 'horn' | RĒS f. 'thing' | DIĒS m. 'day' |
| Singular | Nom | aqua | dominus | dōnum | rēx | homō | corpus | cīvis | mare | frūctus | cornū | rēs | diēs |
| | Voc | aqua | domine | dōnum | rēx | homō | corpus | cīvis | mare | frūctus | cornū | rēs | diēs |
| | Gen | aquae | dominī | dōnī | rēgis | hominis | corporis | cīvis | maris | frūctūs | cornūs | reī | diēī |
| | Dat | aquae | dominō | dōnō | rēgī | hominī | corporī | cīvī | marī | frūctuī | cornū | reī | diēī |
| | Acc | aquam | dominum | dōnum | rēgem | hominem | corpus | civem | mare | frūctum | cornū | rem | diem |
| | Abl | aquā | dominō | dōnō | rēge | homine | corpore | cīve | marī | frūctū | cornū | rē | diē |
| Plural | Nom | aquae | dominī | dōna | rēgēs | hominēs | corpora | cīvēs | maria | frūctūs | cornua | rēs | diēs |
| | Voc | aquae | dominī | dōna | rēgēs | hominēs | corpora | cīvēs | maria | frūctūs | cornua | rēs | diēs |
| | Gen | aquārum | dominōrum | dōnōrum | rēgum | hominum | corporum | cīvium | marium | frūctuum | cornuum | rērum | diērum |
| | Dat | aquīs | dominīs | dōnīs | rēgibus | hominibus | corporibus | cīvibus | maribus | frūctibus | cornibus | rēbus | diēbus |
| | Acc | aquās | dominōs | dōna | rēgēs | hominēs | corpora | cīvēs | maria | frūctūs | cornua | rēs | diēs |
| | Abl | aquīs | dominīs | dōnīs | rēgibus | hominibus | corporibus | cīvibus | maribus | frūctibus | cornibus | rēbus | diēbus |

Latin also has a locative case of rather limited use (mainly for names of places). In the first and second declensions, the locative singular form is identical to the genitive singular form; otherwise, locative forms (singular or plural) are identical to the corresponding ablative forms (singular or plural).

syncretized not with the ablative, but with the genitive. The apparent generalization – that a Latin noun's dative plural form is identical to its ablative
plural form – is an irreducible generalization about paradigm structure: the
paradigm of a nominal lexeme L contains the cell $\langle$L, {dat pl} : $w\rangle$ if and only
if it contains the cell $\langle$L, {abl pl} : $w\rangle$.[11]

The syncretism of dative with ablative in the plural inflection of Latin nouns
is a paradigmatic regularity involving distinct cells in the same paradigm. But
the irreducibility hypothesis also encompasses regularities involving cells in
distinct paradigms. Consider again the characteristics of Latin deponent verbs.
Recall that deponent verbs (i) lack finite passive forms but (ii) exhibit finite
active forms that have the morphology usual for passives (Table 1.3). Observation (ii) is an observation about paradigm structure, relating the inflectional
morphology of a cell $\langle L_n, \sigma_p : w_n\rangle$ (in which $L_n$ is a nondeponent verbal lexeme
and $\sigma_p$ is a passive property set) to that of a cell $\langle L_d, \sigma_a : w_d\rangle$ (in which $L_d$ is
a deponent verbal lexeme and $\sigma_a$ is the active counterpart of $\sigma_p$). Thus, a language's inflectional morphology defines paradigmatic as well as syntagmatic
relations.

The dative/ablative generalization is irreducible because it identifies a pattern that is recurrently instantiated by the same pair of cells from one paradigm
to the next, and this pattern is not tied to any specific piece of morphology; for
instance, the pairs

$\langle$DOMINUS, {da t pl} : *dominīs*$\rangle$ / $\langle$DOMINUS, {abl pl} : *dominīs*$\rangle$

and

$\langle$RĒS, {dat pl} : *rēbus*$\rangle$ / $\langle$RĒS, {a bl pl} : *rēbus*$\rangle$

both fit the pattern. The deponency generalization is irreducible because it
identifies a pattern that is recurrently instantiated by cells in different paradigms whose word forms are morphologically alike but differ in their content,
and this pattern is, again, not tied to any specific piece of morphology; both
the pair

$\langle$MONĒRE, {1sg prs ind pass} : *moneor*$\rangle$ / $\langle$ VERĒRĪ, {1sg prs ind act} : *vereor*$\rangle$

and the pair

$\langle$MONĒRE, {2pl prs ind pass} : *monēminī*$\rangle$ / $\langle$ VERĒRĪ, {2pl prs ind act} :
*verēminī*$\rangle$

fit the pattern.

---

11 In Chapter 11, I return to the status of syncretism as a property of paradigm structure.

The irreducibility hypothesis entails that there are morphologically signifi-cant generalizations that are, irreducibly, about whole word forms and their content (= about paradigm cells). This hypothesis is related to the stronger hypothesis that *all* morphologically significant generalizations are about whole word forms and their content (cf. Blevins 2006, O'Neill 2014, Pirrelli et al. 2015) – that morphology trades in whole word forms rather than in stems, affixes, and morphological operations. As I show below (Section 14.2), the latter hypothesis is ultimately too strong; see also Matthews 1972: 26ff for arguments to this effect.

### 1.3.2    *The interface hypothesis*

According to the interface hypothesis, paradigms serve as the interfaces of a language's inflectional morphology with its syntax and its semantics. Consider first the interface of a language's inflectional morphology with its syntax. Syn-tactic principles determine the distribution of morphosyntactic properties on a sentence's lexical nodes; lexemes provide the lexical content of these nodes. But as we have seen (Section 1.1), lexemes are not, themselves, linguistic forms; as a consequence, when a lexeme provides a node's lexical content, it does so only through the mediation of one of its word forms inserted into that node.

A language's inflectional morphology determines the form of the word real-izing the combination of a particular lexeme with a particular set of morpho-syntactic properties; that is, it defines the word form $w$ in a cell $\langle L, \sigma : w \rangle$ as a function of L and $\sigma$. A lexeme's inflectional paradigm therefore constitutes the nexus of its syntax with its inflectional morphology: inflectional morphology determines the pairing of content and form in a cell $\langle L, \sigma : w \rangle$; syntax employs the cell by inserting $w$ into any node having $\sigma$ as its morphosyntactic content and L as its lexical content. Syntax is insensitive to the details of the function by which the morphology of $w$ is deduced from L and $\sigma$; conversely, inflec-tional morphology is insensitive to the details of the varied syntactic contexts in which $w$ serves to express L and $\sigma$.[12]

Consider now the interface of a language's inflectional morphology with its semantics. The meaning of a word form $w$ in a paradigm cell $\langle L, \sigma : w \rangle$ is, in general, a function of L and $\sigma$; this function is wholly insensitive to the morphology of $w$. Thus, a lexeme's inflectional paradigm also constitutes the nexus of its semantics with its inflectional morphology: given a lexeme L and a complete and compatible morphosyntactic property set $\sigma$, inflectional

---

12 These are, respectively, the principles of morphology-free syntax and syntax-free morphology (Zwicky 1992: 354ff).

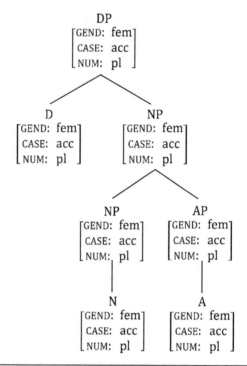

For each lexical node X there is a lexeme L that supplies the lexical content of X through the insertion of the word form *w* from the cell ⟨L, {fem acc pl}: *w*⟩:

| X | L | *w* | ⟨L, {e m acc pl} *w*⟩ |
|---|---|---|---|
| D | ILLE 'that' | *illās* | ⟨ILLE, {e m acc pl} *illās*⟩ |
| N | PUELLA 'girl' | *puellās* | ⟨PUELLA, {e m acc pl} *puellās*⟩ |
| A | BEĀTA 'happy' | *beātās* | ⟨BEĀTA, {e m acc pl} *beātās*⟩ |

Figure 1.6 *A simple example of the interface of syntax with inflectional morphology*

morphology determines the word form *w* realizing L and σ (licensing the cell ⟨L, σ : *w*⟩); correspondingly, semantic principles determine the meaning of *w* as a function of L and σ.

The following example demonstrates these interfaces. The syntax of Latin defines the branching phrase structure in Figure 1.6. One effect of this definition is the association of the property set {fem acc pl} with each of the nonterminal nodes in this structure. Each lexical node gets its lexical content from a lexeme L (ILLE 'that' for node D, PUELLA 'girl' for N, and BEĀTA 'happy' for A). In each case, the appropriate form of lexeme L is the word form *w* supplied by the node

⟨L, {fem acc pl} : *w*⟩ in L's paradigm. The precise form of *w* is spelled out not in the syntax, but in the inflectional morphology; the syntax is insensitive to the internal workings of inflectional morphology, but depends on it to furnish the appropriate realizations at their interface. By the same token, the semantic interpretation of *illās*, *puellās* and *beātās* is insensitive to the morphology of these forms, depending purely on the lexical content of the lexemes ILLE, PUELLA and BEĀTA and on the morphosyntactic content {fem acc pl}.

Thus, besides embodying the paradigmatic dimension defined by a language's inflectional morphology, inflectional paradigms play an essential role in delineating the engagement of inflectional morphology with other grammatical components. Before proceeding, it is important to be clear about the precise content of this conclusion.

First, the conclusion that paradigms are essential to the definition of a language's grammar does not entail that every lexeme's full paradigm is housed in the lexicon. Those parts of a paradigm that are not predictable must naturally be stored, but given that paradigms are often highly predictable (Stump and Finkel 2013), full storage is not logically necessitated by the conclusion that paradigms are essential to a grammar's definition; that is, this conclusion is compatible with psycholinguistic evidence that suggests that only irregular inflected forms are necessarily stored (Clahsen 1999, Pinker 1999) – granting, of course, the experimental evidence that even wholly regular forms may be stored if they are high-frequency (Stemberger and MacWhinney 1988).

Second, the conclusion that paradigms are essential to a grammar's definition does not entail that a language's paradigms have the properties of tables; as we have seen, tables embody ordering relations that are irrelevant to paradigm structure. A paradigm is, again, a set of cells, which may be characterized (for the moment) as the form–content pairings embodied by a lexeme's inflectional realizations. A paradigmatic regularity is an irreducible regularity in the coöccurrence of cells, either within or across paradigms.

I note, in concluding, that paradigm-based approaches to morphology are subject to none of the reservations raised in Sections 1.2.1–1.2.6 about morpheme-based approaches. That is, paradigm-based approaches are compatible with each of the following six common phenomena:

  (i)  *Compatibility with underdetermination.* When the lexical and morphosyntactic content of a cell ⟨L, σ : *w*⟩ determines the form of the realization *w*, there is no expectation that the morphology of *w* will fully determine the identity of either L or σ; that is, the rules of exponence deducing the morphology of *w* from L and σ may simply be insensitive to some of the morphosyntactic distinctions in σ.

(ii)   *Compatibility with form–content mismatches.* In a paradigm-based approach to inflection, the realization $w_1$ of a cell $\langle L_1, \sigma_1 : w_1 \rangle$ may systematically involve the same morphology as the realization $w_2$ of a cell $\langle L_2, \sigma_2 : w_2 \rangle$ even if $\sigma_1 \neq \sigma_2$; that is, the rules of exponence that deduce the morphology of $w_1$ from $L_1$ and $\sigma_1$ may be exactly those that deduce the morphology of $w_2$ from $L_2$ and $\sigma_2$. (Instances of this kind are discussed in detail in Chapter 12.)

*Compatibility with (iii) extended and (iv) overlapping exponence.* When the morphosyntactic content $\sigma$ of the cell $\langle L, \sigma : w \rangle$ determines the form of the realization $w$, there is no expectation that each property in $\sigma$ will have at most one exponent in $w$ nor that the exponence of the properties in $\sigma$ will not overlap; that is, the rules of exponence deducing the morphology of $w$ from L and $\sigma$ may include more than one rule sensitive to the same subset of $\sigma$ as well as rules sensitive to overlapping subsets of $\sigma$.

(v)   *Compatibility with amorphousness.* Given any cell $\langle L, \sigma : w \rangle$, there is no assumption that the form $w$ determined by L and $\sigma$ as the realization of their joint content is anything other than a phonological representation; that is, rules of exponence define a word's form as a phonological representation and not as a representation of morphological constituent structure.

(vi)   *Compatibility with nonconcatenative morphology.* Given any cell $\langle L, \sigma : w \rangle$, there is no expectation that the exponents of $\sigma$ in $w$ are fundamentally affixal; that is, rules of exponence may effect all kinds of inflectional marking, concatenative or nonconcatenative.

# 2   Canonical inflectional paradigms

In order to understand the characteristics of inflectional paradigms in the most systematic way possible, it will frequently be useful to draw upon the assumptions of canonical typology (Corbett 2005, 2009, Brown et al. 2013). The strategy of this approach to typology is

(a)   to identify the dimensions of possible cross-linguistic variation in a given phenomenon and the logical endpoints of these dimensions; and

(b)   to situate canonical types at the extremes of these dimensions, calibrating attested phenomena according to the degree and direction of their deviation from these canonical types.

By postulating the notion of a canonical inflectional paradigm, one can describe different kinds of paradigmatic phenomena as involving different kinds of deviation from this canonical ideal.

In Section 2.1, I discuss the notion of canonical inflection as originally characterized by Corbett 2009; this provides a basis for the narrower notion of a canonical inflectional paradigm, whose characteristics I discuss individually in Section 2.2 and summarize in Section 2.3.

## 2.1    Canonical typology and canonical inflection

I take the notion of **canonical inflection** proposed by Corbett 2009 as a starting point for defining the canonical inflectional paradigm. The characteristics that Corbett associates with canonical inflection involve both a comparison of contrasting cells belonging to the same paradigm and a comparison of corresponding cells across paradigms (of the same category). The three relevant comparisons involve (i) the morphotactics of word forms, (ii) a lexeme's expression as a stem, and (iii) the inflectional exponents of a word form's morphosyntactic properties.

Table 2.1  *The declension of Turkish* ADAM *'man'*

|  | Singular | Plural |
| --- | --- | --- |
| Nominative | *adam* | *adam-lar* |
| Accusative | *adam-ı* | *adam-lar-ı* |
| Dative | *adam-a* | *adam-lar-a* |
| Locative | *adam-da* | *adam-lar-da* |
| Ablative | *adam-dan* | *adam-lar-dan* |
| Genitive | *adam-ın* | *adam-lar-ın* |

Consider first the comparison of cells belonging to a single paradigm. In instances of canonical inflection, the word forms realizing a paradigm's cells all have the same morphotactic structure. The declensional paradigm of Turkish ADAM ɨn an' in Table 2.1 exemplifies this characteristic: every word form in this paradigm has the structure

[ Stem – (NUMBER) – (CASE) ],

where NUMBER and CASE are suffixal expressions of number and case and where the parentheses reflect the absence of overt number marking in the singular and the absence of overt case marking in the nominative. Besides having the same structure, all of the inflected word forms realizing a particular lexeme canonically exhibit the same stem; for example, all of the forms in Table 2.1 exhibit the stem *adam*. Finally, word forms realizing distinct morphosyntactic properties canonically exhibit distinct inflectional marking; thus, no two of the word forms realizing ADAM in Table 2.1 are alike, reflecting the fact that no two express exactly the same morphosyntactic properties of number and case. Together, these three patterns entail that canonically, the word forms realizing a paradigm's cells are all different.

Consider now the comparison of corresponding cells in distinct paradigms (of the same category). Canonically, these exhibit the same morphotactics. For example, each of the forms of TAVAN ɔ̆ eiling' (Table 2.2) exhibits the same [ Stem – (NUMBER) – (CASE) ] structure as its counterpart in the paradigm of ADAM. By contrast, word forms realizing distinct lexemes canonically exhibit distinct stems, e.g. *adam* vs *tavan*. Nevertheless, they canonically exhibit the same inflectional exponents: each form of TAVAN in Table 2.2 exhibits the same inflectional marking as the corresponding form of ADAM in Table 2.1.[1] These

---

1 Vowel harmony causes the exponents of number and case in Turkish declensional paradigms to exhibit a considerable amount of allomorphy determined by a stem's phonology; thus, alongside

Table 2.2 *The declension of Turkish tavan 'ceiling'*

|              | Singular   | Plural         |
|--------------|------------|----------------|
| Nominative   | *tavan*    | *tavan-lar*    |
| Accusative   | *tavan-ı*  | *tavan-lar-ı*  |
| Dative       | *tavan-a*  | *tavan-lar-a*  |
| Locative     | *tavan-da* | *tavan-lar-da* |
| Ablative     | *tavan-dan*| *tavan-lar-dan*|
| Genitive     | *tavan-ın* | *tavan-lar-ın* |

Table 2.3 *Canonical inflection as defined by Corbett (2009: 2)*

|  | Comparison across cells of a lexeme's paradigm | Comparison of corresponding cells across paradigms |
|---|---|---|
| 1. Composition/structure (morphotactics) | same | same |
| 2. Lexical material (≈ shape of stem) | same | different |
| 3. Inflectional material (≈ shape of inflection) | different | same |
| Outcome (≈ shape of inflected word form) | different | different |

three patterns entail that in canonical inflection, each cell in one lexeme's paradigm is realized by a word form distinct from that realizing the corresponding cell in another lexeme's paradigm.

The details of Corbett's conception of canonical inflection may be summarized as in Table 2.3.

The notion of canonical inflection serves as a logical point of reference for the typological comparison of different inflectional systems. Thus, consider the two Sanskrit declensional paradigms in Table 2.4. The morphotactics of the word forms in this table are more or less constant both within and across paradigms: in general, these forms all have the structure

[Stem – (Suffix)],

the genitive singular form *adam-ın* fna n's' are *ev-in* hous e's,' *top-un* ba ll's' and *ön-ün* front' s.' Thus, Turkish declensional paradigms can only be said to exhibit the same inflectional marking if the effects of vowel harmony are abstracted away.

Table 2.4  *The declension of two Sanskrit nouns*

(Hyphens separate stems from suffixes except in cases of sandhi or fusion.)

| | AŚVA hors e' | | | PITAR 'father' | | |
|---|---|---|---|---|---|---|
| | Singular | Dual | Plural | Singular | Dual | Plural |
| Nom | *aśva-s* | *aśvau* | *aśvās* | *pitā* | *pitar-au* | *pitar-as* |
| Voc | *aśva* | *aśvau* | *aśvās* | *pitar* | *pitar-au* | *pitar-as* |
| Acc | *aśva-m* | *aśvau* | *aśvā-n* | *pitar-am* | *pitar-au* | *pitṝ-n* |
| Ins | *aśvena* | *aśvā-bhyām* | *aśvais* | *pitr-ā* | *pitṛ-bhyām* | *pitṛ-bhis* |
| Dat | *aśvāya* | *aśvā-bhyām* | *aśve-bhyas* | *pitr-e* | *pitṛ-bhyām* | *pitṛ-bhyas* |
| Abl | *aśvāt* | *aśvā-bhyām* | *aśve-bhyas* | *pitur* | *pitṛ-bhyām* | *pitṛ-bhyas* |
| Gen | *aśva-sya* | *aśva-yos* | *aśvā-nām* | *pitur* | *pitr-os* | *pitṝ-ṇām* |
| Loc | *aśve* | *aśva-yos* | *aśve-ṣu* | *pitar-i* | *pitr-os* | *pitṛ-ṣu* |

though the suffixal boundary is often obscured by sandhi (e.g. *aśve* 'near a horse' ← *aśva-* + *-i*) or by morphological fusion (*aśvena* 'with a horse'). But while the two paradigms exhibit different stems, there is also considerable variation in stem shape within each paradigm (*aśva-* ~ *aśvā-* ~ *aśve-*, *pitā-* ~ *pitar-* ~ *pitr-* ~ *pitṛ-* ~ *pitṝ-* ~ *pitur-*). Moreover, some cells within the same paradigm exhibit identical inflectional marking (e.g. genitive and ablative singular *pitur*, dative and ablative plural *aśve-bhyas*), and across paradigms, corresponding cells sometimes exhibit distinct inflectional marking (e.g. nominative singular *aśva-s* but *pitā*, instumental plural *aśvais* but *pitṛ-bhis*). Thus, Sanskrit declensional paradigms exhibit a pattern of inflection that is less canonical in various respects than Turkish declensional paradigms. It is important to understand that this means only that Sanskrit paradigms are farther from the logical extreme defined in Table 2.3. It does not mean that they exhibit a less common pattern; indeed, conformity to the canonical pattern in Table 2.3 is surely less common than deviation from it.[2]

## 2.2   *The canonical inflectional paradigm*

I assume that a **canonical inflectional paradigm** is embedded in a system of canonical inflection, but that canonical inflectional paradigms possess some

---

2  See Brown and Chumakina's (2013) discussion of the "Venus principle" in canonical typology.

additional characteristics that do not follow directly from those of canonical inflection. Those characteristics that do follow from the notion of canonical inflection are listed in (1).

(1)     Characteristics of canonical inflectional paradigms that derive from
        Corbett's notion of canonical inflection
        a. Every lexeme has a single stem that is the basis for realizing every cell in
           its paradigm.
        b. Every cell in a lexeme's paradigm has a distinct realization.
        c. The paradigm of a lexeme of category C belongs to a system of para-
           digms for category C such that each paradigm is canonical, no two para-
           digms have the same stem, and corresponding cells in distinct paradigms
           exhibit the same inflectional marking.

I shall assume that in addition to the characteristics in (1), canonical inflectional paradigms possess the following seven characteristics.

*2.2.1     No constraints on combining morphosyntactic properties*
An inflectional category $\alpha$ draws its values from a set $S_\alpha$ of morphosyntactic properties; in French, for example, the inflectional categories PERSON, NUMBER and GENDER draw their values from the respective sets $S_{\text{PERSON}}$ (= {1s t, 2nd, 3rd}, $S_{\text{NUMBER}}$ (= {$s$ ingular, plural} and $S_{\text{GENDER}}$ (= {ma sculine, feminine}). If L is a lexeme belonging to syntactic category C and {$I_1, ,.. I_n$} is the set containing only and all inflectional categories $I_1, ,.. I_n$ for which members of C are specified, a canonical paradigm for L has one cell for each member of

$$\{ p_1,\ldots,p_n \colon p_1 \in s_1 \}.^3$$

Suppose, for instance, that {$Cat_1, Cat_2, Cat_3$} is the set of inflectional categories for which a lexeme L is specified, and that the set of possible values for each of these categories is as in Table 2.5; in that case, the paradigm of L is canonical only if it has a cell for each of the twenty-seven property sets in (2).

(2)     {A ,M, X}, {A, N, X}, {A, O, X}, {B, M, X}, {B, N, X}, {B, O, X},
        {C ,M, X}, {C, N, X}, {C, O, X},
        {A ,M,Y}{ A, N, Y}, {A, O, Y}, {B, M, Y}, {B, N, Y}, {B, O, Y},
        {C ,M,Y}, {C, N, Y}, {C, O, Y}
        {A ,M, Z}{ A, N, Z}, {A, O, Z}, {B, M, Z}, {B, N, Z}, {B, O, Z},
        {C ,M, Z}, {C, N, Z}, {C, O, Z}.

The Sanskrit declensional paradigms in Table 2.4 are canonical in this sense, since each has a cell for every case/number combination. But many

---

3 In the terminology of Spencer 2003, a paradigm that is canonical in this way is an **exhaustive**
  paradigm.

Table 2.5 *Three hypothetical inflectional categories*

| Inflectional category α | Set $S_\alpha$ of morphosyntactic properties from which the value of α is drawn |
|---|---|
| Cat$_1$ | A , B, C} |
| Cat$_2$ | M , N, O} |
| Cat$_3$ | X , Y, Z} |

paradigms are not canonical in this respect; in the paradigms of Latin verbs, for example, there are cells for most tense/mood combinations, but not for the combination of future tense with subjunctive mood; the partial paradigm in Table 2.6 illustrates.

### 2.2.2   No underdetermination

In a canonical paradigm, every property associated with a given cell has an overt exponent in the realization of that cell; that is, the kind of underdetermination observed in Section 1.3.1 is noncanonical. The future-tense paradigm of Sanskrit BHṚ č arry' in Table 2.7 is canonical in this sense: every morphosyntactic property has an overt exponent in every cell. For instance, the second-person plural future medio-passive form *bhariṣyadhve* has *-iṣy(a)* as its exponent of future tense and *-dhve* as its exponent of medio-passive voice (cf. the corresponding active form *bhariṣyatha*), of plural number (cf. the corresponding singular *bhariṣyase* and the corresponding dual *bhariṣyethe*), and of second person (cf. the corresponding first-person form *bhariṣyāmahe* and the corresponding third-person form *bhariṣyante*).[4]

By contrast, the inflectional paradigm of the Old English strong verb SMŪGAN 'creep' is noncanonical with respect to this criterion. Consider, for example, the form *smūgen*. Though this is unambiguously the plural present subjunctive form of SMŪGAN, it is a default form lacking any overt exponent of the subjunctive mood. The stem form *smūg-* does not express the subjunctive mood: it also appears in the imperative, the participles, the infinitives, the plural present indicative form *smūgaþ*, and the first singular present indicative form *smūge*; *smūg-* is apparently the default stem of SMŪGAN, overridden only in the past tense. The suffix *-e* is likewise not an exponent of the subjunctive mood: besides appearing in the subjunctive forms, it appears in the first singular present indicative form *smūge* and the second singular past indicative form

---

4 Note that this criterion does not exclude the possibility that the word forms in a canonical paradigm exhibit cumulative exponence; but see Section 2.2.4.

Table 2.6 *The active inflection of Latin* PARĀRE *'prepare'*

|  |  | Nonperfective | | | | Perfective | | |
|--|--|---------|--------|-----------|---------|--------------|-------------|
|  |  | Present | Future | Imperfect | Perfect | Fut. perfect | Pluperfect |
| Indicative | 1sg | parō | parābō | parābam | parāvī | parāverō | parāveram |
|  | 2sg | parās | parābis | parābās | parāvistī | parāveris | parāverās |
|  | 3sg | parat | parābit | parābat | parāvit | parāverit | parāverat |
|  | 1pl | parāmus | parābimus | parābāmus | parāvimus | parāverimus | parāverāmus |
|  | 2pl | parātis | parābitis | parābātis | parāvistis | parāveritis | parāverātis |
|  | 3pl | parant | parābunt | parābant | parāvērunt | parāverint | parāverant |
| Subjunctive | 1sg | parem |  | parārem | parāverim |  | parāvissem |
|  | 2sg | parēs |  | parārēs | parāverīs |  | parāvissēs |
|  | 3sg | paret |  | parāret | parāverit |  | parāvisset |
|  | 1pl | parēmus |  | parārēmus | parāverīmus |  | parāvissēmus |
|  | 2pl | parētis |  | parārētis | parāverītis |  | parāvissētis |
|  | 3pl | parent |  | parārent | parāverint |  | parāvissent |

Table 2.7   *The future-tense inflection of Sanskrit* BHṚ *'carry'*

|                |     | Singular    | Dual          | Plural        |
|----------------|-----|-------------|---------------|---------------|
| Active         | 1st | *bhariṣyāmi* | *bhariṣyāvas*  | *bhariṣyāmas*  |
|                | 2nd | *bhariṣyasi* | *bhariṣyathas* | *bhariṣyatha*  |
|                | 3rd | *bhariṣyati* | *bhariṣyatas*  | *bhariṣyanti*  |
| Medio-passive  | 1st | *bhariṣye*   | *bhariṣyāvahe* | *bhariṣyāmahe* |
|                | 2nd | *bhariṣyase* | *bhariṣyethe*  | *bhariṣyadhve* |
|                | 3rd | *bhariṣyate* | *bhariṣyete*   | *bhariṣyante*  |

*smuge*; in the inflection of weak verbs, it appears throughout the singular past indicative. To all appearances, *-e* is a suffix without content which appears by default whenever its appearance is not overridden by a suffix realizing specific content. And the suffix *-n* does not express the subjunctive mood: besides appearing in plural subjunctives, it appears in the plural past indicative. It is a default plural suffix, overridden only by *-aþ* in the present indicative. Thus, even though the content of *smūgen* can be determined by a kind of process of elimination, the individual inflectional exponents of *smūgen* underdetermine its content.

### 2.2.3   No extended exponence
In a canonical paradigm, every morphosyntactic property associated with a given cell has only one overt exponent in the realization of that cell. Thus, in the traditional analysis of the future-tense paradigm of Sanskrit BHṚ č arry' in Table 2.7, no morphosyntactic property has more than one exponent: in each form, future tense has the exponent *-iṣy(a)* and voice, person and number are expressed by a terminal suffix. On the other hand, the plural past indicative form *smugon* in the paradigm of Old English SMŪGAN č reep' in Table 2.8 exhibits extended exponence: the short stem *smug-* and the suffix *-o* both express past tense, and the suffix *-o* and the suffix *-n* both express plural number.

### 2.2.4   No cumulative or overlapping exponence
In a canonical paradigm, no two properties associated with a cell are simultaneously expressed by a single exponent. The paradigm of Turkish ADAM ma n' in Table 2.1 is canonical with respect to this criterion, since each affix expresses either case or plural number, never a combination of case and number. By contrast, the Sanskrit declensional paradigms in Table 2.4 exhibit cumulative exponence: every mark of case is also a mark of number. The declensional paradigm of Old English SMŪGAN č reep' in Table 2.8 presents instances of

Table 2.8 *The inflection of Old English* SMŪGAN *'creep'*

|  |  |  | Present | Past |
|---|---|---|---|---|
| Indicative | Singular | 1st | *smūge* | *smēag* |
|  |  | 2nd | *smȳhst* | *smuge* |
|  |  | 3rd | *smȳhþ* | *smēag* |
|  | Plural |  | *smūgaþ* | *smugon* |
| Subjunctive | Singular |  | *smūge* | *smuge* |
|  | Plural |  | *smūgen* | *smugen* |
| Participle |  |  | *smūgende* | *smogen* |
| Infinitive |  |  | *smūgan* |  |
| Inflected infinitive |  |  | *tō smūganne* |  |
| Imperative | Singular |  | *smūg, smūh* |  |
|  | Plural |  | *smūgaþ* |  |

Table 2.9 *The declension of Sanskrit* RĀJAN *'king'*

|  | Singular | Dual | Plural |
|---|---|---|---|
| Nominative | *rājā* | *rājān-au* | *rājān-as* |
| Vocative | *rājan* | *rājān-au* | *rājān-as* |
| Accusative | *rājān-am* | *rājān-au* | *rājñ-as* |
| Instrumental | *rājñ-ā* | *rāja-bhyām* | *rāja-bhis* |
| Dative | *rājñ-e* | *rāja-bhyām* | *rāja-bhyas* |
| Ablative | *rājñ-as* | *rāja-bhyām* | *rāja-bhyas* |
| Genitive | *rājñ-as* | *rājñ-os* | *rājñ-ām* |
| Locative | *rājñ-i (rājan-i)* | *rājñ-os* | *rāja-su* |

overlapping exponence; for instance, the *-n* in the plural indicative form *smu-gon* ʻ rept' is a default expression of plural number, while the *-o* expresses plural number as well as past tense and indicative mood.

### 2.2.5 No homophonous exponents

In a canonical paradigm, no two distinct properties have exponents that are phonologically identical. The exponents of case and number in the Turkish paradigm in Table 2.1 are canonical in this regard. By contrast, the exponents of case and number in the paradigm of Sanskrit RĀJAN kingʼ exhibit considerable homophony (Table 2.9); for instance, the suffix *-as* may express the ablative

Table 2.10 *The personal future- and past-tense inflection of Swahili*
TAKA *'want'*

|  |  | Positive | | | Negative | | | |
|---|---|---|---|---|---|---|---|---|
| Future tense | 1sg | *ni-* | *ta-* | *taka* | *si-* | | *ta-* | *taka* |
| | 2sg | *u-* | *ta-* | *taka* | *ha-* | *u-* | *ta-* | *taka*( → *hutataka*) |
| | 3sg (class 1) | *a-* | *ta-* | *taka* | *ha-* | *a-* | *ta-* | *taka*( → *hatataka*) |
| | 1pl | *tu-* | *ta-* | *taka* | *ha-* | *tu-* | *ta-* | *taka* |
| | 2pl | *m-* | *ta-* | *taka* | *ha-* | *m-* | *ta-* | *taka* |
| | 3pl (class 2) | *wa-* | *ta-* | *taka* | *ha-* | *wa-* | *ta-* | *taka* |
| Past tense | 1sg | *ni-* | *li-* | *taka* | *si-* | | *ku-* | *taka* |
| | 2sg | *u-* | *li-* | *taka* | *ha-* | *u-* | *ku-* | *taka*( → *hukutaka*) |
| | 3sg (class 1) | *a-* | *li-* | *taka* | *ha-* | *a-* | *ku-* | *taka*( → *hakutaka*) |
| | 1pl | *tu-* | *li-* | *taka* | *ha-* | *tu-* | *ku-* | *taka* |
| | 2pl | *m-* | *li-* | *taka* | *ha-* | *m-* | *ku-* | *taka* |
| | 3pl (class 2) | *wa-* | *li-* | *taka* | *ha-* | *wa-* | *ku-* | *taka* |

or genitive singular as well as the accusative plural and (with a different stem) the nominative and vocative plural.

### 2.2.6   No allomorphy

For every property associated with two or more cells in a canonical paradigm, the exponent of that property is invariant across those cells.[5] Thus, in the paradigm of Turkish ADAM ḟna n' (Table 2.1), no morphosyntactic property exhibits any allomorphy; in this paradigm, "plural" is always expressed by *-lar*, "accusative" is always expressed by *-ı*, and so on. By contrast, the property "past" exhibits two distinct exponents in the inflection of a Swahili verb, *li-* in affirmative forms, *ku-* in negative forms (Table 2.10).

### 2.2.7   The dual function of morphosyntactic property sets

In each cell $\langle$L, σ : w$\rangle$ of a canonical inflectional paradigm, the morphosyntactic property set σ has a dual function, on the one hand determining *w*'s syntax and semantics and on the other hand determining *w*'s inflectional realization. Thus, in the Turkish paradigm in Table 2.1, the property set {abl pl} determines the syntax and semantics of the word form *adamlardan* from  men' as well as its

---

5 This criterion relates to a morphosyntactic property's exponence within a single paradigm; for this reason, it does not itself entail that a paradigm is noncanonical if the exponent that it exhibits for some property is distinct from that property's exponent in another paradigm. But this is in any event entailed by criterion (1c).

Table 2.11  *Characteristics of canonical inflectional paradigms*

|  | Comparison across cells of a canonical paradigm | Comparison across canonical paradigms |
|---|---|---|
| Stem | same | different |
| Inflectional marking | different | same |
| Realization | different | different |
| Combinations of morphosyntactic properties | unconstrained | |
| Underdetermination | none | |
| Extended exponence | none | |
| Cumulative or overlapping exponence | none | |
| Homophonous exponents | none | |
| Allomorphy | none | |
| Dual function of property sets | yes | |

inflectional realization by means of the plural suffix -*lar* and the ablative suffix -*dan*. Yet, there are complex cases in which a word form's inflectional realization seems to be driven by morphosyntactic properties distinct from those that determine its syntax and semantics; for example, the Latin deponent verb form *vereor* I fear' (Section 1.2.2) has active syntax and semantics (comparable to the syntax and semantics of *moneō* 'I warn') but passive morphology (comparable to that of *moneor* I am warned').

## *2.3   Summary*

The characteristics assumed for canonical inflectional paradigms are summarized in Table 2.11.

As characterized in this way, canonical inflectional paradigms are very orderly things. If all inflectional paradigms were canonical, it would be difficult to argue against a morpheme-based theory of inflection. But we do not live in the world of canonical inflectional paradigms: in one language after another, inflectional paradigms prove to be noncanonical in more than one way, and it is this fact that motivates the postulation of a paradigm-based theory of inflection. This is not simply true of fusional languages; as I will show, even highly agglutinating languages such as Turkish present inflectional paradigms whose structure is noncanonical.

In Chapters 7 through 13, I examine a range of inflectional phenomena whose incidence causes a language's inflectional paradigms to deviate from

the canonical characteristics in Table 2.11; these deviations make it desirable
to rethink some unexamined assumptions about the nature of a language's inflectional morphology. In order to be precise about such deviations, it is essential to have a precise understanding of four key components of an inflectional
paradigm – the morphosyntactic property sets that it subsumes, the lexeme that
it expresses, that lexeme's stem(s), and a stem's inflection-class membership;
these components are successively discussed in Chapters 3 through 6.

# 3 *Morphosyntactic properties*

Each cell in a lexeme's inflectional paradigm is distinguished by its association with a particular set of morphosyntactic properties. As observed in Section 1.3.2, the morphology, syntax and semantics of the word form realizing a particular cell may all depend on that cell's morphosyntactic properties. In syntax, a word form's morphosyntactic properties identify the grammatical characteristics that it possesses, either inherently or as an effect of its syntactic context; these properties determine the particular syntactic relations in which the word form may participate within a sentence. Some such properties (e.g. plural number in most languages) have specific semantic correlates, while others (e.g. masculine gender in many languages) do not. In morphology, a word form's morphosyntactic properties determine the inflectional exponents involved in its realization.

In this chapter, I consider the role of morphosyntactic properties in the structure of inflectional paradigms. I begin by examining the ways in which inflectional categories may vary, with respect to both the complexity of their values and the syntactic categories with which they are associated (Section 3.1). I then discuss the different ways in which morphosyntactic properties may be associated with word forms (Section 3.2); the combinations into which morphosyntactic properties enter (Section 3.3); the kinds of relations that exist between morphosyntactic property sets (Section 3.4); constraints on morphosyntactic property sets and the satisfaction of these constraints (Section 3.5); and the realization of morphosyntactic properties by their exponents (Section 3.6). I conclude by discussing a puzzle concerning the representation of morphosyntactic properties in noncanonical paradigms (Section 3.7).

## 3.1    *Different kinds of inflectional categories*

An inflectional category has a set of related but mutually exclusive values; in formal terms, a morphosyntactic property is the pairing of an inflectional category

43

Table 3.1 *Some common associations of inflectional categories with syntactic categories*

|  | Common inflectional categories | Commonly associated syntactic categories |
|---|---|---|
| Atom-valued | CASE | Noun, Pronoun, Adjective, Determiner |
|  | NUMBER | Noun, Pronoun, Verb, Adjective, Determiner |
|  | GENDER | Noun, Pronoun, Adjective, Determiner |
|  | PERSON | Verb, Pronoun |
|  | INCLUSIVENESS | Verb, Pronoun |
|  | HONORIFICITY | Verb, Pronoun |
|  | TENSE | Verb |
|  | ASPECT | Verb |
|  | MOOD | Verb |
|  | VOICE | Verb |
|  | POLARITY | Verb |
| Set-valued | AGREEMENT |  |
|  | • with a head noun | Determiner, Numeral, Adjective, Possessive pronoun |
|  | • with an argument | Verb, Adposition |
|  | • with a possessor | Noun |

with one of its values, e.g. "TENSE:past." Inflectional categories vary with respect to the complexity of their values. **Atom-valued** inflectional categories have simple values, such as "past," "accusative" or "plural." But it is sometimes desirable to postulate **set-valued** inflectional categories whose values are themselves sets of morphosyntactic properties (Gazdar et al. 1985: 25); for instance, an inflectional category AGR might have values such as {PERSON:3, NUMBER:pl, GENDER:fem}

Every inflectional category I is associated with at least one syntactic category C such that members of C inflect for I. Table 3.1 lists some cross-linguistically recurrent inflectional categories and the syntactic categories with which they are often associated in this way.

## 3.2   *The association of word forms with morphosyntactic properties*

A word form may be associated with a morphosyntactic property in at least three ways. On one hand, a word form may be associated with a morphosyntactic property by virtue of its appearance in a particular syntactic context. For example, it may appear in a context in which, as an agreement target, it must match the corresponding trigger with respect to one or more properties; thus, French *national* must match the gender and number of the noun it modifies (as in *musées nationaux* 'national museums,' where noun and adjective are both masculine and plural). Or it may appear in a syntactic context in which a governing phrasal head imposes a particular morphosyntactic property on it (as *to* imposes object case: *to them*). These kinds of associations of a morphosyntactic property with a word form are described as **relational** (Anderson 1985) or **contextual** (Booij 1994, 1996).

A word form's association with a particular morphosyntactic property may, alternatively, be a function not of its syntactic context but of its intended interpretation; thus, *aime* 'likes' and *aimait* 'liked' both appear in the context *Niki ___ ce musée* but their contrasting specifications for tense yield a semantic difference in that context – 'likes this museum' (present) vs 'liked this museum' (imperfect). In such cases, the association of the morphosyntactic property set with the word form that expresses it is an **inherent** one (Anderson and Booij, *operibus citatis*).

Finally, a word form's association with a particular morphosyntactic property may be purely a matter of lexical stipulation; thus, the word forms realizing the French lexeme MUSÉE are masculine because that is how MUSÉE is lexically specified.

## 3.3    *Morphosyntactic property sets*

The morphology, syntax and semantics of an inflected word form very often depend on its simultaneous association with more than one morphosyntactic property; in French, for example, the grammatical characteristics of *nationaux* reflect its association with the morphosyntactic property set {GENDER:masc, NUMBER:pl}  (Henceforth, I shall sometimes abbreviate the representation of a morphosyntactic property set by omitting the name of a morphosyntactic property's inflectional category if this is unambiguously recoverable, e.g. {ma  sc pl.}) Canonically, a lexeme that inflects for *n* inflectional categories $I_1, \ldots, I_n$ has a paradigm in which there is a cell for every member of

$$\left\{ \{p_1, \ldots, p_n\}\text{:}\ \ p_i \in S_{I_i} \right\}, \text{ where } S_{I_i} \text{ is the set of values for } I_i.$$

It is very common, however, for combinations of morphosyntactic properties to be constrained in various ways. In some instances, these constraints are simply a matter of logic; for instance, the properties "inclusive" and "third person" are inherently incompatible. Other constraints are more arbitrary in character, such as the fact that in Latin, the properties "subjunctive" and "future" are mutually exclusive, even though properties of tense and mood are generally combinable (Section 2.2.1). Constraints on the ways in which morphosyntactic properties combine can be formulated as **property coöccurrence restrictions**. Such restrictions may be formulated as explicit prohibitions or as implicational relations; for instance, the Latin future/subjunctive restriction might be formulated either as (1a) or as (1b).

(1)    A Latin property coöccurrence restriction
    a. There is no well-formed property set $\sigma$ such that {future subjunctive} $\subseteq \sigma$.
    b. For any well-formed property set $\sigma$, if TENSE:future $\in \sigma$, then
       MOOD:indicative $\in \sigma$.

A morphosyntactic property set is **well-formed** in some language if and only if it conforms to every one of that language's property coöccurrence restrictions. A well-formed morphosyntactic property set $\sigma$ is **complete** in some language if and only if there is no well-formed morphosyntactic property set $\tau$ such that $\sigma$ is a proper subset of $\tau$. Thus, the inflectional paradigm of a lexeme L is customarily seen as having one cell for each of the complete morphosyntactic property sets for which L is inflectable.

### 3.4    *Relations b̶ tween morphosyntactic property sets*

The definition of a language's inflectional morphology is frequently sensitive to relations between morphosyntactic property sets; as I will show in this section, such relations determine a realization rule's applicability and resolve competition among such rules. Logically, such relations might be of two kinds: set-theoretic and unification-based.

One can distinguish a variety of set-theoretic relations and operations among morphosyntactic property sets, including (among others)

- the identity relation, e.g. the relation between {acc pl} and {acc pl}
- the proper subset relation, e.g. the relation between {acc pl} and {f m acc pl}
- the intersection relation, e.g. the relation between {acc pl} and {f m pl}
- the disjoint relation, e.g. the relation between {acc pl} and {na sc sg} and
- the union operation, where the union of {acc pl} and {f m pl} (i.e. {acc pl} $\cup$ {f m pl} is {f m acc pl}

Set-valued inflectional categories, however, make it preferable to refer to unification-based relations among morphosyntactic property sets. Consider, for example, the property sets in (2). It would be inaccurate to say that (2b) is a subset of (2a), since AGR:{PERSON:3} is a member of (2b) but not of (2a). But (2a) is an extension of (2b), where "extension" is recursively defined as in (3).

(2)      a. {TENSE:pst, POLARITY:neg, AGR:{PERSON:3, NUMBER:pl}}
         b. {TENSE:pst, AGR:{PERSON:3}

(3)      Where $\sigma$ and $\tau$ are well-formed morphosyntactic property sets, $\sigma$ is an
**extension** of $\tau$ (i.e. $\tau \sqsubseteq \sigma$) if and only if (i) for any atom-valued inflectional category F and any value v for F, if F:v $\in$ $\tau$, then F:v $\in$ $\sigma$; and (ii) for any set-valued inflectional category F and any permissible value $\rho$ for F, if F:$\rho$ $\in$ $\tau$, then F:$\acute{\rho}$ $\in$ $\sigma$, where $\acute{\rho}$ is an extension of $\rho$. (Cf. Gazdar et al. 1985: 27, Stump 2001: 41.)

The related operation of unification may be defined as in (4); according to this definition, the unification of {TENSE:pst, AGR:{PERSON:3} and {POLARITY:neg, AGR:{NUMBER:pl} is the set in (2a).

(4)      Where $\sigma$ and $\tau$ are well-formed morphosyntactic property sets, the **unification** of $\sigma$ and $\tau$ (i.e. $\sigma \sqcup \tau$) is the smallest well-formed morphosyntactic property set $\rho$ such that $\rho$ is an extension of both $\sigma$ and $\tau$.

In specifying relations between morphosyntactic property sets, the extension relation is clearly more versatile than the subset relation: where $\sigma$ and $\tau$ are morphosyntactic property sets, $\tau$ is an extension of $\sigma$ whenever $\sigma$ is a subset of $\tau$, but $\sigma$ isn't necessarily a subset of $\tau$ whenever $\tau$ is an extension of $\sigma$. My practice will therefore generally be to employ the notion of extension in specifying relations between morphosyntactic property sets. For similar reasons, I shall prefer the operation of unification to that of set union.

### 3.5 *Property constraints*

Many generalizations about the realization of a language's inflectional paradigms may be stated with reference to sets of morphosyntactic properties. But some generalizations are more easily stated with reference to **property constraints**[1] – constraints that may be satisfied by some number of property sets. Property constraints are useful for formulating property coöccurrence restrictions (Section 3.3)[2], and as I will show (Section 3.6), they are also helpful for stating rules of exponence.

     Given a set P of morphosyntactic properties, the set $C_P$ of property constraints for P is defined recursively as in (5). By (5a), a morphosyntactic property set itself

---

1   For discussion, see Kasper and Rounds 1986 and Gazdar et al. 1988.
2   Thus, the property coöccurrence restrictions in (18) below are formulated as property constraints.

counts as a property constraint; by (5b), Boolean operations on property constraints (the "and," "or" and "not" operations) also count as property constraints.

(5)  a. If $\sigma \subseteq P$, then $\sigma \in C_P$.
  b. If $\kappa_1, \kappa_2 \in C_P$, then $[\kappa_1 \wedge \kappa_2]$, $[\kappa_1 \vee \kappa_2]$, $\neg\kappa_1 \in C_P$.

Property constraints may be satisfied by morphosyntactic property sets. This satisfaction relation between subsets of a set P of morphosyntactic properties and members of the set $C_P$ of property constraints for P is defined recursively in (6). By (6), the property set {s g} satisfies both of the constraints in (7).

(6)  Where $\sigma \subseteq P$ and $\kappa_1, \kappa_2 \in C_P$,
  a. $\sigma$ satisfies $[\kappa_1 \wedge \kappa_2]$ if and only if $\sigma$ satisfies both $\kappa_1$ and $\kappa_2$.
  b. $\sigma$ satisfies $[\kappa_1 \vee \kappa_2]$ if and only if $\sigma$ satisfies either $\kappa_1$ or $\kappa_2$ (or both).
  c. $\sigma$ satisfies $\neg\kappa_1$ if and only if $\sigma$ doesn't satisfy $\kappa_1$.
  d. If $\kappa_1 \subseteq P$, then $\sigma$ satisfies $\kappa_1$ if and only if $\kappa_1 \subseteq \sigma$.

(7)  a. [{ } ∨ {pl}]
  b. [{ g} ∧ {}]

All morphosyntactic property sets are property constraints, but not all property constraints are morphosyntactic property sets. For this reason, generalizations stated in terms of property sets can always be stated in terms of property constraints, but the reverse is not true.

### 3.6 How morphosyntactic properties are realized

In paradigm-based theories of inflection, it is customary to assume that the association of morphosyntactic properties with their exponents is made not in the lexicon, but by **rules of exponence** (Zwicky 1985, Anderson 1992, Stump 2001). One possible format for rules of exponence is (8), where X is a variable over stems, C is a class of stems, $\kappa$ is a property constraint and $f$ is an operation on stems.

(8)  $X, C, \kappa \rightarrow f(X)$

A rule of exponence in this format is to be interpreted as follows:

  (i)  where $\langle Y, \sigma \rangle$ is a **stem pairing** (the pairing of a stem Y with a complete morphosyntactic property set $\sigma$), rule (8) is applicable to $\langle Y, \sigma \rangle$ if Y belongs to class C and $\sigma$ satisfies $\kappa$;
  (ii)  in that case, the result of applying rule (8) to the stem pairing $\langle Y, \sigma \rangle$ is the pairing $\langle f(Y), \sigma \rangle$.

Consider an example from French. As the (phonetically transcribed) forms in Table 3.2 show, a default rule of exponence for the inflection of a French verb stem associated with any extension of {pl} is (9).

Table 3.2 *The first-person plural inflection of seven French verbs*

| | Indicative | | | | | Subjunctive | |
|---|---|---|---|---|---|---|---|
| | Present | Imperfect | Simple past | Future | Conditional | Present | Past |
| AIMER 'like' | aimons / ɛm-ɔ̃ / | aimions ɛm-j-ɔ̃ | aimâmes ɛma-m | aimerons ɛmə-ʁ-ɔ̃ | aimerions ɛmə-ʁ-j-ɔ̃ | aimions ɛm-j-ɔ̃ | aimassions ɛma-s-j-ɔ̃ / |
| CONNAÎTRE 'be acquainted with' | connaissons / kɔnɛs-ɔ̃ | connaissions kɔnɛs-j-ɔ̃ | connûmes kɔny-m | connaîtrons kɔnɛt-ʁ-ɔ̃ | connaîtrions kɔnɛt-ʁ-ij-ɔ̃ | connaissions kɔnɛs-j-ɔ̃ | connussions kɔny-s-j-ɔ̃ / |
| FAIRE 'do, make' | faisons / fəz-ɔ̃ | daisions fəz-j-ɔ̃ | fîmes fi-m | ferons f-ʁ-ɔ̃ | ferions f-ʁ-j-ɔ̃ | fassions fas-j-ɔ̃ | fissions fi-s-j-ɔ̃ / |
| CUEILLIR 'pick' | cueillons / kœj-ɔ̃ | cueillions køj-ɔ̃ | cueillîmes køji-m | cueillerons kœjə-ʁ-ɔ̃ | cueillerions kœjə-ʁ-j-ɔ̃ | cueillions køj-ɔ̃ | cueillissions køji-s-j-ɔ̃ / |
| ALLER 'go' | allons / al-ɔ̃ | allions al-j-ɔ̃ | allâmes ala-m | irons i-ʁ-ɔ̃ | irions i-ʁ-j-ɔ̃ | allions al-j-ɔ̃ | allassions ala-s-j-ɔ̃ / |
| LEVER 'raise' | levons / ləv-ɔ̃ | levions ləv-j-ɔ̃ | levâmes ləva-m | leverons ləvə-ʁ-ɔ̃ | leverions ləvə-ʁ-j-ɔ̃ | levions ləv-j-ɔ̃ | levassions ləva-s-j-ɔ̃ / |
| CÉDER 'give up' | cédons / sed-ɔ̃ | cédions sed-j-ɔ̃ | cédâmes seda-m | céderons sɛdə-ʁ-ɔ̃ | céderions sɛdə-ʁ-j-ɔ̃ | cédions sed-j-ɔ̃ | cédassions seda-s-j-ɔ̃ / |

N.B. The first-person plural imperative forms of these verbs are identical to their present indicative counterparts.

(9)      X, V, { pl} → Xɔ̃

Thus, in realizing the lexical content AIMER ʎik e' and the morphosyntactic property set {pl  prs ind} (9) applies to the stem pairing (10a) to yield the pairing (10b).

(10)     a. ⟨/ɛm/, {pl prs  ind}⟩
         b. ⟨/ɛmɔ̃/, {pl prs  ind}⟩

Two rules of exponence may compete in the sense that they specify alternative ways of realizing the same content. In French, the default rule in (9) competes with rule (11), which suffixes /-m/ rather than /-ɔ̃/ in first-person plural forms of the simple past indicative; see again Table 3.2. The competition between (9) and (11) is resolved in favor of (11), in accordance with Pāṇini's principle (12). Thus, in realizing the lexical content AIMER ʎik e' and the morphosyntactic property set {pl  simple.pst ind} (11) overrides (9), applying to the stem pairing (13a) to yield the pairing (13b).

(11)     X, V, { pl simple.pst ind} → Xm

(12)     Pāṇini's principle (cf. Stump 2001: 22)
         When two rules compete, the narrower rule overrides the more general rule.
         (Rule A is **narrower** than Rule B if and only if the set of stem pairings to which A is applicable is a proper subset of those to which B is applicable.)

(13)     a. ⟨/ɛma/, {pl s  imple.pst ind}⟩
         b. ⟨/ɛmam/, {pl s  imple.pst ind}⟩

In the rules of exponence in (9) and (11), the property constraints are also property sets; but some rules of exponence must be stated in terms of property constraints that are not simply property sets. Consider, for example, the rules in (14). Rule (14a) realizes both future and conditional property sets through the suffixation of /-ʁ/;[3] (14b) realizes property sets that are either imperfect or nonindicative by the suffixation of /-j/. These examples are typical of the kinds of cases that require reference to a property constraint rather than to a property set: in such cases, the class of property sets satisfying the constraint is not a natural class – that is, it cannot be seen as the class containing all extensions of some particular property set.

(14)     a. X, V, [{future } ∨ {conditional} → Xʁ
         b. X, V, [{imperfect} ∨ {ind}     → Xj

---

3 As an alternative, one might try to motivate the postulation of a property "irrealis" shared by
  future-tense and conditional forms (but not by subjunctive forms); if one could do so, then (14a)
  could be reformulated more simply as realizing the property set {irre alis}

Rules of exponence are interpreted as applying to a ⟨form, property set⟩ pairing to yield a ⟨form, property set⟩ pairing. This is a desirable assumption, because the definition of an inflected word form often involves the successive application of more than one rule of exponence; in French, for example, the conditional form *aimerions* /ɛmə-ʁ-j-ɔ̃/ involves three different suffixation rules. Such forms show that rules of exponence are organized in the syntagmatic dimension: in the definition of an inflected word form, rules of exponence must apply in a particular order. But rules of exponence are also organized in the paradigmatic dimension; that is, certain rules of exponence are paradigmatically opposed in the sense that (a) their application is mutually exclusive and (b) they exhibit the same syntagmatic ordering with respect to other rules of exponence. For example, the rule of exponence that realizes the first person plural through the suffixation of /-ɔ̃/ and the rule realizing the second person plural through the suffixation of /-e/ are mutually exclusive in their application, but they apply in the same sequence in the series of rule applications defining a French verb's inflectional morphology.

One way of accounting for both the syntagmatic ordering and the paradigmatic opposition of rules of exponence is to assume that a language's rules of exponence are grouped into ordered **blocks** such that members of the same block are in competition (with their mutual exclusion mediated by Pāṇini's principle) and are alike in their order of application relative to rules in other blocks (Anderson 1992: 129). One way of executing this idea is through the postulation of paradigm functions (Stump 2001). A language's **paradigm function** applies to the content of a given cell in the paradigm of a lexeme L to yield the realization of that cell; in formal terms, the definition of a language's paradigm function PF is such that for any cell ⟨L, σ : w⟩ in any of that language's inflectional paradigms, PF(⟨L, σ⟩) = ⟨w, σ⟩. The definition of a language's inflectional morphology may therefore be equated with the definition of its paradigm function.

The three suffixes of French *aimerions* /ɛmə-ʁ-j-ɔ̃/ imply that French verb inflection involves three rule blocks – Block I (whose rules include the rule (14a) of /ʁ/-suffixation), Block II (containing the rule (14b) of /j/-suffixation), and Block III (whose rules include the rule of /ɔ̃/-suffixation in (9)). The ordering of these rule blocks is specified by the definition of the French paradigm function in (15). In this definition, the notation [ *n* : ⟨X, σ⟩] represents the result of applying the narrowest applicable rule in Block *n* to the stem pairing ⟨X, σ⟩; if Block *n* has no rule that is applicable to ⟨X, σ⟩, then [ *n* : ⟨X, σ⟩] = ⟨X, σ⟩, in accordance with the Identity Function Default (Stump 2001: 53).

(15)     PF($\langle$L, σ$\rangle$) = $_{def}$ [ III : [ II : [ I : $\langle$X, σ$\rangle$]]], where X is the stem of L that is
         appropriate[4] for σ.

This definition of the French paradigm function entails equations such as

$$PF(\langle\text{AIMER}, \{\text{pl c onditional}\}\rangle) = \langle/\text{ɛmə-ʁ-j-ɔ̃/}, \{\text{pl c onditional}\}\rangle.$$

## 3.7     A puzzle concerning the representation of morphosyntactic properties in noncanonical inflectional paradigms

According to the conception of canonical inflectional paradigms proposed
in Chapter 2, a canonical paradigm possesses the two characteristics in (16),
among others. An important issue for morphological theory is that of distinguishing deviations from (16a) and deviations from (16b).

(16)     Two of the characteristics of canonical inflectional paradigms
         a. A canonical paradigm exhibits no constraints on the combination of
            morphosyntactic properties (Section 2.2.1).
         b. Every cell in a canonical paradigm has a distinct realization
            (cf. Table 2.3).

To see the significance of this issue, consider the inflectional paradigm of the
verb DĒKH $ ee' in Bhojpuri (Indo-Iranian; India). This may be represented in
at least two ways. In the representation in Table 3.3, there is a cell corresponding to each possible combination of a person (1, 2 or 3), a number (singular
or plural), a gender (masculine or feminine), a mood (indicative or optative),
and – in the indicative – a tense (past, present or future). Although there are
forty-eight such combinations, there are only twenty-four distinct forms in the
paradigm, as Table 3.4 more clearly shows; thus, one might instead suppose
that the paradigm actually only has twenty-four cells. In the more numerously
celled representation in Table 3.3, each cell has a morphosyntactic property set
containing either five properties (a set belonging to (17a)) or four (a set belonging to (17b)). In the representation in Table 3.4, by contrast, many of the cells
have smaller property sets; these are listed in Table 3.5.

(17)[5]    a. { $p, n, g, t,$ ind} $p \in S_{\text{PERSON}}, n \in S_{\text{NUMBER}}, g \in S_{\text{GENDER}}, t \in S_{\text{TENSE}}$
           b. { $p, n, g,$ optative} $p \in S_{\text{PERSON}}, n \in S_{\text{NUMBER}}, g \in S_{\text{GENDER}}$

The puzzle, then, is whether the noncanonical paradigm of Bhojpuri DĒKH
has the structure in Table 3.3 or the one in Tables 3.4/3.5. If it has the structure
in Table 3.3, then it deviates from the canonical property in (16b) but not from
the one in (16a). But if it instead has the structure in Tables 3.4/3.5, then it

4 The notion of stem appropriateness is sharpened in Chapter 5.
5 In (17), $S_\alpha$ represents the set of values for the inflectional category $\alpha$.

Table 3.3  *The inflection of Bhojpuri DĒKH 'see' (48 cells)*

|  |  | Present indicative | | Past indicative | | Future indicative | | Optative | |
|---|---|---|---|---|---|---|---|---|---|
|  |  | sg | pl | sg | pl | sg | pl | sg | pl |
| 1 | masc | dēkh-īl-ā | dēkh-īl-ā | dekh-al-ĩ | dekh-al-ĩ | dēkh-ab | dekh-ab-ǣ | dēkh-ĩ | dēkh-ĩ |
|  | fem | dēkh-īl-ā | dēkh-īl-ā | dekh-al-ĩ | dekh-al-ĩ | dēkh-ab | dekh-ab-ǣ | dēkh-ĩ | dēkh-ĩ |
| 2 | masc | dēkh-āl-ā | dēkh-āl-ā | dekh-al-ā | dekh-al-ā | dekh-ab-ā | dekh-ab-ā | dēkh-ā | dēkh-ā |
|  | fem | dēkh-æl-iu | dēkh-æl-iu | dekh-al-iu | dekh-al-iu | dekh-ab-iu | dekh-ab-iu | dēkh-ā | dēkh-ā |
| 3 | masc | dēkh-āl-ā | dēkh-æl-ǣ | dēkh-al | dekh-al-ǣ | dēkh-ĩ | dekh-ih-ǣ | dēkh-æ | dēkh-ǣ |
|  | fem | dēkh-æl-ē | dēkh-æl-ini | dēkh-al-i | dekh-al-ini | dēkh-ĩ | dekh-ih-ǣ | dēkh-æ | dēkh-ǣ |

*Source:* Shukla 1981

Table 3.4  *The inflection of Bhojpuri DĒKH 'see' (24 cells)*

|  |  | Present indicative | | Past indicative | | Future indicative | | Optative | |
|---|---|---|---|---|---|---|---|---|---|
|  |  | sg | pl | sg | pl | sg | pl | sg | pl |
| 1 | masc, fem | dēkh-īl-ā | | dekh-al-ĩ | | dēkh-ab | dekh-ab-ǣ | dēkh-ĩ | |
| 2 | masc | dēkh-āl-ā | | dekh-al-ā | | dekh-ab-ā | | dēkh-ā | |
|  | fem | dēkh-æl-iu | | dekh-al-iu | | dekh-ab-iu | | | |
| 3 | masc | dēkh-āl-ǣ | dēkh-æl-ǣ | dēkh-al | dekh-al-ǣ | dēkh-ī | dekh-ih-ǣ | dēkh-œ | dēkh-ǣ |
|  | fem | dēkh-ēl-ē | dēkh-æl-ini | dēkh-al-i | dekh-al-ini | | | | |

*Source:* Shukla 1981

Table 3.5 *The morphosyntactic property sets associated with the cells in Table 3.4*

| | Present indicative | | Past indicative | | Future indicative | | Optative | |
| --- | --- | --- | --- | --- | --- | --- | --- | --- |
| | sg | pl | sg | pl | sg | pl | sg | pl |
| 1 masc, fem | {1 prs ind} | | {1 pst ind} | | {1sg fut ind} | {1pl fut ind} | | {1 opt} |
| 2 masc | {2 masc prs ind} | | {2 masc pst ind} | | {2 masc fut ind} | | | {2 opt} |
| fem | {2 fem prs ind} | | {2 fem pst ind} | | {2 fem fut ind} | | | |
| 3 masc | {3sg masc prs ind} | {3pl masc prs ind} | {3sg masc pst ind} | {3pl masc pst ind} | {3sg fut ind} | {3pl fut ind} | {3sg opt} | {3pl opt} |
| fem | {3sg fem prs ind} | {3pl fem prs ind} | {3sg fem pst ind} | {3pl fem pst ind} | | | | |

exhibits the property coöccurrence restrictions in (18), deviating from (16a) but not from (16b). Is there any reason for preferring one or the other representation of the paradigm of DĒKH?

(18)    Property coöccurrence restriction exhibited by Tables 3.4/3.5.
        A morphosyntactic property set σ is well-formed if and only if

        for some τ ∈ {{p, n, g, t, m}: p ∈ $S_{\text{PERSON}}$, n ∈ $S_{\text{NUMBER}}$, g ∈ $S_{\text{GENDER}}$,
                t ∈ $S_{\text{TENSE}}$, m ∈ $S_{\text{MOOD}}$},

        σ is the largest subset of τ that satisfies all of the following property constraints:
        a.  [{ ind} ∧ [[prs  } ∨ [ps t} ∨ [ut}]]
        b.  [[p   t} ∧ [[prs  } ∨ [ps t} ∨ [ut}]]
        c.  [{ 1} ∧ [[ma sc} ∨ [e m}]]
        d.  [{ 1} ∧ [[prs  } ∨ [ps t} ∨ [pt}   ∧ [[ g} ∨ {pl}]]]
        e.  [{ 2} ∧ [[ g} ∨ [pl}]]
        f.  [{ 2} ∧ [pt}  ∧ [[ma sc} ∨ [e m}]]
        g.  [{ 3} ∧ [[ut}  ∨ [pt}  ∧ [[ma sc} ∨ [e m}]]].

    There are two apparent reasons for preferring the representation in Table 3.3 over that of Tables 3.4/3.5. The first is the fact that the logic guiding the latter representation cannot be fully applied in any event. In Tables 3.4/3.5, property coöccurrence restrictions are employed to eliminate syncretism from the paradigm of DĒKH. But this is only possible because each group of complete property sets whose realization is syncretized in Table 3.3 constitutes a natural class; for instance, the four property sets in (19) are realized syncretically in Table 3.3, and they constitute the natural class of complete extensions of {1 prs ind}. But property sets whose realizations are syncretized do not always constitute a natural class (a point to which I return in Chapter 10). For example, the Sanskrit genitive is ordinarily syncretized with the ablative in the singular and with the locative in the dual; and the ablative, besides being ordinarily syncretized with the genitive in the singular, is syncretized with the dative in the plural and with both the dative and the instrumental in the dual. The paradigm of AGNI 'fire' in Table 3.6 illustrates. As this example shows, there is no consistent way to portray these instances of syncretism by appealing to natural classes of case properties.

(19)    a. {s g masc prs ind}       c. {pl  masc prs ind}
        b. {s g fem prs ind}        d. {1pl fem prs ind}

    The second reason for preferring the representation in Table 3.3 over that of Tables 3.4/3.5 is the fact that there is no syntactic motivation for the property coöccurrence restrictions in (18). In the third person of the present and past indicative, a verb's subject-agreement inflection is sensitive to distinctions of

Table 3.6 *The declension of Sanskrit* AGNI *'fire'*

(Boxes enclose syncretized genitives; shading encloses syncretized ablatives.)

|              | Sg      | Du        | Pl       |
| ------------ | ------- | --------- | -------- |
| Nominative   | agnis   | agnī      | agnayas  |
| Vocative     | agne    | agnī      | agnayas  |
| Accusative   | agnim   | agnī      | agnīn    |
| Instrumental | agninā  | agnibhyām | agnibhis |
| Dative       | agnaye  | agnibhyām | agnibhyas |
| Ablative     | agnes   | agnibhyām | agnibhyas |
| Genitive     | agnes   | agnyos    | agnīnām  |
| Locative     | agnau   | agnyos    | agniṣu   |

both number and gender. There is no syntactic counterevidence to the simple
assumption that number and gender are subject-agreement categories in all
persons, tenses and moods – that finite verbs invariably carry properties of
number and gender. On this hypothesis, the fact that *dēkhæ̃ the* y should see'
doesn't distinguish gender is not a sign that a verb's paradigm has a single
third-plural optative cell (in accordance with the property coöccurrence restriction in (18g)); rather, it reflects the fact that the rules of exponence realizing the
optative mood happen to be insensitive to gender distinctions. Thus, consider
the partial analysis of Bhojpuri verb inflection in Table 3.7. In this analysis,
only four rules of exponence serve in the realization of optative forms: these
are rules (a), (e), (l) and (m) in Block II, none of which realizes gender.

The relation between optative mood and properties of gender in Bhojpuri is
therefore wholly unlike the relation (1) of future tense to subjunctive mood in
Latin. Contra (18), nothing in Bhojpuri syntax excludes the free combination
of optative mood with subject-agreement properties of gender; one need only
assume that the inflectional morphology of Bhojpuri fails to realize gender
distinctions in the optative, where masculine and feminine are therefore syncretized.[6] In Latin, by contrast, the absence of any specific exponence for the
future subjunctive isn't simply compensated for by a syncretism of the future
subjunctive with some other tense/mood combination; rather, it is a reflection
of the fact that in Latin syntax, future tense and subjunctive mood do not
combine – that in order to express the meaning of a future subjunctive, some
kind of circumlocution has to be resorted to.[7]

6  In Section 10.1, I will propose a refinement of this analysis of Bhojpuri syncretism.
7  Typically, this circumlocution is the use of a future active participle together with a present
   subjunctive form of be ': *Incertus sum quid facturus sim* I a m uncertain what I shall do.'

Table 3.7 *Analysis of a fragment of Bhojpuri verb inflection*

**Paradigm function:**
PF($\langle$L, σ$\rangle$) $=_{def}$ II : [ I : $\langle$X, σ$\rangle$]], where X is the stem of L appropriate for the realization of σ.

**Stems of the lexeme DĒKH 'see':**
- *dēkh* is appropriate for realizing extensions of the following property sets –
  {PERS:3 NUM:sg}   {TNS:fut PERS:1 NUM:sg}
  {TNS:prs}          {MOOD:opt}
- otherwise, *dekh* is the appropriate stem.

**Rules of exponence:**

| **Block I** | **Block II** |
|---|---|
| a. X, V, {prs } → Xāl | a. X, V, {} → Xĩ |
| b. X, V, { prs} → Xīl | b. X, V, { prs} → Xā |
| c. X, V, [{prs } ∧ [{2 fe m} ∨ {3pl}]] → Xæl | c. X, V, { fut} → X |
| d. X, V, {3s g fem prs} → Xēl | d. X, V, {pl fut} → Xæ̃ |
| e. X, V, {ps t} → Xal | e. X, V, {2} → Xā |
| f. X, V, {ut} → Xab | f. X, V, {2 fem ind} → Xiu |
| g. X, V, {3 fut} → X | g. X, V, {3sg prs} → Xā |
| h. X, V, {3pl fut} → Xih | h. X, V, {3s g fem prs} → Xē |
| | i. X, V, {3sg pst} → X |
| | j. X, V, {3sg fem pst} → Xi |
| | k. X, V, {3s g fut} → Xī |
| | l. X, V, {3sg opt} → Xæ |
| | m. X, V, {3pl} → Xæ̃ |
| | n. X, V, [{3pl fem} ∧ [{prs} ∨ {pst}]] → Xini |

## 3.8 Conclusion

The conception of morphosyntactic properties presented so far is essentially quite simple, and the simplest hypothesis is that this conception affords a satisfactory account of inflectional morphology. We will, however, find that certain kinds of inflectional paradigms motivate a fundamental revision of this conception.

# 4    *Lexemes*

An inflectional paradigm specifies the word forms realizing a particular lexeme. Like phonemes in phonology, lexemes are a theoretical abstraction: Just as phonemes serve to classify the speech sounds composing a spoken utterance (allowing, for example, the [tʰ] in [tʰɑp], the [t] in [stɑp], the [ɾ] in [ˈbɛɾ ɚ] and the [ʔ] in [ˈbʌʔn̩] to be classified as instances of the English phoneme /t/), so lexemes serve to classify the word forms composing a sentence (allowing, for example, the word forms *go, goes, went, gone* and *going* to be classified as instances of the English lexeme GO). The term "lexeme" is therefore only meaningful in the context of a theory of the lexicon and its interface with morphology, syntax and semantics. Here, I discuss the fundamental properties of lexemes within this theoretical context (Section 4.1), the relation between lexemes and lexical entries (Section 4.2), and the incidence of noncanonical lexical entries (Section 4.3), briefly summarizing in Section 4.4.

## 4.1    *What is a lexeme?*

A **lexeme** is (i) a lexical abstraction that (ii) has either a meaning (ordinarily) or a grammatical function, (iii) belongs to a syntactic category (most often a lexical category), and (iv) is realized by one or more phonological forms (canonically, by morphosyntactically contrasting word forms). All four components of this characterization have been sources of misunderstanding and sometimes disagreement, and therefore deserve some elaboration. (See also Bauer 2000.)

### 4.1.1    *A lexeme is a lexical abstraction*
Lexemes are sometimes equated with lexical entries, but there are lexical entries that aren't lexemes (e.g. multiword idioms) as well as lexemes that don't exist as lexical entries (e.g. productively created lexemes such as the compound noun

*city garbage report*); see Di Sciullo and Williams (1987: Ch. 1). Lexemes are lexical abstractions in the sense that

(a) lexemes themselves have no phonological form, but they are realized by expressions that do have phonological form – by word forms, ordinarily;

(b) a lexeme's syntactic category and semantic content are either listed in its lexical entry or are determined by the properties of other lexemes in accordance with rules of "word formation" (a potentially misleading term intended to subsume the phenomena of compounding and derivation); and

(c) the expressions that realize a lexeme may be listed as part of its lexical entry or may be determined by inflectional rules.

### 4.1.2 A lexeme has a meaning or grammatical function

Ordinarily, the word forms in a lexeme L's paradigm exhibit systematic differences in meaning, yet they simultaneously share an important core of meaning; this core is regarded as the meaning of L, and is sometimes referred to as the **lexical meaning** of its word forms. In the default case, the meaning of a word form realizing a lexeme L is simply L's lexical meaning; for instance, the meaning of *sleep* in *I can't sleep* is plausibly just that of the verbal lexeme SLEEP. But the meaning of a word form realizing L may instead be the value of some function/operation applied to L's lexical meaning; thus, the meaning of *slept* in *I slept* involves the application of a past-tense operator to the meaning of SLEEP. On the assumption that lexemes may belong to functional as well as lexical categories (Section 4.1.3), a lexeme may have a purely grammatical function rather than any lexical meaning (Spencer 2013: 46ff); thus, if the main verb DO of *Do your homework* and the auxiliary DO of *I don't know* are both lexemes, the first seemingly expresses a lexical meaning, and the second, a purely grammatical function.

### 4.1.3 A lexeme belongs to a syntactic category

A lexeme's syntactic category membership determines that of the forms that realize it. This does not entail that all of the forms realizing a lexeme necessarily belong to the same syntactic category, since there are familiar instances in which that is not the case; for instance, the realizations of verbal lexemes can be plausibly assumed to include participles and infinitives, even though in many languages, these are respectively adjectival and nominal rather than verbal. A lexeme's category membership does, however, make it possible to deduce the category membership of each of the forms realizing it.

Although lexemes are sometimes thought of as members of lexical categories (e.g. verb, noun, adjective) and not of functional categories (e.g. conjunction, determiner, complementizer), it is not clear what the rationale for this idea is.

It might be that this idea follows from the assumption that members of lexical categories are realized by more than one word form (i.e. have paradigms), but that functional categories are not; that assumption, however, is not factual. There are inflectionally invariant members of lexical categories (e.g. adjectives such as *daily* and *asleep*) as well as inflectable members of functional categories (e.g. determiners that inflect for gender, case and number; complementizers that inflect for agreement (cf. Haegeman 1992: 47ff, Weiss 2005, de Haan 2010: Ch.10, and so on)).

Perhaps the idea that lexemes are restricted to lexical categories stems from the assumption that members of lexical categories have independently specifiable meanings, but that members of functional categories only have a grammatical function, and can therefore only be meaningful in combination with members of lexical categories. But this assumption is questionable. While some "function words" have grammatical functions that cannot be easily construed as independently specifiable meanings (e.g. the use of *of* to mark a noun's direct argument: *destroy the building*, but *the destruction of the building*), this is not invariably the case. In a Fregean approach to semantics (e.g. that of Montague 1973), both "content words" (SEEK, UNICORN) and "function words" (AND, THE) may denote functions (one-place operations) whose evaluation depends on their combination with other meaningful expressions; in such an approach, the assumption that the function/operation denoted by SEEK is somehow independently specifiable in a way that the function/operation denoted by THE is not has no clear basis.

For present purposes, I see no compelling obstacle to assuming that any lexical unit that can be realized as a word form is a lexeme.

### 4.1.4  *A lexeme is realized by one or more phonological forms*

In the simplest cases, a lexeme is realized by a single word form, as in the case of *daily* and *asleep*. Most lexemes, however, are not this simple: a lexeme may be realized by two or more alternative word forms, which may or may not contrast morphosyntactically; and lexemes may be realized by phonological forms that are larger than or smaller than a simple word form – that is, by a combination of word forms or by a clitic. Consider each of these cases.

Canonically, a lexeme may be realized by alternative word forms that contrast in their morphosyntactic content, as in Table 4.1. In exceptional cases, some of the word forms realizing a lexeme may be associated with a specialization of its lexical meaning. Thus, although *brethren* and *brothers* express the same morphosyntactic properties, *brethren* additionally involves a specialization of the meaning of the lexeme BROTHER; similar remarks apply to such pairs as *hung/hanged*, *worst/baddest*, *farther/further* and *older/elder*.

Table 4.1 *Some English lexemes realized by morphosyntactically contrasting word forms*

| Lexeme L | Word forms realizing L that contrast morphosyntactically | | | |
|---|---|---|---|---|
| CHILD | /ˈʧaɪld/ | *child* | /ˈʧɪldɹən/ | *children* |
| | /ˈʧaɪldz/ | *child's* | /ˈʧɪldɹənz/ | *children's* |
| TEACHER | /ˈtiʧɚ/ | *teacher* | | |
| | /ˈtiʧɚz/ | *teachers,* | | |
| | | *teacher's,* | | |
| | | *teachers'* | | |
| SING | /ˈsɪŋ/ | *sing* | /ˈsʌŋ/ | *sung* |
| | /ˈsɪŋz/ | *sings* | /ˈsɪŋɪŋ/ | *singing* |
| | /ˈsæŋ/ | *sang* | | |
| UNTIE | /ənˈtaɪ/ | *untie* | /ənˈtaɪd/ | *untied* |
| | /ənˈtaɪz/ | *unties* | /ənˈtaɪjɪŋ/ | *untying* |
| BE | /ˈbi/ | *be* | /ˈwʌz/ | *was* | /ˈwʌznt/ | *wasn't* |
| | /ˈɛm/ | *am* | /ˈwɝ/ | *were* | /ˈwɝnt/ | *weren't* |
| | /ˈɑɹ/ | *are* | /ˈbɪn/ | *been* | /ˈɑɹnt/ | *aren't* |
| | /ˈɪz/ | *is* | /ˈbijɪŋ/ | *being* | /ˈɪznt/ | *isn't* |
| SLEEPY | /ˈslipi/ | *sleepy* | /ˈslipijəst/ | *sleepy* |
| | /ˈslipijɚ/ | *sleepier* | | |

A lexeme may also be realized by alternative word forms that contrast phonologically but not grammatically or semantically. These may be in free variation or in overlapping environments, or they may have a complementary distribution conditioned by factors of a phonological, prosodic or syntactic nature;[1] the forms in Table 4.2 illustrate.

In the foregoing cases, the word forms realizing a given lexeme are in paradigmatic opposition in the sense that they constitute alternative realizations. But a lexeme may also be realized periphrastically, by a combination of two or more word forms. In Latin, for example, verbs inflect synthetically in the imperfective active and passive as well as in the perfective active, but not in the perfective passive, where periphrastic inflection instead appears (Börjars, Vincent and Chapman 1997); the partial paradigm in Table 4.3 illustrates.[2]

1 Instances of free variation or overlapping distribution constitute instances of overabundance (Thornton 2012), a topic to which I return in Chapter 9. Instances of complementary distribution have sometimes been described as the effect of shape conditions; see Asudeh and Klein 2002 and the references cited there.
2 Inflectional periphrasis has been the focus of extensive investigation in recent years; see, for example, Börjars, Vincent and Chapman 1997, Sadler and Spencer 2001, Ackerman and Stump 2004, Ackerman, Stump and Webelhuth 2011, Bonami and Webelhuth 2012, Spencer 2013, Chumakina and Corbett 2013.

Table 4.2 *Some English lexemes realized by phonologically contrasting but synonymous word forms*

| Lexeme L | Phonologically contrasting synonyms realizing L | | Distribution |
|---|---|---|---|
| DREAM | /dɹimd/ ~ /dɹɛmt/ | *dreamed, dreamt* | free variation |
| PROVE | /pɹuvən/ ~ /pɹuvd/ | *proven, proved* (as ptcp.) | or overlapping |
| TOWARD | /twɔɹd/ ~ /twɔɹdz/ | *toward, towards* | environments |
| A | /eɪ/ ~ /ə/ ~ /æn/ ~ /ən/ | | complementary |
| THE | /ð̆/ ~ /ðə/ | *a, an* | phonological or |
| HAVE | /hæz/ ~ /(h)əz/ ~ /z/ *has, 's* | *the* | prosodic environments |
| I | /maɪ/ ~ /maɪn/ | *my, mine* | complementary |
| THEY | /ðɛɹ/ ~ /ðɛɹz/ | *their, theirs* | syntactic |
| LONE | /loʊn/ ~ /əloʊn/ | *lone, alone* | environments |

Table 4.3 *The indicative inflection of Latin* PARĀRE *'prepare'*

| | Nonperfective | | | Perfective | | |
|---|---|---|---|---|---|---|
| | Present | Future | Imperfect | Perfect | Future Perfect | Pluperfect |
| Active | *parō* | *parābō* | *parābam* | *parāvī* | *parāverō* | *parāveram* |
| | *parās* | *parābis* | *parābās* | *parāvistī* | *parāveris* | *parāverās* |
| | *parat* | *parābit* | *parābat* | *parāvit* | *parāverit* | *parāverat* |
| | *parāmus* | *parābimus* | *parābāmus* | *parāvimus* | *parāverimus* | *parāverāmus* |
| | *parātis* | *parābitis* | *parābātis* | *parāvistis* | *parāveritis* | *parāverātis* |
| | *parant* | *parābunt* | *parābant* | *parāvērunt* | *parāverint* | *parāverant* |
| Passive | *paror* | *parābor* | *parābar* | *parātus sum* | *parātus erō* | *parātus eram* |
| | *parāris* | *parāberis* | *parābāris* | *parātus es* | *parātus eris* | *parātus erās* |
| | *parātur* | *parābitur* | *parābātur* | *parātus est* | *parātus erit* | *parātus erat* |
| | *parāmur* | *parābimur* | *parābāmur* | *parātī sumus* | *parātī erimus* | *parātī erāmus* |
| | *parāminī* | *parābiminī* | *parābāminī* | *parātī estis* | *parātī eritis* | *parātī erātis* |
| | *parantur* | *parābuntur* | *parābantur* | *parātī sunt* | *parātī erunt* | *parātī erant* |

Finally, a lexeme may be realized by a clitic, which is not itself a word form but requires a word form as its host; for instance, the clitic *-s* /z/ may serve as a realization for the lexemes BE (*He's sick*), HAVE (*He's had lunch*) and DO (*What's he want?*).[3]

---

3 Clitics are sometimes assumed not to belong to any syntactic category (Spencer 2013: 50f); under that assumption, a lexeme realized as a clitic would therefore seemingly fail to satisfy the expectation (Section 4.1.2) that lexemes belong to syntactic categories. For detailed discussion of the range of clitic–host relations, see Anderson 2005: 37ff.

*4.1.5    Lexemes and the distinction between inflection and word formation*

Logically, the notion "lexeme" is bound to the distinction between inflection and word formation (Spencer 2013: 38ff). Inflection is seen as determining the morphological realization of the cells in a lexeme's paradigm; the function of inflection is therefore not to create new lexemes, but to spell out the inventory of word forms available for expressing an existing lexeme. By contrast, word formation creates new lexemes from existing lexemes, either by deriving one lexeme from another or by compounding two lexemes.

A leitmotif in the morphological literature is the question of whether the traditional distinction between inflection and word formation is theoretically defensible. Arguments against the distinction have taken various forms, generally asserting the inadequacy of the various practical criteria[4] that are sometimes invoked in attempts to delineate the boundary between inflection and word formation. But if the distinction between inflection and word formation is seen as a canonical opposition relative to which a continuum of noncanonical phenomena may be defined, then arguments of this sort tend to lose their force. (See Spencer 2013: 38ff for relevant discussion.)

## 4.2    Lexical entries

Discussions of the notion "lexical entry" become unnecessarily complex when logically distinct conceptions of the lexicon are casually conflated, making it desirable to distinguish among the two notions "mental lexicon" and "stipulated lexicon."

A language user's **mental lexicon** is a system in which specific linguistic forms and their associated grammatical and semantic content are stored in that language user's brain; thus, the mental lexicon is a part of a person's linguistic knowledge. It is customary to assume that in the mental lexicon, associations of linguistic forms with grammatical and semantic content are compartmentalized as discrete entries. Many of these entries correspond to specific lexemes, but not all do. Some entries house combinations of words, including rote memorizations (e.g. song lyrics, commercial slogans, etc.), idioms (*jump the shark*, *nip in the bud*), conventionalized expressions (*get going*, *make a false move*), and so on; other entries list lexeme-like bound elements whose stems are employed in productive compounding (*astro-*, *-meister*).[5] A true lexeme's entry

---

4  Discussions of these criteria include those of Anderson 1985, Stump 1998, and Booij 2000.
5  Di Sciullo and Williams (1987) coin the term LISTEME to refer to any of the range of expressions listed in a language user's mental lexicon.

includes at least one form (a stem or a word form), but it may include multiple word forms; multiple forms must obviously be specified in cases of suppletion or irregularity, but experimental psycholinguistic evidence shows that high-frequency forms may be stored even if they are regular in every way (Stemberger and MacWhinney 1988). Thus, the mental lexicon is in some ways redundant. There is no expectation that different speakers' mental lexicons are identical, nor must one assume that a lexeme is listed in the mental lexicon simply because it is interpretable, since interpretation may result from analysis rather than retrieval (as in the case of newly encountered compound lexemes such as *city garbage report*).

A language's **stipulated lexicon** is the body of lexical information that is presupposed by the definition of a language's grammar. The stipulated lexicon may therefore be seen as containing a part of the information in a language user's mental lexicon. In particular, it contains information about stems and word forms that is necessary for the systematic definition of more complex expressions by the language's morphology and syntax and for the interpretation of these expressions by the language's semantics. While the mental lexicon is redundant, there is no obstacle to assuming that a language's stipulated lexicon never lists information that the language's grammar is independently capable of inducing by productive means.

A complete entry for a lexeme L in the stipulated lexicon may be assumed to contain information about the word forms realizing L, the grammatically significant categories to which L belongs, L's semantics and the morphosyntactic content of its individual word forms. But lexical entries aren't necessarily complete in this sense. A language's inflectional morphology makes it possible to simplify a lexeme's lexical entry by minimizing the amount of information listed about its word forms; and a language's word-formation principles make it possible to minimize the amount of grammatical or semantic information listed in the lexical entry of a derived or compound lexeme. As a consequence, a lexeme's entry in the stipulated lexicon mainly specifies aspects of its form or content that are not independently deducible by grammatical means. The vivid metaphor for the lexicon proposed by Di Sciullo and Williams 1987 ("a prison for the lawless") seems somewhat apt as a characterization of the stipulated lexicon,[6] though it might be wrongly taken to imply that the lexicon's inmates remain lawless even once they are released into the society of morphosyntax; a better metaphor might be a dot-to-dot puzzle, the location and numbering

6  It is less appropriate for the mental lexicon, in which high-frequency forms may be stored even if they are grammatically regular and hence entirely lawful.

of whose dots cannot be deduced by any rule, but whose use as the basis for deducing a particular image depends on its compatibility with a regular system of line-drawing rules.

## 4.3 Noncanonical entries in the stipulated lexic on

Canonically, entries in the stipulated lexicon differ in certain ways: they correspond to lexemes that differ both in their lexical meaning and in the forms by which they are realized. Thus, in the canonical case, there is no synonymy among distinct lexemes and no homophony among the realizations of distinct lexemes. There are, of course, various kinds of deviations from these canonical properties. Synonymous lexemes do exist (e.g. the compound lexemes WOODCHUCK and GROUNDHOG), though it is striking how few of the candidate examples are truly synonymous. Homophones, by contrast, positively abound: the singular form of the noun SAW and the past-tense form of the verb SEE; the infinitive of GROAN and the past participle of GROW; and so on and on. The explanation resides at least partly in the fact that the small size of a language's inventory of phonological segments and the inevitable restrictiveness of its phonotactics together make it necessary to employ at least some word forms in more than one function.

What is perhaps more striking than the widespread incidence of homophony is that of **homomorphy**: homomorphic lexemes are lexically and semantically distinct but alike in every detail of their morphology. In English, the verbs WEAR$_1$ 'have on (an article of clothing)' and WEAR$_2$ 'erode' are absolutely alike in their morphology; the same is true of STICK$_1$ 'adhere' and STICK$_2$ 'jab'; of CAST$_1$ 'throw, project,' CAST$_2$ 'assign a role (in acting),' and CAST$_3$ 'create by means of a liquid substance hardened in a mold'; and so on. The examples in (1) illustrate.[7] We will return to the significance of homomorphic lexemes in Chapter 7.[8]

---

7 The boundary between homomorphy and polysemy is a fuzzy one. In the clearest cases of polysemy, a class of lexemes is used systematically to express two or more related kinds of meanings. In English, for example, intransitive verbs with an inchoative meaning ("become X") can also be used transitively with a causative meaning ("cause to become X"), e.g. ACCELERATE, COOL, DARKEN, INTENSIFY, VAPORIZE. The clearest cases of homomorphy, by contrast, appear to involve nothing more than a coincidental similarity in the realization of two unrelated lexemes. Between these extremes are less clearcut cases such as that of DRAW, where drawing a picture, drawing a curtain, drawing a wagon and drawing a number out of a hat all entail moving something across or along or out of something else (be it a pencil across paper, a curtain across a window, a wagon along a road or a number out of a hat); or that of French VOLER, whose meanings to fly' and to steal' are historically linked by a once-common metaphor likening stealing to making something fly away (Bernard Fradin, personal communication).

8 The examples in (1) involve lexemes all of whose word forms are alike. There are, however, instances of what might be called **restricted homomorphy** – cases in which two lexemes are

(1)     Some examples of homomorphy in English
        a. He **wears/wore/has worn** the same shirt every day.
           His backpack **wears/wore/has worn** holes in all his shirts.
        b. He **sticks/stuck/has stuck** me in the side with his pen.
           Your gum **sticks/stuck/has stuck** to the inside of the waste basket.
        c. He **casts/cast/has cast** spells on everyone.
           In every film, he **casts/cast/has cast** us as a bunch of hoods.
           He **casts/cast/has cast** his sculptures in bronze.

## *4.4     Conclusion*

Summarizing, lexemes are lexical abstractions. A lexeme belongs to a syntactic category, has a meaning or grammatical function, and has one or more phonological realizations (typically word forms). Canonical inflectional morphology defines a lexeme's phonological realizations; canonical word formation defines new lexemes on the basis of existing lexemes. Although lexical entries ordinarily correspond to lexemes, not all do, nor do all lexemes have corresponding lexical entries. Canonically, distinct lexical entries exhibit neither synonymy nor homophony, but noncanonical entries may exhibit either phenomenon, homophony being significantly more common than true synonymy.

 In the two chapters that follow, we will consider two characteristics of lexemes that are central to the definition of their inflectional paradigms: their stems and the inflection classes to which they belong.

---

alike in their morphology in only part of their paradigms. In Spanish, for example, the verbs IR 'go' and SER 'be' are alike in the preterite indicative and in the imperfect and future subjunctive (where they exhibit identical forms based on the stem *fu-*); otherwise, they inflect differently.

# 5    *Stems*

The definition of a lexeme's inflectional paradigm makes essential reference to that lexeme's stem(s). Canonically, a single stem serves as the basis for every word form in a lexeme's paradigm, as in Table 5.1. Very often, however, a lexeme's paradigm is based on more than one stem. In such cases, the difference in form between the stems is logically independent of their difference in distribution (Section 5.1). Formal variation among a lexeme's stems may be attributable to sandhi processes, may be an inherent property of a particular inflection class or may reflect a juxtaposition of independent inflection classes (Section 5.2). The distribution of stems within a lexeme's inflectional paradigm may be conditioned in a variety of ways (Section 5.3): Phonologically conditioned distribution may be purely an effect of automatic sandhi processes or may be nonautomatic; grammatically conditioned distribution may be sensitive to morphosyntactic or morphomic properties of a lexeme's word forms. I exemplify the various possibilities with evidence from Sanskrit, whose inflectional morphology is particularly rich in stem alternations. I summarize the ways in which the different kinds of alternation in stem form crosscut the different patterns of stem distribution (Section 5.4). As will become increasingly clear in subsequent chapters, an understanding of the factors that determine the form and choice of a lexeme's stems

Table 5.1 *The declension of Turkish* ADAM *'man'*

|            | Singular   | Plural         |
|------------|------------|----------------|
| Nominative | *adam*     | *adam-lar*     |
| Accusative | *adam-ı*   | *adam-lar-ı*   |
| Dative     | *adam-a*   | *adam-lar-a*   |
| Locative   | *adam-da*  | *adam-lar-da*  |
| Ablative   | *adam-dan* | *adam-lar-dan* |
| Genitive   | *adam-ın*  | *adam-lar-ın*  |

Table 5.2  *The neuter declension of Sanskrit* ŚUCI
*'bright' and* BALIN *'powerful'*

| Singular | Nominative | śuci | bali |
|---|---|---|---|
| | Vocative | śuci | bali(n) |
| | Accusative | śuci | bali |
| | Instrumental | śucin-ā | balin-ā |
| | Dative | śucin-e | balin-e |
| | Ablative, Genitive | śucin-as | balin-as |
| | Locative | śucin-i | balin-i |
| Dual | Nom, Voc, Acc | śucin-ī | balin-ī |
| | Instr, Dat, Abl | śuci-bhyām | bali-bhyām |
| | Genitive, Locative | śucin-os | balin-os |
| Plural | Nom, Voc | śucīn-i | balīn-i |
| | Accusative | śucīn-i | balīn-i |
| | Instrumental | śuci-bhis | bali-bhis |
| | Dative, Ablative | śuci-bhyas | bali-bhyas |
| | Genitive | śucīn-ām | balin-ām |
| | Locative | śuci-ṣu | bali-ṣu |

is central to understanding the structure of inflectional paradigms. I therefore propose a precise way of modeling a stem's formal and distributional properties by means of two operations (Section 5.5): a function **Stem** mapping a paradigm cell's lexical and morphosyntactic content to a stem form (cf. Stump 2001: 183ff); and an operation **SC** whose value for a particular stem varies according to its syntagmatic context. I summarize in Section 5.6.

## 5.1    *Stem form and stem distribution*

An alternation among the members of some set of inflectional stems is a correlation of the difference in form among these stems with the difference in their paradigmatic distribution. In an alternation of this sort, the dimensions of form and distribution are in principle independent; one reflection of this separation is the fact that two lexemes may exhibit stem alternations that are alike with respect to form but different with respect to distribution, or conversely, stem alternations that are different with respect to form but alike with respect to distribution.

Thus, consider the neuter declension of the Sanskrit adjectives ŚUCI 'bright' and BALIN þo werful' in Table 5.2. They exhibit the same alternation in stem form (śuci- ~ śucin- ~ śucīn-, bali- ~ balin- ~ balīn-), but they differ with respect to the distribution of these stems: ŚUCI uses its *īn* stem śucīn- in realizing

Table 5.3 *The declension of Sanskrit* RĀJAN *'king' and*
PANTHAN *'road'*

| Singular | Nominative | *rājā* | *panthā-s* |
|---|---|---|---|
| | Vocative | *rājan* | *panthā-s* |
| | Accusative | *rājān-am* | *panthān-am* |
| | Instrumental | *rājñ-ā* | *path-ā* |
| | Dative | *rājñ-e* | *path-e* |
| | Ablative, Genitive | *rājñ-as* | *path-as* |
| | Locative | *rājñ-i* | *path-i* |
| Dual | Nom, Voc, Acc | *rājān-au* | *panthān-au* |
| | Instr, Dat, Abl | *rāja-bhyām* | *pathi-bhyām* |
| | Genitive, Locative | *rājñ-os* | *path-os* |
| Plural | Nom, Voc | *rājān-as* | *panthān-as* |
| | Accusative | *rājñ-as* | *path-as* |
| | Instrumental | *rāja-bhis* | *pathi-bhis* |
| | Dative, Ablative | *rāja-bhyas* | *pathi-bhyas* |
| | Genitive | *rājñ-ām* | *path-ām* |
| | Locative | *rāja-su* | *pathi-ṣu* |

the genitive plural, whereas BALIN instead uses its *in* stem *balin-*; and BALIN, unlike ŚUCI, has the option of using its *in* stem in the vocative singular.

The converse situation is exemplified by the paradigms of Sanskrit PAN-THAN 'road' and RĀJAN 'king' in Table 5.3. These paradigms exhibit a widely observed distributional pattern in Sanskrit declension (Whitney 1889: Section 311). This pattern involves a "Strong" stem (exemplified by *rājān-* and *panthān-* and their sandhi forms *rājā-* and *panthā-*), a "Middle" stem (exemplified by *rāja-* and *pathi-*) and a "Weakest" stem (*rājñ-* and *path-*); the Strong stem is used to realize morphosyntactic property sets that satisfy the property constraint (1) and the Middle and Weakest stems are used otherwise[1] (the Weakest stem prevocalically, the Middle stem elsewhere). Although the Strong stems of PANTHAN and RĀJAN are alike in form (both end in *ān*, typically for *n*-stem nouns), their Middle and Weakest stems are different; while those of RĀJAN are usual for an *n*-stem noun, those of PANTHAN are exceptional. Yet, as Table 5.3 shows, the Middle and Weakest stems of PANTHAN exhibit precisely the same distribution as those of RĀJAN. Thus, the stems in Table 5.2 are alike with respect to form but different with

1 In the declension to which RĀJAN king' belongs, masculine vocative singular forms have their own stem (e.g. *rājan*).

Table 5.4  *The declension of Sanskrit* MARUT
*'wind'*

|          |                     |              |
| -------- | ------------------- | ------------ |
| Singular | Nom, Voc            | *marut*      |
|          | Accusative          | *marut-am*   |
|          | Instrumental        | *marut-ā*    |
|          | Dative              | *marut-e*    |
|          | Ablative, Genitive  | *marut-as*   |
|          | Locative            | *marut-i*    |
| Dual     | Nom, Voc, Acc       | *marut-au*   |
|          | Instr, Dat, Abl     | *marud-bhyām* |
|          | Genitive, Locative  | *marut-os*   |
| Plural   | Nom, Voc, Acc       | *marut-as*   |
|          | Instrumental        | *marud-bhis* |
|          | Dative, Ablative    | *marud-bhyas* |
|          | Genitive            | *marut-ām*   |
|          | Locative            | *marut-su*   |

respect to distribution, while the Middle and Weakest stems in Table 5.3 are different with respect to form but alike with respect to distribution. These facts suggest the need to define rules for the formation of stems separately from rules determining the distribution of stems: Stems whose formation is determined by the same rules may be subject to different distributional rules, and vice versa.

(1)      [[{ɲom} ∨ {ʋ oc} ∨ {ɑ̣ cc} ∧ [{ɦe ut pl} ∨ [[{masc} ∨ {fem}] ∧ {ɬ acc pl}]]]

## 5.2     *Sources of formal differences among alternating stems*

Some of the alternations in stem form exhibited by a language's inflectional paradigms may be necessitated by the phonology of the language. The declensional paradigm of the Sanskrit noun MARUT 'w ind' in Table 5.4 exhibits two stem forms: *marut-* and *marud-*. The latter stem appears before a suffix beginning with a voiced obstruent; elsewhere, the former stem is used. This alternation is necessitated by the phonology of Sanskrit, which invariably requires that /t/ be voiced before a voiced obstruent (Whitney 1889: Section 159). The stem forms *marut-* and *marud-* should therefore be seen as **sandhi alternants**: forms whose distinction is purely a response to the phonological requirements of the language.

Not all alternations in stem form are sandhi alternations. The alternation of the stem forms *anaiṣ-* and *aneṣ-* in the aorist paradigm of Sanskrit NĪ 'lead'

Table 5.5 *The aorist inflection of Sanskrit* NĪ *'lead'*

|        |   | Singular | Dual | Plural |
|--------|---|----------|------|--------|
| Active | 1 | *anaiṣ-am* | *anaiṣ-va* | *anaiṣ-ma* |
|        | 2 | *anaiṣ-īs* | *anaiṣ-ṭam* | *anaiṣ-ṭa* |
|        | 3 | *anaiṣ-īt* | *anaiṣ-ṭām* | *anaiṣ-us* |
| Middle | 1 | *aneṣ-i* | *aneṣ-vahi* | *aneṣ-mahi* |
|        | 2 | *aneṣ-ṭhās* | *aneṣ-āthām* | *aneḍhvam*( ← *aneṣ-dhvam*) |
|        | 3 | *aneṣ-ṭa* | *aneṣ-ātām* | *aneṣ-ata* |

(Table 5.5) cannot be attributed to sandhi, since the stems contrast before the suffix *-ta*: active *anaiṣ-ṭa* 'you led,' but middle *aneṣ-ṭa* ŝ he led.'[2] In this case, the alternation in stem form is simply necessitated by the lexeme NĪ's membership in the *s*-aorist conjugation, whose members exhibit a "strong" root vowel in the active voice and a "weaker" vowel in the middle voice. Because the alternation of *anaiṣ-* and *aneṣ-* is dictated by the membership of NĪ 'lead' in the *s*-aorist conjugation, I call this a **class-determined** alternation in stem form; I shall refer to the participants in such a class-determined stem alternation as **kindred** stems.

Some alternations in stem form are neither sandhi alternations nor class-determined alternations. Consider, for example, the present-system conjugation of the verb NĪ 'lead' in Table 5.6. All of the forms in this table are based on a stem *naya-* whose form is typical of verbs belonging to Sanskrit's first present-system conjugation. The alternation of *naya-* with NĪ's aorist stems *anaiṣ-/aneṣ-* is not a sandhi alternation; note, for example, that like *anaiṣ-* and *aneṣ-*, *naya-* combines with a suffix *-ta* (in the second-person plural forms of the imperfect and imperative active). Nor is the alternation a class-determined alternation: In Sanskrit, a verb's membership in a particular aorist-system conjugation class is logically independent of its membership in a particular present-system conjugation class; that is, the alternation of *naya-* with *anaiṣ-/aneṣ-* is not a feature of membership in either the first present-system conjugation or the *s*-aorist conjugation. Rather, it is a consequence of the fact that Sanskrit conjugation classes are segregated (in the terminology of Section 6.2). Thus, *naya-* and *anaiṣ-/aneṣ-* are **independent** stems belonging to two distinct inflectional patterns; the alternation of *naya-* with

2 The principles of Sanskrit sandhi require the suffix *-ta* to appear as *-ṭa* after *ṣ* (Whitney 1889: Section 226).

Table 5.6 *The present-system inflection of Sanskrit* NĪ *'lead'*

|  | Active | | | Middle | | |
|---|---|---|---|---|---|---|
|  | Singular | Dual | Plural | Singular | Dual | Plural |
| Present indicative | *nayāmi* | *nayāvas* | *nayāmas* | *naye* | *nayāvahe* | *nayāmahe* |
|  | *nayasi* | *nayathas* | *nayatha* | *nayase* | *nayethe* | *nayadhve* |
|  | *nayati* | *nayatas* | *nayanti* | *nayate* | *nayete* | *nayante* |
| Imperfect indicative | *anayam* | *anayāva* | *anayāma* | *anaye* | *anayāvahi* | *anayāmahi* |
|  | *anayas* | *anayatam* | *anayata* | *anayathās* | *anayethām* | *anayadhvam* |
|  | *anayat* | *anayatām* | *anayan* | *anayata* | *anayetām* | *anayanta* |
| Optative | *nayeyam* | *nayeva* | *nayema* | *nayeya* | *nayevahi* | *nayemahi* |
|  | *nayes* | *nayetam* | *nayeta* | *nayethās* | *nayeyāthām* | *nayedhvam* |
|  | *nayet* | *nayetām* | *nayeyus* | *nayeta* | *nayeyātām* | *nayeran* |
| Imperative | *nayāni* | *nayāva* | *nayāma* | *nayai* | *nayāvahai* | *nayāmahai* |
|  | *naya* | *nayatam* | *nayata* | *nayasva* | *nayethām* | *nayadhvam* |
|  | *nayatu* | *nayatām* | *nayantu* | *nayatām* | *nayetām* | *nayantām* |

*anaiṣ-/aneṣ-* is a **class-independent alternation**. In general, then, stem alternations may be a reflection of sandhi, of the morphological pattern proper to a particular inflection class, or of the stems' membership in independent inflection classes.

## 5.3   Stem distribution

The choice between two alternating stems may be determined purely by their phonological context or may instead be sensitive to grammatical information of some kind (either in addition to or instead of information about their phonological surroundings). Phonologically conditioned alternations can, in turn, be of two different kinds, as can grammatically conditioned alternations.

### 5.3.1   *Phonologically conditioned stem alternations:*
### *automatic vs nonautomatic*

On first consideration, one might suppose that phonologically conditioned stem alternants always arise as an effect of automatic sandhi operations (as in the case of *marut- ~ marud-* in Table 5.4). Closer consideration, however, reveals that although sandhi alternations are (by definition) phonologically conditioned, not all phonologically conditioned alternations can be seen as an effect of automatic sandhi. The declensional paradigm of Sanskrit GĪR ś ong'

Table 5.7 *The declension of Sanskrit* GĪR *'song'*

| Singular | Nom, Voc | *gīr* |
|---|---|---|
| | Accusative | *gir-am* |
| | Instrumental | *gir-ā* |
| | Dative | *gir-e* |
| | Ablative, Genitive | *gir-as* |
| | Locative | *gir-i* |
| Dual | Nom, Voc, Acc | *gir-au* |
| | Instr, Dat, Abl | *gīr-bhyām* |
| | Genitive, Locative | *gir-os* |
| Plural | Nom, Voc, Acc | *gir-as* |
| | Instrumental | *gīr-bhis* |
| | Dative, Ablative | *gīr-bhyas* |
| | Genitive | *gir-ām* |
| | Locative | *gīr-ṣu* |

in Table 5.7 exhibits two stems: Because the stem *gir-* appears before vowels and the stem *gīr-* elsewhere, the alternation of *gīr-* with *gir-* is phonologically conditioned. Yet, *gīr-* and *gir-* are not sandhi alternants. Sanskrit phonology allows the sequence /īr/ before vowels and the sequence /ir/ before consonants (e.g. *vīras* he ro,' *nirgacchati* § he goes out'). Thus, although the alternation of *gīr-* and *gir-* is phonologically conditioned, it is not automatic.[3]

### 5.3.2 Grammatically conditioned stem alternations: morphosyntactic vs morphomic

As Table 5.5 shows, the alternation of *anaiṣ-* and *aneṣ-* in the aorist paradigm of Sanskrit NĪ le ad' is grammatically conditioned. Specifically, it is morpho-syntactically conditioned, since *anaiṣ-* is used to express a morphosyntactic property ("active voice") and *aneṣ-*, to express a contrasting property ("middle voice"). One might suppose that in grammatically conditioned stem alterna-tions, each alternant invariably serves to realize a particular morphosyntactic

3 Crosscutting the segmental alternation of *gīr-* with *gir-* is an accentual alternation: direct-case (nominative, vocative and accusative) forms have stem accent, while oblique-case forms have suffixal accent: *gír* (nom sg), *gíras* (nom pl), but *giré* (dat sg), *gīrbhyás* (dat pl).The *gīr-/gir-* alternation is an example of inward phonological conditioning – the conditioning of a stem alternation by the phonological context created by the affixes with which the stem joins. Paster (2006, 2009 and 2015) argues that there are no genuine instances of inward phonological con-ditioning; nevertheless, there do seem to be robust examples of it (Anderson 2008, Carstairs 1987: 179–88, 1988, Round 2009: 227f, Stump 2001: 173ff, Wolf 2013), including the *gīr-/gir-* alternation.

Table 5.8 *The present-system inflection of Sanskrit* KRĪ *'buy'*
(Shaded cells are based on the strong stem *krīṇā-*.)

|  |  |  | Singular | Dual | Plural |
|---|---|---|---|---|---|
| Active voice | Present indicative | 1 | *krīṇā-mi* | *krīṇī-vas* | *krīṇī-mas* |
|  |  | 2 | *krīṇā-si* | *krīṇī-thas* | *krīṇī-tha* |
|  |  | 3 | *krīṇā-ti* | *krīṇī-tas* | *krīṇ-anti* |
|  | Imperfect indicative | 1 | *akrīṇā-m* | *akrīṇī-va* | *akrīṇī-ma* |
|  |  | 2 | *akrīṇā-s* | *akrīṇī-tam* | *akrīṇī-ta* |
|  |  | 3 | *akrīṇā-t* | *akrīṇī-tām* | *akrīṇ-an* |
|  | Optative | 1 | *krīṇī-yām* | *krīṇī-yāva* | *krīṇī-yāma* |
|  |  | 2 | *krīṇī-yās* | *krīṇī-yātam* | *krīṇī-yāta* |
|  |  | 3 | *krīṇī-yāt* | *krīṇī-yātām* | *krīṇī-yus* |
|  | Imperative | 1 | *krīṇā-ni* | *krīṇā-va* | *krīṇā-ma* |
|  |  | 2 | *krīṇī-hi* | *krīṇī-tam* | *krīṇī-ta* |
|  |  | 3 | *krīṇā-tu* | *krīṇī-tām* | *krīṇ-antu* |
| Middle voice | Present indicative | 1 | *krīṇ-e* | *krīṇī-vahe* | *kriṇī-mahe* |
|  |  | 2 | *krīṇī-ṣe* | *krīṇ-āthe* | *krīṇī-dhve* |
|  |  | 3 | *krīṇī-te* | *krīṇ-āte* | *krīṇ-ate* |
|  | Imperfect indicative | 1 | *akrīṇ-i* | *akrīṇī-vahi* | *akrīṇī-mahi* |
|  |  | 2 | *akrīṇī-thās* | *akrīṇ-āthām* | *akrīṇī-dhvam* |
|  |  | 3 | *akrīṇī-ta* | *akrīṇ-ātām* | *akrīṇ-ata* |
|  | Optative | 1 | *krīṇ-īya* | *krīṇ-īvahi* | *krīṇ-īmahi* |
|  |  | 2 | *krīṇ-īthās* | *krīṇ-īyāthām* | *krīṇ-īdhvam* |
|  |  | 3 | *krīṇ-īta* | *krīṇ-īyātām* | *krīṇ-īran* |
|  | Imperative | 1 | *kriṇai (← kriṇā-ai)* | *krīṇā-vahai* | *krīṇā-mahai* |
|  |  | 2 | *krīṇī-ṣva* | *krīṇ-āthām* | *krīṇī-dhvam* |
|  |  | 3 | *krīṇī-tām* | *krīṇ-ātām* | *krīṇ-atām* |

property set; but such is not always the case. In particular, there are grammatically conditioned stem alternations whose condition is **morphomic** (Aronoff 1994) – whose alternants follow a distributional pattern whose significance is purely morphological, having no invariant correlation with phonology, syntax or semantics. In the present-system inflection of Sanskrit KRĪ b uy' (Table 5.8), the alternation of the "strong" stem form *krīṇā-* with the "weak" stem form *krīṇī-* is morphomically conditioned: The strong stem appears in the realization of morphosyntactic property sets satisfying the property constraint in (2) – that is, it appears in the singular active of the present indicative and imperfect, in the first person (active and middle) of the imperative, and in the third-person singular imperative active, with the weak stem appearing elsewhere. There is no morphosyntactic property or set of properties whose realization is a necessary and sufficient correlate of the appearance of either stem; rather, the alternation of *krīṇā-* and *krīṇī-* follows a pattern whose condition is purely morphomic. Although this pattern has no phonological, syntactic or semantic significance, it has considerable morphological significance in Sanskrit: indeed, it conditions the alternation of strong and weak stems in all six athematic conjugations of the present system (the conjugations traditionally numbered 2, 3, 5, 7, 8 and 9).[4]

(2)      [{ ingular indicative active} ∨ [{mpe rative} ∧ [{1} ∨ {3 singular active}]]]]

## 54     *Kinds of stem alternations*

The different sources of alternation in stem form crosscut the different factors that condition stem distribution. That is, one may classify the alternation of two stems both in formal terms (as embodying a class-determined or class-independent difference in form or as an effect of automatic sandhi) and in distributional terms (as being phonologically conditioned, morphosyntactically conditioned, or morphomically conditioned).

As we have seen, a phonologically conditioned alternation may be automatic (as in the case of *marut-* with *marud-* in Table 5.4) or it may be class-determined, embodying a nonautomatic pattern peculiar to a particular inflection class (as in the case of *gīr-* and *gir-* in Table 5.7). A phonologically conditioned alternation may also be class-independent, embodying a nonautomatic pattern of alternation between stems belonging to distinct inflection classes. In the inflection of Sanskrit PANTHAN ʈoa d,' the alternation of *pathi-* and *path-* is phonologically conditioned (the Weakest stem *path-* appears prevocalically, the Middle stem *pathi-* otherwise) and is also class-independent: As Table 5.9 shows, *pathi-* follows the declension of *i*-stem nouns (e.g. AGNI fi re'), but *path-* follows the declension of consonant-stem nouns (e.g. PAD foot'). [5]

---

4 The property constraint given earlier in (1) defines another prominent morphomic pattern in Sanskrit.

5 In other words, PANTHAN is heteroclite. The phenomenon of heteroclisis is examined in greater detail in Chapter 11.

Table 5.9  *The declension of Sanskrit* PAD *'foot,'* PANTHAN *'road,'* RĀJAN *'king'*
*and* AGNI *'fire'*

| | | | | | |
|---|---|---|---|---|---|
| Singular | Nominative | *pād* | *panthā-s* | *rājā* | *agni-s* |
| | Vocative | *pād* | *panthā-s* | *rājan* | *agne* |
| | Accusative | *pād-am* | *panthān-am* | *rājān-am* | *agni-m* |
| | Instrumental | *pad-ā* | *path-ā* | *rājñ-ā* | *agnin-ā* |
| | Dative | *pad-e* | *path-e* | *rājñ-e* | *agnay-e* |
| | Ablative, Genitive | *pad-as* | *path-as* | *rājñ-as* | *agne-s* |
| | Locative | *pad-i* | *path-i* | *rājñ-i* | *agnau* |
| Dual | Nom, Voc, Acc | *pād-au* | *panthān-au* | *rājān-au* | *agnī* |
| | Instr, Dat, Abl | *pad-bhyām* | *pathi-bhyām* | *rāja-bhyām* | *agni-bhyām* |
| | Genitive, Locative | *pad-os* | *path-os* | *rājñ-os* | *agny-os* |
| Plural | Nom, Voc | *pād-as* | *panthān-as* | *rājān-as* | *agnay-as* |
| | Accusative | *pad-as* | *path-as* | *rājñ-as* | *agnī-n* |
| | Instrumental | *pad-bhis* | *pathi-bhis* | *rāja-bhis* | *agni-bhis* |
| | Dative, Ablative | *pad-bhyas* | *pathi-bhyas* | *rāja-bhyas* | *agni-bhyas* |
| | Genitive | *pad-ām* | *path-ām* | *rājñ-ām* | *agnī-n-ām* |
| | Locative | *pat-su* | *pathi-ṣu* | *rāja-su* | *agni-ṣu* |

Table 5.10  *Kinds of stem alternations*

| Distributional condition | Source of variation in stem form | | |
|---|---|---|---|
| | automatic sandhi | class-determined | class-independent |
| Phonological | *marut- / marud-* | *gīr- / gir-* | *pathi- / path-* |
| Morphosyntactic | | *anaiṣ- / aneṣ-* | *naya- / anaiṣ-* |
| Morphomic | | *krīṇā- / krīṇī-* | *panthān- / path(i)-* |

Morphosyntactically conditioned alternations may be class-determined (as
in the case of *anaiṣ-* and *aneṣ-* in Table 5.5) or class-independent (as with
*naya-* and *anaiṣ-* in Tables 5.5, 5.6). We have seen that morphomically conditioned alternations may be class-determined (as with *krīṇā-* and *krīṇī-* in
Table 5.8). They may also be class-independent: In the exceptional inflection of
PANTHAN, the Strong stem *panthān-*, the Middle stem *pathi-* and the Weakest
stem *path-* conform to different declensions (those of RĀJAN, AGNI and PAD,
respectively), and the alternation among these stems is conditioned (in part) by
the morphomic pattern defined by property constraint (1); see again Table 5.9.

These different kinds of stem alternations are represented schematically in
Table 5.10.

Table 5.11 *The singular indicative active inflection of five Latin verbs*

|  |  |  | I<br>'prepare' | II<br>'remind' | III<br>'rule' | III (-*iō*)<br>'take' | IV<br>'hear' |
|---|---|---|---|---|---|---|---|
| Imperfect | Present | 1sg | *parō* | *moneō* | *regō* | *capiō* | *audiō* |
|  |  | 2sg | *parās* | *monēs* | *regis* | *capis* | *audīs* |
|  |  | 3sg | *parat* | *monet* | *regit* | *capit* | *audit* |
|  | Future | 1sg | *parābō* | *monēbō* | *regam* | *capiam* | *audiam* |
|  |  | 2sg | *parābis* | *monēbis* | *regēs* | *capiēs* | *audiēs* |
|  |  | 3sg | *parābit* | *monēbit* | *reget* | *capiet* | *audiet* |
|  | Preterite | 1sg | *parābam* | *monēbam* | *regēbam* | *capiēbam* | *audiēbam* |
|  |  | 2sg | *parābās* | *monēbās* | *regēbās* | *capiēbās* | *audiēbās* |
|  |  | 3sg | *parābat* | *monēbat* | *regēbat* | *capiēbat* | *audiēbat* |
| Perfect | Present | 1sg | *parāvī* | *monuī* | *rēxī* | *cēpī* | *audīvī* |
|  |  | 2sg | *parāvistī* | *monuistī* | *rēxistī* | *cēpistī* | *audīvistī* |
|  |  | 3sg | *parāvit* | *monuit* | *rēxit* | *cēpit* | *audīvit* |
|  | Future | 1sg | *parāverō* | *monuerō* | *rēxerō* | *cēperō* | *audīverō* |
|  |  | 2sg | *parāveris* | *monueris* | *rēxeris* | *cēperis* | *audīveris* |
|  |  | 3sg | *parāverit* | *monuerit* | *rēxerit* | *cēperit* | *audīverit* |
|  | Preterite | 1sg | *parāveram* | *monueram* | *rēxeram* | *cēperam* | *audīveram* |
|  |  | 2sg | *parāverās* | *monuerās* | *rēxerās* | *cēperās* | *audīverās* |
|  |  | 3sg | *parāverat* | *monuerat* | *rēxerat* | *cēperat* | *audīverat* |

## 5 Formalizing conditions on stem alternation

In the ensuing chapters, it will be important to represent the conditions on a language's stem alternations in a precise way. I therefore introduce two operations that make this possible: a function **Stem** accounting for a language's grammatically conditioned alternations, and an operator **SC** accounting for its nonautomatic phonologically conditioned alternations.

### 5.5.1 The Stem function

A language's grammatically conditioned stem alternations may be defined by means of a function **Stem** such that for any cell $\langle L, \sigma : w \rangle$ in any paradigm, **Stem** applies to the cell's lexical and morphosyntactic content to yield the stem form Y employed in its realization: $\textbf{Stem}(\langle L, \sigma \rangle) = Y$.[6] In the canonical case, every cell in a lexeme's paradigm is mapped onto the same stem form.

---

6 This formalism helps define a language's paradigm function in a precise way. In Section 3.6, for example, the French paradigm function is defined as in (i). I now assume that the French **Stem** function is defined so as to allow the italicized portion of (i) to be replaced with (ii).

(i) PF($\langle L, \sigma \rangle$) =def [ III : [ II : [ I : $\langle X, \sigma \rangle$ ]]], *where X is the stem of L that is appropriate for $\sigma$.*

(ii) ... where **Stem**($\langle L, \sigma \rangle$) =X .

In the partial Latin verb paradigms in Table 5.11, each verb has two stems, one imperfective and the other perfective. To provide for this grammatically conditioned alternation, the Latin **Stem** function is defined so that each of the equations in (3) holds true.

(3)   a.   Where {imperfective} ⊆ σ,   b.   Where {perfective} ⊆ σ,
          **Stem**(⟨PARĀRE, σ⟩) = *parā*           **Stem**(⟨PARĀRE, σ⟩) = *parāv*
          **Stem**(⟨MONĒRE, σ⟩) = *monē*        **Stem**(⟨MONĒRE, σ⟩) = *monu*
          **Stem**(⟨REGERE, σ⟩) = *reg*           **Stem**(⟨REGERE, σ⟩) = *reks*
          **Stem**(⟨CAPERE, σ⟩) = *capi*         **Stem**(⟨CAPERE, σ⟩) = *cēp*
          **Stem**(⟨AUDĪRE, σ⟩) = *audī*       **Stem**(⟨AUDĪRE, σ⟩) = *audīv*

It is not, in general, necessary to include all of these equations in the lexicon, since some of them embody default patterns. For instance, most first-conjugation verbs conform to the **stem-formation rule** in (4); here and throughout, σ:{*x*}e presents a property set σ such that {*x*} ⊆ σ.

(4)       Stem-formation rule
       Where L is a first-conjugation verb such that **Stem**(⟨L, σ:{imperfective}⟩) = X*ā*, **Stem**(⟨L, σ:{perfective}⟩) ⇒ X *āv* by default.

There are some first-conjugation verbs that do not conform to (4); for example, the perfective stem of SECĀRE ċ ut' is *secu-* rather than *\*secāv-*. For such verbs, one must assume that the default pattern in (4) is overridden by a lexical stipulation such as the one in (5).

(5)       **Stem**(⟨SECĀRE, σ:{perfective}⟩) = *secu*

In cases of gross suppletion, the value of **Stem** must of course be lexically listed. For example, the lexical listing of FERRE ċ arry' *(ferō* I carry,' *tulī* I have carried') must include the specifications in (6).

(6)       a.   **Stem**(⟨FERRE, σ:{imperfective}⟩) = *fer*
          b.   **Stem**(⟨FERRE, σ:{perfective}⟩) = *tul*

Consider also the Old English paradigms in Table 5.12, which exhibit two to four stems. The strong verb BERSTAN b urst' distinguishes all four of these: a default stem (used in the shaded cells), a singular past stem (used in the first and third singular of the past indicative), a default past stem (used elsewhere in the past) and a past participial stem. In the inflection of the strong verbs SMĪTAN ş mite' and SINGAN ş ing,' the past participial stem is not distinguished from the default past stem; in that of the weak verb LEORNIAN le arn,' neither the past participial stem nor the singular past stem is distinguished from the default past stem. These facts are summarized in Table 5.13.

The stem-formation rules appropriate for the verbs in Table 5.13 might be plausibly formulated as in Table 5.14.

Table 5.12 *The inflection of four Old English verbs*

|  |  |  | SMĪTAN 'smite' (strong–1) | SINGAN 'sing' (strong–3a) | BERSTAN 'burst' (strong–3c) | LEORNIAN 'learn' (weak–2) |
|---|---|---|---|---|---|---|
| Present | Indicative | 1sg | *smīte* | *singe* | *berste* | *leornie* |
|  |  | 2sg | *smītest* | *singest* | *berstest* | *leornast* |
|  |  | 3sg | *smīteþ* | *singeþ* | *bersteþ* | *leornaþ* |
|  |  | pl | *smītaþ* | *singaþ* | *berstaþ* | *leorniaþ* |
|  | Subjunctive | sg | *smīte* | *singe* | *berste* | *leornie* |
|  |  | pl | *smīten* | *singen* | *bersten* | *leornien* |
| Past | Indicative | 1sg | *smāt* | *sang* | *bærst* | *leornode* |
|  |  | 2sg | *smite* | *sunge* | *burste* | *leornodest* |
|  |  | 3sg | *smāt* | *sang* | *bærst* | *leornode* |
|  |  | pl | *smiton* | *sungon* | *burston* | *leornodon* |
|  | Subjunctive | sg | *smite* | *sunge* | *burste* | *leornode* |
|  |  | pl | *smiten* | *sungen* | *bursten* | *leornoden* |
| Present participle |  |  | *smītende* | *singende* | *berstende* | *leorniende* |
| Past participle |  |  | *(ge)smiten* | *(ge)sungen* | *(ge)borsten* | *(ge)leornod* |
| Infinitive |  |  | *smītan* | *singan* | *berstan* | *leornian* |
| Inflected infinitive |  |  | *tō smītanne* | *tō singanne* | *tō berstanne* | *tō leornianne* |
| Imperative | sg |  | *smīt* | *sing* | *berst* | *leorna* |
|  | pl |  | *smītaþ* | *singaþ* | *berstaþ* | *leorniaþ* |

Table 5.13 *The stems of four Old English verbal lexemes*

| Lexeme L |  | By default | Value of **Stem**($\langle$L, $\sigma\rangle$) | | |
|---|---|---|---|---|---|
|  |  |  | Where {ps t} $\subseteq \sigma$ | | |
|  |  |  | if $\sigma$ satisfies [{ g ind} $\wedge$ [{ } $\vee$ ]] | otherwise | Where {pst ptcp} $\subseteq \sigma$ |
| BERSTAN | 'burst' | *berst* | *bærst* | *burst* | *borst* |
| SMĪTAN | 'smite' | *smīt* | *smāt* | *smit* | |
| SINGAN | 'sing' | *sing* | *sang* | *sung* | |
| LEORNIAN | 'learn' | *leorn* | *leornod* | | |

Table 5.14 *Stem-formation rules for four Old English conjugations*

| Conjugation | strong–1 | strong–3a | strong–3c | weak–2 |
|---|---|---|---|---|
| Default stem | X$\bar{\imath}$Y | X$i$Y | X$e$Y | X |
| **Stem**(⟨L, σ:{3sg pst ind}⟩)* | ⇒X $\bar{a}$Y | = X$a$Y | = X$æ$Y | = X$od$ |
| **Stem**(⟨L, σ:þs t⟩) | ⇒X $i$Y | = X$u$Y | = X$u$Y | (id.) |
| **Stem**(⟨L, σ:þs t ptcp⟩) | (id.) | (id.) | ⇒X $o$Y | (id.) |
| Otherwise, **Stem**(⟨L, σ⟩) | = default stem | = default stem | = default stem | = default stem |

*An independent principle causes the first singular past indicative form to be syncretized with the third singular past indicative form; see Stump: to appear, b; see also Chapter 10.

### 5.5.2   The SC operation

The **Stem** function accounts for grammatical conditions on stem alternation; it does not, however, account for phonological conditions. Stem alternations that are conditioned by a language's automatic phonology are not strictly the province of its morphology in any event; that is, automatic alternants such as those of Sanskrit MARUT ẇ ind' (Table 5.4) are not distinguished by a language's morphology, but are only distinguished once the applicable phonological rules are taken into account. But what of nonautomatic phonological conditions? These are formalized in the definition of a language's syntagmatic context (*SC*) operation: This is an operation whose application to a stem varies in its value according to the stem's surroundings – in the case at hand, its phonological surroundings. In Sanskrit, the *SC* operation is defined so that in the inflection of GĪR ṣ ong,' *SC*(*gīr*) is evaluated as *gir* in the presence of a vowel-initial suffix, and otherwise as *gīr*; *SC* functions similarly in modeling other instances of inward phonological conditioning.[7]

Consider the interaction of **Stem** and *SC* in the following example. In Sanskrit, the masculine and neuter forms[8] of perfect active participles employ four stems (Whitney 1889: Sections 458ff). For example, in the inflection of TASTHIVAMS 'having stood,' the Strong stem *tasthivāṃs* (sandhi form *tasthivān*) is employed in the realization of any morphosyntactic property set satisfying the property constraint (1) and thus appears above the dashed lines in Table 5.15; the stem *tasthivaṃs* (sandhi form *tasthivan*) is restricted to

7   In his model of Kayardild inflection, Round (2013: 37) employs an allomorphy feature whose effect is closely comparable to the *SC* operation.
8   The feminine forms are not included here because they are based on an *ī*-stem derivative whose inflection belongs to an entirely different declension.

Table 5.15 *The masculine and neuter declension of the Sanskrit perfect active participle* TASTHIVAṂS *'having stood'*

|  | Singular | | Dual | | Plural | |
|---|---|---|---|---|---|---|
|  | Masculine | Neuter | Masculine | Neuter | Masculine | Neuter |
| Nominative | *tasthivān* | *tasthivat* | *tasthivāṁs-au* | *tasthuṣ-ī* | *tasthivāṁs-as* | *tasthivāṁs-i* |
| Vocative | *tasthivan* | *tasthivat* | *tasthivāṁs-au* | *tasthuṣ-ī* | *tasthivāṁs-as* | *tasthivāṁs-i* |
| Accusative | *tasthivāṁs-am* | *tasthivat* | *tasthivāṁs-au* | *tasthuṣ-ī* | *tasthuṣ-as* | *tasthivāṁs-i* |
| Instrumental | *tasthuṣ-ā* | | *tasthivad-bhyām* | | *tasthivad-bhis* | |
| Dative | *tasthuṣ-e* | | *tasthivad-bhyām* | | *tasthivad-bhyas* | |
| Ablative | *tasthuṣ-as* | | *tasthivad-bhyām* | | *tasthivad-bhyas* | |
| Genitive | *tasthuṣ-as* | | *tasthuṣ-os* | | *tasthuṣ-ām* | |
| Locative | *tasthuṣ-i* | | *tasthuṣ-os* | | *tasthivat-su* | |

the masculine vocative singular (boxed in Table 5.15); the stems *tasthuṣ* and *tasthivat* (sandhi form *tasthivad*) appear otherwise – the Weakest stem *tasthuṣ* before a suffixal vowel and the Middle stem *tasthivat* elsewhere (in the shaded cells in Table 5.15).

Thus, the definition of the Sanskrit **Stem** function is subject to the stem-formation rules in (7),[9] and those values of the **Stem** function defined by rule (7c) depend on the definition of the **SC** operation in (8).

(7)   Stem-formation rules for perfect active participles in Sanskrit
      Where L is a perfect active participle with Strong stem X*vāṁs*,
      a.   Where σ satisfies the property constraint (1), **Stem**($\langle$L, σ$\rangle$) = L's Strong stem
      b.   **Stem**($\langle$L, {na sc voc sg}$\rangle$) = X *vaṁs*
      c.   Otherwise, **Stem**($\langle$L, σ$\rangle$) = **SC**(X*vat*)
      [N.B.: By Pāṇini's principle, (7b) overrides (7a) and (7a,b) override (7c).]

(8)   **SC** operation
      Where L is a perfect active participle with Strong stem X*vāṁs*,
      **SC**(X*vat*) = X*uṣ* before a vowel-initial suffix
               = X*vat* otherwise.

## 5̃6   Summary

The facts presented here show that any two alternating stems Y and Z stand in exactly one of three possible relations.

---

9  The stem-formation rules in (7) are restated in a more general form in Section 6.4.

Table 5.16 *The declension of Sanskrit* KROṢṬṚ *'jackal' alongside that of* KARTṚ *'maker' and* GURU *'elder'*
(Unshaded forms follow the *r*-stem declension; shaded forms follow the *u*-stem declension.)

|          |                   | KARTṚ      | KROṢṬṚ       | GURU       |
|----------|-------------------|------------|--------------|------------|
| Singular | Nominative        | *kartā*    | *kroṣṭā*     | *gurus*    |
|          | Vocative          | *kartar*   | *kroṣṭo*     | *guro*     |
|          | Accusative        | *kartāram* | *kroṣṭāram*  | *gurum*    |
|          | Instrumental      | *kartrā*   | *kroṣṭrā*    | *guruṇā*   |
|          | Dative            | *kartre*   | *kroṣṭre*    | *gurave*   |
|          | Ablative, Genitive| *kartur*   | *kroṣṭur*    | *guros*    |
|          | Locative          | *kartari*  | *kroṣṭari*   | *gurau*    |
| Dual     | Nom, Voc, Acc     | *kartārau* | *kroṣṭārau*  | *gurū*     |
|          | Instr, Dat, Abl   | *kartṛbhyām* | *kroṣṭubhyām* | *gurubhyām* |
|          | Genitive, Locative| *kartros*  | *kroṣṭros*   | *gurvos*   |
| Plural   | Nom, Voc          | *kartāras* | *kroṣṭāras*  | *guravas*  |
|          | Accusative        | *kartṝn*   | *kroṣṭūn*    | *gurūn*    |
|          | Instrumental      | *kartṛbhis*| *kroṣṭubhis* | *gurubhis* |
|          | Dative, Ablative  | *kartṛbhyas* | *kroṣṭubhyas* | *gurubhyas* |
|          | Genitive          | *kartṝṇām* | *kroṣṭūnām*  | *gurūṇām*  |
|          | Locative          | *kartṛṣu*  | *kroṣṭuṣu*   | *guruṣu*   |

- Stem Y and stem Z are **sandhi alternants** if principles of automatic phonology determine the choice between them. Thus, in the inflection of Sanskrit KARTṚ 'ma ker' in the first paradigm in Table 5.16, the Middle stem *kartṛ*- and the Weakest stem *kartr*- are sandhi alternants: *kartr*- appears before vowels and *kartṛ*- elsewhere. The same is true of the stems *gurv*- and *guru*- in the inflection of GURU è lder' in the table's third paradigm.
- Stem Y and stem Z are **kindred stems** if they form part of the inflectional pattern of a single inflection class, with the choice between them being either grammatically conditioned or phonologically conditioned but nonautomatic. Thus, in the inflection of KARTṚ, the Strong stem *kartār*- and the Weakest stem *kartr*- are kindred stems, since both are required by the inflectional pattern of the *r*-stem declension; every ordinary member of this declension has both a stem in *-ār* (paralleling *kartār*-) in some forms and a stem in *-r* (paralleling *kartr*-) in other forms. In this particular example, the alternation between *kartār*- and

*kartr-* is morphomically conditioned by the property constraint in (1).

- Stem Y and stem Z are **independent stems** if each forms part of the inflectional pattern of a distinct inflection class. The inflection of the Sanskrit noun KROṢṬṚ Ja ckal' is based on independent stems, as Table 5.16 shows: In some forms, the inflection of KROṢṬṚ involves (a) the kindred stems *kroṣṭā(r)-*, *kroṣṭar-*, *kroṣṭr-* and *kroṣṭur-*, which follow the pattern of the *r*-stem declension; but in other forms, the inflection of KROṢṬṚ involves (b) the kindred stems *kroṣṭo-* and *kroṣṭŭ-*, which follow the pattern of the *u*-stem declension. Thus, members of the set (a) are independent of the members of the set (b).[10]

This classification depends on the notion of inflection classes, whose characteristics we now consider in detail.

---

10 Like PANTHAN 'road,' KROṢṬṚ 'jackal' is heteroclite; see Chapter 11 for detailed discussion of heteroclisis.

# 6 *Inflection classes*

Languages with rich inflectional morphology frequently exhibit inflection-class systems, in which the same morphosyntactic property sets are realized differently in the inflection of stems belonging to the same syntactic category but to distinct inflection classes. Drawing on the notion of canonical inflection classes proposed by Corbett 2009 (Section 6.1), I highlight three facts about inflection classes that have important implications for an adequate theory of inflection: These are the fact that inflection classes may be global or segregated (Section 6.2), the fact that inflection classes are classes of stems rather than classes of lexemes (Section 6.3), and the fact that inflection classes are often most easily distinguished by their patterns of stem formation and stem alternation (Section 6.4).

## 6 *Canonical inflection classes*

Corbett (2009) proposes a list of canonical characteristics of inflection classes. These are subsumed by two general principles: a principle of **distinctiveness**, according to which "Canonical inflectional classes are fully comparable and are distinguished as clearly as possible," and a principle of **independence**, by which "The distribution of lexical items over canonical inflectional classes is synchronically unmotivated." These principles characterize a canonical ideal from which many varied deviations are observable in the inflection-class systems of the world's languages.

Consider first the four criteria subsumed by the principle of distinctiveness, quoted in (1). According to Criterion 1, contrasts among canonical inflection classes are manifested in every cell of their members' paradigms. This criterion is rarely satisfied; in the Sanskrit paradigms in Table 6.1, for example, the consonant-stem declension of MARUT 'wind' and the *a*-stem declension of GAJA 'elephant' are inflectionally alike in the cells shaded in Table 6.2, and are therefore noncanonical with respect to Criterion 1.

Table 6.1 *The declension of Sanskrit* MARUT *'wind' and* GAJA *'elephant'*

|  | Singular | Dual | Plural | Singular | Dual | Plural |
|---|---|---|---|---|---|---|
| Nominative | marut | marutau | marutas | gajas | gajau | gajās |
| Vocative | marut | marutau | marutas | gaja | gajau | gajās |
| Accusative | marutam | marutau | marutas | gajam | gajau | gajān |
| Instrumental | marutā | marudbhyām | marudbhis | gajena | gajābhyām | gajais |
| Dative | marute | marudbhyām | marudbhyas | gajāya | gajābhyām | gajebhyas |
| Ablative | marutas | marudbhyām | marudbhyas | gajāt | gajābhyām | gajebhyas |
| Genitive | marutas | marutos | marutām | gajasya | gajayos | gajānām |
| Locative | maruti | marutos | marutsu | gaje | gajayos | gajeṣu |

Table 6.2 *The declension of Sanskrit* MARUT *'wind' and* GAJA *'elephant'*
*(with stems and sandhi abstracted away)*

|  | Singular | Dual | Plural | Singular | Dual | Plural |
|---|---|---|---|---|---|---|
| Nominative | X | Xau | Xas | Xs | Xau | Xas |
| Vocative | X | Xau | Xas | X | Xau | Xas |
| Accusative | Xam | Xau | Xas | Xm | Xau | Xan |
| Instrumental | Xā | Xbhyām | Xbhis | Xina* | Xābhyām | Xais |
| Dative | Xe | Xbhyām | Xbhyas | Xāya | Xābhyām | Xibhyas* |
| Ablative | Xas | Xbhyām | Xbhyas | Xāt | Xābhyām | Xibhyas* |
| Genitive | Xas | Xos | Xām | Xsya | Xyos | Xānām |
| Locative | Xi | Xos | Xsu | Xi* | Xyos | Xiṣu* |

Sa ndhi: $a + i \rightarrow e$

(1)  Characteristics of canonical inflection classes subsumed by the principle of distinctiveness (Corbett 2009: 3–5)

*Criterion 1:* In the canonical situation, forms differ as consistently as possible *across* inflectional classes, cell by cell.

*Criterion 2:* Canonical inflectional classes realize the same morphosyntactic or morphosemantic distinctions (they are of the same structure).

*Criterion 3:* *Within* a canonical inflectional class each member behaves identically.

*Criterion 4:* *Within* a canonical inflectional class each paradigm cell is of equal status.

By Criterion 2, contrasting inflection classes canonically determine the morphology of the same morphosyntactic property sets. This criterion is more commonly satisfied; for example, the consonant-stem and *a*-stem declensions exemplified in Table 6.1 provide inflectional exponents for exactly the same morphosyntactic property sets, and are therefore canonical with respect to Criterion 2.

By Criterion 3, the members of a canonical inflection class exhibit the same inflectional morphology. The *a*-stem declension of GAJA is close to being canonical with respect to Criterion 3: the innumerable nouns in this declension are alike in their inflection (Whitney 1889: Section 331), though *a*-stem numerals, pronouns and pronominal adjectives do exhibit some peculiarities.

According to Criterion 4, membership in a canonical inflection class is revealed equally clearly by the morphology of every cell in a member's paradigm. The GAJA declension clearly fails this test of canonicity, since some of the cells in the paradigm of GAJA exhibit morphology that is diagnostic of this declension (e.g. the instrumental, dative, ablative and genitive cells of the singular), while other cells exhibit the default exponents for their property sets (e.g. the locative singular cell and the nominative cells of the dual and plural).

Consider now four[1] criteria subsumed by the principle of independence, in (2). According to Criterion 5, inflection classes with many members are more canonical than those with few (but not if they have more than their share of members). A language's inflection classes typically vary in size and therefore vary in their canonicity with respect to this criterion. French, for example, has dozens of conjugation classes – seventy-two, according to the breakdown in Table 6.3 (in which each conjugation is named for an exemplar). Among these, the variation in type frequency is considerable (Table 6.4): AIMER 'like' has 4,139 members, while VOULOIR 'want' has a single member. Given the 6,484 types tallied in Table 6.4, an equal share for each of the seventy-two conjugations would be ninety members; six conjugations far exceed this share, but among those that do not, there is considerable variation in canonicity with respect to Criterion 5.

(2)     Four characteristics of canonical inflection classes subsumed by the principle of independence (Corbett 2009: 5–7)

*Criterion 5:*   The larger the number of members of an inflectional class (up to an equal "share" of the available items) the more canonical that class.

*Criterion 6:*   In the canonical situation, the distribution of lexical items over inflectional classes is not phonologically motivated.

*Criterion 7:*   In the canonical situation, the distribution of lexical items over inflectional classes is not syntactically motivated.

*Criterion 8:*   In the canonical situation, the distribution of lexical items over inflectional classes is not motivated by Part of Speech.

---

1  Corbett subsumes a fifth criterion under the principle of independence according to which "the distribution of lexical items over inflectional classes is [in the canonical case] not motivated by pragmatics (including information structure)"; see Corbett (2009: 7) for discussion.

Table 6.3 *Seventy-two French conjugations (each named for an exemplar)*

| ÊTRE | be ' | CUEILLIR | pic k' | PEINDRE | 'paint' |
|---|---|---|---|---|---|
| AVOIR | ha ve' | ASSAILLIR | a ssail' | JOINDRE | 'join' |
| AIMER | lik e' | BOUILLIR | boil' | CRAINDRE | 'fear' |
| COLLER | pa ste' | DORMIR | s leep' | VAINCRE | 'conquer' |
| BEURRER | b utter' | COURIR | tun' | FAIRE | 'do' |
| DÉJEUNER | ha ve lunch' | MOURIR | die ' | PLAIRE | 'please' |
| ÉCROUER | lmpris on' | SERVIR | s erve' | CONNAÎTRE | 'be acquainted with' |
| ÉCHOUER | f ail' | FUIR | fl ee' | NAÎTRE | 'be born' |
| REFLUER | è bb' | RECEVOIR | te ceive' | REPAÎTRE | 'feed' |
| REMUER | s tir' | VOIR | s ee' | CROÎTRE | 'grow' |
| LEVER | ta ise' | POURVOIR | pro vide' | CROIRE | 'believe' |
| CÉDER | gi ve up' | SAVOIR | kno w' | BOIRE | 'drink' |
| COPIER | c opy' | DEVOIR | ha ve to' | CONCLURE | 'end' |
| APPUYER | pre ss' | POUVOIR | c an' | INCLURE | 'include' |
| BROYER | grind' | MOUVOIR | mo ve' | COUDRE | 'sew' |
| ENVOYER | s end' | VALOIR | be worth' | MOUDRE | 'grind' |
| FINIR | fi nish' | VOULOIR | w ant' | SUIVRE | 'follow' |
| HAÏR | ha te' | ASSEOIR$_1$ | s eat' | VIVRE | 'live' |
| ALLER | go' | ASSEOIR$_2$ | s eat' | LIRE | 'read' |
| TENIR | hold' | SURSEOIR | s tay' | DIRE | 'say' |
| ACQUÉRIR | a cquire' | RENDRE | gi ve back' | RIRE | 'laugh' |
| SENTIR | fe el' | PRENDRE | ta ke' | ÉCRIRE | 'write' |
| VÊTIR | c lothe' | BATTRE | be at' | CONFIRE | 'preserve' |
| COUVRIR | c over' | METTRE | put' | CUIRE | 'cook' |

By Criterion 6, membership in an inflection class is not predictable from the phonology of a lexeme's stem(s). In some languages, inflection classes are noncanonical with respect to this criterion, since inflection-class membership is phonologically determined. For example, verbs in Moru (Nilo-Saharan; Sudan) fall into three inflection classes according to whether their stems are monosyllabic, disyllabic and vowel-initial, or disyllabic and consonant-initial; the verbs in Table 6.5 illustrate. In most languages, however, inflection-class membership is only partially predictable on phonological grounds. In Sanskrit, for example, nouns with stems ending in short *a* invariably belong to the *a*-stem declension, but this declension has two subtypes, one for masculine nouns (such as GAJA è lephant,' Table 6.1), the other for neuters, such as ĀSYA tnouth'; for these nouns, inflection-class membership depends on gender as well as phonology.

According to Criterion 7, membership in an inflection class is not predictable from a lexeme's syntactic properties. The inflection of GAJA and ĀSYA is

Table 6.4 *Type frequency of French conjugations*

| | | | | | | | |
|---|---|---|---|---|---|---|---|
| AIMER | 4139 | CONNAÎTRE | 11 | VÊTIR | 4 | CROIRE | 2 |
| CÉDER | 499 | ÉCRIRE | 11 | VOIR | 4 | DEVOIR | 2 |
| COLLER | 423 | ÉCROUER | 11 | COUDRE | 3 | ENVOYER | 2 |
| FINIR | 332 | FAIRE | 11 | CRAINDRE | 3 | FUIR | 2 |
| COPIER | 262 | PRENDRE | 11 | CUEILLIR | 3 | NAÎTRE | 2 |
| LEVER | 196 | COUVRIR | 10 | DORMIR | 3 | POURVOIR | 2 |
| APPUYER | 83 | BATTRE | 9 | INCLURE | 3 | RIRE | 2 |
| REMUER | 63 | COURIR | 8 | MOUDRE | 3 | VAINCRE | 2 |
| BROYER | 53 | JOINDRE | 8 | MOUVOIR | 3 | ALLER | 1 |
| RENDRE | 52 | DIRE | 7 | SERVIR | 3 | DÉJEUNER | 1 |
| ÉCHOUER | 33 | ACQUÉRIR | 5 | SUIVRE | 3 | ÊTRE | 1 |
| BEURRER | 31 | CONFIRE | 5 | VIVRE | 3 | HAÏR | 1 |
| TENIR | 30 | RECEVOIR | 5 | ASSEOIR1 | 2 | MOURIR | 1 |
| CUIRE | 24 | ASSAILLIR | 4 | ASSEOIR2 | 2 | POUVOIR | 1 |
| PEINDRE | 17 | CROÎTRE | 4 | AVOIR | 2 | REPAÎTRE | 1 |
| METTRE | 15 | LIRE | 4 | BOIRE | 2 | SAVOIR | 1 |
| REFLUER | 12 | PLAIRE | 4 | BOUILLIR | 2 | SURSEOIR | 1 |
| SENTIR | 12 | VALOIR | 4 | CONCLURE | 2 | VOULOIR | 1 |

*Source:* Stump and Finkel 2013: 254.

Table 6.5 *The general inflection of three Moru verbs (Miza dialect)*

| | | Class i<br>zɪ ċ all' | Class ii<br>ɛmɛ ɦe at' | Class iii<br>KANDA 'shake' |
|---|---|---|---|---|
| Singular | 1 | *mă-zi* | *m-ɛ́mɛ* | *má-kanda* |
| | 2 | *mí-zi* | *ny-ɛ́mɛ* | *nyá-kanda* |
| | 3 | *ányä zi* | *ány-ɛmɛ* | *ánya kanda* |
| Plural | 1 | *mà-zi* | *m-èmɛ* | *mà-kanda* |
| | 2 | *mì-zi* | *ny-èmɛ* | *nyà-kanda* |
| | 3 | *ànyä zi* | *àny-ɛmɛ* | *ànya kanda* |

Where v is a vowel symbol, v́ indicates high tone, v̀ low tone, and v mid tone; *ä* represents a high central vowel.

*Source:* Tucker 1940.

noncanonical by this criterion, since the declensional difference between GAJA and ĀSYA reflects the different patterns of gender agreement in which they participate in syntax. By contrast, neither gender nor phonology is sufficient to predict the inflection-class difference between the *r*-stem masculines PITAR 'father' and NAPTAR 'grandson,' which differ with respect to the vowel grade (*ar* vs *ār*) of their strong stem (Whitney 1889: Section 370); compare the shaded cells of Table 6.6.

Table 6.6 *The declension of Sanskrit* PITAR *'father' and* NAPTAR *'grandson'*

|  | Singular | Dual | Plural | Singular | Dual | Plural |
|---|---|---|---|---|---|---|
| Nominative | pitā | pitarau | pitaras | naptā | naptārau | naptāras |
| Vocative | pitar | pitarau | pitaras | naptar | naptārau | naptāras |
| Accusative | pitaram | pitarau | pitṝn | naptāram | naptārau | naptṝn |
| Instrumental | pitrā | pitṛbhyām | pitṛbhis | naptrā | naptṛbhyām | naptṛbhis |
| Dative | pitre | pitṛbhyām | pitṛbhyas | naptre | naptṛbhyām | naptṛbhyas |
| Ablative | pitur | pitṛbhyām | pitṛbhyas | naptur | naptṛbhyām | naptṛbhyas |
| Genitive | pitur | pitros | pitṝṇām | naptur | naptros | naptṝṇām |
| Locative | pitari | pitros | pitṛṣu | naptari | naptros | naptṛṣu |

Table 6.7 *Three Sanskrit declensional paradigms*

|  |  | GAJA 'elephant' (masc.) | PRIYA 'dear' (masc. forms) | Demonstrative pronoun 'that' (masc. forms) |
|---|---|---|---|---|
| Singular | Nominative | gajas | priyas | sas |
|  | Vocative* | gaja | priya | – |
|  | Accusative | gajam | priyam | tam |
|  | Instrumental | gajena | priyena | tena |
|  | Dative | gajāya | priyāya | tasmai |
|  | Ablative | gajāt | priyāt | tasmāt |
|  | Genitive | gajasya | priyasya | tasya |
|  | Locative | gaje | priye | tasmin |
| Dual | Nom, Voc,* Acc | gajau | priyau | tau |
|  | Ins, Dat, Abl | gajābhyām | priyābhyām | tābhyām |
|  | Gen, Loc | gajayos | priyayos | tayos |
| Plural | Nom, Voc* | gajās | priyās | te |
|  | Accusative | gajān | priyān | tān |
|  | Instrumental | gajais | priyais | tais |
|  | Dat, Abl | gajebhyas | priyebhyas | tebhyas |
|  | Genitive | gajānām | priyānām | teṣām |
|  | Locative | gajeṣu | priyeṣu | teṣu |

* The demonstrative pronoun naturally lacks vocative forms.

Criterion 8 specifies that membership in a canonical inflection class is not a function of part of speech. In Sanskrit, the declension class to which *a*-stem nouns belong also includes ordinary adjectives, and is to that extent canonical. By contrast, pronouns having stems in *a*, though they have some inflectional characteristics in common with *a*-stem nouns and adjectives, follow a distinct declension (Table 6.7), contrary to Criterion 8.[2]

In summary, a canonical inflection class comprises members that are alike in their inflection; any two classes in a canonical system determine distinct inflectional realizations for the same morphosyntactic property sets and are alike in the number of members that they comprise; and the membership of a canonical inflection class cannot, in general, be deduced from independent phonological or grammatical characteristics of candidate members. In the chapters that follow, I will examine a number of inflection-class systems that deviate in one or more ways from these canonical properties. My discussion of these deviations will presuppose three important observations about inflection classes; these are discussed in the following sections.

## *6.2   Global vs segregated inflection classes*

It is usual to think of inflection-class membership as being **global** in its effects, in the sense that membership in a given inflection class determines the realization of every cell of a member's paradigm (whether or not that realization is in all cases diagnostic of class membership). In Sanskrit, for example, the MARUT and GAJA declensions represented in Table 6.1 each determine the inflectional exponence of all twenty-four case/number pairings for which a member noun inflects. Yet, inflection classes are not invariably global in this way. Consider, for example, the inflection of Latin verbs.

The traditional Latin conjugations classify verbs according to their imperfective inflection; a verb's perfective inflection depends on its membership in a different, crosscutting conjugation class. As Table 6.8 shows, verbs whose inflection follows the same imperfective conjugation (I, II, III, III (-*iō*), or IV) need not follow the same perfective conjugation (e.g. *u*-stem, $\emptyset$ stem, *v*-stem, *s*-stem, or reduplicated), and the reverse is likewise true. Neither the imperfective nor the perfective conjugations should therefore be seen as global; instead, they are **segregated** – that is, they only determine the exponence of a proper subset of the cells in a paradigm. As I show in the following section, the existence of segregated inflection classes helps reveal an important insight into the nature of inflection classes.

---

2 There is a closed class of "pronominal adjectives" (e.g. ANYA òthe r,' SARVA à ll') that follow the pronominal *a*-stem declension (Whitney 1889: Sections 522ff).

Table 6.8 *Imperfective and perfective stems in Latin*

| Verbal lexeme | | Imperfective | | Perfective conjugation and stem | | | | |
|---|---|---|---|---|---|---|---|---|
| | | Conjugation | Stem | Root + -u | Root + ∅ | Imperfective stem + -v | Root + -s | Reduplicated root |
| CREPĀRE | 'rattle' | I | crepā- | crepu- | | | | |
| IUVĀRE | 'help' | | iuvā- | | iūv- | | | |
| LAUDĀRE | 'praise' | | laudā- | | | laudāv- | | |
| MONĒRE | 'warm' | II | monē- | monu- | | | | |
| VIDĒRE | 'see' | | vidē- | | vid- | | | |
| DĒLĒRE | 'destroy' | | dēlē- | | | dēlēv- | | |
| LŪGĒRE | 'mourn' | | lūgē- | | | | lūx- /luːks/ | |
| SPONDĒRE | 'pledge' | | spondē- | | | | | spopond- |
| ALERE | 'nourish' | III | al- | alu- | | | | |
| DĒCERNERE | 'decide' | | dēcern- | | | dēcrēv-* | | |
| DŪCERE | 'lead' | | dūc- | | | | dūx- /duːks/ | |
| CADERE | 'fall' | | cad- | | | | | cecid- |
| CAPERE | 'take' | III (-iō) | capi- | | cēp- | | | |
| SALĪRE | 'jump' | IV | salī- | salu- | | | | |
| VENĪRE | 'come' | | venī- | | vēn- | | | |
| AUDĪRE | 'hear' | | audī- | | | audīv- | | |
| VINCĪRE | 'bind' | | vincī- | | | | vinx- /vinks/ | |

* with stem suppletion

## *β*      *Inflection classes are classes of stems (not of lexemes)*

It is customary to think of inflection classes as classes of lexemes (Carstairs-McCarthy 2000), but in fact, they are classes of stems. Various kinds of evidence demonstrate this.

The first is the existence of segregated inflection classes (Section 6.2). If inflection classes were classes of lexemes, one might expect a lexeme's inflection-class membership to be reflected throughout its paradigm, but in the case of segregated inflection classes, this is precisely what we do not find. Consider again the case of Latin verbs (Table 6.8). An ordinary Latin verb has an imperfective stem and a perfective stem, and these do not, in general, belong to a single conjugational pattern but instead embody two independent inflection classes.

This fact might lead one to suppose that each Latin verbal lexeme belongs to two conjugations, one of which determines its imperfective inflection (including the formation of its imperfective stem) and the other of which determines its perfective inflection (including the formation of its perfective stem); on this hypothesis, a lexeme L's inflection-class membership is in effect conditioned by the morphosyntactic property set with which L is associated in any given case. But this hypothesis cannot be plausibly extended to certain instances of heteroclisis (Stump 2006). Consider, for example, the inflection of Sanskrit ASTHI bone ,' some of whose forms follow the *i*-stem declension of VĀRI 'w a-ter' but whose other forms follow the *n*-stem declension of NĀMAN 'ha me.' As Table 6.9 shows, ASTHI's *n*-stem *asthn-* appears prevocalically and its *i*-stem *asthi-* elsewhere. This alternation is therefore comparable to nonautomatic phonologically conditioned stem choice in paradigms that aren't heteroclite (e.g. the choice between prevocalic *gir-* and default *gīr-* in the inflection of Sanskrit GĪR 'song'; Table 5.7). It is not reasonable to see it as involving a lexeme's phonologically conditioned membership in a particular declension class, since lexemes are abstractions and do not join with affixes; phonological conditioning is a property of stem alternations.

Another apparent advantage of the stem-class conception of inflection classes is that it affords a simpler format for rules of exponence. Recall the format (3) proposed in Section 3.6. A rule in this format is applicable to the pairing $\langle Z, \sigma \rangle$ of stem Z with property set $\sigma$ only if Z belongs to C and $\sigma$ satisfies the property constraint $\kappa$; if applicable, the rule applies to $\langle Z, \sigma \rangle$ to yield $\langle f(Z), \sigma \rangle$, where $f$ is a function on stem forms. With this rule format, the class restriction C on the rule's application and the morphological operation $f$ apply to the same entity, a stem. Under the lexeme-class conception, by contrast, the application of a rule of exponence must refer directly both to a lexeme and to the stem that realizes it.

Table 6.9 *The heteroclite declension of Sanskrit* ASTHI *'bone'*

| | | VĀRI 'water' | ASTHI 'bone' | | NĀMAN 'name' | |
|---|---|---|---|---|---|---|
| | | *i*-stem declension | | *n*-stem declension | | |
| Singular | Nom, Voc, Acc | *vāri* | *asthi* | | *nām-a* | |
| | Instr | *vāriṇ-ā* | | *asthn-ā* | *nāmn-ā* | |
| | Dat | *vāriṇ-e* | | *asthn-e* | *nāmn-e* | |
| | Abl, Gen | *vāriṇ-as* | | *asthn-as* | *nāmn-as* | |
| | Loc | *vāriṇ-i* | | *asthn-i* | *nāmn-i (nāman-i)* | |
| Dual | Nom, Voc, Acc | *vāri-ṇī* | *asthi-nī* | | *nāmn-ī, nāman-ī* | |
| | Instr, Dat, Abl | *vāri-bhyām* | *asthi-bhyām* | | *nāma-bhyām* | |
| | Gen, Loc | *vāriṇ-os* | | *asthn-os* | *nāmn-os* | |
| Plural | Nom, Voc, Acc | *vārī-ṇi* | *asthī-ni* | | *nāmān-i* | |
| | Instr | *vāri-bhis* | *asthi-bhis* | | *nāma-bhis* | |
| | Dat, Abl | *vāri-bhyas* | *asthi-bhyas* | | *nāma-bhyas* | |
| | Gen | *vārīṇ-ām* | | *asthn-ām* | *nāmn-ām* | |
| | Loc | *vāri-ṣu* | *asthi-ṣu* | | *nāma-su* | |

*Source:* Whitney 1889: 122, 160

(3)     X, C, κ → *f*(X)

One might counter this observation by arguing that reference to the lexeme realized by a stem is sometimes necessary anyway. Consider, for example, the verbs RING₁ put or make a ring around' and RING₂ to (cause to) sound' (of a bell). One might suppose that in order to guarantee that

PF(⟨RING₁, {pst}⟩) = ⟨*ringed*, {ps t}⟩

but that

PF(⟨RING₂, {pst}⟩) = ⟨*rang*, {ps t}⟩,

the rule of exponence that suffixes *-ed* in the definition of *ringed* and the rule of stem ablaut in the definition of *rang* must be sensitive to a lexemic distinction. But this assumption simply begs the question; in fact, these rules need only be sensitive to the possibility that homophonous stems may belong to different inflection classes.

The phenomenon of **overabundance** (Section 9.1) makes this point more clearly. Overabundance is the property of a lexeme whose paradigm has at least one cell that may be realized in at least two ways (Thornton 2012). In some instances, overabundance is an intrinsic characteristic of a single inflection class (as in the case of Spanish past subjunctives discussed in Section 9.1); in others,

Table 6.10 *The overabundant declension of neuter **i**-stem adjectives in Sanskrit*

(Shaded forms function as masculines and may also serve as alternatives to the neuter forms to their right; arrows indicate cells where masculine forms and neuter forms exhibit the same exponence.)

|  | | masculine | ŚUCI 'pure' | | neuter |
|---|---|---|---|---|---|
|  | | MUNI Ś age' | masculine | neuter | VĀRI 'water' |
| Sg | Nom | *munis* | *śucis* | *śuci* | *vāri* |
|  | Voc | *mune* | *śuce* | *śuci* | *vāri* |
|  | Acc | *munim* | *śucim* | *śuci* | *vāri* |
|  | Inst | *muninā* | ← *śucinā* → | | *vāriṇā* |
|  | Dat | *munaye* | *śucaye* | *śucine* | *vāriṇe* |
|  | Abl, Gen | *munes* | *śuces* | *śucinas* | *vāriṇas* |
|  | Loc | *munau* | *śucau* | *śucini* | *vāriṇi* |
| Du | Nom, Voc, Acc | *munī* | *śucī* | *śucinī* | *vāriṇī* |
|  | Inst, Dat, Abl | *munibhyām* | ← *śucibhyām* → | | *vāribhyām* |
|  | Gen, Loc | *munyos* | *śucyos* | *śucinos* | *vāriṇos* |
| Pl | Nom, Voc | *munayas* | *śucayas* | *śucīni* | *vārīṇi* |
|  | Acc | *munīn* | *śucīn* | *śucīni* | *vārīṇi* |
|  | Inst | *munibhis* | ← *śucibhis* → | | *vāribhis* |
|  | Dat, Abl | *munibhyas* | ← *śucibhyas* → | | *vāribhyas* |
|  | Gen | *munīnām* | ← *śucīnām* → | | *vārīṇām* |
|  | Loc | *muniṣu* | ← *śuciṣu* → | | *vāriṣu* |

it arises because a cell's realization may be determined by either of two com-peting inflection classes. An example of this latter sort of overabundance is the neuter inflection of Sanskrit *i*-stem adjectives (e.g. ŚUCI ṗure '), which exhibits two alternative forms for certain case/number combinations: In each such case, one form follows the declension of masculine *i*-stems (e.g. MUNI Ś age') while the other form follows the declension of neuter *i*-stems (e.g. VĀRI ẁ ater'); the paradigms in Table 6.10 illustrate. As this example shows, two contrasting inflection classes may compete to realize the very same cell in the paradigm of a single lexeme; the stems involved in these alternative realizations may perfectly well be homophonous.

It is redundant to assume that lexemes belong to inflection classes, since one must assume that their stems belong to inflection classes in any event, and nothing actually requires lexemes to do so as well. As a kind of shorthand, one can certainly say that L belongs to an inflection class, but this just means that it has a stem (or a set of kindred stems) belonging to that class. In the case of segregated inflection classes, no ambiguity can result; but this shorthand is potentially misleading in the cases of heteroclisis and overabundance, since in such cases, a lexeme's paradigm juxtaposes inflection classes that are ordinarily in competition.

## 6.4 Stems and inflection classes

The conclusion that inflection classes are classes of stems rather than of lexemes leads to the expectation that inflection-class distinctions will often take the form of distinctions in the form and distribution of stems. The following Sanskrit example confirms this expectation especially clearly.

Table 6.11 shows the paradigms of four masculine nouns and the masculine paradigms of four adjectives; each nominal embodies a different declension. These eight declensions are related in various ways. All are C(onsonant)-stem declensions, insofar as some if not all of their alternating stems end in consonants; in addition, all exhibit a distinctive pattern of stem alternation, and their inflectional endings are largely the same.

Using the formal notation introduced in Section 3.6, we can describe the inflectional endings in Table 6.11 by means of the paradigm function defined in (4) and the rules of exponence in (5). The rules in (5) are organized into two blocks, the first of which houses a single rule; this rule introduces the $n$ appearing in the accusative plural and genitive plural forms and concomitantly syllabifies and lengthens the stem-final resonant. All of the other endings in Table 6.11 are introduced by Block II. As the rules in (5) show, the endings are not sensitive to all of the inflection-class distinctions among the eight paradigms in Table 6.11. Instead, it is the patterns of stem alternation that distinguish these declensions most fully.

(4)    $PF(\langle L, \sigma \rangle) =_{def}$ **Block II**: [ **Block I**: $\langle Z, \sigma \rangle$]], where $Stem(\langle L, \sigma \rangle) = Z$

(5)[3]   **Block I**  a.   XR, [Nominal $r$-stems and V-stems], [[{acc} ∨
                      {gen}] ∧ pl}                          → $X\bar{R}n$[4]
         **Block II** b.   XR, [Nominal $n$-stems and $r$-stems], {nom sg}   → X
                      c.   X, [Nominal C-stems], {cc sg}                     → $Xam$
                      d.   X, Nominals, {ins  sg}                            → $X\bar{a}$
                      e.   X, Nominals, {da t sg}                            → $Xe$
                      f.   X, [Nominal C-stems], [[{ bl} ∨ {gen}] ∧ {sg}]    → $Xas$

---

3  In rules (5a) and (5b), R represents a resonant.
4  By automatic sandhi, the -$n$ suffix becomes retroflex after $\bar{r}$ when followed by a vowel. Thus, *pitṝṇām* ôf the  fathers,' but *pitṝn* f athers' (accusative).

g.   X*r*, [Nominal *r*-stems], [[ä bl} ∨ {gen}] ∧ {sg}]   → X*ur*
h.   X, Nominals, {oc  sg}   → X*i*
i.   X, Nominals, [[ñom}  ∨ ( oc} ∨ {acc}] ∧ {du}]   → X*au*
j.   X, Nominals, [[ïns } ∨ ḍa t} ∨ {abl}] ∧ {du}]   → X*bhyām*
k.   X, Nominals, [[ǵe n} ∨ {oc }] ∧ {du}]   → X*os*
l.   X, Nominals, [[ñom}  ∨ ( oc} ∨ {acc}] ∧ {pl}]   → X*as*
m.   X, [Nominal *r*-stems and V-stems], {acc pl}   → X
n.   X, Nominals, {ns  pl}   → X*bhis*
o.   X, Nominals, [[ḍa t} ∨ ä bl}] ∧ {pl}]   → X*bhyas*
p.   X, Nominals, ǵe n pl}   → X*ām*
q.   X, Nominals, {oc  pl}   → X*su*[5]

In order to understand the patterns of stem alternation in Table 6.11, it is important to understand the Sanskrit system of vowel gradation (Whitney 1889: Sections 235ff). This system distinguishes three vowel grades, traditionally known as the Vṛddhi, Guṇa and Zero grades. In the simplest cases, a member of a set of alternating stems is in the Guṇa grade if the vowel in its final syllable is a short *a*; it is in the Vṛddhi grade if the vowel in its final syllable is a long *ā*; and it is in the Zero grade if the alternating *ă* is absent – thus, Guṇa *kartar-*, Vṛddhi *kartār-*, Zero *kartr-*. If the alternating vowel happens to precede a resonant consonant, then in the Zero grade, this resonant becomes syllabic in preconsonantal positions to compensate for the absence of the alternating vowel, as in the instrumental plural form *kartṛ-bhis*. These characteristics of Sanskrit vowel gradation are summarized in Table 6.12. An important wrinkle in this system is that in the prehistory of Sanskrit, syllabic nasals developed into *a*, so that (for example) Guṇa-grade *rājan-* and Vṛddhi-grade *rājān-* correspond to Zero-grade *rāja-* in preconsonantal position. (Compare the prevocalic Zero-grade form *rājñ-*, in which the *n* is preserved, palatalized by the adjoining *j*.)

Each of the nominals in Table 6.11 exhibits at least two stem grades, as Table 6.13 shows. The declensions of VIDVAṂS 'knowing' and PRATYAÑC 'westerly' also exhibit stems (*viduṣ-*, *vidvat-* and *pratīc-*) that are not simple vowel-grade alternants of their Guṇa-grade stems; these, in effect, take the place of the stems that would otherwise occupy the shaded cells in Table 6.13. Though I refer to these special stems as suppletive stems, it should be noted that the patterns that they embody are typical of all members of the declensions to which they belong.

Although all of the declensions in Table 6.11 exhibit stem forms participating in the system of vowel gradation, they differ with respect to the ways in which these stems are distributed in their paradigms. In Sanskrit, many C-stems exhibit the distinctive pattern of stem distribution schematized in Figure 6.1. In this

5  By automatic sandhi, the *s* in -*su* becomes retroflex after *ṛ*. Thus: *pitṛṣu* à t the fathers.'

Table 6.11  *The declension of eight Sanskrit nominals*
(Nouns are masculine; adjectives* are in their masculine forms.)

| | | RĀJAN 'king' | VIDVĀMS* 'knowing' | ĀTMAN 'self' | KARTAR 'maker' | PITAR 'father' | BHAGAVANT* 'fortunate' | PRATYAÑC* 'westerly' | NAYANT* 'leading' |
|---|---|---|---|---|---|---|---|---|---|
| Declension: | | n-stem-1 | vāṃs-stem | n-stem-2 | r-stem-1 | r-stem-2 | vant-stem | añc-stem | ant-stem |
| Sg | Nom | rājā | vidvān | ātmā | kartā | pitā | bhagavān | pratyaṅ | nayan |
| | Voc | rājan | vidvan | ātman | kartar | pitar | bhagavan | pratyaṅ | nayan |
| | Acc | rājān-am | vidvāṃs-am | ātmān-am | kartār-am | pitar-am | bhagavant-am | pratyañc-am | nayant-am |
| | Ins | rājñ-ā | viduṣ-ā | ātman-ā | kartr-ā | pitr-ā | bhagavat-ā | pratīc-ā | nayat-ā |
| | Dat | rājñ-e | viduṣ-e | ātman-e | kartr-e | pitr-e | bhagavat-e | pratīc-e | nayat-e |
| | Abl | rājñ-as | viduṣ-as | ātman-as | kartur | pitur | bhagavat-as | pratīc-as | nayat-as |
| | Gen | rājñ-as | viduṣ-as | ātman-as | kartur | pitur | bhagavat-as | pratīc-as | nayat-as |
| | Loc | rājñ-i | viduṣ-i | ātman-i | kartar-i | pitar-i | bhagavat-i | pratīc-i | nayat-i |
| Du | Nom | rājān-au | vidvāṃs-au | ātmān-au | kartār-au | pitar-au | bhagavant-au | pratyañc-au | nayant-au |
| | Voc | rājān-au | vidvāṃs-au | ātmān-au | kartār-au | pitar-au | bhagavant-au | pratyañc-au | nayant-au |
| | Acc | rājān-au | vidvāṃs-au | ātmān-au | kartār-au | pitar-au | bhagavant-au | pratyañc-au | nayant-au |
| | Ins | rāja-bhyām | vidvad-bhyām | ātma-bhyām | kartr-bhyām | pitr-bhyām | bhagavad-bhyām | pratyag-bhyām | nayad-bhyām |
| | Dat | rāja-bhyām | vidvad-bhyām | ātma-bhyām | kartr-bhyām | pitr-bhyām | bhagavad-bhyām | pratyag-bhyām | nayad-bhyām |
| | Abl | rāja-bhyām | vidvad-bhyām | ātma-bhyām | kartr-bhyām | pitr-bhyām | bhagavad-bhyām | pratyag-bhyām | nayad-bhyām |
| | Gen | rājñ-os | viduṣ-os | ātman-os | kartr-os | pitr-os | bhagavat-os | pratīc-os | nayat-os |
| | Loc | rājñ-os | viduṣ-os | ātman-os | kartr-os | pitr-os | bhagavat-os | pratīc-os | nayat-os |
| Pl | Nom | rājān-as | vidvāṃs-as | ātmān-as | kartār-as | pitar-as | bhagavant-as | pratyañc-as | nayant-as |
| | Voc | rājān-as | vidvāṃs-as | ātmān-as | kartār-as | pitar-as | bhagavant-as | pratyañc-as | nayant-as |
| | Acc | rājñ-as | viduṣ-as | ātman-as | kartṝ-n | pitṝ-n | bhagavat-as | pratīc-as | nayat-as |
| | Ins | rāja-bhis | vidvad-bhis | ātma-bhis | kartṛ-bhis | pitṛ-bhis | bhagavad-bhis | pratyag-bhis | nayad-bhis |
| | Dat | rāja-bhyas | vidvad-bhyas | ātma-bhyas | kartṛ-bhyas | pitṛ-bhyas | bhagavad-bhyas | pratyag-bhyas | nayad-bhyas |
| | Abl | rāja-bhyas | vidvad-bhyas | ātma-bhyas | kartṛ-bhyas | pitṛ-bhyas | bhagavad-bhyas | pratyag-bhyas | nayad-bhyas |
| | Gen | rājñ-ām | viduṣ-ām | ātman-ām | kartṝ-ṇ-ām | pitṝ-ṇ-ām | bhagavat-ām | pratīc-ām | nayat-ām |
| | Loc | rāja-su | vidvat-su | ātma-su | kartṛ-ṣu | pitṛ-ṣu | bhagavat-su | pratyak-su | nayat-su |

Table 6.12 *Sanskrit vowel gradation*

| Grade | Stem form | With a following resonant | |
|---|---|---|---|
| Guṇa | X$a$C$^n$- | X$a$RC$^1$-, | X$a$R- |
| Vṛddhi | X$\bar{a}$C$^n$- | X$\bar{a}$RC$^1$-, | X$\bar{a}$R- |
| Zero | XC$^n$- | XṚC$^1$- | ⎰ XṚ- before a consonant |
|  |  |  | ⎱ XR- before a vowel |

C$^n$: string of $n$ consonants ($n \geq 0$)
R: resonant consonant

Table 6.13 *Grade forms of eight nominal stems in Sanskrit (masculine forms)*

|  |  | RĀJAN 'king' | VIDVAṂS 'kno wing' | ĀTMAN 's elf' | KARTAR 'ma ker' | PITAR 'f ather' | BHAGAVANT 'fortuna te' | PRATYAÑC 'w esterly' | NAYANT 'le ading' |
|---|---|---|---|---|---|---|---|---|---|
| Guṇa |  | *rājan* | *vidvaṃs* | *ātman* | *kartar* | *pitar* | *bhagavant* | *pratyañc* | *nayant* |
| Vṛddhi |  | *rājan* | *vidvāṃs* | *ātmān* | *kartār* | *pitār* | *bhagavānt* | – | – |
| Zero | _V | *rājñ* |  | – | *kartr* | *pitr* | *bhagavat* |  | *nayat* |
|  | _C | *rāja* |  | *ātma* | *kartṛ* | *pitṛ* | *bhagavat* | *pratyac* | *nayat* |

Figure 6.1 *The default distribution of the Strong, Middle and Weakest stems in Sanskrit*

pattern, three stems are distinguished: a Strong stem, a Middle stem and a Weakest stem (Whitney 1889: Section 311). In masculine and feminine paradigms participating in this pattern of stem distribution, the Strong stem appears in the nominative, vocative and accusative cases (except in the accusative plural and, in some cases, in the vocative singular); otherwise, the Weakest stem appears before vowel-initial endings, and the Middle stem appears elsewhere. In neuter paradigms, the pattern is different: There, the Strong stem appears in the nominative,

Table 6.14  *Alternating stems in eight Sanskrit declensions*

|        | RĀJAN 'king' | | VIDVAṂS kno wing' | | ĀTMAN 'self' | | KARTAR 'maker' | |
|--------|--------|---|--------|---|--------|----|--------|-----|
| Strong | rājān | V | vidvāṃs | V | ātmān | V | kartār | V |
| Middle | rāja | 0 | vidvat | x | ātma | 0 | kartṛ | 0 |
| Weakest | rājñ | 0 | vidus | x | ātman | G | kartr | 0 |
| Nom sg | rājā | Vtr | vidvāṃs | V | ātmā | Vtr | kartā | Vtr |
| Voc sg | rājan | G | vidvaṃs | G | ātman | G | kartar | G |
| Loc sg | rājan | G | viduṣ | x | ātman | G | kartar | G |

|        | PITAR f ather' | | BHAGAVANT fortuna te' | | PRATYAÑC ẁ esterly' | | NAYANT 'leading' | |
|--------|--------|---|----------|---|----------|---|--------|---|
| Strong | pitar | G | bhagavant | G | pratyañc | G | nayant | G |
| Middle | pitṛ | 0 | bhagavat | 0 | pratyac | 0 | nayat | 0 |
| Weakest | pitr | 0 | bhagavat | 0 | pratīc | x | nayat | 0 |
| Nom sg | pitā | Vtr | bhagavānt | V | pratyañc | G | nayant | G |
| Voc sg | pitar | G | bhagavant | G | pratyañc | G | nayant | G |
| Loc sg | pitar | G | bhagavat | 0 | pratīc | x | nayat | 0 |

V: Vṛddhi grade    0: Zero grade    G: Guṇa grade    x: suppletive stem
Vtr: Vṛddhi grade, with morphological truncation of a stem-final resonant in
accordance with the rule of exponence (5b).

vocative and accusative plural, with the Weakest stem again appearing in the
remaining prevocalic positions and the Middle stem again elsewhere.

Each of the declensions in Table 6.11 participates in this pattern of stem distribution (in some cases with minor deviations). One might accordingly anticipate
that the three vowel grades (Guṇa, Vṛddhi and Zero) and the three distribution
classes (Strong, Middle and Weakest) will correspond in the same way in each
of the eight declensions. Examination of Table 6.11 reveals that they do not. If
the stems in these declensions are classified by both form and distribution, they
fall into the seven different patterns in Table 6.14.[6] (In this table, the patterns of

6  Principles of automatic sandhi cause the stem forms listed in Table 6.14 to be modified in certain
   phonological contexts. Word-finally, *vidvāṃs-*, *vidvaṃs-*, *bhagavānt-*, *bhagavant-*, *pratyañc-*
   and *nayant-*, become *vidvān*, *vidvan*, *bhagavān*, *bhagavan*, *pratyaṇ* and *nayan*; before a voiced
   obstruent, *vidvat-*, *bhagavat-*, *pratyac-* and *nayat-* become *vidvad-*, *bhagavad-*, *pratyag-* and
   *nayad-*; before a voiceless obstruent, *pratyac-* becomes *pratyak-*.

RĀJAN 'king' and KARTAR 'maker' are alike; their declensions must neverthe-less be distinguished, since they exhibit different endings in the ablative/genitive singular and in the accusative and genitive plural; see again the rules of ex-ponence in (5a, g, m).) The cross-classification of alternations in stem form with alternations in stem distribution is summarized in Table 6.15.

An ordinary C-stem nominal's lexical entry need only list its Strong stem, since the corresponding Middle and Weakest stems are deducible from the Strong stem's inflection-class membership by the stem-formation rules in Table 6.16, which determine a particular pattern of vowel gradation for each declension and, in the case of the VIDVAṂS and PRATYAÑC declensions, a particular pattern of stem suppletion. The stem-formation rules in the bottom row of Table 6.16 are a refine-ment of those proposed for perfect active participles in Section 5.5.2.

The stem-formation rules in Table 6.16 are unlike those proposed in Sec-tion 5.5 because they are not stated directly in terms of values of the *Stem* function, but rather in terms of the morphomic stem categories Strong, Middle and Weakest. Nevertheless, the paradigmatic distribution of stems still depends on the definition of the Sanskrit *Stem* function. The relevant clauses in this definition are given in (6).

(6)　　Clauses in the definition of the Sanskrit *Stem* function
　　　a.　Where σ satisfies property constraint (7), *Stem*(⟨L, σ⟩) = L's Strong stem
　　　b.　*Stem*(⟨L, {na sc voc sg}⟩) = L 's Guṇa-grade stem
　　　c.　Where L's Strong stem belongs to the PITAR or BHAGAVANT declension, *Stem*(⟨L, σ:{na sc nom sg}⟩) = L 's Vṛddhi-grade stem.
　　　d.　*Stem*(⟨L, σ⟩) = *SC*(Z), where Z is L's Middle stem
　　　e.　Where L's Strong stem belongs to the RĀJAN, KARTAR or PITAR declen-sion,
　　　　　*Stem*(⟨L, σ:{oc sg}⟩) = L 's Guṇa-grade stem.
(7)　　[[{nom} ∨ {voc} ∨ {cc} ∧ [{ne ut pl} ∨ [[{masc} ∨ {fem}] ∧ {acc pl}]]]]

By (6a), the Strong stem is used by default in the realization of property sets satisfying the property constraint in (7). This clause is, however, overridden by the two more specific clauses in (6b, c). Clause (6b) captures the generaliza-tion that in each of the declensions in Table 6.11, the vocative singular form is based on the Guṇa-grade stem, regardless of whether or not this is the Strong stem; cf. again Table 6.15. By (6c), masculine nominative singular forms are based on the Vṛddhi-grade stem in the PITAR and BHAGAVANT declensions (*pitā, bhagavān*) even though the Strong stem is not the Vṛddhi-grade stem in these declensions.

Clause (6d) specifies that a C-stem nominal's ultimate default stem is *SC*(Z), where Z is the nominal's Middle stem and the definition (8) of the *SC* function

Table 6.15 Cross-classification of eight Sanskrit nominals by stem grade and Strong/Middle/Weakest alternation

| | | | | | | Deviations | | |
|---|---|---|---|---|---|---|---|
| | Strong | Middle | Weakest | | | Nominative singular | Vocative singular | Locative singular |
| Vṛddhi | RĀJAN: rājān<br>VIDVAMS: vidvāṃs<br>ĀTMAN: ātmān<br>KARTAR: kartār | | | PITAR:<br>BHAGAVANT: | pitār<br>bhagavānt | | |
| Guṇa | PITAR: pitar<br>ĀTMAN:<br>BHAGAVANT: bhagavant<br>PRATYAÑC: pratyañc<br>NAYANT: nayant | | ātman | RĀJAN:<br>VIDVAMS:<br>KARTAR: | | ātman<br>rājan<br>vidvams<br>kartar | pitar<br>rājan<br>kartar |
| Zero | | rāja<br>ātma<br>kartṛ<br>pitṛ<br>bhagavat<br>pratyac<br>nayat | rājñ<br>kartṛ<br>pitṛ<br>bhagavat<br>nayat | RĀJAN:<br>ĀTMAN:<br>KARTAR:<br>PITAR:<br>BHAGAVANT:<br>PRATYAÑC:<br>NAYANT: | | | |
| Suppletive | | vidvat | viduṣ<br>pratīc | VIDVAMS:<br>PRATYAÑC: | | | |

Table 6.16 *Stem-formation rules for some Sanskrit C-stem declensions*

| Declension | Stems | | |
|---|---|---|---|
| | Strong | Middle | Weakest |
| RĀJAN | V: X$\bar{a}$n | 0: X$a$ | 0: X$n$ |
| KARTAR | V: X$\bar{a}$r ⎫ | | |
| PITAR | G: X$ar$ ⎭ | 0: X$ṛ$ | 0: X$r$ |
| VIDVAṂS | V: X$v\bar{a}$ṃs | X$vat$ | X$uṣ$ |
| ĀTMAN | V: X$\bar{a}$n | 0: X$a$ | G: X$an$ |
| BHAGAVANT, NAYANT | G: X$ant$ | 0: X$at$ | |
| PRATYAÑC | G: X$añc$ | 0: X$ac$ | X$\bar{i}c$ |

restricts the Middle stem to nonprevocalic contexts by causing it to yield to the Weakest stem in prevocalic positions. Clause (6d) is overridden by (6a–c); that is, the default stem *SC* (Z) is the value of ***Stem***($\langle$L, σ$\rangle$) only if σ doesn't satisfy (7). In addition, (6d) is overridden by (6e), according to which members of the RĀJAN, KARTAR and PITAR declensions have locative singular forms based on their Guṇa-grade stem (*rājan-i, kartar-i, pitar-i*).

(8)    Where L has Z as its Middle stem,
       *SC*(Z) ⊥ 's Weakest stem before a vowel-initial suffix
          = Z otherwise.

As this example shows, patterns of stem formation and stem distribution play a central role in distinguishing inflection classes in Sanskrit. This fact, together with (i) the fact that inflection classes are classes of stems rather than of lexemes as well as (ii) the fact that a lexeme's stems may participate in segregated inflection classes, helps to motivate a more explicit conception of inflectional paradigms and of the inflectional systems that define them. In the following chapter, I begin articulating this new conception of inflectional morphology.

# 7 A conception of the relation of content to form in inflectional paradigms

If all inflectional paradigms conformed to the canonical ideal described in Chapter 2, there would be no reason to attribute any theoretical significance to them, since each of a lexeme's word forms could be seen as arising through a simple "spelling out" of its associated morphosyntactic properties. But inflectional paradigms rarely conform to the canonical ideal; on the contrary, there are numerous ways in which content and form may be misaligned in a lexeme's inflectional realization; such misalignments very often involve patterns defined not over individual word forms but over groups of cells within and across inflectional paradigms and potentially over entire paradigms.

A naïve inclination is to see all such cases as aberrations – that is, to see "canonical" as "normal." But "canonical" does not mean "normal," nor "most usual," nor "most stable." A canonical inflectional paradigm is like the winter solstice – a well-defined seasonal extreme relative to which a year's 364 other days can be calendrically compared, but by no means the most common or the most typical of days.

We have already seen several cases of noncanonical inflection – of mismatch between form and content in the realization of a paradigm's cells:

- Lexemes with distinct lexical meanings may have paradigms whose inflected word forms are alike in every detail (Section 4.3).
- Paradigms often exhibit morphomic patterns of exponence or stem alternation (Sections 3.6, 5.3).
- Word forms realizing the same property sets in the paradigms of different lexemes may exhibit distinct exponents for those property sets (Section 6.1).
- Paradigms may exhibit heteroclisis (Section 6.3).

Although the canonical relation between content and form in inflectional paradigms is direct and transparent (Section 2.2), deviations such as those bulleted above suggest the need for a richer architecture for modeling inflectional systems. Up to now, we have been assuming that a paradigm is a set of cells, where each cell is the pairing of a particular content with a particular word form $w$, and a cell's content comprises both the lexical content of a lexeme L and the morphosyntactic content of a property set $\sigma$; that is, we have been regarding a paradigm as a set of cells of the form $\langle L, \sigma : w \rangle$. Henceforth, however, we will pursue the richer hypothesis in (1).[1]

(1)    The paradigm-linkage hypothesis
       The content and form of a lexeme L's realizations involve three distinct but corresponding paradigms.
       - A lexeme L's **content paradigm** lists the morphosyntactic property sets with which L may be associated in syntax and which determine L's semantic interpretation in a particular sentential context. Accordingly, the cells in this paradigm (**content cells**) are pairings of the lexeme L with each such property set $\sigma$: $\langle L, \sigma \rangle$. A lexeme L's content paradigm constitutes L's interface with syntax and semantics.
       - Each lexeme L possesses a set $S_L$ of one or more stems, and the **form paradigm** associated with $S_L$ specifies the range of property sets that may be realized morphologically through the inflection of the stem(s) in $S_L$. Accordingly, each of the cells in this paradigm (its **form cells**) is the pairing of a stem Z belonging to $S_L$ with a property set $\tau$ for which Z inflects: $\langle Z, \tau \rangle$. The form paradigm of $S_L$ serves as the basis for defining L's inflected forms.
       - The **realized paradigm** of a lexeme L is a set of **realized cells** of the form $\langle w, \tau \rangle$ in which $w$ is the word form that realizes a cell $\langle Z, \tau \rangle$ in the form paradigm of $S_L$.

In general, each content cell is realized by being linked to a form cell whose realization it shares; this form cell is the content cell's **form correspondent**, and the pairing of content cells with their form correspondents is defined by a language-specific principle of paradigm linkage.[2] Accordingly, the definition

---

1 This hypothesis was first proposed, in a somewhat different form, by Stump 2002, and was subsequently developed by Ackerman and Stump 2004, Ackerman, Stump and Webelhuth 2011, Spencer and Stump 2013, Stewart and Stump 2007, Stump 2006, 2010, 2012, 2014a, 2015, Stump: to appear A, Stump: to appear B. See Walther 2013, O'Neill 2011, 2013 and Round 2013 for the development of comparable hypotheses; see also the analysis of Nepali verb inflection proposed by Bonami and Boyé (2008, 2010), which I discuss in the next chapter.
2 The relation between a content cell and its form correspondent, formulated below as a function *Corr*, is closely comparable to the ΣM mapping in the framework of constraint-based realizational morphology developed by Round (2013: Ch. 11).

Table 7.1 *Three types of paradigms*

| The content paradigms of the lexemes SING and EAT | The form paradigms of the stem sets $\mathbf{S}_{\text{SING}}$ and $\mathbf{S}_{\text{EAT}}$ | The realized paradigms of the lexemes SING and EAT |
|---|---|---|
| ⟨SING, {prs }⟩ | ⟨*sing*, {prs }⟩ | ⟨*sing*, {prs}⟩ |
| ⟨SING, {3s g prs ind}⟩ | ⟨*sing*, {3s g prs ind}⟩ | ⟨*sings*, {3sg prs ind}⟩ |
| ⟨SING, {ps t}⟩ | ⟨*sing*, {ps t}⟩ | ⟨*sang*, {pst}⟩ |
| ⟨SING, {prs  ptcp}⟩ | ⟨*sing*, {prs  ptcp}⟩ | ⟨*singing*, {prs ptcp}⟩ |
| ⟨SING, {ps t ptcp}⟩... | ⟨*sing*, {ps t ptcp}⟩... | ⟨*sung*, {pst ptcp}⟩... |
| | | |
| ⟨EAT, {prs }⟩ | ⟨*eat*, {prs }⟩ | ⟨*eat*, {prs}⟩ |
| ⟨EAT, {3s g prs ind}⟩ | ⟨*eat*, {3s g prs ind}⟩ | ⟨*eats*, {3sg prs ind}⟩ |
| ⟨EAT, {ps t}⟩ | ⟨*eat*, {ps t}⟩ | ⟨*ate*, {pst}⟩ |
| ⟨EAT, {prs  ptcp}⟩ | ⟨*eat*, {prs  ptcp}⟩ | ⟨*eating*, {prs ptcp}⟩ |
| ⟨EAT, {ps t ptcp}⟩... | ⟨*eat*, {ps t ptcp}⟩... | ⟨*eaten*, {pst ptcp}⟩... |
| | ↑ | ↑ |
| | Each form cell is the form correspondent of the content cell to its left. | Each realized cell realizes the cells to its left. |

of a language's morphology determines not only the morphological realization of the cells in its form paradigms but also the linkage of these form paradigms to the content paradigms constituting its syntactic and semantic interfaces.

The implications of the paradigm-linkage hypothesis for the definition of a language's inflectional morphology are simple but far-reaching. According to this hypothesis, the definition of an inflectional paradigm's content is logically independent of the definition of its form. In the canonical case, this independence is not apparent, since the three sorts of paradigm are simply isomorphic, as for example in Table 7.1: here, a lexeme L has a single stem Z such that each content cell ⟨L, σ⟩ in L's content paradigm has ⟨Z, σ⟩ as its form correspondent, so that ⟨L, σ⟩ and ⟨Z, σ⟩ share a realization ⟨w, σ⟩. Nevertheless, noncanonical patterns involve sometimes dramatic deviations from this canonical isomorphism. When seen in the context of the paradigm-linkage hypothesis, such deviations have important consequences for understanding the irreducibility and interface hypotheses discussed in Section 1.3:

- **The irreducibility hypothesis:** Some morphological regularities are, irreducibly, regularities in paradigm structure.
- **The interface hypothesis:** Paradigms are the interfaces of inflectional morphology with syntax and semantics.

Table 7.2  *The declension of Turkish* ADAM *'man'*

|            | Singular  | Plural        |
|------------|-----------|---------------|
| Nominative | *adam*    | *adam-lar*    |
| Accusative | *adam-ı*  | *adam-lar-ı*  |
| Dative     | *adam-a*  | *adam-lar-a*  |
| Locative   | *adam-da* | *adam-lar-da* |
| Ablative   | *adam-dan*| *adam-lar-dan*|
| Genitive   | *adam-ın* | *adam-lar-ın* |

In this chapter, I focus on the canonical relation of content to form in morphology (Section 7.1); the details of the paradigm-linkage hypothesis (Section 7.2); and the relevance of this hypothesis for modeling a stem's inflection-class membership and its paradigmatic distribution (Section 7.3).

## 7.1    *The canonical relation of content to form in morphology*

In the morphology of natural languages, the canonical relation of content to form is straightforward: Sameness of content is expressed as sameness of form, and difference of content is expressed as difference of form. This canonical relation is manifested both internally to a lexeme's paradigm of word forms and across paradigms. Paradigm-internally, the lexical content common to a lexeme's word forms is canonically expressed by a shared stem form, and across paradigms, differences in the lexical content of word forms are canonically expressed as a difference in their stem forms. Both within and across paradigms, the similarities and differences in word forms' morphosyntactic content are expressed by similarities and differences in their inflectional exponence.[3]

Thus, consider the declensional paradigm of the Turkish noun ADAM 'man' in Table 7.2. The members of this paradigm exhibit a canonical paradigm-internal content–form relation. This relation is diagrammed in Figure 7.1: (i) the shared lexical content of *adamdan* 'from the man,' *adamlardan* 'from the men' and *adamların* 'of the men' is expressed by the shared stem *adam*; (ii) the ablative

---

3 Stump 2015 distinguishes two models of the interface of inflectional morphology with syntax and semantics – the **cell interface model** (which presumes that the morphosyntactic property set that determines a word form's syntax and semantic is identical to the property set that determines its inflectional exponence) and the **paradigm-linkage model** (which accommodates differences between these two property sets) – and presents evidence from Latin and Kashmiri that is compatible with the latter model but not the former.

Table 7.3 *The declension of Turkish* TAVAN *'ceiling'*

|  | Singular | Plural |
|---|---|---|
| Nominative | *tavan* | *tavan-lar* |
| Accusative | *tavan-ı* | *tavan-lar-ı* |
| Dative | *tavan-a* | *tavan-lar-a* |
| Locative | *tavan-da* | *tavan-lar-da* |
| Ablative | *tavan-dan* | *tavan-lar-dan* |
| Genitive | *tavan-ın* | *tavan-lar-ın* |

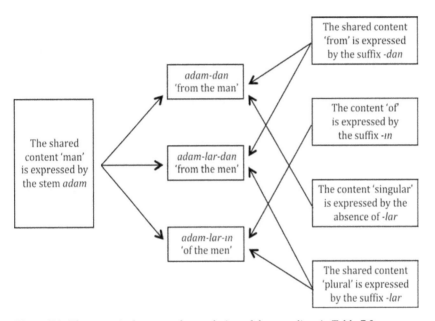

Figure 7.1 *The canonical content–form relation of the paradigm in Table 7.2*

case shared by *adamdan* and *adamlardan* is expressed by the shared suffix *-dan*; (iii) the contrasting genitive case of *adamların* is expressed by the contrasting suffix *-ın*; (iv) the shared plural number of *adamlardan* and *adamların* is expressed by the shared suffix *-lar*; and (v) the contrasting singular number of *adamdan* is expressed by the contrasting absence of the *-lar* suffix.

A comparison of the paradigm of ADAM with that of TAVAN 'ceiling' (Table 7.3) reveals a canonical cross-paradigmatic content–form relation: The paradigms are built upon the distinct stems *adam* and *tavan* (reflecting their distinct lexical content), but the parallel sets of morphosyntactic properties for which these stems inflect are realized by the same suffixal exponents.

Table 7.4 *The declension of Turkish* EV *'house,'* ÖN *'front' and* TOP *'ball'*

| | EV hous e' | | ÖN front ' | | TOP 'ball' | |
|---|---|---|---|---|---|---|
| | Singular | Plural | Singular | Plural | Singular | Plural |
| Nominative | *ev* | *ev-ler* | *ön* | *ön-ler* | *top* | *top-lar* |
| Accusative | *ev-i* | *ev-ler-i* | *ön-ü* | *ön-ler-i* | *top-u* | *top-lar-ı* |
| Dative | *ev-e* | *ev-ler-e* | *ön-e* | *ön-ler-e* | *top-a* | *top-lar-a* |
| Locative | *ev-de* | *ev-ler-de* | *ön-de* | *ön-ler-de* | *top-ta* | *top-lar-da* |
| Ablative | *ev-den* | *ev-ler-den* | *ön-den* | *ön-ler-den* | *top-tan* | *top-lar-dan* |
| Genitive | *ev-in* | *ev-ler-in* | *ön-ün* | *ön-ler-in* | *top-un* | *top-lar-ın* |

Inflectional systems are rarely this orderly. Indeed, if one looks at Turkish inflection in greater detail, one finds a number of deviations from the canonical content–form relation. Some such deviations have a phonological motivation, as in the case of EV hous e,' ÖN front, ' and TOP ba ll.' As the paradigms in Table 7.4 show, the principles of Turkish vowel harmony cause case suffixes with high vowels to exhibit four alternating forms (e.g. accusative *-ı, -i, -ü, -u*) and cause the remaining suffixes to have two alternating forms (e.g. plural *-lar*, *-ler*). Moreover, a principle of voicing assimilation causes a suffix with initial *d* to exhibit an alternant with initial *t*: *tavan-dan* 'from the ceiling,' but *top-tan* 'from the  ball.'

Because of these phonological phenomena, the morphosyntactic property "ablative" has at least four exponents in Turkish (*-dan*, *-den*, *-tan* and *-ten*); ablative nouns therefore participate in a content–form relation that is not canonical. But because the allomorphy of the ablative suffix is regular, one can postulate a single underlying form whose ultimate realization is determined by phonological rules; for instance, one might postulate the underlying representation *-dAn*, whose *d* is subject to voicing assimilation and in which A is a morphophoneme realized as *a* or *e*, according to context. This approach makes it possible to say that at an underlying level of phonological analysis, ablatives in *-dAn* exhibit a canonical content–form relation after all.

I will return to Turkish in Chapter 10 to discuss another striking deviation from the canonical content–form relation in its system of nominal inflection – a deviation that cannot be resolved phonologically.

Table 7.5 *The declension of Sanskrit* KARTṚ *'maker'*

|              | Singular  | Dual        | Plural      |
|--------------|-----------|-------------|-------------|
| Nominative   | *kartā*   | *kartār-au* | *kartār-as* |
| Vocative     | *kartar*  | *kartār-au* | *kartār-as* |
| Accusative   | *kartār-am* | *kartār-au* | *kartṝn*  |
| Instrumental | *kartr-ā* | *kartṛ-bhyām* | *kartṛ-bhis* |
| Dative       | *kartr-e* | *kartṛ-bhyām* | *kartṛ-bhyas* |
| Ablative     | *kartur*  | *kartṛ-bhyām* | *kartṛ-bhyas* |
| Genitive     | *kartur*  | *kartr-os*  | *kartṝṇām*  |
| Locative     | *kartar-i* | *kartr-os* | *kartṛ-ṣu*  |

Table 7.6 *The declension of Sanskrit* GAJA *'elephant'*

|              | Singular   | Dual         | Plural       |
|--------------|------------|--------------|--------------|
| Nominative   | *gaja-s*   | *gajau*      | *gajās*      |
| Vocative     | *gaja*     | *gajau*      | *gajās*      |
| Accusative   | *gaja-m*   | *gajau*      | *gajān*      |
| Instrumental | *gajena*   | *gajābhyām*  | *gajais*     |
| Dative       | *gajāya*   | *gajābhyām*  | *gajebhyas*  |
| Ablative     | *gajāt*    | *gajābhyām*  | *gajebhyas*  |
| Genitive     | *gaja-sya* | *gajay-os*   | *gajānām*    |
| Locative     | *gaje*     | *gajay-os*   | *gajeṣu*     |

Languages exhibit a wide variety of such nonphonological deviations. Consider, for example, the declensional paradigm of the Sanskrit noun KARTṚ 'maker' in Table 7.5. In this paradigm,

- the same lexical content ('maker') is expressed by a variety of stem forms: *kartār-* (truncated as *kartā* in the nominative singular), *kartar-*, *kartr-*, *kartṛ-* (lengthened to *kartṝ-* in the accusative and genitive plural) and *kartur-*. Moreover,
- similarities in morphosyntactic content are not expressed by similarities in inflectional exponence; to cite but two examples, there is no constant morphology shared by all dual forms or by all accusative forms. And
- differences in morphosyntactic content are not invariably expressed by differences in inflectional exponence; thus, in the dual and the plural (though not the singular), the ablative form is not distinguished from the dative form.

Table 7.7 *The content paradigm of the Turkish lexeme* ADAM *'man'*

| | |
|---|---|
| ⟨ADAM, {nom s g}⟩ | ⟨ADAM, {nom pl}⟩ |
| ⟨ADAM, {cc sg}⟩ | ⟨ADAM, {cc pl}⟩ |
| ⟨ADAM, {da t sg}⟩ | ⟨ADAM, {da t pl}⟩ |
| ⟨ADAM, {loc sg}⟩ | ⟨ADAM, {lo c pl}⟩ |
| ⟨ADAM, {bl sg}⟩ | ⟨ADAM, {bl pl}⟩ |
| ⟨ADAM, {ge n sg}⟩ | ⟨ADAM, {ge n pl}⟩ |

If we now compare the declension of KARTṚ with that of GAJA è lephant' (Table 7.6), we find additional, cross-paradigmatic deviations from the canonical content–form relation. In particular, the same morphosyntactic content does not receive the same morphological expression; for instance, the paradigm of KARTṚ exhibits an unsuffixed, truncated stem in *ā* in the nominative singular and a suffixal *-ā* in the instrumental singular, whereas the paradigm of GAJA presents a suffix *-s* in the nominative singular and a fusional form in *ena* in the instrumental singular.

These examples only scratch the surface of the extremely varied ways in which inflectional paradigms may deviate from the canonical relation between content and form.[4] Such content–form mismatches reveal important aspects of the architecture of the morphological component that remain concealed in paradigms that more closely approximate the canonical ideal. In particular, they reveal the fundamental autonomy of a language's system of inflectional morphology.

Certain conceptual distinctions greatly simplify the task of describing – and theorizing about – the various kinds of content–form mismatches that arise in inflectional paradigms. Most fundamentally, it is helpful to distinguish the three different notions of paradigm in (1); consider now the details of this essential component of the paradigm-linkage hypothesis.

## 2 *Content paradigms, form paradigms, realized paradigms, and the relations between them*

It is customary to assume that a paradigm is a set of cells and that each such cell is a pairing; but it is useful to postulate at least three different sorts of

---

4 Walther (2013) provides an exceptionally detailed and precise account of the dimensions of such deviations from the canonical ideal in inflectional morphology.

Table 7.8 *The form paradigm of the Turkish stem* **adam** *'man'*

| | |
|---|---|
| ⟨*adam*, {nom s g}⟩ | ⟨*adam*, {nom pl} ⟩ |
| ⟨*adam*, { cc sg}⟩ | ⟨*adam*, { cc pl}⟩ |
| ⟨*adam*, {da t sg}⟩ | ⟨*adam*, {da t pl}⟩ |
| ⟨*adam*, {oc  sg}⟩ | ⟨*adam*, {oc  pl}⟩ |
| ⟨*adam*, { bl sg}⟩ | ⟨*adam*, { bl pl}⟩ |
| ⟨*adam*, {ge n sg}⟩ | ⟨*adam*, {ge n pl}⟩ |

Table 7.9 *The realized paradigm of the Turkish stem* **adam** *'man'*

| | |
|---|---|
| ⟨*adam*, {nom s g}⟩ | ⟨*adamlar*, {nom pl }⟩ |
| ⟨*adamı*, { cc sg}⟩ | ⟨*adamları*, { cc pl}⟩ |
| ⟨*adama*, {da t sg}⟩ | ⟨*adamlara*, {da t pl}⟩ |
| ⟨*adamda*, {oc  sg}⟩ | ⟨*adamlarda*, {oc  pl}⟩ |
| ⟨*adamdan*, { bl sg}⟩ | ⟨*adamlardan*, { bl pl}⟩ |
| ⟨*adamın*, {ge n sg}⟩ | ⟨*adamların*, {ge n pl}⟩ |

pairing, and correspondingly, three different sorts of paradigm. In the content paradigm of the Turkish lexeme ADAM ‘ma n’ (Table 7.7), each cell is the pairing of ADAM with a complete morphosyntactic property set with which this lexeme may be associated at a node in syntactic structure and relative to which it is semantically interpreted in that context.

The form paradigm of ADAM's stem set {*adam*} lists the property sets for which a morphological realization of ADAM is defined. Thus, each cell in the form paradigm of the stem set {*adam*} is the pairing of *adam* with a property set σ, as in Table 7.8.

The morphology of Turkish defines a realization for each of the form cells in Table 7.8. Thus, this form paradigm gives rise to the realized paradigm in Table 7.9: each cell in this realized paradigm is the pairing ⟨*w*, σ⟩ of a word form *w* with the morphosyntactic property set σ that it realizes.

The intuition underlying this way of modeling inflection is that each content cell is linked to a form correspondent, a form cell with which it shares its realization. The canonical relation between content paradigms and form paradigms is one in which (i) each lexeme L has a single stem Z and (ii) each cell ⟨L, σ⟩ in the content paradigm of L has ⟨Z, σ⟩ as its form correspondent.

Table 7.10 *The canonical relation between content paradigms and form paradigms, exemplified by the declension of Turkish* ADAM *'man'*

| Content paradigm | | Form paradigm | | Realized paradigm |
|---|---|---|---|---|
| ⟨ADAM, {nom s g}⟩ | ⟹ | ⟨*adam*, {nom s g}⟩ | → | ⟨*adam*, {nom sg}⟩ |
| ⟨ADAM, {cc sg}⟩ | ⟹ | ⟨*adam*, {cc sg}⟩ | → | ⟨*adamı*, {acc sg}⟩ |
| ⟨ADAM, {da t sg}⟩ | ⟹ | ⟨*adam*, {da t sg}⟩ | → | ⟨*adama*, {dat sg}⟩ |
| ⟨ADAM, {oc sg}⟩ | ⟹ | ⟨*adam*, {oc sg}⟩ | → | ⟨*adamda*, {loc sg}⟩ |
| ⟨ADAM, {bl sg}⟩ | ⟹ | ⟨*adam*, {bl sg}⟩ | → | ⟨*adamdan*, {abl sg}⟩ |
| ⟨ADAM, {ge n sg}⟩ | ⟹ | ⟨*adam*, {ge n sg}⟩ | → | ⟨*adamın*, {gen sg}⟩ |
| ⟨ADAM, {nom pl}⟩ | ⟹ | ⟨*adam*, {nom p l}⟩ | → | ⟨*adamlar*, {nom pl}⟩ |
| ⟨ADAM, {cc pl}⟩ | ⟹ | ⟨*adam*, {cc pl}⟩ | → | ⟨*adamları*, {acc pl}⟩ |
| ⟨ADAM, {da t pl}⟩ | ⟹ | ⟨*adam*, {da t pl}⟩ | → | ⟨*adamlara*, {dat pl}⟩ |
| ⟨ADAM, {oc pl}⟩ | ⟹ | ⟨*adam*, {oc pl}⟩ | → | ⟨*adamlarda*, {loc pl}⟩ |
| ⟨ADAM, {bl pl}⟩ | ⟹ | ⟨*adam*, {bl pl}⟩ | → | ⟨*adamlardan*, {abl pl}⟩ |
| ⟨ADAM, {ge n pl}⟩ | ⟹ | ⟨*adam*, {ge n pl}⟩ | → | ⟨*adamların*, {gen pl}⟩ |

The Turkish declensional paradigms in Tables 7.7–9 exemplify this canonical relation, as in Table 7.10. In this table, the double-shafted arrow represents the relation of form correspondence and the single-shafted arrow, the realization relation. Thus, the notation '⟨L, σ⟩ ⟹ ⟨Z, σ⟩ → ⟨w, σ⟩' means that ⟨Z, σ⟩ is the form correspondent of ⟨L, σ⟩ and that ⟨Z, σ⟩ (hence also ⟨L, σ⟩) has ⟨w, σ⟩ as its realization.

According to this way of conceiving of inflectional paradigms, the definition of a language's inflectional morphology comprises that of both the form-correspondence relation and the realization relation. These relations can be most easily defined by distinguishing three functions.

First, I use PF to represent the paradigm function such that for any content cell ⟨L, σ⟩ and any form cell ⟨Z, τ⟩, PF(⟨L, σ⟩) is the realized cell that realizes ⟨L, σ⟩ and PF(⟨Z, τ⟩) is the realized cell that realizes ⟨Z, τ⟩. In addition, I use *Corr* to represent that function such that for any content cell ⟨L, σ⟩, *Corr*(⟨L, σ⟩) is the form correspondent of ⟨L, σ⟩; *Corr* is a **form-correspondence function**. By definition, PF(⟨L, σ⟩) = PF(*Corr*(⟨L, σ⟩)). Finally, we use *pm* to represent that function such that for some content cell ⟨L, σ⟩ having ⟨Z, τ⟩ as its form correspondent, *pm*(σ) = τ; *pm* is a **property mapping**.[5] A language's inflectional

---

5 The notion of *règles de transfert* developed by Walther (2013) is closely similar to that of property mappings. In the framework of constraint-based realizational morphology developed by Round (2013: Ch. 11), the ΣM lexicon serves as a kind of extensional definition of the relation formulated as a property mapping in the paradigm-linkage approach.

morphology comprises definitions determining the language-specific evaluation of each of these three functions.

The realization relation between a form cell and the corresponding realized cell is mediated by rules of exponence, whose interaction conforms to a paradigm function (Section 3.6). The relation of paradigm linkage between a content cell and its form correspondent is mediated by the correspondence function **Corr**, whose definition typically involves one or more property mappings and the **Stem** function (Section 5.5.1.).

We can use **Corr** and **pm** to give a precise characterization of the canonical relation between content paradigms and form paradigms. We will say that the relation between a set of content paradigms and a set of form paradigms is canonical if and only if it possesses the following five characteristics:

(2)  Canonical paradigm linkage
   a. **Property-set preservation.** Content cells and their form correspondents have the same property set; that is, for any property set $\sigma$ associated with a content cell, $pm(\sigma) = \sigma$.
   b. **Stem invariance.** All of a lexeme's inflected forms are based on the same stem; that is, each lexeme L has a single stem Z such that for each cell $\langle L, \sigma \rangle$ in L's content paradigm, $Corr(\langle L, \sigma \rangle) = \langle Z, \sigma \rangle$.
   c. **Unambiguity.** Distinct lexemes do not have identical realizations; that is, there are no two lexemes $L_1$, $L_2$ such that for some morphosyntactic property set $\sigma$, $Corr(\langle L_1, \sigma \rangle) = Corr(\langle L_2, \sigma \rangle)$.
   d. **Isomorphism of paradigms belonging to the same part of speech.** Lexemes belonging to the same syntactic category have isomorphic paradigms; that is, if two lexemes $L_1$, $L_2$ belong to the same syntactic category, then $\langle L_1, \sigma \rangle$ is a cell in $L_1$'s content paradigm if and only if $\langle L_2, \sigma \rangle$ is a cell in $L_2$'s content paradigm.
   e. **Non-isomorphism of paradigms belonging to distinct parts of speech.** Lexemes belonging to distinct syntactic categories inflect for distinct property sets; that is, if two lexemes $L_1$, $L_2$ belong to distinct syntactic categories, then there is no morphosyntactic property set $\sigma$ such that $\langle L_1, \sigma \rangle$ is a cell in $L_1$'s content paradigm and $\langle L_2, \sigma \rangle$ is a cell in $L_2$'s content paradigm.

Logically, a canonical relation of paradigm linkage must be manifested at several levels of "granularity":

(3)  a. *At the level of morphosyntactic property sets:* a content cell's morphosyntactic property set contains a property p if and only if the property set of that cell's form correspondent also contains p.
   b. *At the level of stems:* A lexeme L has a single stem Z by which it is expressed in the form correspondents of its content cells, and this stem expresses no lexeme other than L.
   c. *At the level of paradigms:* A lexeme's content paradigm is isomorphic to the form paradigm of its stem.

Table 7.11 *The formal components of the paradigm-linkage hypothesis*

| | |
|---|---|
| Content paradigm: | A set of content cells. |
| Content cell: $\langle L, \sigma \rangle$ | $\langle L, \sigma \rangle$ determines the lexical insertion and semantic interpretation of its realization.<br>L is a lexeme.<br>$\sigma$ is a morphosyntactic property set appropriate for L.<br>PF($\langle L, \sigma \rangle$), the realization of $\langle L, \sigma \rangle$, is defined as the realization of ***Corr***($\langle L, \sigma \rangle$).<br>***Corr***($\langle L, \sigma \rangle$) is the form correspondent of $\langle L, \sigma \rangle$; its value is defined by means of ***Stem*** and ***pm***.<br>Most often, ***Corr*** is defined so that ***Corr***($\langle L, \sigma \rangle$) = $\langle$***Stem***($\langle L, \sigma \rangle$), ***pm***($\sigma$)$\rangle$; occasionally, however, the definition of ***Corr*** instead entails that ***Corr***($\langle L, \sigma \rangle$) = $\langle$***Stem***($\langle L,$ ***pm***($\sigma$)$\rangle$), ***pm***($\sigma$)$\rangle$.[6] |
| Form paradigm: | A set of form cells. |
| Form cell: $\langle Z, \tau \rangle$ | Where $\langle Z, \tau \rangle$ = ***Corr***($\langle L, \sigma \rangle$) for some content cell $\langle L, \sigma \rangle$, $\langle Z, \tau \rangle$ determines the inflectional realization of $\langle L, \sigma \rangle$.<br>$Z$ = ***Stem***($\langle L, \sigma \rangle$), the stem appropriate for the realization of $\langle L, \sigma \rangle$.<br>$\tau$ = ***pm***($\sigma$); canonically, ***pm***($\sigma$) = $\sigma$, but often, ***pm***($\sigma$) $\neq \sigma$.<br>PF($\langle Z, \tau \rangle$), the realization of $\langle Z, \tau \rangle$, is defined by blocks of rules of exponence. |
| Realized paradigm: | A set of realized cells. |
| Realized cell: $\langle w, \tau \rangle$ | For some content cell $\langle L, \sigma \rangle$, $\langle w, \tau \rangle$ is the inflectional realization of ***Corr***($\langle L, \sigma \rangle$), hence also of $\langle L, \sigma \rangle$.<br>$w$ is a word form. |

d. ***At the level of memb rs of a single syntactic category:*** The paradigms of lexemes belonging to the same syntactic category are isomorphic.

e. ***At the level of memb rs of distinct syntactic categories:*** Where $L_1, L_2$ belong to distinct syntactic categories, if $\langle L_1, \sigma \rangle$ belongs to the content paradigm of $L_1$, then $\langle L_2, \sigma \rangle$ does not belong to the content paradigm of $L_2$.

Actual inflectional systems may deviate from any or all of the canonical characteristics (2a–e), as the coming chapters will demonstrate.

The key characteristics of the proposed formalization of the paradigm-linkage hypothesis are summarized in Table 7.11; this formalization entails that content

6 An example of the former sort of value for ***Corr*** is given in (6) below; an example of the latter sort of value is given in definition (20) in Section 12.4.

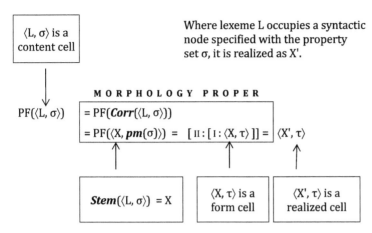

Figure 7.2 *The interface of content paradigms and form paradigms*

paradigms, form paradigms and realized paradigms possess the interface schematized in Figure 7.2.

In what follows, I shall sometimes refer to the **paradigm-linkage theory**. By this I mean an inferential-realizational theory of inflectional morphology in which the paradigm-linkage hypothesis is assumed. In this theory, the realization relation between form paradigms and realized paradigms is defined in fundamentally the same way as realization is defined in Paradigm Function Morphology (Stump 2001); but the paradigm-linkage theory additionally assumes a form-correspondence relation between content paradigms and form paradigms, and this relation is defined by means of the **Corr**, **Stem** and **pm** functions described above. One might therefore think of the paradigm-linkage theory as an extension of Paradigm Function Morphology whose objective is to provide a systematic and general account of the interface of inflectional morphology with syntax and semantics – an account that explains the wide variety of ways in which the relation between words' content and form may deviate from a relation of pure isomorphism.

## 7.3    Inflection classes and stem distribution under the paradigm-linkage hypothesis

The functions **Stem**, **pm** and **Corr** afford an enlightening account of the relationship between a stem's inflection-class membership and its distribution. Consider, for example, the patterns of stem alternation exhibited by the Latin verbs in Table 7.12. Each of these partial paradigms exhibits four stems: an

Table 7.12 *Stems in the active inflection of five Latin verbs (Finite forms are indicative.)*

| | | | First | Second | Third | Third (-io) | Fourth |
|---|---|---|---|---|---|---|---|
| Conjugation: | | | PARĀRE 'prepare' | MONĒRE 'warn' | REGERE 'rule' | CAPERE 'take' | AUDĪRE 'hear' |
| Verbal lexeme: | | | | | | | |
| Imperfective | Present | 1sg | [ par] ō | [ mone] ō | [ reg] ō | [ capi] ō | [ audi] ō |
| | | 2sg | [ parā] s | [ monē] s | [ regi] s | [ capi] s | [ audī] s |
| | | 3sg | [ para] t | [ mone] t | [ regi] t | [ capi] t | [ audī] t |
| | Future | 1sg | parāb-ō | monēb-ō | [ reg] am | [ capi] am | [ audi] am |
| | | 2sg | parāb-is | monēb-is | [ reg] ēs | [ capi] ēs | [ audi] ēs |
| | | 3sg | parāb-it | monēb-it | [ reg] et | [ capi] et | [ audi] et |
| | Preterite | 1sg | parāb-am | monēb-am | regēb-am | capiēb-am | audiēb-am |
| | | 2sg | parāb-ās | monēb-ās | regēb-ās | capiēb-ās | audiēb-ās |
| | | 3sg | parāb-at | monēb-at | regēb-at | capiēb-at | audiēb-at |
| Perfective | Present | 1sg | { parāv} ī | { monu} ī | { rēx} ī | { cēp} ī | { audīv} ī |
| | | 2sg | { parāv} istī | { monu} istī | { rēx} istī | { cēp} istī | { audīv} istī |
| | | 3sg | { parāv} it | { monu} it | { rēx} it | { cēp} it | { audīv} it |
| | Future | 1sg | { parāv} erō | { monu} erō | { rēx} erō | { cēp} erō | { audīv} erō |
| | | 2sg | { parāv} eris | { monu} eris | { rēx} eris | { cēp} eris | { audīv} eris |
| | | 3sg | { parāv} erit | { monu} erit | { rēx} erit | { cēp} erit | { audīv} erit |
| | Preterite | 1sg | { parāv} eram | { monu} eram | { rēx} eram | { cēp} eram | { audīv} eram |
| | | 2sg | { parāv} erās | { monu} erās | { rēx} erās | { cēp} erās | { audīv} erās |
| | | 3sg | { parāv} erat | { monu} erat | { rēx} erat | { cēp} erat | { audīv} erat |
| Participles | Present | | [ parā] ns | [ monē] ns | [ reg] ēns | [ capi] ēns | [ audi] ēns |
| | Future | | \|parāt\|ūrus | \|monit\|ūrus | \|rēct\|ūrus | \|capt\|ūrus | \|audīt\|ūrus |

Table 7.13 *Stems in Latin conjugation*

| Example | Imperfective | | {Pe rfective Stem} | \| Third Stem \| | *b* Stem |
| | [ Stem] | Conjugation | | | |
|---|---|---|---|---|---|
| PARĀRE þre pare' | [ *parā*] | ∈ First | { *parā* } | \| *parāt*\| | *parāb-* |
| MONĒRE ẁ arn' | [ *monē*] | ∈ Second | { *monu* } | \| *monit*\| | *monēb-* |
| REGERE ŧule ' | [ *reg*] | ∈ Third | { *rēx* } | \| *rēct*\| | *regēb-* |
| CAPERE ŧa ke' | [ *capi*] | ∈ Third –*io* | { *cēp* } | \| *capt*\| | *capiēb-* |
| AUDĪRE ħe ar' | [ *audī*] | ∈ Fourth | { *audīv* } | \| *audīt*\| | *audiēb-* |

imperfective stem (enclosed in []), a perfective stem (enclosed in { }, a *b*-stem (ending with a hyphen, in a boxed cell), and what Aronoff (1994: Ch. 2) calls a "third stem" (enclosed in ⎸).

The five verbal lexemes in Table 7.12 have the stem inventories in Table 7.13. In many cases, one stem form is deducible from another by means of a stem-formation rule; for example, a verb's *b*-stem is in general deducible from its imperfective stem. But given that our present concern is with stems' inflection-class membership and their distribution, I here make the simplifying assumption that a Latin verbal lexeme's four stems are listed in its lexical entry. In the present context, nothing hinges on this assumption.

Under the paradigm-linkage hypothesis, the inflection-class membership of a stem Z has the same status as a morphosyntactic property: It is one of the members of the property set paired with Z in a form cell. Inflection-class indices are different from morphosyntactic properties in that they are restricted to form paradigms, where they are incapable of conditioning either the syntax or the semantics of a cell's realization; unlike morphosyntactic properties, they are introduced by a language's property mappings. The property mapping $pm_c$ defined in (4) accounts for the five conjugations in Table 7.13. Where c indexes an inflection class and σ is a morphosyntactic property set, $pm_c(σ)$ is the union of σ with ⊄ } for example, where **conj1** is the property associated with the first conjugation in Latin, $pm_{conj1}(\{s \; g \; fut \; pfv \; ind \; act\}) = \{s \; g \; fut \; pfv \; ind \; act$ **conj1**} The property mapping $pm_c$ enters into the definition of the **Corr** function discussed below.

(4)    Property mapping $pm_c$ for Latin verbs[7]
For any inflection-class index c and any well-formed morphosyntactic property set $\sigma$, $pm_c(\sigma) = \sigma \cup \{\ \}$

The Latin **Stem** function accounts for the choice of stem in the realization of each cell in a verbal lexeme's content paradigm. Those clauses in the definition of **Stem** that are relevant to verb inflection are given in (5).

(5)    Partial definition of the Latin **Stem** function
a.    Where $\langle L, \sigma \rangle$ is a cell in a verbal lexeme's content paradigm, **Stem**($\langle L, \sigma \rangle$) has the value Z if $\sigma$ satisfies the property constraint κ:

| Z | κ |
|---|---|
| L's Imperfective Stem | [{ipfv} ∨ {prs ptcp}] |
| L's Perfective Stem | {pfv} |
| L's Third Stem | {ut ptcp} |
| L's *b* Stem | {pre t ipfv} |

b.    But: **Stem**($\langle L, \sigma$:{ut ipfv}$\rangle$) = L's *b* Stem Z if Z belongs to the first or second conjugation.

Finally, the Latin **Corr** function draws upon **Stem** and the property mappings in (4) to determine a content cell's form correspondent, as in (6).

(6)    Where **Stem**($\langle L, \sigma \rangle$) belongs to conjugation c, **Corr**($\langle L, \sigma \rangle$) = $\langle$**Stem**($\langle L, \sigma \rangle$), $pm_c(\sigma)\rangle$

In accordance with this analysis, the content cell (7a) has the form correspondent (7b). Inflection-class indices such as **conj1** condition the realization of the form cells in which they appear; for instance, **conj1** conditions the suffixation of -$\bar{o}$ in the realization of (7b).

(7)    a.    $\langle$PARĀRE, {s g fut ipfv act ind}$\rangle$
b.    $\langle$*parāb*, {s g fut ipfv act ind **conj1**}$\rangle$

This model of the inflection-class membership and distribution of Latin verb stems exemplifies one kind of deviation from the canonical pattern of paradigm linkage characterized in Section 7.1: By virtue of the nontrivial property mappings in (4), it exhibits neither (2a), the characteristic of property-set preservation, nor (2b), that of stem invariance.

   In the chapters that follow, I examine numerous additional kinds of deviation, for each of which the paradigm-linkage hypothesis affords a coherent explanation. In Chapters 8–11, I look at deviations that are observable within a single paradigm. The most basic of these are mismatches between the property

---

7  In precise terms, $pm_c$ is not itself a property mapping, but a property-mapping schema defining a class of property mappings, one for each conjugation whose inflection-class index is a possible value for the metalinguistic variable c.

sets that define a word form's syntax and semantics and those that define its inflectional realization; canonically, these are the same property set, but morphomic properties (Chapter 8) entail a deviation from this idealization. I then examine mismatches between the number of content cells required for syntactic and semantic purposes and the number of form cells available for their inflectional realization. Canonically, these numbers are equal, but in instances of defectiveness, there are "too few" form cells, and in some instances of overabundance, there are "too many" (Chapter 9); in addition, syncretism involves a many-to-one relation between content cells and their form correspondents (Chapter 10). By contrast, suppletion involves one-to-many relations between lexemes and their stems, a deviation from the canonical expectation that every lexeme has a single stem (Chapter 11).

In Chapters 12 and 13, I examine mismatches that emerge once one begins comparing distinct paradigms. In instances of deponency and metaconjugation, the same morphology is put to different uses in the paradigms of lexemes belonging to the same category (Chapter 12); in instances of polyfunctionality, the same morphology is put to different uses in the paradigms of lexemes belonging to distinct categories (Chapter 13).

# 8  *Morphomic properties*

Canonically, the system of grammatical contrasts relevant to a lexeme's syntax and semantics is exactly the system relevant for the inflectional realization of that lexeme's word forms. In Turkish, for instance, a noun's syntax and semantics involve six distinct case properties (nominative, accusative, dative, locative, ablative and genitive) and two number properties (singular and plural), and a noun's inflectional morphology realizes exactly these properties, as in Table 8.1.

Many languages, however, possess noncanonical systems of inflection in which the grammatical distinctions relevant for a lexeme's syntax and semantics are neither identical nor isomorphic to those relevant for its inflectional realization (Stump 2012, 2014a, 2014b, 2015, Stump: to appear A). In examining content–form mismatches in inflectional paradigms, we have already seen various ways in which the morphosyntactic property set S determining a word form's syntax and semantics differs from the property set M determining its inflectional form. Typically, set S and set M draw upon the same inventory of morphosyntactic properties, a part of the shared vocabulary of morphology, syntax and semantics; but unlike set S, set M may also contain an inflection-class index (Section 7.3). In this chapter, I examine a larger class of properties available to set M but not to set S.

Aronoff 1994 introduces the term **morphomic** to describe elements of pure morphology, to which other grammatical components are simply blind. A wide variety of phenomena have been recognized as morphomic. See, for example, Cruschina et al. 2013, Maiden 2005, Maiden et al. 2011, O'Neill 2014, and the various contributions to Baerman et al. 2007; see Round 2013 for a particularly detailed account of the richly morphomic agreement system of Kayardild.

Under the assumptions of the paradigm-linkage hypothesis, such morphomic phenomena can all be seen as an effect of properties that are restricted to the level of form paradigms. That is, we can distinguish two types of grammatical properties: **morphosyntactic properties**, to which morphology, syntax and

Table 8.1 *The declension of Turkish* ADAM *'man'*

|  | Singular | Plural |
|---|---|---|
| Nominative | *adam* | *adam-lar* |
| Accusative | *adam-ı* | *adam-lar-ı* |
| Dative | *adam-a* | *adam-lar-a* |
| Locative | *adam-da* | *adam-lar-da* |
| Ablative | *adam-dan* | *adam-lar-dan* |
| Genitive | *adam-ın* | *adam-lar-ın* |

semantics may all be sensitive, and **morphomic properties**, to which morphology alone is sensitive.[1] Content cells are pairings of lexemes with sets of morphosyntactic properties; form cells, by contrast, are pairings of stems with sets of properties of which some may be morphosyntactic and others morphomic.

In this chapter, I develop this distinction. In Section 8.1, I draw a distinction between morphomic properties whose incidence is lexically conditioned and morphomic properties whose incidence is morphosyntactically conditioned; I illustrate with an example from Sanskrit. In Sections 8.2–8.6, I examine several examples of morphomic properties whose incidence is morphosyntactically conditioned. In Section 8.2, I discuss the striking example of verb agreement in Hua, for which I propose a formal account in Section 8.3. In Sections 8.4–8.6, I discuss similar phenomena in Noon, Twi, and Nepali. In each of the systems under discussion, the property set S distinguishing a particular cell of a lexeme's content paradigm differs from the property set M distinguishing the corresponding cell of its stem's form paradigm, and the source of this difference is the presence of one or more morphomic properties in M. I summarize these findings in Section 8.6.

## 8.1  Lexical and morphosyntactic conditioning of morphomic properties

Some morphomic properties are **lexically conditioned**: The appearance of a lexically conditioned morphomic property μ in a form cell $\langle X, \{\mu \quad \}.. \rangle$ is sensitive to the identity of X. Morphomic properties may also be **morphosyntactically conditioned**: The appearance of a morphosyntactically conditioned

---

1 This distinction may be likened to if not equated with the distinction between s-features and m-features (drawn by Sadler and Spencer 2001 and Spencer 2013: 219ff), between morphosyntactic and morphological features (drawn by Corbett and Baerman 2006), and between morphosyntactic and morphomic features (as drawn by Bonami and Boyé 2008). For detailed discussion, see Corbett 2012: 42ff.

morphomic property μ in the property set σ of a form cell ⟨X, σ⟩ is sensitive to other properties in σ.[2] Consider, as an example, the first-person plural aorist indicative active cell (1a) in the content paradigm of Sanskrit RUDH ὸbs truct'; the realization of this cell (as *arautsma* ẁ e obstructed') is determined by the form correspondent of (1a), namely (1b). This form correspondent contains three morphomic properties: **s-aor**, **strong** and **2ary**. As the following facts show, the first of these is lexically conditioned, and the remaining two are morphosyntactically conditioned.

(1)     a. ⟨RUDH, {pl a or ind act}⟩
        b. ⟨*arauts-*, {pl a or ind act **s-aor strong 2ary**}⟩

The morphomic property **s-aor** in (1b) conditions the aorist realizations of verb stems belonging to the *s*-aorist conjugation; thus, **s-aor** is what was called an inflection-class index in Section 7.3. The fact that the aorist stem of RUDH belongs to the *s*-aorist conjugation is a matter of lexical stipulation; given this fact, the form of this aorist stem is deducible from RUDH's root *rudh* (as *arauts-*). Because of this lexical conditioning, content cells that share the morphosyntactic property set in (1a) may have form correspondents whose property sets are different from that of (1b); for example, the content paradigm of the verb DĀ 'give' contains the cell (2a), but its form correspondent is (2b), reflecting the fact that the lexical entry of DĀ specifies that its aorist stem belongs to the root-aorist conjugation.

(2)     a. ⟨DĀ, {pl a or ind act}⟩
        b. ⟨*adā-*, {pl a or ind act **ROOT 2ary**}⟩

The morphomic property **strong** in (1b) conditions the aorist active-voice realizations of verb stems belonging to the *s*- and *iṣ*-aorist conjugations; the property **weak** conditions the corresponding middle-voice realizations. Thus, while the form correspondent (1b) has the morphomic property **strong**, the form correspondent of the middle-voice content cell (3a) has the property **weak**, as in (3b). A rule of exponence conditioned by the property **weak** causes RUDH's aorist stem *arauts-* to be weakened to *aruts-*, as in the middle form *arutsmahi* ẁ e obstructed.'

(3)     a. ⟨RUDH, {pl a or ind mid}⟩
        b. ⟨*arauts-*, {pl a or ind mid **s-aor weak 2ary**}⟩

The morphomic property **2ary** in (1b) conditions the expression of agreement in all aorist forms. More generally, Sanskrit verbs draw upon different sets of

---

2 A priori, nothing excludes the possibility that a morphomic property may be conditioned both lexically and morphosyntactically.

Table 8.2 *Sanskrit primary and secondary verb endings*

|  |  |  | Singular | Dual | Plural |
|---|---|---|---|---|---|
| Primary endings | Active | 1st | *-mi* | *-vas* | *-mas* |
|  |  | 2nd | *-si* | *-thas* | *-tha* |
|  |  | 3rd | *-ti* | *-tas* | *-a(n)ti* |
|  | Middle | 1st | *-e* | *-vahe* | *-mahe* |
|  |  | 2nd | *-se* | *-āthe* | *-dhve* |
|  |  | 3rd | *-te* | *-āte* | *-a(n)te* |
| Secondary endings | Active | 1st | *-(a)m* | *-va* | *-ma* |
|  |  | 2nd | *-s* | *-tam* | *-ta* |
|  |  | 3rd | *-t* | *-tām* | *-(a)n, -us* |
|  | Middle | 1st | *-i, -a* | *-vahi* | *-mahi* |
|  |  | 2nd | *-thās* | *-āthām* | *-dhvam* |
|  |  | 3rd | *-ta* | *-ātām* | *-a(n)ta, -ran* |

agreement suffixes, of which the principal sets are the so-called primary and secondary sets of suffixes in Table 8.2: The primary suffixes are used in the present indicative and future indicative; the secondary suffixes are used in the imperfect indicative, the present optative, the conditional and the aorist indicative.[3] Thus, the morphomic property **2ary** in the aorist form cell (3b) induces the appearance of the secondary suffix in *arautsma* 'w e obstructed'; but the morphomic property **1ary** in the corresponding present-tense form cell (4b) induces the appearance of the primary suffix in *rundhmas* 'w e obstruct.'

(4)     a. ⟨RUDH, { pl prs ind act}⟩
        b. ⟨*rundh-*, {1pl prs ind act **weak VII 1ary**}⟩

The morphomic property **s-aor** in (1b) is lexically conditioned because its appearance depends on the lexeme RUDH 'obstruct'; the lexeme DĀ 'give' fails to condition it. By contrast, the morphomic properties **strong** and **2ary** in (1b) are morphosyntactically conditioned: The appearance of the former is induced by the cell's aorist active specification, and that of the latter, by its aorist specification.

In formal terms, we can think of the inflection of RUDH as involving the lexical specifications in (5), the property mapping $pm_c$ in (6), and the form-correspondence function *Corr* in (7). Together with RUDH's root *rudh*, the lexical specifications in (5) determine the form of RUDH's stems; in particular, the *Stem* function may be defined so that

---

3 The imperative and the perfect have their own sets of suffixes whose membership partially overlaps that of the primary and secondary sets.

$Stem(\langle \text{RUDH}, \sigma\rangle) = arauts$- if σ satisfies ⟨ or}
$= ruṇadh$- if σ instead satisfies [prs } ∨ impf]).

(5)    If σ satisfies ⟨ or}        then $Stem(\langle\text{RUDH}, \sigma\rangle)$   the *s*-aorist
                                    belongs to                conjugation.

       [prs } ∨ {impf}],                                      Conjugation **VII**.

(6)    For each inflection-class index c, there is a property mapping $pm_c$ such that
       for any well-formed morphosyntactic property set σ, $pm_c(\sigma)$ is the smallest
       set τ such that

       $\sigma \subseteq \tau$;
       $c \in \tau$;
       **strong** $\in \tau$ if σ satisfies
              [⟨ or act} ∨ [prs } ∧ [⟨ g ind act} ∨ [{impv} ∧ [{1} ∨
              ⟩s g act}]]]]
       and **weak** $\in \tau$ if not; and
       **1ary** $\in \tau$ if σ satisfies
              [ind} ∧ [prs } ∨ {ut}]]
       and **2ary** $\in \tau$ if not.

(7)    Where $Stem(\langle L, \sigma\rangle)$ belongs to the conjugation associated with the
       inflection-class index c, $Corr(\langle L, \sigma\rangle) = \langle Stem(\langle L, \sigma\rangle), pm_c(\sigma)\rangle$

In accordance with the definition in (6), the property mapping $pm_{\text{s-aor}}$ (for the
*s*-aorist conjugation) applies to the morphosyntactic property set {1pl aor ind
act} to yield the property set {pl  aor ind act **s-aor strong 2ary**} thus, in accordance with definition (7),

       $Corr(\langle\text{RUDH}, \{\text{pl a  or ind act}\}\rangle)$
       $= \langle Stem(\langle\text{RUDH}, \{\text{pl a  or ind act}\}\rangle), pm_c(\{\text{1pl aor ind act}\})\rangle$
       $= \langle Stem(\langle\text{RUDH}, \{\text{1pl aor ind act}\}\rangle), \{\text{1pl aor ind act } \textbf{s-aor strong 2ary}\}\rangle$
       $= \langle arauts\text{-}, \{\text{pl a  or ind act } \textbf{s-aor strong 2ary}\}\rangle$

– in this way associating the content cell (1a) with its form correspondent (1b).

As the property mapping $pm_c$ in (6) is defined, it distinguishes strong and
weak property sets in the present system as well as in the aorist system. In the
present system, the distinction between strong and weak property sets is massively morphomic; in the realized present-system paradigm of RUDH, for example, the strong cells are those shaded in Table 8.3, and the weak cells are those
that remain. Yet, although the distribution of RUDH's strong and weak present-
systems stems (*ruṇadh*- and *rundh*-, respectively) is incoherent with respect to
the morphosyntactic property sets in RUDH's content paradigm, it is coherent
with respect to the partially morphomic property sets in the corresponding form

Table 8.3 *The finite inflection of Sanskrit root √rudh 'obstruct'*

| Tense system | Conjugation Stem | Tense | Person | Active Singular | Active Dual | Active Plural | Middle Singular | Middle Dual | Middle Plural |
|---|---|---|---|---|---|---|---|---|---|
| Present | 7th STRONG: *ruṇadh* WEAK: *rundh* | Present | 1st | *ruṇadhmi* | *rundhvas* | *rundhmas* | *rundhe* | *rundhvahe* | *rundhmahe* |
| | | | 2nd | *ruṇatsi* | *runddhas* | *runddha* | *runtse* | *rundhāthe* | *rundhve* |
| | | | 3rd | *ruṇaddhi* | *runddhas* | *rundhanti* | *runddhe* | *rundhāte* | *rundhate* |
| | | Imperfect | 1st | *aruṇadham* | *arundhva* | *arundhma* | *arundhi* | *arundhvahi* | *arundhmahi* |
| | | | 2nd | *aruṇas*[1] | *arunddham* | *arunddha* | *arunddhās* | *arundhāthām* | *arunddhvam* |
| | | | 3rd | *aruṇat* | *arunddhām* | *arundhan* | *arunddha* | *arundhātām* | *arundhata* |
| | | Imperative | 1st | *ruṇadhāni* | *ruṇadhāva* | *ruṇadhāma* | *ruṇadhai* | *ruṇadhāvahai* | *ruṇadhāmahai* |
| | | | 2nd | *runddhi* | *runddham* | *runddha* | *runtsva* | *rundhāthām* | *rundhdhvam* |
| | | | 3rd | *ruṇaddhu* | *runddhām* | *rundhantu* | *runddhām* | *rundhātām* | *rundhatām* |
| | STRONG: *rundhyā* WEAK: *rundhī(y)* | Optative | 1st | *rundhyām* | *rundhyāva* | *rundhyāma* | *rundhīya* | *rundhīvahi* | *rundhīmahi* |
| | | | 2nd | *rundhyās* | *rundhyāta* | *arundhyāta* | *rundhīthās* | *rundhīyāthām* | *rundhīdhvam* |
| | | | 3rd | *rundhyāt* | *mrundhyātām* | *rundhyus* | *rundhīta* | *rundhīyātām* | *rundhīran* |
| Aorist | s-Aorist STRONG: *rauts* WEAK: *ruts* | Aorist | 1st | *arautsam* | *arautsva* | *arautsma* | *arutsi* | *arutsvahi* | *arutsmahi* |
| | | | 2nd | *arautsīs* | *arauddham* | *arauddha* | *arudhdhās* | *arutsāthām* | *arudhdhvam* |
| | | | 3rd | *arautsīt* | *arauddhām* | *arautsus* | *arudhdha* | *arutsātām* | *arutsata* |
| Perfect | Synthetic STRONG: *rurodh* WEAK: *rurudh* | Perfect | 1st | *rurodha* | *rurudhiva* | *rurudhima* | *rurudhe* | *rurudhivahe* | *rurudhimahe* |
| | | | 2nd | *rurodhitha* | *rurudhathus* | *rurudha* | *rurudhiṣe* | *rurudhāthe* | *rurudhidhve* |
| | | | 3rd | *rurodha* | *rurudhatus* | *rurudhus* | *rurudhe* | *rurudhāte* | *rurudhire* |
| Future | s-Future *rotsya* | Future | 1st | *rotsyāmi* | *rotsyāva* | *rotsyāmas* | *rotsye* | *rotsyāvahe* | *rotsyāmahe* |
| | | | 2nd | *rotsyasi* | *rotsyathas* | *rotsyatha* | *rotsyase* | *rotsyethe* | *rotsyadhve* |
| | | | 3rd | *rotsyati* | *rotsyatas* | *rotsyanti* | *rotsyate* | *rotsyete* | *rotsyante* |
| | | Conditional | 1st 2nd | *arotsyam* *arotsyas* | *arotsyāva* *arotsyatam* | *arotsyāma* *arotsyata* | *arotsye* *arotsyathās* | *arotsyāvahi* *arotsyethām* | *arotsyāmahi* *arotsyadhvam* |
| | | | 3rd | *arotsyat* | *arotsyatām* | *arotsyan* | *arotsyata* | *arotsyetām* | *arotsyanta* |

Source: Whitney 1889: Sections 683ff.

1 Also *aruṇat*.

paradigm, in which the cells containing the strong stem constitute the natural class of cells bearing the morphomic property **strong** (and similarly for the weak stem and the morphomic property **weak**). Thus, the rule of nonconcatenative exponence weakening the strong stem *ruṇadh-* to its weak kindred stem *rundh-* applies to the natural class of form cells bearing the property **weak**.[4]

Lexically conditioned morphomes such as **s-aor** and **VII** are familiar, since, again, these amount to inflection-class specifications (Section 7.3). Because morphosyntactically conditioned morphemes are less familiar, I now examine several examples, demonstrating that the paradigm-linkage hypothesis affords a straightforward account of their rather striking mismatches between content and form.

**8.2    *Verbagr eement inflections in Hua (Trans-New-Guinea;*
***Papua New Guinea)***

In the Hua language (Haiman 1980), verbs inflect for the twelve modal properties listed in (1) as well as for the person and number of their subject. This agreement is expressed by both a suffix and stem ablaut. Verbs fall into three classes according to the type of ablaut pattern exhibited in their conjugation: Type I verbs exhibit an *u–a–i* ablaut pattern; Type II verbs, an *o–a–e* pattern; and Type III verbs, an *u–i–i* pattern. The interrogative forms of the verbs HU do, ' DO è at' and MI ĝi ve' in Table 8.4 exemplify these three ablaut patterns. (I have purposely omitted glosses for the individual word forms in Table 8.4 in order to focus attention entirely on their form; we will come to the glosses below.)

(8)    Modal properties expressed by verb inflection in Hua

| | |
|---|---|
| Indicative | Inconsequential |
| Interrogative | Medial: a. Coordinate b. Subordinate |
| Relative | Exclamatory |
| Purposive | Assertive |
| Concessive-expectant | Counterfactual: a. Protasis b. Apodosis |

If one assumes that a Type I verb has a root in *u* (e.g. *hu*), that a Type II verb has a root in *o* (e.g. *do*), and that a Type III verb has a root in *i* (e.g. *mi*), then the ablaut alternations exhibited by the stems in Table 8.4 are systematic. In the first ablaut grade (that of rows a, d and f in Table 8.4, with stems *hu-*, *do-* and *mu-*), the root vowel becomes a back vowel (if it is not already back); in

---

4 In this way, the analysis proposed here allows the scope of a morphomic pattern to be characterized *en bloc*; cf. O'Neill 2011, 2013.

Table 8.4 *Three verb types in Hua (interrogative forms)*

|     | Type I:<br>HU ɗo'<br>D id I do? ˀ... | Type II:<br>DO ɛ̀ at'<br>D id I eat? ˀ... | Type III:<br>MI 'give'<br>'Did I give?'... |
| --- | --- | --- | --- |
| a.  | *hu-ve* | *do-ve* | *mu-ve* |
| b.  | *ha-ve* | *da-ve* | *mi-ve* |
| c.  | *hi-ve* | *de-ve* | *mi-ve* |
| d.  | *hu-'ve* | *do-'ve* | *mu-'ve* |
| e.  | *ha-'ve* | *da-'ve* | *mi-'ve* |
| f.  | *hu-pe* | *do-pe* | *mu-pe* |
| g.  | *ha-pe* | *da-pe* | *mi-pe* |

Table 8.5 *Stem ablaut in Hua verbs*

| Ablaut<br>grade | Type I:<br>HU ɗo'<br>(root *hu*) | Type II:<br>DO ɛ̀ at'<br>(root *do*) | Type III:<br>MI ɡi ve'<br>(root *mi*) | Operation on root vowel |
| --- | --- | --- | --- | --- |
| 1 | *hu-* | *do-* | *mu-* | root vowel → [−front] |
| 2 | *ha-* | *da-* | *mi-* | [−front] root vowel → [+low] |
| 3 | *hi-* | *de-* | *mi-* | root vowel → [+front] |

the second ablaut grade (that of rows b, e and g in Table 8.4, with stems *ha-*, *da-* and *mi-*), the root vowel becomes low if it is back; and in the third ablaut grade (that of row c in Table 8.4, with stems *hi-*, *de-* and *mi-*), the root vowel becomes a front vowel (if it is not already front). These regularities are summarized in Table 8.5.

Although the interrogative forms in Table 8.4 aren't glossed, the systematicity of their morphology is nevertheless very clear. Each verb has its first ablaut grade (*hu-*, *do-*, *mu-*) in three forms, its second ablaut grade (*ha-*, *da-*, *mi-*) in three forms, and its third ablaut grade (*hi-*, *de-*, *mi-*) in one form. (The only wrinkle is that for the Type III verb MI, the second and third ablaut grades are alike.) Moreover, all three verbs exhibit the suffix *-ve* in combination with all three stem grades and the suffixes *-'ve* and *-pe* in combination with the first and second stem grades. Thus, purely on the basis of form, one might arrange the interrogative forms in Table 8.4 as in Table 8.6, where each row corresponds to a different ablaut grade and each column corresponds to a different suffix. The row labels 1–3 and the column labels *a–c* are arbitrarily chosen; they simply index formal properties.

Table 8.6 *Interrogative verb forms in Hua, arranged according to form*

| Type I: HU do' | | | Type II: DO è at' | | | Type III: MI 'give' | | |
|---|---|---|---|---|---|---|---|---|
| *A* | *B* | *C* | *A* | *B* | *C* | *A* | *B* | *C* |
| 1 *hu-ve* | *hu-'ve* | *hu-pe* | 1 *do-ve* | *do-'ve* | *do-pe* | 1 *mu-ve* | *mu-'ve* | *mu-pe* |
| 2 *ha-ve* | *ha-'ve* | *ha-pe* | 2 *da-ve* | *da-'ve* | *da-pe* | 2 *mi-ve* | *mi-'ve* | *mi-pe* |
| 3 *hi-ve* | | | 3 *de-ve* | | | 3 *mi-ve* | | |

Table 8.7 *Interrogative verb forms in Hua, arranged according to content*

| | Type I: HU do' | | | Type II: DO è at' | | | Type III: MI 'give' | | |
|---|---|---|---|---|---|---|---|---|---|
| | Sg | Du | Pl | Sg | Du | Pl | Sg | Du | Pl |
| 1st person | *hu-ve* | *hu-'-ve* | *hu-pe* | 1st *do-ve* | *do-'-ve* | *do-pe* | 1st *mu-ve* | *mu-'-ve* | *mu-pe* |
| 2nd person | *ha-pe* | *ha-'-ve* | *ha-ve* | 2nd *da-pe* | *da-'-ve* | *da-ve* | 2nd *mi-pe* | *mi-'-ve* | *mi-ve* |
| 3rd person | *hi-ve* | " | " | 3rd *de-ve* | " | " | 3rd *mi-ve* | " | " |

When the interrogative forms in Table 8.6 are rearranged according to content, as in Table 8.7, some unexpected complications arise. The least problematic label in Table 8.6 is that of the *B* column: this corresponds to dual number. The labels 1, 2 and 3 in Table 8.6 correspond to the first, second and third persons (respectively), but in the dual and plural columns of Table 8.7, the third person is syncretized with the second person. (This is why the *B*3 and *C*3 cells in Table 8.6 are empty.) For present purposes, however, the most salient complication in Table 8.7 is that neither label *A* nor label *C* has an invariant morphosyntactic interpretation in Table 8.6: While the first and third cells in the *A* column are singular, the second is instead plural; and while the first cell in the *C* column is plural, the second is instead singular. Thus, the *-ve* suffix in the *A* columns and the *-pe* suffix in the *C* columns are morphosyntactically incoherent.

One might suppose that this unexpected mismatch between content and form is an idiosyncrasy of the interrogative mood – and one would be wrong in that supposition. In every one of the twelve moods listed in (8), there are three suffixes whose distribution parallels that of *-ve*, *-'ve* and *-pe* in Table 8.7. That is, every mood has its own dual suffix and its own (morphosyntactically incoherent) *A* and *C* suffixes; the full inventory of these agreement suffixes is presented in Table 8.8. In each mood, the first-person plural form contrasts in number with the second-person singular form, but they are invariably alike in their suffixal exponence; similarly, the first-person singular and third-person

Table 8.8 *Hua mood/agreement suffixes*

| | Indicative | Interrogative | Relative | Purposive | Concessive-expectant | Inconsequential | Medial | | | Assertive | Counterfactual | |
|---|---|---|---|---|---|---|---|---|---|---|---|---|
| | | | | | | | Coordinate | Subordinate | Exclamatory | | Protasis | Apodosis |
| A | -e | -ve | -ma' | -mi' | -va | -mana | -ga | -ma | -mane | -mae | -hipana | -hine |
| du | -'e | -'ve | -'ma' | -'mi' | -'va | -'mana | -'ga | -'ma | -'mane | -'mae | -'hipana | -'hine |
| C | -ne | -pe | -pa' | -pi' | -pa | -pana | -na | -pa | -pane | -pae | -sipana | -sine |

Table 8.9 *The mismatch of content and form in the interrogative subparadigm of Hua HU 'do'*

| | arranged by form | | | | arranged by content | | |
|---|---|---|---|---|---|---|---|
| | *A* | *B* | *C* | | sg | du | pl |
| 1 | *hu-ve* | *hu-'-ve* | *hu-pe* | *1* | *hu-ve* | *hu-'-ve* | *hu-pe* |
| 2 | *ha-ve* | *ha-'-ve* | *ha-pe* | 2 | *ha-pe* | *ha-'-ve* | *ha-ve* |
| 3 | *hi-ve* | | | 3 | *hi-ve* | " | " |

singular forms contrast in number with the syncretic form of the second and third persons plural, but they are likewise invariably alike in their suffixal exponence. Thus, Hua verbs show a recurring mismatch between content and form, as exemplified in Table 8.9. The paradigm-linkage hypothesis affords a precise account of this mismatch.

## 8   Content and form in Hua verb agreement

We can think of the content paradigm of a Hua verb as having 108 cells, corresponding to the combination of 12 moods × 3 persons × 3 numbers; these content cells are represented schematically in Figure 8.1.

The 108 content cells in Figure 8.1 correspond to the 84 form cells in Figure 8.2. The morphosyntactic property sets labeling the columns of content cells in Figure 8.1 and those labeling the columns of form cells in Figure 8.2

| Person: | 1 | | | 2 | | | 3 | | |
|---|---|---|---|---|---|---|---|---|---|
| Mood　Number: | sg | du | pl | sg | du | pl | sg | du | pl |
| indicative | | | | | | | | | |
| interrogative | | | | | | | | | |
| relative | | | | | | | | | |
| purposive | | | | | | | | | |
| concessive-expectant | | | | | | | | | |
| inconsequential | | | | | | | | | |
| medial-coordinate | | | | | | | | | |
| medial-subordinate | | | | | | | | | |
| exclamatory | | | | | | | | | |
| assertive | | | | | | | | | |
| protasis | | | | | | | | | |
| apodosis | | | | | | | | | |

Figure 8.1　*Content cells for Hua verbs*

| Person: | 1 | | | 2 | | | 3 |
|---|---|---|---|---|---|---|---|
| Mood　"Number": | other | du | $c$ | other | du | $c$ | other |
| indicative | | | | | | | |
| interrogative | | | | | | | |
| relative | | | | | | | |
| purposive | | | | | | | |
| concessive-expectant | | | | | | | |
| inconsequential | | | | | | | |
| medial-coordinate | | | | | | | |
| medial-subordinate | | | | | | | |
| exclamatory | | | | | | | |
| assertive | | | | | | | |
| protasis | | | | | | | |
| apodosis | | | | | | | |

Figure 8.2　*Form cells for Hua verbs*

are alike with respect to properties of person and the property of dual number. Nevertheless, the property $c$ in Figure 8.2 doesn't have a coherent syntactic or semantic interpretation: It corresponds to plural number in the first person but to singular number in the second person. Property $c$ therefore isn't a morphosyntactic property at all, but a morphomic property, relevant only for morphological realization. In each mood, property sets containing $c$ are realized

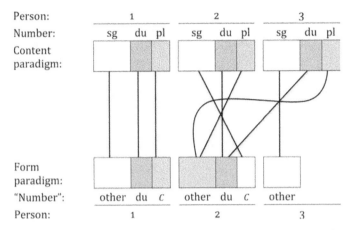

Figure 8.3 *Mismatch between content and form in the person/number morphology of Hua verbs*

by means of the same agreement suffix, one shared by second-person singular forms and first-person plural forms; for example, $c$ is realized by the suffix -*pe* in the interrogative mood. The columns of form cells labeled "other" in Figure 8.2 are those that were labeled $A$ in Section 8.1; the new label "other" is meant to account for the fact that these form cells are realized by default morphology because they are associated neither with dual number nor with the morpheme $c$.

The morphology of Hua defines the correspondence between the 108 content cells in Figure 8.1 and the 84 form cells in Figure 8.2. Within a given mood, the first- and second-person dual content cells respectively correspond to the first- and second-person dual form cells. The first-person plural content cell corresponds to the first-person $c$ form cell, but it is the second-person singular content cell that corresponds to the second-person $c$ form cell. The third-person dual and plural content cells correspond to the same form cells as their second-person counterparts. In all remaining cases, a content cell specified for a particular number and a particular mood corresponds to the "other" (non-dual, non-$c$) form cell specified for the same number and mood. These facts are represented schematically in Figure 8.3.

The correspondences schematized in Figure 8.3 embody the property mapping ***pm*** defined in Table 8.10; that is, for any verbal lexeme L with stem Z, each cell $\langle L, \sigma \rangle$ in L's content paradigm corresponds to the form cell $\langle Z, \textbf{\textit{pm}}(\sigma) \rangle$. As the extensional definition shows most clearly, the Hua property mapping causes two content cells whose morphosyntactic property sets do not constitute a natural class to have form correspondents whose property sets do constitute a

Table 8.10 *The Hua property mapping* ***pm***

| | Extensional definition<br>Where α is any mood, | |
|---|---|---|
| | σ | *pm*(σ) |
| Intensional definition | {1sg α} | {1sg α} |
| *pm*(σ:{s g} = σ[sg/c] | {2sg α} | {2 c α} |
| *pm*(σ:{pl} = σ[pl/c] | {3sg α} | {3sg α} |
| *pm*(σ:{s g} = σ | {1 du α} | {1 du α} |
| *pm*(σ:{} = σ[3/2] | {2 du α} | {2 du α} |
| *pm*(σ:{ = σ | {3 du α} | {2 du α} |
| (σ:K {is a variable over | {1pl α} | {1 c α} |
| supersets of K } σ[a/b] | {2pl α} | {2pl α} |
| is the result of replacing *a* | {3pl α} | {2pl α} |
| with *b* in σ.) | | |

natural class. This, I claim, is a general feature of morphomic categories: Their membership is heterogeneous at the level of content paradigms and homogeneous at the level of form paradigms.[5]

Given this definition of ***pm***, the relevant clause of the Hua form-correspondence function ***Corr*** may be defined as in (9).

(9)   The Hua form-correspondence function ***Corr***:
      ***Corr***(⟨L, σ⟩) = ⟨Z, ***pm***(σ)⟩, where Z is L's root.
      *Example:*   ⟨HU, {intr g 2sg}⟩              content cell
                  ***Corr***(⟨HU, {intr g 2sg}⟩)   its form correspondent
                  = ⟨*hu*, ***pm***({intr g 2sg} ⟩   "          [by (9)]
                  = ⟨*hu*, {intr g 2 c}⟩           "          [by Table 8.10]

The inflectional realization of each cell depends on the Hua paradigm function PF, whose partial definition is given in (10).

(10)   The Hua paradigm function PF:
       a.   PF(⟨L, σ⟩) = PF(***Corr***(⟨L, σ⟩))

       b.   PF(⟨X, σ⟩) = [ III : [ II : [ I : ⟨X, σ⟩]]]
            (Recall that [ *n* : ⟨X, σ⟩] represents the result of applying the
            narrowest applicable rule in Block *n* to ⟨X, σ⟩; Section 3.6.)
            *Example:*   ⟨HU, {intr g 2sg}⟩         content cell
                        PF(⟨HU, {intr g 2sg}⟩)     its realization

5 In this particular case, there is also a kind of "opposite reaction": whereas ρ:{s g} σ:{s g} and τ:{s g}form a natural class, *pm*(ρ), *pm*(σ) and *pm*(τ) do not.

$$= \text{PF}(\textbf{\textit{Corr}}(\langle\text{HU, intr g 2sg}\rangle))) \qquad \text{[by (10a)]}$$
$$= \text{PF}(\langle\textit{hu}, \text{intr g 2 } c\rangle)) \qquad \text{[by (9), Table 8.10]}$$
$$= [\text{ III} : [\text{ II} : [\text{ I} : \langle\textit{hu}, \{\text{intrg 2 } c\}\rangle]]] \qquad \text{[by (10b)]}$$

For the fragment of Hua verb morphology that is at issue here, three blocks of rules of exponence are necessary (as definition (10b) implies); the relevant rules are formulated in (11).

(11)     Hua rules of exponence

**Block I.** (stem ablaut)

a. X, V, { } → the result of applying to X:     root vowel → [–front]
b. X, V, { } → the result of applying to X:     [–front] root vowel → [+low]
c. X, V, { } → the result of applying to X:     root vowel → [+front]

**Block II.** (dual subject-agreement suffix)

d. X, V, {du} → X'

**Block III.** (remaining subject-agreement suffixes)

e. X, V, {ntr g}     → X*ve*
f. X, V, {ntr g c}     → X*pe*
g. X, V, { xclam}     → X*mana*
h. X, V, { xclam c}     → X*pana*
        etc.

*Example:*   ⟨HU, intr g 2sg⟩                    content cell
        PF(⟨HU, intrg 2sg⟩))                its realization
        = [ III : [ II : [ I : ⟨*hu*, intr g 2 *c*⟩]]]      [by (10), (9), Table 8.10]
        = [ III : [ II : ⟨*ha*, {intrg 2 *c*}⟩]]        [by (11b)]
        = [ III : ⟨*ha*, intr g 2 *c*⟩]          [by default]
        = ⟨*hape*, {intrg 2 *c*}⟩          [by (11f)]
        *hape* 'do you (s g) do?'

These Hua facts provide strong evidence for the irreducibility hypothesis (Section 1.3). In particular, the definition of the Hua property mapping in Table 8.10 expresses an irreducible regularity in paradigm structure: In every mood in the inflection of a Hua verb, the second-person singular cell and the first-person plural cell are alike in their suffixal realization, irrespective of the particular suffix that is involved. That is, the morphome *c* defines a paradigmatic pattern encompassing two cells in each mood.

The Hua facts likewise support the paradigm-linkage hypothesis, showing that the representations of morphosyntactic content that are relevant for a lexeme's insertion into syntactic structure and for its semantic interpretation are not always the representations that determine the inflectional realization of its word forms.

**8⁄**      *Verb inflection in Noon (Niger-Congo: Senegal)*

The Noon language (Soukka 2000) exhibits a verbal suffix -*us* participating in a distinctive pattern of alternation. In word-final position, it appears as -*u*; thus, it only appears as -*us* in the presence of a subsequent suffix. Moreover, in certain phonological contexts, its vowel is predictably elided. Finally, it doesn't appear in perfect verb forms, where its place is taken by a portmanteau suffix -*uunun* subsuming both the content "perfect" and that of the -*us* suffix.

In some instances, -*us* and its alternants express passive voice, as in each of the examples in (12). Yet, in other instances, they serve to express agreement with a plural subject, as in each of (13a–c). (In this function, it only expresses the plural number of a nonpronominal subject; thus, it is absent from the verb in (13d).) One could, of course, assume that there are two homophonous -*us* suffixes; this, however, would portray as coincidental both the identical patterns of alternation in (12) and (13) and the fact that the morphotactics of -*us* and its alternants remain the same whether they express passive voice or plural subject agreement. Note, indeed, that sentence (14) is ambiguous between the two possible interpretations of this suffix (Maria Soukka, personal communication).

(12)  a. *Mi      lím-u              ga          Padee.*
         I        have.child-PASS    in          Fandène
         I  was born in Fandène.'

      b. *Jën-aa        ñamsi (<       ñam-us-i)       na        maalu.*
         fish-DEF                       eat-PASS-HAB    with      rice
         Fis h is eaten (habitually) with rice.'

      c. *Jën-aa        tóoh       ñam-uunun.*
         fish-DEF       all        eat-PASS.PERF
         Th e whole fish has been eaten.'

(13)  a. *Beti-caa         ham-u        ga       feet-aa.*
         women-DEF        dance-PL     at       feast-DEF
         Th e women dance at the feast.'

      b. *Yaal-caa        ka'seera (<       kaɗ-us-ee-ra   )        Dakaa'.*
         men-DEF                           leave.for-PL-PST-PUNCT    Dakar
         Th e men had left for Dakar.'

      c. *Oomaa-caa        fool-uunun        bes-ii      tóoh.*
         children-DEF     run-PL.PERF       day-DEF     all
         Th e children have run all day.'

      d. *Ba       ham        ga       feet-aa.*
         they     dance      at       feast-DEF
         Th ey dance at the feast.'

(14)  *Pe'-caa         ñam-uunun.*
       goats-DEF       eat-P.PERF
       Ambiguous: 'The goats have eaten.' / 'The goats have been eaten.'

Table 8.11 *The property mapping **pm** for Noon verbs*

| σ | $pm(\sigma)$ |
|---|---|
| σ:{SBJ:pl} | $pm((\sigma \cup \{P\}\backslash\{$ SBJ:pl$\}$ |
| σ:{VCE:{pass} | $pm((\sigma \cup \{P\}\backslash\{$ VCE:pa ss$\}\})$ |
| Otherwise: σ | σ |

N.B. Given the property sets σ, τ: σ\τ is the set of members of σ that are not members of τ.

Under the paradigm-linkage hypothesis, the *-us* suffix has a unitary function at the level of form even though it serves to express two distinct kinds of content. In particular, Noon has a property mapping that causes the distinct properties of plural subject agreement and passive voice in content paradigms to be mapped onto a single morpheme *P* in the corresponding form paradigms, in accordance with the definition in Table 8.11; according to this definition, property sets that do not form a natural class at the level of content cells do so at the level of their form correspondents. Thus, the rules of exponence for Noon verbs include the rules in (15), which realize the morpheme *P* whether its source is a property of plural subject agreement or of passive voice.

(15)  a. X, V, {P} → X*u*S [sandhi: $S \to \emptyset/\_\#$ → *s* otherwise]
   b. X, V, pe rf, P} → X*uunun*
   c. X, V, pe rf} → X*in*

Like the Hua evidence, the Noon evidence shows that the property sets that license lexical insertion and semantic interpretation may be distinct from those that determine inflectional realization; in particular, property sets of the former kind may make distinctions that are simply neutralized in property sets of the latter kind.

## 8  *Verb inflection in Twi (Niger-Congo:Ghana)*

Asante Twi verb inflection (Paster 2010, Stump 2009) exhibits a striking interaction between tense and polarity. In examining this interaction, I take the four verbs in Table 8.12 as a basis for discussion; these verbs exemplify the four[6] root shapes to which most verbs conform in Twi. The tense/polarity interaction exhibited by these verbs is presented in Table 8.13.

6 There is also a fifth form, which I omit because it involves phonological phenomena that are not at issue here; nothing hinges on this omission. See Paster (2010) for detailed discussion of the interaction of the morphology described here with the principles of Twi phonology.

Table 8.12  *Four root shapes in Asante Twi (Paster 2010)*

| Root shape | Root tone | Sample root |
|---|---|---|
| CV | H | *tɔ́* 'buy' |
| CVR(V) | LH | *dàné* 'turn' |
| CVV | LH | *kàé* 'remember' |
| CVOV | LH | *bìsá* 'ask' |
| C = consonant | O = obstruent | H = high tone |
| V = vowel | R = sonorant consonant | L = low tone |

Where v is a vowel or syllabic nasal, v́ represents high-toned v and v̀ represents low-toned v.

Table 8.13  *Partial paradigms of four Twi verbs*

| | | Affirmative | | Negative | |
|---|---|---|---|---|---|
| Present | 'buys' | *tɔ́* | | *ǹ-tɔ́* | |
| | 'turns' | *dàné* | | *ǹ-dàné* | |
| | 'remembers' | *kàé* | | *ŋ̀-kàé* | |
| | 'asks' | *bìsá* | | *m̀-mìsá* | |
| | | when a complement follows | when no complement follows | | |
| Past | 'bought' | *tɔ̀-ɔ́* | *tɔ̀-ɔ́-yɛ̀* | *à-ǹ-tɔ́* | |
| | 'turned' | *dàné-è* | *dàné-è-yɛ̀* | *à-ǹ-dàné* | |
| | 'remembered' | *kàé-è* | *kàé-è-yɛ̀* | *à-ŋ̀-kàé* | |
| | 'asked' | *bìsá-à* | *bìsá-à-yɛ̀* | *è-m̀-mìsá* | |
| | | | | when a complement follows | when no complement follows |
| Perfect | 'has bought' | *à-tɔ́* | | *ǹ-tɔ́-ɔ́* | *ǹ-tɔ́-ɔ́-yɛ̀* |
| | 'has turned' | *à-dáné* | | *ǹ-dáné-è* | *ǹ-dáné-è-yɛ̀* |
| | 'has remembered' | *à-káé* | | *ŋ̀-káé-è* | *ŋ̀-káé-è-yɛ̀* |
| | 'has asked' | *è-bísá* | | *m̀-mísá-à* | *m̀-mísá-à-yɛ̀* |

Consider first the present-tense forms. In the affirmative present, each verb simply assumes its root form. The corresponding negative forms are marked by the low-toned *ǹ*- prefix, whose allomorphy is an effect of the phonological modifications in (16).

(16)    *ǹ-bX → m̀-mX*; otherwise, *ǹ-CX → Ǹ-CX*, where Ǹ is a low-toned nasal homorganic to C.

The past-tense forms in Table 8.13 are more complex. Affirmative forms assume two shapes, whose use in syntax depends on the presence or absence of a following complement. In either case, the root's first syllable is low-toned and its final vowel is doubled by a low-toned vowel; in the absence of any complement, affirmative past-tense forms additionally exhibit a final suffix -yè. Negative past-tense forms exhibit rather different morphology: a prefix à- followed by the negative prefix ǹ-; these forms show the effects of the phonological modifications in (16) and (17).

(17)    $à → è$    $/\underline{\quad}$    $C\begin{bmatrix} V \\ \text{front} \end{bmatrix}X$

Consider finally the perfect forms. The affirmative forms exhibit the prefix à-. The negative forms are again marked by the prefix ǹ-. As in the affirmative past tense, the negative perfect forms have two different shapes depending on the presence or absence of a following complement; in either case, the root's final vowel is doubled by a low-toned vowel, and in the absence of any complement, negative perfect forms exhibit a final suffix -yè.

What is striking is that (leaving aside the obvious difference that only negative forms exhibit the prefix ǹ-) the affirmative perfect forms have essentially the same morphology as the negative past-tense forms, while the negative perfect forms have essentially the same morphology as the affirmative past-tense forms. One difference nevertheless jumps out: The perfect forms, affirmative and negative, differ from their past-tense counterparts in that they have high tone on the root's first syllable. Thus, in negative perfect forms, the root-initial syllable does not exhibit the tone lowering typical of the affirmative past, nor do the negative past-tense forms exhibit the tone raising observed on the root-initial syllable in the affirmative perfect. Thus, an adequate account of Twi verb morphology must explain both (a) the reversal of past and perfect morphology associated with negative polarity, and (b) the lack of any reversal in the incidence of root-initial tone raising, a mark of the perfect.

Under the paradigm-linkage hypothesis, the reversal of past and perfect morphology can be seen as the effect of two morphomic tense properties – a property $D$ shared by affirmative past-tense and negative perfect forms, and a property $E$ shared by negative past-tense and affirmative perfect forms. That is, verbal lexemes exhibit the pattern of form correspondence schematized in Table 8.14. On this analysis, the morphology shared by the affirmative past and the negative perfect realizes the morphome $D$; that shared by the negative past and the affirmative perfect realizes the morphome $E$.

This pattern of form correspondence is effected by means of the property mapping defined in (18); here again, content cells whose morphosyntactic

Table 8.14 *Form correspondence in the inflection of Twi* tɔ́ *'buy'*

| Content cells | ⟨tɔ́,ǽ ff past}⟩ | ⟨tɔ́,ǽ ff perfect}⟩ | ⟨tɔ́,{neg past}⟩ | ⟨tɔ́,{neg perfect}⟩ |
|---|---|---|---|---|
| | ↓ | ↓ | ↓ | ↓ |
| Form correspondents | ⟨tɔ́, ǽ ff *D*}⟩ | ⟨tɔ́, ǽ ff *E*}⟩ | ⟨tɔ́, {neg *E*}⟩ | ⟨tɔ́, {neg *D*}⟩ |

property sets are not alike have form correspondents whose property sets are alike.[7] The paradigm function and rules of exponence for Twi verbs are accordingly formulated as in (19) and (20); the application of the rules in (20) is conditioned not by the morphosyntactic properties "past" and "perfect," but by the morphomic properties *D* and *E*.

(18)  The Twi property mapping ***pm***
  ***pm***(σ:{aff past} = σ[past/*D*]   ***pm***(σ:ǽ ff perfect}) = σ[perfect/*E*]
  ***pm***(σ:{neg past} = σ[past/*E*]   ***pm***(σ:ɧe g perfect}) = σ[perfect/*D*]
  Otherwise, ***pm***(σ) = σ.
  [N.B. Given a property set σ, σ[*x*/*y*] is the result of replace *x* with *y* in σ.]

(19)  The Twi paradigm function PF
  PF(⟨L, σ⟩) = PF(***Corr***(⟨L, σ⟩))
  PF(⟨X, σ⟩) = [ v : [ iv : [ iii : [ ii : [ i : ⟨X, σ⟩]]]]]

(20)  Twi rules of exponence
  a.  Block i:      CVX, Verb, {aff, *D*} → CV́X
  b.  Block ii:     X, Verb, ɧe g} → ǹ-X
  c.  Block iii:    X, Verb, {*E*} → à-X
  d.  Block iv:     $X\begin{bmatrix} Y \\ \text{sonorant} \end{bmatrix}$, Verb, {*D*} → XYỲ
  e.  Block v:      X, Verb, {*D*, PHRASE-FINAL:ǂ → X-yὲ

The definitions in (18)–(20) account for the reversal of past and perfect morphology associated with negative polarity. Turn now to the lack of any reversal in the incidence of the root-initial tone raising observed throughout the perfect. Under the paradigm-linkage hypothesis, this can be attributed to the interaction of a stem-formation rule with the definition of the form-correspondence function ***Corr***. In this analysis, a Twi verb has two alternating stems – a default stem and a high stem – such that a verb's high stem is deduced from its default stem by the stem-formation rule in (21); according to this rule, a verb's high stem has high tone on its first syllable. Thus, if a verb's default stem also has initial high tone (as in the case of tɔ́ 'buy'), then its high stem is identical to its default stem. The definition of the ***Corr*** function in (22) then requires the use of the high stem in

---

7  And here again, as in the Hua case, there is also an "opposite reaction."

realizing a perfect content cell, regardless of whether that cell's form correspondent has *D* or *E* as its tense morphome; according to this definition, a non-default high stem is only used in the realization of a content paradigm's perfect cells.

(21)    Twi stem-formation rule
        If L has CVX as its default stem, it has CV́X as its high stem.

(22)    The Twi form-correspondence function ***Corr***
        a. ***Corr***($\langle$L, σ:þe rfect$\}\rangle$) = $\langle$X, ***pm***(σ)$\rangle$, where X is L's high stem.
        b. Otherwise, ***Corr***($\langle$L, σ$\rangle$) = $\langle$X, ***pm***(σ)$\rangle$, where X is L's default stem.

The Twi facts examined here are one instance of a more general phenomenon, that of morphological reversals (Baerman 2007). As a class, morphological reversals provide especially strong evidence for the paradigm-linkage hypothesis; as Baerman puts it, they constitute "strong evidence for the separateness of morphological paradigms from the features that they encode" (p. 33).

## 8.6    Verb inflection in Nepali

The analysis of Hua verb morphology developed above (Section 8.1) recalls a similar analysis proposed by Bonami and Boyé (2010) for Nepali verb inflection. Like the Hua analysis, their Nepali analysis is based on the observation that if a verb's inflectional realizations are organized according to their form, the resulting paradigm is distinct in its structure from the paradigm resulting from an organization of these same realizations according to their content. For illustration, consider the representative subparadigm in Table 8.15: the long negative present-tense subparadigm of the Nepali verb BIRSANU for get.' As this example shows, Nepali verbs inflect for three persons and two numbers; singular forms distinguish masculine and feminine genders; and the second and third persons distinguish three honorific grades (low, mid and high). The high honorific form (e.g. *birsanuhūdajna*) stands apart, since it neutralizes gender, number and (second and third) person. If it is left aside, the subparadigm in Table 8.15 presents fifteen cells; it does not, however, contain fifteen distinct forms, since several forms are syncretic. In fact, only ten forms are distinguished, as shown in Table 8.16.

Table 8.16 reflects the organization of BIRSANU's long negative present-tense realizations according to their morphosyntactic content; but as Bonami and Boyé observe, the three columns in Table 8.16 can be collapsed into two columns if these realizations are organized according to their morphological form. In particular, they can be collapsed as in Table 8.17, whose cells are distinguished not by PERSON, NUMBER, GENDER and HONORIFIC GRADE, but by PER(SON), ROW and COL(UMN), where the possible values of ROW are the

Table 8.15  *The long negative present-tense*
*inflection of Nepali* BIRSANU *'forget'*

|  |  | Singular | Plural |
|---|---|---|---|
|  | Feminine | Masculine |  |
| 1 | *birsādinā* | *birsādinā* | *birsādajnaũ* |
| 2.low | *birsādinas* | *birsādajnas* | *birsādajnau* |
| 2.mid | *birsādinau* | *birsādajnau* | *birsādajnau* |
| 3.low | *birsādina* | *birsādajna* | *birsādajnan* |
| 3.mid | *birsādinan* | *birsādajnan* | *birsādajnan* |
| (high | *birsanuhũdajna*) |  |  |

Table 8.16  *Syncretism in the long negative*
*present-tense inflection of Nepali* BIRSANU *'forget'*

|  | Singular | | Plural |
|---|---|---|---|
|  | Feminine | Masculine |  |
| 1 | *birsādinā* | | *birsādajnaũ* |
| 2.low | *birsādinas* | *birsādajnas* | |
| 2.mid | *birsādinau* | | *birsādajnau* |
| 3.low | *birsādina* | *birsādajna* | |
| 3.mid | *birsādinan* | | *birsādajnan* |

Table 8.17  *The long negative present-tense inflection of Nepali*
BIRSANU *'forget,' arranged by form (exploded view)*

| prefinal suffix sequence: | | *-d-i-na* | *-d-aj-na* | |
|---|---|---|---|---|
|  |  | COL *a* | COL *b* | final suffix |
| PER 1 | ROW α | *birsā-d-i-na-ā* | – | *-ā* |
|  | ROW β | – | *birsā-d-aj-na-aũ* | *-aũ* |
| PER 2 | ROW α | *birsā-d-i-na-s* | *birsā-d-aj-na-s* | *-s* |
|  | ROW β | *birsā-d-i-na-au* | *birsā-d-aj-na-au* | *-au* |
| PER 3 | ROW α | *birsā-d-i-na* | *birsā-d-aj-na* | – |
|  | ROW β | *birsā-d-i-na-n* | *birsā-d-aj-na-n* | *-n* |

Table 8.18 *The correspondence of content to form in Table 8.17*

|        |       | COL *a*        | COL *b*                                      |
|--------|-------|----------------|----------------------------------------------|
| PER 1  | ROW α | {s g}          | –                                            |
|        | ROW β | –              | {pl}                                         |
| PER 2  | ROW α | {2s g fem low} | {2sg masc low}                               |
|        | ROW β | {2s g fem mid} | {2s g masc mid} or {2pl low} or {2pl mid}    |
| PER 3  | ROW α | {3s g fem low} | {3sg masc low}                               |
|        | ROW β | {3s g fem mid} | {3s g masc mid} or {3pl low} or {3pl mid}    |

properties α and β, and those of COL, the properties *a* and *b*. The COL *a* forms share the prefinal suffix sequence *-d-i-na*; the COL *b* forms instead share the sequence *-d-aj-na*. Each combination of a PER property with a ROW property is distinguished by its final suffix: {PER 1, ROW α} is distinguished by the final suffix *-ã*; {PER 1, ROW β} by the final suffix *-aũ*; {PER 2, ROW α} by the suffix *-s*; {PER 2, ROW β} by the suffix *-au*; {PER 3, ROW α} by the absence of any corresponding final suffix; and {PER 3, ROW β} by the suffix *-n*.

Crucially, the properties α, β, *a* and *b* are morphomic. As Table 8.18 shows, none is morphosyntactically coherent:

- The forms bearing the property α are heterogeneous with respect to person and gender; they include only singular forms, but they do not include all singular forms; and while most of the forms that they include are low in honorificity, the first-person α form does not distinguish honorific grade.
- The forms bearing β are mixed with respect to person, number, gender and honorific grade.
- The forms bearing the property *a* are mixed with respect to person and honorific grade; they include only singular forms, but they do not include all singular forms; and while they include all feminine forms, the first-person *a* form does not distinguish gender.
- The forms bearing the property *b* are heterogeneous with respect to person, number and honorific grade; the singular forms are all masculine, but the plural forms do not distinguish gender.

Under the paradigm-linkage hypothesis, the long negative present-tense inflection of the Nepali verb BIRSANU for get' involves the three paradigms in Table 8.19. The content paradigm determines the syntax and semantics of

Table 8.19 *The long negative present-tense inflection of Nepali* BIRSANU *'forget' under the paradigm-linkage hypothesis* (lnp = long negative present)

| Content paradigm | ⟨BIRSANU, {1sg fem lnp}⟩ | ⟨BIRSANU, {1sg masc lnp}⟩ | ⟨BIRSANU, {1pl lnp}⟩ |
|---|---|---|---|
| | ⟨BIRSANU, {2sg fem low lnp}⟩ | ⟨BIRSANU, {2sg masc low lnp}⟩ | ⟨BIRSANU, {2pl low lnp}⟩ |
| | ⟨BIRSANU, {2sg fem mid lnp}⟩ | ⟨BIRSANU, {2sg masc mid lnp}⟩ | ⟨BIRSANU, {2pl mid lnp}⟩ |
| | ⟨BIRSANU, {3sg fem low lnp}⟩ | ⟨BIRSANU, {3sg masc low lnp}⟩ | ⟨BIRSANU, {3pl low lnp}⟩ |
| | ⟨BIRSANU, {3sg fem mid lnp}⟩ | ⟨BIRSANU, {3sg masc mid lnp}⟩ | ⟨BIRSANU, {3pl mid lnp}⟩ |
| Form paradigm | ⟨*birs*, {PER 1, COL *a*, ROW α, lnp}⟩ | | ⟨*birs*, {PER 1, COL *b*, ROW β, lnp}⟩ |
| | ⟨*birs*, {PER 2, COL *a*, ROW α, lnp}⟩ | | ⟨*birs*, {PER 2, COL *b*, ROW α, lnp}⟩ |
| | ⟨*birs*, {PER 2, COL *a*, ROW β, lnp}⟩ | | ⟨*birs*, {PER 2, COL *b*, ROW β, lnp}⟩ |
| | ⟨*birs*, {PER 3, COL *a*, ROW α, lnp}⟩ | | ⟨*birs*, {PER 3, COL *b*, ROW α, lnp}⟩ |
| | ⟨*birs*, {PER 3, COL *a*, ROW β, lnp}⟩ | | ⟨*birs*, {PER 3, COL *b*, ROW β, lnp}⟩ |
| Realized paradigm | ⟨*birsādinā*, {PER 1, COL *a*, ROW α, lnp}⟩ | | ⟨*birsādajnaũ*, {PER 1, COL *b*, ROW β, lnp}⟩ |
| | ⟨*birsādinas*, {PER 2, COL *a*, ROW α, lnp}⟩ | | ⟨*birsādajnas*, {PER 2, COL *b*, ROW α, lnp}⟩ |
| | ⟨*birsādinau*, {PER 2, COL *a*, ROW β, lnp}⟩ | | ⟨*birsādajnau*, {PER 2, COL *b*, ROW β, lnp}⟩ |
| | ⟨*birsādina*, {PER 3, COL *a*, ROW α, lnp}⟩ | | ⟨*birsādajna*, {PER 3, COL *b*, ROW α, lnp}⟩ |
| | ⟨*birsādinan*, {PER 3, COL *a*, ROW β, lnp}⟩ | | ⟨*birsādajnan*, {PER 3, COL *b*, ROW β, lnp}⟩ |

Table 8.20 *Extensional definition of the Nepali property mapping **pm***

| σ | $pm(σ)$ |
|---|---|
| {PER 1, NUM sg, GEND mascfe m} | {PER 1, COL a, ROW α} |
| {PER 1, NUM pl} | {PER 1, COL b, ROW β} |
| {PER 2, NUM sg, GEND fem, HON low} | {PER 2, COL a, ROW α} |
| {PER 2, NUM sg, GEND fem, HON mid} | {PER 2, COL a, ROW β} |
| {PER 2, NUM sg, GEND masc, HON low} | {PER 2, COL b, ROW α} |
| {PER 2, NUM sg, GEND masc, HON mid} {PER 2, NUM pl, HON lowhmid} | {PER 2, COL b, ROW β} |
| {PER 3, NUM sg, GEND fem, HON low} | {PER 3, COL a, ROW α} |
| {PER 3, NUM sg, GEND fem, HON mid} | {PER 3, COL a, ROW β} |
| {PER 3, NUM sg, GEND masc, HON low} | {PER 3, COL b, ROW α} |
| {PER 3, NUM sg, GEND masc, HON mid} {PER 3, NUM pl, HON lowhmid} | {PER 3, COL b, ROW β} |

BIRSANU; the form paradigm determines what the inflectional morphology will realize; and the realized paradigm is the result of this realization.

The relation between the content cells in Table 8.19 and their form correspondents is defined by the Nepali form-correspondence function *Corr* in (23). The definition of *Corr* presumes definitions for both the *Stem* function and the property mapping *pm*. For present purposes, I simply assume that *Stem*(⟨BIRSANU, σ⟩) = *birs* for any relevant property set σ. The property mapping *pm* may be defined intensionally (as in (24)) or extensionally (as in Table 8.20). As these definitions show, *pm* effectively replaces properties of number, gender and honorificity with morphomic values of COL and ROW; in the now-familiar pattern, the property mapping applies to property sets that do not constitute a natural class to yield property sets that do.

(23)    The Nepali form-correspondence function *Corr*
        *Corr*(⟨L, σ⟩) = ⟨*Stem*(⟨L, σ⟩), *pm*(σ)⟩

(24)    Intensional definition of Nepali property mapping *pm* (where σ\τ = {x | x ∈ σ & x ∉ τ}
        a. *pm*(σ:{NUM pl} = (σ\{ NUM pl, HON X} ∪ {COL *b*, ROW β}
        b. *pm*(σ:{NUM sg, GEND fem} = *g*((σ\{ GEND fem}) ∪ {COL *a*})
        c. *pm*(σ:{PER 1, NUM sg} = (σ\{ NUM sg, GEND X}) ∪ {COL *a*, ROW α}
        d. otherwise, *pm*(σ) = *g*((σ\{ GEND masc} ∪ {COL *b*}))
        e. *g*(σ:{NUM sg, HON mid} = (σ\{ NUM sg, HON mid}) ∪ {ROW β}
        f. *g*(σ:{NUM sg, HON low} = (σ\{ NUM sg, HON low}) ∪ {ROW α}

Table 8.21 *Rule blocks for Nepali verbs (adapted from Bonami and Boyé 2010)*

(A partial list, including only the rules necessary for the long negative present tense.)

| Block 1: | Block 7 |
|---|---|
| X, σ:{CLASS cc, ASP ipfv} → X*a* | ... |
| X, σ:{CLASS vv, ASP ipfv} → X*u* | Block 8: |
| **Block 2:**\* | X, σ:{MOOD ind, PER 1, ROW α} → X*ā* |
| X, σ:{ASP ipfv} → X$^{\triangleleft}$*n* | X, σ:{PER 1, ROW β, COL b} → X*aũ* |
| **Block 3:** | X, σ:{MOOD ind, PER 2, ROW β} → X*au* |
| X, σ:{ASP ipfv, FORM long} → X*d* | Block 9 |
| **Block 4:** | ... |
| X, σ:{POL neg, FORM long, COL a} → X*i* | **Block 10:** |
| X, σ:{ASP ipfv, FORM long, POL neg, COL b} → X*aj* | X, σ:{PER 2, ROW α} → X*s* |
| **Block 5:**† | |
| X, σ:{POL neg} → X*na*$^{\triangleright}$ | X, σ:{PER 3, ROW β} → X*n* |
| **Block 6** | |
| ... | |

\* In the notation of Boyé 2000, $^{\triangleleft}$[α voc, β cons] → ∅ / [α voc, β cons] __; $^{\triangleleft}$X → X elsewhere.

† In the notation of Boyé 2000, [α voc, β cons]$^{\triangleright}$ → ∅ / __ [α voc, β cons]; X$^{\triangleright}$ → X elsewhere.

With the correspondence between content cells and form cells defined in this way, the Nepali paradigm function may be defined as in (25). This definition assumes ten blocks of rules of exponence (Bonami and Boyé 2010); not every rule block, however, is necessary for realizing long negative present-tense forms. In Table 8.21, I list only those rules that are relevant for these forms. Together with these rules of exponence, the paradigm function in (25) defines the mapping from the content and form paradigms in Table 8.19 to the corresponding realized paradigm.

(25)    The Nepali paradigm function PF:
  a. PF($\langle$L, σ$\rangle$) = PF(Corr($\langle$L, σ$\rangle$))
  b. PF($\langle$Z, σ$\rangle$)
    = [ 10 : [ 9 : [ 8 : [ 7 : [ 6 : [ 5 : [ 4 : [ 3 : [ 2 : [ 1 : $\langle$Z, σ$\rangle$]]]]]]]]]]

This analysis is essentially a recasting of Bonami and Boyé's analysis under the assumptions of the paradigm-linkage hypothesis. This recasting differs from their analysis in one crucial way: In their approach, content paradigms are not distinguished from form paradigms; as a consequence, the morphomic properties "ROW α," "ROW β," "COL a" and "COL b" are not substituted for morphosyntactic properties of number, gender and honorificity, but instead simply combine with them, in accordance with the property coöccurrence restrictions in (26). For this reason, the modification proposed here is preferable: Unlike Bonami and Boyé's original analysis, the present analysis predicts that syntax and semantics should be insensitive to the four morphomic properties, because these properties are absent from content paradigms and hence inaccessible at the interface of morphology with syntax and semantics. In addition, the original analysis portrays as coincidence the fact that the rules of exponence in Table 8.21 make no reference to gender, number or honorificity; the present analysis, by contrast, predicts that these rules are not conditioned by gender, number or honorificity, since the properties in these inflectional categories are absent from form paradigms (having been replaced with combinations of morphomes).

(26)    a. Property coöccurrence restrictions for COL
$$\{\text{NUM } pl\} \supset \{\text{COL } b\}$$
$$\{\text{GEND } fem, \text{NUM } sg\} \supset \{\text{COL } a\}$$
$$\{\text{GEND } masc, \text{NUM } sg\} \supset (\{\text{PER } 1\} \equiv \{\text{COL } a\})$$

   b. Property coöccurrence restrictions for ROW
$$\{\text{NUM } pl\} \supset \{\text{ROW } \beta\}$$
$$\{\text{HON } mid\} \supset \{\text{ROW } \beta\}$$
$$\{\text{HON } low, \text{NUM } sg\} \supset \{\text{ROW } \alpha\}$$
$$\{\text{PER } 1, \text{NUM } sg\} \supset \{\text{ROW } \alpha\}$$

## 8    Conclusion

In this chapter, I have examined several morphomic phenomena. On the surface, these seem quite varied: Some seemingly involve morphomic classes (e.g. Sanskrit Class VII verbs), others seem to involve morphomic stems (e.g. a Sanskrit verb's strong stem), and still others seem to involve morphomic affixes (e.g. the Sanskrit secondary affixes). Under the assumptions of the paradigm-linkage hypothesis, all of these morphomic phenomena are defined by means of morphomic properties (e.g. **VII**, **strong**, **2ary**), whose essential difference from morphosyntactic properties is that they are restricted to form paradigms (and are therefore invisible at the interface of inflectional morphology with syntax and semantics). Thus, an important feature of property mappings is their capacity to map morphosyntactic properties to morphomic properties as part of the mapping from content cells to their form correspondents. In the examples discussed above, we have seen evidence for property mappings introducing the morphomic properties in Table 8.22.

Table 8.22 *Morphomic properties in four languages*

| Language | morphomic property | subsumes | sensitive to |
|----------|-------------------|----------|--------------|
| Hua | C | NUM | PER |
| Noon | P | VCE, NUM | – |
| Twi | D,E | TNS | POL |
| Nepali | ROW a, b; COL α, β | NUM, GEND, HON | PER |

Table 8.23 *Kinds of property mappings*

| | Morphosyntactic property sets in content cells | Property sets in form cells |
|----------|------------------------------------------------|------------------------------|
| Canonical | σ | σ (identity mapping) |
| Noncanonical | σ | $pm(σ)$ contains ≥1 morphomic property |
| | | (Hua, Noon, Twi, Nepali; cf. also Section 7.3) |
| | σ, τ such that σ ≠ τ | $pm(σ) = pm(τ)$ (Chapters 10, 13) |
| | σ, τ such that σ ≠ τ | $pm(σ) = τ$, $pm(τ)$ is undefined (Chapter 12) |

The introduction of morphomic properties is not the only way in which property mappings may give rise to noncanonical patterns of paradigm linkage. In later chapters, I will examine other kinds of effects; these are represented schematically in Table 8.23. These varied patterns of property mapping reflect the numerous ways in which the properties that condition a word form's inflectional realization may diverge from the properties that determine its lexical insertion and its semantic interpretation.

# 9 *Too many cells, too few cells*

In the canonical case, paradigms exhibit a kind of symmetry in two dimensions. On one hand, there is a one-to-one correspondence between the cells in a lexeme's content paradigm and the cells in the form paradigm with which it shares its realizations. On the other hand, different lexemes in the same syntactic category have content paradigms that have the same number of cells. But there are deviations from these canonical symmetries. An exceptional lexeme may have a content paradigm with more or fewer cells than the content paradigms of other lexemes belonging to the same syntactic category; moreover, a form paradigm may have more or fewer cells than the content paradigm that it realizes, and this may be true not merely exceptionally, but as a general pattern for the paradigms of lexemes belonging to a particular syntactic category. In this chapter, I examine such departures from canonical symmetry. Overabundance is a surfeit of form cells or of realized cells in comparison with the content cells that they realize; this can arise in more than one way (Section 9.1). Where overabundance involves word forms that are identical in content and consequently freely interchangeable, shape alternants are word forms that, despite the identity of the content that they express, are restricted to complementary phonological or syntactic environments (Section 9.2). Overdifferentiation is a surplus of cells in the content paradigm of an exceptional lexeme (Section 9.3). Defectiveness is an exceptional shortage of cells; such shortages arise in both content paradigms and form paradigms, though for different reasons (Section 9.4). A content paradigm may also be realized by a form paradigm with fewer cells as a consequence of syncretism, discussion of which I defer to Chapter 10.

## 9.1 Overabundance

Canonically, a content cell has a single form correspondent; but there are noncanonical cases in which one content cell has more than one form correspondent.

Table 9.1 *The inflection of* SEEM, MEAN *and* DREAM

|  | Weak conjugation |  |  | T conjugation |  |
|---|---|---|---|---|---|
| SEEM | *seem* | /sim/ | MEAN | *mean* | /min/ |
|  | *seems* | /simz/ |  | *means* | /minz/ |
|  | *seemed* | /simd/ |  | *meant* | /mɛnt/ |
|  | *seeming* | /simɪŋ/ |  | *meaning* | /minɪŋ/ |
|  | *seemed* | /simd/ |  | *meant* | /mɛnt/ |
| DREAM | *dream* | /dɹim/ | DREAM | *dream* | /dɹim/ |
|  | *dreams* | /dɹimz/ |  | *dreams* | /dɹimz/ |
|  | *dreamed* | /dɹimd/ |  | *dreamt* | /dɹɛmt/ |
|  | *dreaming* | /dɹimɪŋ/ |  | *dreaming* | /dɹimɪŋ/ |
|  | *dreamed* | /dɹimd/ |  | *dreamt* | /dɹɛmt/ |

Consider, for example, the lexemes SEEM and MEAN in Table 9.1. The lexeme SEEM inflects as an ordinary weak verb; MEAN, by contrast, belongs to what might be called the "T conjugation," whose past tense is marked by a *-t* suffix (rather than by *-d*)[1] as well as by a laxing and lowering of its stem vowel. The lexeme DREAM, however, can (in many people's speech) inflect either like SEEM or like MEAN; that is, the content cell ⟨DREAM, þa st}⟩ may have either ⟨*dream*₁, þa st}⟩ or ⟨*dream*₂, þa st}⟩ as its form correspondent, where the stem *dream*₁ belongs to the weak conjugation, and *dream*₂ to the T conjugation. This example illustrates the phenomenon of overabundance (Thornton 2012), the availability of more than one realization for the same content cell; in this case, the availability of more than one realization for the content cell ⟨DREAM, þa st}⟩ reflects the availability of more than one form correspondent for this cell.

Here, the overabundance is exceptional; DREAM is the sole example in my speech of a verb that has alternative past-tense forms in the weak and T conjugations. But this exceptionality is not a necessary characteristic of overabundance. Many languages present instances of overabundance that are exhibited by whole classes of lexemes. In Sanskrit, for example, adjectives agree with the modified noun's case, number and gender. In the inflection of *i*-stem adjectives (e.g. ŚUCI þure '), neuter forms in the oblique cases (i.e. in cases other than the nominative, vocative and accusative) may follow either of two patterns: that of masculine *i*-stems (i.e. that of masculine nouns such as MUNI ş age' and of an

---

1 Because the *t* in *meant* does not come from *-d* by assimilative devoicing, it cannot be identified with the /t/ in *walked* /wɔkt/.

Table 9.2 *The overabundant declension of neuter* i-*stem adjectives in Sanskrit*

(Forms in shaded cells may express neuter agreement; arrows indicate cells where masculine and neuter *i*-stems are invariably alike in their inflection.)

|     |     | masculine | ŚUCI ɲur e' | | neuter |
| --- | --- | --- | --- | --- | --- |
|     |     | MUNI ʂ age' | masculine | neuter | VĀRI 'water' |
| Sg | Nom | munis | śucis | śuci | vāri |
|    | Voc | mune | śuce | śuci | vāri |
|    | Acc | munim | śucim | śuci | vāri |
|    | Inst | muninā | ← śucinā → | | vāriṇā |
|    | Dat | munaye | śucaye | śucine | vāriṇe |
|    | Abl, Gen | munes | śuces | śucinas | vāriṇas |
|    | Loc | munau | śucau | śucini | vāriṇi |
| Du | Nom, Voc, Acc | munī | śucī | śucinī | vāriṇī |
|    | Inst, Dat, Abl | munibhyām | ← śucibhyām → | | vāribhyām |
|    | Gen, Loc | munyos | śucyos | śucinos | vāriṇos |
| Pl | Nom, Voc | munayas | śucayas | śucīni | vārīṇi |
|    | Acc | munīn | śucīn | śucīni | vārīṇi |
|    | Inst | munibhis | ← śucibhis → | | vāribhis |
|    | Dat, Abl | munibhyas | ← śucibhyas → | | vāribhyas |
|    | Gen | munīnām | ← śucīnām → | | vārīṇām |
|    | Loc | muniṣu | ← śuciṣu → | | vāriṣu |

In the inflection of VĀRI ɲv ater,' *n → ṇ* as an effect of sandhi.

*i*-stem adjective's masculine forms) or that of neuter *i*-stem nouns such as VĀRI ɲv ater.' The paradigms in Table 9.2 illustrate.

This example differs from the DREAM example in two ways. First, the overabundance is not exceptional, but is typical of the neuter forms of *i*-stem adjectives. Second, the overabundance does not reflect a choice between competing inflection classes (e.g. the weak conjugation and the T conjugation), but instead reflects a choice within the *i*-stem declension, between explicitly neuter forms and default, syncretic forms in which the morphosyntactic distinction between the masculine and neuter genders is neutralized. But this example is also like the DREAM example in the sense that the overabundance can be attributed to the availability of more than one form correspondent for the

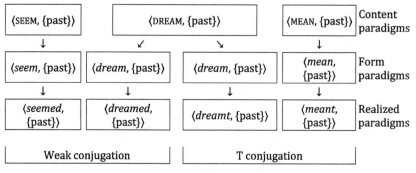

Figure 9.1 *Overabundance engendered by **Corr** in English*

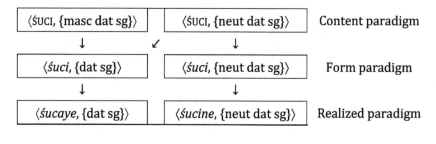

Figure 9.2 *Overabundance and syncretism engendered by **Corr** in Sanskrit*

same content cell: With DREAM, the content cell ⟨DREAM, ɸa st}⟩ may have either ⟨*dream₁*, ɸa st}⟩ or ⟨*dream₂*, ɸa st}⟩ as its form correspondent; and with ŚUCI ɸu re,' the content cell ⟨ŚUCI, ɦe ut dat sg}⟩ may have either (a) ⟨*śuci*, ɦe ut dat sg}⟩ or (b) ⟨*śuci*, ɖa t sg}⟩ as its form correspondent, receiving a neuter-specific realization from (a), and receiving from (b) a default realization that it shares with the masculine content cell ⟨ŚUCI, ɱa sc dat sg}⟩.

In formal terms, these examples show that a language's form-correspondence function ***Corr*** may, in fact, be merely a relation rather than a true function; that is, ***Corr***(⟨L, σ⟩) may in some cases have more than one possible value. In such instances, it is the relational status of ***Corr*** that gives rise to overabundance, as in Figures 9.1 and 9.2.

A slightly different example of nonexceptional overabundance is that of the Spanish past subjunctive (Alcoba 1999); as Table 9.3 shows, it is generally possible for a Spanish verb to form its past subjunctive forms in either of two

Table 9.3 *The past subjunctive inflection of two Spanish verbs*

| | CORTAR to c ut' | | VIVIR 'to live' | |
|---|---|---|---|---|
| | Form 1 | Form 2 | Form 1 | Form 2 |
| 1sg | cortara | cortase | viviera | viviese |
| 2sg | cortaras | cortases | vivieras | vivieses |
| 3sg | cortara | cortase | viviera | viviese |
| 1pl | cortáramos | cortásemos | viviéramos | viviésemos |
| 2pl | cortarais | cortaseis | vivierais | vivieseis |
| 3pl | cortaran | cortasen | vivieran | viviesen |

Figure 9.3 *Overabundance engendered by realization rules in Spanish*

ways. What makes this instance of overabundance different from that of English DREAM is that here, the overabundance is not the effect of two competing inflection classes. What makes it different from the overabundance of neuter *i*-stem adjectives in Sanskrit is that here, the overabundance does not reflect a choice between default, syncretic forms and more specific nonsyncretic forms. In this case, each conjugation simply supplies two alternative ways of realizing past subjunctive forms.

In formal terms, this example shows that a language's paradigm function PF may, in fact, be merely a relation rather than a true function (Bonami and Boyé 2007); in such cases, overabundance arises because different combinations of rules of exponence do not in fact compete, but simply yield alternative values for PF($\langle X, \sigma \rangle$). Thus, overabundance may arise either as part of the mapping from content cells to form cells (as in Figures 9.1 and 9.2) or as part of the mapping from form cells to realized cells (as in Figure 9.3).

### ℒ   *The qe stion of shape alternants*

In instances of overabundance, the alternative realizations of a given content cell are generally in free variation. But among instances in which a content cell has more than one realization, there are also cases in which, despite the identity of their lexical and morphosyntactic content, the realizations appear in complementary contexts. Realizations of this sort, which have been called **shape alternants** (Zwicky 1990, 1992), are quite varied in their behavior: In some cases, the choice among shape alternants is determined by their phonological context; in others, by the presence or absence of a neighboring "trigger" in their syntactic context.

Consider first the case of French adjectives. In French, adjectives agree in gender and number with the modified noun, as in (1). But when an adjective with a final vowel immediately precedes a vowel-initial masculine noun, the hiatus between the two vowels is often circumvented by the use of an alternative, consonant-final shape for the adjective matching that of the corresponding feminine form, as in (2).

(1)   a. *un beau* [bo] *tableau* à  fine painting'
      b. *une belle* [bɛl] *peinture* à  fine painting'

(2)   a. *un bel* [bɛl] *ami* à  fine friend (male)'
      b. *une belle* [bɛl] *amie* à  fine friend (female)'

Consider next the case of Breton consonant mutations. In the earlier history of Breton (as in that of other Celtic languages), sandhi processes caused initial consonants to assimilate to a preceding sound in particular contexts. Ultimately, these changes were reanalyzed as having a kind of syntactic significance, so that even though their original phonological motivation has withered away with the passage of time, they persist to the present day, triggered not by a word's phonological context, but by its syntactic proximity to a preceding trigger. Consider, for example, the possessive pronouns. These have the effect of triggering the three mutations in Table 9.4 in the initial consonant of a following noun: *penn* he ad,' *e benn* his  head,' *va fenn* my  head'; *bara* bre ad,' *e vara* his  bread,' *ho para* your  (pl) bread.'

Consider finally the English possessive pronouns. In English, ordinary possessive noun phrases carry the possessive marker *'s*, whose morphosyntactic status has been variously analyzed (Zwicky 1987, Miller 1992, Halpern 1995, Anderson 2005: 89ff, Spencer and Luís 2012: 287ff); such noun phrases may appear in any of the four environments in (3).

Table 9.4 *Breton initial consonant mutations triggered by possessive pronouns*

| Base form | Lenition | Spirantization | Fortition |
|---|---|---|---|
| p<br>   *penn* he ad' | b<br>   *benn* | f<br>   *fenn* | |
| t<br>   *tad* f ather' | d<br>   *dad* | z<br>   *zad* | |
| k<br>   *kalon* he art' | g<br>   *galon* | c'h [x]<br>   *c'halon* | |
| b<br>   *bara* bre ad' | v<br>   *vara* | | p<br>   *para* |
| d<br>   *dant* tooth' | z<br>   *zant* | | t<br>   *tant* |
| g<br>   *gar* le g' | c'h [γ]<br>   *c'har* | | k<br>   *kar* |
| gw<br>   *gwad* blood' | w<br>   *wad* | | kw<br>   *kwad* |
| m<br>   *mamm* mothe r' | v<br>   *vamm* | | |
| Triggers | *da* your (s g)'<br>*e* his ' | *va* my'<br>*he* he r'<br>*o* the ir' | *ho* 'your (pl)' |

(3)    a. In prenominal position, e.g. ***John's*** *car is missing.*
        b. Before N′ ellipsis, e.g. *Mary's car is here, but* ***John's*** ____ *is missing.*
        c. In predicative position, e.g. *This car is* ***John's***.
        d. As a postnominal possessive marked by *of*, e.g. *A friend of* ***John's***
           *arrived.*

The possessive pronoun *his* appears in all of these same environments. Most possessive pronouns, however, have two forms, one appearing in prenominal position (environment (3a)), the other appearing before N′ ellipsis, in predicative position, and as a postnominal possessive marked by *of* (environments (3b–d)); these are listed in Table 9.5.

Should the masculine adjectival forms *beau* and *bel* be seen as realizing distinct form cells in French? What about the Breton nominal forms *penn*, *benn* and *fenn*, or English possessive pronominal forms such as *my* and *mine*? Although these three cases are not alike in all ways, they are alike in that their alternating forms express precisely the same lexical and morphosyntactic

Table 9.5 *Shape alternants of English possessive pronouns*

| | Ordinary possessive noun phrase *John's* | Possessive pronoun | | | | | | |
| | | 1st person | | 2nd person | 3rd person | | | |
| | | sg | pl | | sg | | | pl |
| | | | | | masc | fem | neut | |
|---|---|---|---|---|---|---|---|---|
| In prenominal position | | *my* | *our* | *your* | *his* | *her* | *its* | *their* |
| Before N′ ellipsis | | *mine* | *ours* | *yours* | | *hers* | ? | *theirs* |
| In predicative position | *John's* | | | | | | | |
| As postnominal possessive | | | | | | | | |

content and the conditions on their alternation depend on their syntagmatic context.

In Section 5.5.2, I proposed to analyze instances of phonologically conditioned stem alternation by means of a syntagmatic context operator *SC*. This same operator may be plausibly claimed to regulate shape alternations. Thus, I assume that

- in French, the realized paradigm of the adjective BEAU fi ne' has *SC(beau)* in its masculine singular cell, where the definition of *SC* is such that *SC(beau)* = *bel* in prevocalic position, and otherwise *beau*;
- in Breton, *SC(penn)* = *benn* in the context of a lenition trigger, *fenn* in the context of a spirantization trigger, and otherwise *penn*;
- in English, *SC(mine)* = *my* as the modifier of an overt head noun, and otherwise *mine*.

As these examples suggest, a language's *SC* operation may be sensitive to various aspects of its argument's syntagmatic context, including phonological aspects (as in the case of *bel*), lexical aspects (as in the case of Breton mutations), and syntactic aspects (as in the case of English possessive pronouns). An important question awaiting future research concerns the limits on such sensitivity.[2]

---

2 A reasonable hypothesis is that *SC* is only sensitive to its argument's immediately adjacent context; but see Stump 1988 for discussion of a counterexample.

Table 9.6 *The fourteen morphosyntactic properties for which ordinary English verbs inflect*

| Finite forms | Tense | past, nonpast/present |
|---|---|---|
| | Mood | indicative, subjunctive, irrealis, imperative |
| | Person | 1, 2, 3 |
| | Number | singular, plural |
| Nonfinite forms | | infinitive, present participle, past participle |

## 9 Overdifferentiation

Canonically, the lexemes in a given syntactic category have isomorphic paradigms – they have the same number of cells, and any morphosyntactic property set associated with a cell in one lexeme's paradigm is associated with a parallel cell in the paradigm of every other lexeme. But while the inflectional morphology of lexemes belonging to the same syntactic category tends to realize the same morphosyntactic distinctions from one paradigm to the next, there are some lexemes that make additional distinctions; that is, the paradigms of some lexemes may exhibit **overdifferentiation** (Brown 2007, Corbett 2007). In fact, overdifferentiation may be of either of two kinds. On one hand, a lexeme may exhibit overdifferentiation because its inflection expresses an inflectional category that has no place in the inflection of ordinary lexemes. On the other hand, a lexeme may exhibit overdifferentiation because it doesn't participate in an otherwise general pattern of syncretism – that is, its inflection may involve the overt morphological expression of morphosyntactic distinctions that ordinarily remain unexpressed. In the former case, overdifferentiation is an exceptional property of content paradigms (more inflectional categories); in the latter case, it is an exceptional property of form paradigms and their realization (more morphological distinctions).

Consider, for example, the inflection of English verbs. Ordinarily, an English verb inflects for various combinations of the fourteen morphosyntactic properties in Table 9.6. But in addition to inflecting for these properties, the English copula expresses three additional distinctions. Typically of English auxiliary verbs, it inflects for polarity: thus, the positive finite forms *is*, *are*, *was* and *were* have the negative counterparts *isn't*, *aren't*, *wasn't* and *weren't*; in addition, the positive forms *am*, *is* and *are* share the stigmatized negative form *ain't* with *has* and *have* (e.g. *I ain't goin'* but *I ain't seen it*). These negative forms have sometimes been seen as clitic groups, but the relevant criteria reveal that they are inflected forms (Zwicky and Pullum 1983).

Present indicative forms of BE also exhibit clitic alternants: *am* ~ *'m*, *is* ~ *'s*, *are* ~ *'re*. These cannot be convincingly seen as shape alternants, since they are not restricted to complementary syntagmatic environments (*She is here* ~ *She's here*).

Finally, informal English presents special inverted alternants for first-person singular indicative forms of BE (Gazdar et al. 1982): *Aren't I invited?* vs *\*I aren't invited*, and for some speakers, *Weren't I good?* vs *\*I weren't good*. Like the clitic alternants, these inverted alternants are not obviously shape alternants: For many speakers, *aren't I* lacks any uninverted negative counterpart (other than the stigmatized *ain't*), whereas *weren't I* is apparently in free variation with *wasn't I* (for those that accept it).

Because they do not simply amount to shape distinctions (Section 9.2), distinctions such as *is* vs *isn't* and *am* vs *'m* vs *aren't (I)* can be plausibly represented in the realized paradigm of BE. Because of its obvious syntactic and semantic relevance, the distinction between *is* and *isn't* in the realized paradigm of BE must be assumed to reflect a polarity distinction in the content paradigm that it realizes. That is, the *is/isn't* distinction entails that the inflection of BE expresses an inflectional category that is foreign to the inflection of most English verbs.

To be sure, the distinction between *am* and *are* must also be represented in the content paradigm of BE, in this case as a distinction between the property set in (4a) and those in (4b); but this alone does not have to be seen as an instance of overdifferentiation, since the distinction in (4) might be assumed to be represented in the content paradigms of nearly all English verbs. But the morphological distinction between *am* and *are* has no parallel in the inflection of any verb other than BE in English. Thus, although the content cells in (5a, b) may be assumed to have the default present indicative form cell in (5c) as their shared form correspondent in the inflection of an ordinary verbal lexeme L in English, the content cell in (6a) and those in (6b) must have the distinct form correspondents in (6c) in the inflection of BE. Similarly, an ordinary English verbal lexeme L has the default past-tense form cell in (7a) as the form correspondent of each of its past-tense content cells; BE, by contrast, has the two form cells in (7b) as form correspondents for its past-tense content cells.

(4)    a. {s g prs ind}

b. {s g prs ind} {pl prs    ind} {pl prs    ind}, {3pl prs ind}

(5)    a. ⟨L, {s g prs ind}⟩

b. ⟨L, {2sg prs ind}⟩, ⟨L, {pl prs    ind}⟩, ⟨L, {2pl prs ind}⟩, ⟨L, {3pl prs ind}⟩

c. ⟨X, {prs ind}⟩, where X is L's present-tense stem

Table 9.7 *The five forms of* SING *and their eight functions*

|        |                        |                       |
|--------|------------------------|-----------------------|
|        | a. infinitive          | *to* **sing**         |
| 1: *sing* | b. subjunctive      | *that she* **sing**   |
|        | c. default present     | *we* **sing**         |
| 2: *sings* | d. 3sg present indicative | *he* **sings**  |
|        | e. past                | *she* **sang**        |
| 3: *sang* | f. irrealis         | *if he* **sang** *tomorrow* |
| 4: *singing* | g. present participle | *is* **singing**  |
| 5: *sung* | h. past participle  | *has* **sung**        |

(6)    a. ⟨BE, {s g prs ind}⟩
      b. ⟨BE, {s g prs ind}⟩, ⟨L, {pl prs ind}⟩, ⟨L, {p 1 prs ind}⟩, ⟨L, {3pl prs ind}⟩
      c. ⟨*am*, {s g prs ind}⟩, ⟨*are*, prs ind}⟩

(7)    a. ⟨X, {pa st}⟩, where X is L's past-tense stem
      b. ⟨*was*, { g past}⟩, ⟨*were*, pl pa st}⟩[3]

English verbs ordinarily have five distinct forms performing the eight functions exemplified in Table 9.7. But because it exhibits overdifferentiation both in its content paradigm and in its form paradigm, English BE has sixteen distinct forms performing the eighteen functions in Table 9.8.

The overdifferentiation of content and form in the inflection of English BE is partly an effect of its status as an auxiliary verb;[4] thus, as a historical consequence of their special syntax, most auxiliary verbs inflect for negative polarity. But BE is also by far the most frequent verb in English, a fact which very likely accounts for its unique preservation of three present indicative forms (*am, are, is*) and two past-tense forms (*was, were*).

## 9.4    Defectiveness

In the most general sense, defectiveness is the characteristic of an inflectional paradigm that is exceptional because one or more of its cells lack any realization. Defectiveness is observed by comparing the paradigms of distinct members

---

3 The assumption here is that the inflection of BE depends on a property mapping **pm** such that **pm**({s g past}) = {pl pa st}.

4 The verb BE does not function as an auxiliary in all of its uses; for example, it fails to invert or to support negation in the "active *be*" construction (Partee 1977, Stump 1985: 76ff).

Table 9.8 *The sixteen forms of* BE *and their eighteen functions*

|  |  |  | Nonclitic | Clitic |
|---|---|---|---|---|
| 1: *be* | a. infinitive<br>b. subjunctive |  | *to b*<br>*that she b* |  |
| 2/3: *are / 're* | c. default present |  | *we **are*** | *'re* |
| 4/5: *am / 'm* | d. 1sg present indicative |  | *I **am*** | *'m* |
| 6/7: *is / 's* | e. 3sg present indicative |  | *she **is*** | *'s* |
| 8: *were* | f. default past<br>g. irrealis |  | *we **were***<br>*if she **were*** |  |
| 9: *was* | h. sg past |  | *I **was*** |  |
| 10: *being* | i. present participle |  | *being* |  |
| 11: *been* | j. past participle |  | *been* |  |
| 12: *aren't* | k. default present negative<br>l. %1sg present indicative negative inverted |  | *we **aren't***<br>*% **aren't** I* |  |
| 13: *ain't* | m. default present negative (informal) |  | *he **ain't*** |  |
| 14: *isn't* | n. 3sg present indicative negative |  | *he **isn't*** |  |
| 15: *weren't* | o. default past negative<br>p. irrealis negative<br>q. % 1sg past negative inverted |  | *we **weren't***<br>*if he **weren't***<br>*% **weren't** I* |  |
| 16: *wasn't* | r. sg past negative |  | *I **wasn't*** |  |

of the same syntactic category; the number of realized cells in a defective paradigm falls short of the norm.

### 9.4.1    *Defective verbs in French*

In French, a typical verb's synthetic paradigm distinguishes the forty-eight content cells in Table 9.9. Thus, the synthetic paradigm of the verb ALLER ğo' in Table 9.10[5] is not defective; it supplies a realization for every one of the content cells in Table 9.9. French does, however, possess a number of verbs whose paradigms are defective because they have a gap in the realization of one or more of these forty-eight cells.

It is important, at the outset, to distinguish true defectiveness from a semantically motivated shortage of realizations: In instances of true defectiveness, there is no reasonable semantic explanation for the gaps in a paradigm's

---

5 Here and below, I represent French paradigms in phonemic transcription, which allows exponence relations to be identified more easily than ordinary spelling does.

Table 9.9 *The forty-eight cells in a French verb's synthetic paradigm*

| | | | | | | | | | | |
|---|---|---|---|---|---|---|---|---|---|---|
| | Finite forms | | | | | | | | Nonfinite forms | |
| | Present | | Imperfect | | | | | | | |
| | Ind | Sbjv | Ind | Sbjv | Preterite | Future | Cond | Imperative | | |
| 1sg | 1 | 7 | 13 | 19 | 25 | 31 | 37 | | Infinitive | 46 |
| 2sg | 2 | 8 | 14 | 20 | 26 | 32 | 38 | 43 | Pres ptcp | 47 |
| 3sg | 3 | 9 | 15 | 21 | 27 | 33 | 39 | | Past ptcp | 48 |
| 1pl | 4 | 10 | 16 | 22 | 28 | 34 | 40 | 44 | | |
| 2pl | 5 | 11 | 17 | 23 | 29 | 35 | 41 | 45 | | |
| 3pl | 6 | 12 | 18 | 24 | 30 | 36 | 42 | | | |

Table 9.10 *The synthetic inflection of French* ALLER *'go'*

| | | | | | | | | | | |
|---|---|---|---|---|---|---|---|---|---|---|
| | Finite forms | | | | | | | | Nonfinite forms | |
| | Present | | Imperfect | | | | | | | |
| | Ind | Sbjv | Ind | Sbjv | Preterite | Future | Cond | Imperative | | |
| 1sg | vɛ | aj | alɛ | alas | alɛ | iʁɛ | iʁɛ | | Infinitive | ale |
| 2sg | va | aj | alɛ | alas | ala | iʁa | iʁɛ | va | Pres ptcp | alɑ̃ |
| 3sg | va | aj | alɛ | ala | ala | iʁa | iʁɛ | | Past ptcp | ale |
| 1pl | alɔ̃ | aljɔ̃ | aljɔ̃ | alasjɔ̃ | alam | iʁɔ̃ | iʁjɔ̃ | alɔ̃ | | |
| 2pl | ale | alje | alje | alasje | alat | iʁe | iʁje | ale | | |
| 3pl | vɔ̃ | aj | alɛ | alas | alɛʁ | iʁɔ̃ | iʁɛ | | | |

realization. Thus, consider the paradigm of the French verb FALLOIR be neces-sary' (Table 9.11). On first consideration, this paradigm seems massively de-fective, but most if not all of its unrealized cells are unrealized for good reason. As the examples in (8)–(9) suggest, the verb FALLOIR does not take a subject argument, but instead requires a third-person singular dummy subject; its com-plement names what is necessary, with an optional argument naming the one for whom it is necessary. Thus, the gaps among the finite forms in Table 9.11 correspond to hypothetical forms for which there is no coherent interpretation. In instances of true defectiveness, by contrast, the missing forms would have reasonable interpretations if they existed.[6]

6 The paradigm of FALLOIR may contain at least one instance of true defectiveness, namely the lack of a present participle, though other kinds of semantic considerations may account for the absence of this form as well.

Table 9.11 *The synthetic inflection of French* FALLOIR *'be necessary'*

| | Finite forms | | | | | | | | Nonfinite forms | |
| | Present | | Imperfect | | Preterite | Future | Cond | Imperative | | |
| | Ind | Sbjv | Ind | Sbjv | | | | | | |
|---|---|---|---|---|---|---|---|---|---|---|
| 1sg | – | – | – | – | – | – | – | | Infinitive | falwaʁ |
| 2sg | – | – | – | – | – | – | – | – | Pres ptcp | – |
| 3sg | fo | faj | falɛ | faly | faly | fodʁa | fodʁɛ | | Past ptcp | faly |
| 1pl | – | – | – | – | – | – | – | – | | |
| 2pl | – | | – | – | – | – | – | – | | |
| 3pl | – | – | – | – | – | – | – | | | |

(8)   a. *Il        me        faut        aller.*
3SG.PRON  1SG.PRON  is.necessary  go.INF
It is necessary for me to go.'
   b. *Il        faut        que  j'        aille.*
3SG.PRON  is.necessary  that  1SG.PRON  go
It is necessary that I go.'

(9)   a. *\*Aller faut.*        (Putatively: 'To go is necessary.')
   b. *\*Que j'aille faut.*     (Putatively: 'That I go is necessary.')

French verb inflection provides many instances of true defectiveness, and these are quite varied. A defective verb may lack comparatively few forms or a great many. For instance, the verb TRAIRE 'milk,' for many speakers, lacks twelve of its forty-eight synthetic forms (Table 9.12); by contrast, for

Table 9.12 *The synthetic inflection of French* TRAIRE *'milk'*

| | Finite forms | | | | | | | | Nonfinite forms | |
| | Present | | Imperfect | | Preterite | Future | Cond | Imperative | | |
| | Ind | Sbjv | Ind | Sbjv | | | | | | |
|---|---|---|---|---|---|---|---|---|---|---|
| 1sg | tʁɛ | tʁɛ | tʁɛjɛ | – | – | tʁɛʁɛ | tʁɛʁɛ | | Infinitive | tʁɛʁ |
| 2sg | tʁɛ | tʁɛ | tʁɛjɛ | – | – | tʁɛʁa | tʁɛʁɛ | tʁɛ | Pres ptcp | tʁɛjɑ̃ |
| 3sg | tʁɛ | tʁɛ | tʁɛjɛ | – | – | tʁɛʁa | tʁɛʁɛ | | Past ptcp | tʁɛ(t) |
| 1pl | tʁɛjɔ̃ | tʁɛjɔ̃ | tʁɛjɔ̃ | – | – | tʁɛʁɔ̃ | tʁɛʁjɔ̃ | tʁɛjɔ̃ | | |
| 2pl | tʁɛje | tʁɛje | tʁɛje | – | – | tʁɛʁe | tʁɛʁje | tʁɛje | | |
| 3pl | tʁɛ | tʁɛ | tʁɛjɛ | – | – | tʁɛʁɔ̃ | tʁɛʁɛ | | | |

Table 9.13 *The synthetic inflection of French* GÉSIR *'lie' (in restricted senses, applied to the ailing or deceased)*

| | Finite forms | | | | | | | | Nonfinite forms | |
|---|---|---|---|---|---|---|---|---|---|---|
| | Present | | Imperfect | | Preterite | Future | Cond | Imperative | | |
| | Ind | Sbjv | Ind | Sbjv | | | | | | |
| 1sg | ʒi | – | ʒizɛ | – | – | – | – | | Infinitive | ʒeziʁ |
| 2sg | ʒi | – | ʒizɛ | – | – | – | – | – | Pres ptcp | ʒizɑ̃ |
| 3sg | ʒi | – | ʒizɛ | – | – | – | – | | Past ptcp | – |
| 1pl | ʒizɔ̃ | – | ʒizjɔ̃ | – | – | – | – | – | | |
| 2pl | ʒize | – | ʒizje | – | – | – | – | – | | |
| 3pl | ʒiz | – | ʒizɛ | – | – | – | – | | | |

many speakers, the verb GÉSIR lie ' (in restricted senses, applied to the ailing or deceased) has only fourteen of the forty-eight possible synthetic forms (Table 9.13). Numerous verbs exhibit varying degrees of defectiveness intermediate between those of TRAIRE and GÉSIR; Table 9.14 compares the patterns of defectiveness exhibited by four such verbs.

Patterns of defectiveness such as those represented in Table 9.14 are not simply random in their shape. Boyé (2000) demonstrates that the patterns in Table 9.14 are directly related to a verb's inventory of stems. At the most abstract level of analysis, an ordinary French verbal lexeme may be seen as having sixteen stems; these are distributed as in Table 9.15, in which the stems are distinguished by the labels employed by Boyé. Some of these stems are morphomic, lacking any coherent morphosyntactic interpretation. For example, Su6 is the stem of the singular present subjunctive together with the third-person plural present subjunctive; Ps4 is the stem of the imperfective subjunctive together with the preterite (or simple past); and so on.

This classification of stems illuminates the patterns of defectiveness in Table 9.14 in a very straightforward way: Each of the defective verbs in this table is defective because it lacks some of the sixteen stems on which nondefective paradigms are based. For example, BRAIRE bra y' is defective because it lacks Pr4, Pr5, Su4, Imp, Ps4, Ju4, Ju5 and Ger.

Although a nondefective verb ordinarily has all sixteen of the stems in Table 9.15, there is always a good deal of syncretism among a verb's stems; the sixteen stems of the verb ALLER ğo, ' for example, are realized by only seven distinct forms, as in Table 9.16. French conjugation classes are in general distinguished not by contrasting sets of endings, but by contrasting patterns of

Table 9.14 *Patterns of defectiveness in six French verbs*

| | | TRAIRE ‘milk’ | PAÎTRE ‘graze’ | CLORE ‘close’ | BRAIRE ‘bray’ | FRIRE ‘fry’ | GÉSIR ‘lie’ | Boyé's stems |
|---|---|---|---|---|---|---|---|---|
| Pres ind | 1sg | tʁɛ | pɛ | klo | bʁɛ | fʁi | ʒi | Pr1 |
| | 2–3sg | tʁɛ | pɛ | klo | bʁɛ | fʁi | ʒi | Pr3 |
| | 1pl | tʁɛ | pɛs | – | – | – | ʒiz | Pr4 |
| | 2pl | tʁɛ | pɛs | – | – | – | ʒiz | Pr5 |
| | 3pl | tʁɛ | pɛs | kloz | bʁɛ | – | ʒiz | Pr6 |
| Pres sbjv | 1–3sg | tʁɛ | pɛs | kloz | bʁɛ | – | – | Su6 |
| | 1–2pl | tʁɛ | pɛs | kloz | – | – | – | Su4 |
| | 3pl | tʁɛ | pɛs | kloz | bʁɛ | – | – | Su6 |
| Impf ind | 1sg–3pl | tʁɛj | pɛs | – | – | – | ʒiz | Imp |
| Impf sbjv | 1sg–3pl | – | – | – | – | – | – | Ps4 |
| Preterite | 1sg–3pl | | | | | | | |
| Future | 1sg–3pl | tʁɛ | pɛt | klo | bʁɛ | fʁi | – | Fut |
| Conditional | 1sg–3pl | | | | | | | |
| Imperative | 2sg | tʁɛ | pɛ | klo | bʁɛ | fʁi | – | Ju2 |
| | 1pl | tʁɛj | pɛs | – | – | – | – | Ju4 |
| | 2pl | tʁɛj | pɛs | – | – | – | – | Ju5 |
| Infinitive | | tʁɛʁ | pɛtʁ | kloʁ | bʁɛʁ | fʁiʁ | ʒeziʁ | Inf |
| Pres ptcp | | tʁɛj | pɛs | kloz | – | – | ʒiz | Ger |
| Past ptcp | | tʁɛ(t) | – | klo(z) | bʁɛ | fʁi(t) | – | Pps |
| Number of missing forms: | | 12 | 13 | 22 | 25 | 30 | 34 | |

Table 9.15 *The sixteen stems of a French verb (Boyé 2000)*

| | Finite forms | | | | | | | | Nonfinite forms | |
|---|---|---|---|---|---|---|---|---|---|---|
| | Present | | Imperfect | | Preterite | Future | Cond | Imperative | | |
| | Ind | Sbjv | Ind | Sbjv | | | | | | |
| 1sg | Pr1 | Su6 | Imp | Ps4 | | Fut | | | Infinitive | Inf |
| 2sg | Pr3 | | | | | | | Ju2 | Pres ptcp | Ger |
| 3sg | | | | | | | | | Past ptcp | Pps |
| 1pl | Pr4 | Su4 | | | | | | Ju4 | | |
| 2pl | Pr5 | | | | | | | Ju5 | | |
| 3pl | Pr6 | Su6 | | | | | | | | |

Table 9.16 *The sixteen stems of French* ALLER *'go'*

| | | Finite forms | | | | | | | | Nonfinite forms | |
|---|---|---|---|---|---|---|---|---|---|---|---|
| | | Present | | Imperfect | | | | | | | |
| | | Ind | Sbjv | Ind | Sbjv | Preterite | Future | Conditional | Imperative | | |
| SG | 1st | vε | aj | al | al | | i | | | Infinitive | ale |
| | 2nd | va | | | | | | | va | Pres ptcp | al |
| | 3rd | | | | | | | | | Past ptcp | ale |
| PL | 1st | al | al | | | | | | al | | |

Table 9.17 *Terminations of French verbs*

| | Finite forms | | | | | | | | Nonfinite forms | |
|---|---|---|---|---|---|---|---|---|---|---|
| | Present | | Imperfect | | | | | | | |
| | Ind | Sbjv | Ind | Sbjv | Preterite | Future | Cond | Imperative | | |
| 1sg | – | – | ε | (a)s | (ε) | ʁε | ʁε | | Infinitive | – |
| 2sg | – | – | ε | (a)s | (a) | ʁa | ʁε | – | Pres ptcp | ɑ̃ |
| 3sg | – | – | ε | (a) | (a) | ʁa | ʁε | | Past ptcp | – |
| 1pl | ɔ̃[1] | jɔ̃ | jɔ̃ | (a)sjɔ̃ | (a-)m | ʁɔ̃ | ʁjɔ̃ | ɔ̃ | | |
| 2pl | e[2] | je | je | (a)sje | (a-)t | ʁe | ʁje | e[3] | | |
| 3pl | – | – | ε | (a)s | (ε-)ʁ | ʁɔ̃ | ʁε | | | |

[1] But ÊTRE: /sɔm/ 'we are.'
[2] But ÊTRE: /ɛt/ 'you (pl) are'; FAIRE: /fɛt/ 'you (pl) do'; DIRE: /dit/ 'you (pl) say.'
[3] But FAIRE: /fɛt/ 'you (pl) do!'; DIRE: /dit/ 'you (pl) say!'

stem formation and stem alternation. In fact, most verbs exhibit exactly the system of endings in Table 9.17; but their patterns for stem formation and stem alternation are quite diverse, as the stems of the twelve more or less randomly chosen verbal lexemes in Table 9.18 show.

As Boyé shows, the patterns of stem syncretism in Table 9.18 are not random and unstructured, but form a very specific system. In particular, twelve of the sixteen stems in a verb's paradigm participate in the inheritance relations schematized in Boyé's diagram in Figure 9.4. The stems in this diagram participate in two sorts of relations, which Boyé labels **hierarchical inheritance** and **non-hierarchical inheritance**; relations of the latter sort are represented as curved arrows, while those of the former kind are represented as branches in a conventional tree diagram. These two kinds of relations among stems are defined in (10).

Table 9.18 *Stems of twelve verbal lexemes in French*

| | AIMER | FINIR | COUVRIR | RECEVOIR | CONNAÎTRE | FAIRE | ALLER | ÊTRE | AVOIR | CUEILLIR | LEVER | CÉDER |
|---|---|---|---|---|---|---|---|---|---|---|---|---|
| Pr1 | ɛm | fini | kuvʁ | ʁəswa | konɛ | fɛ | vɛ | sɥi | ɛ | kœj | lɛv | sɛd |
| Pr3 | = Pr1 | = Pr1 | = Pr1 | = Pr1 | = Pr1 | = Pr1 | va | ɛ | a | = Pr1 | = Pr1 | = Pr1 |
| Pr4 | = Pr1 | finis | = Pr1 | ʁəsəv | konɛs | fəz | al | sɔm | av | køj | lav | sed |
| Pr5 | = Pr1 | = Pr4 | = Pr1 | = Pr4 | = Pr4 | fɛt | = Pr4 | ɛt | = Pr4 | = Pr4 | = Pr4 | = Pr4 |
| Pr6 | = Pr1 | = Pr4 | = Pr1 | ʁəswav | = Pr4 | fɔ̃ | vɔ̃ | sɔ̃ | ɔ̃ | = Pr1 | = Pr1 | = Pr1 |
| Su4 | = Pr1 | = Pr4 | kuvʁi | = Pr4 | = Pr4 | fas | = Pr4 | swa | = Pr1 | køji | = Pr4 | = Pr4 |
| Su6 | = Pr1 | = Pr4 | = Pr1 | = Pr6 | = Pr4 | = Su4 | aj | = Su4 | = Pr1 | = Pr1 | = Pr1 | = Pr1 |
| Imp | = Pr1 | = Pr4 | = Pr1 | = Pr4 | = Pr4 | = Pr4 | = Pr4 | et | = Pr4 | = Pr4 | = Pr4 | = Pr4 |
| Ps4 | = Pr1 | = Pr1 | = Su4 | ʁəsy | kony | fi | = Pr4 | fy | y | køji | = Pr4 | = Pr4 |
| Fut | ɛmɛ | = Pr1 | = Su4 | = Pr4 | konɛt | fə | i | sə | o | kœjɛ | lɛvɛ | sɛdə |
| Ju2 | = Pr1 | = Pr1 | = Pr1 | = Pr1 | = Pr1 | = Pr1 | = Pr3 | = Su4 | = Pr1 | = Pr1 | = Pr1 | = Pr1 |
| Ju4 | = Pr1 | = Pr4 | = Pr1 | = Pr4 | = Pr4 | = Pr4 | = Pr4 | swaj | ɛj | = Pr4 | = Pr4 | = Pr4 |
| Ju5 | = Pr1 | = Pr4 | = Pr1 | = Pr4 | = Pr4 | = Pr5 | = Pr4 | = Ju4 | = Ju4 | = Pr4 | = Pr4 | = Pr4 |
| Inf | ɛme | finiʁ | kuvʁiʁ | ʁəsəvwaʁ | konɛtʁ | fɛʁ | ale | etʁ | avwaʁ | køjiʁ | ləve | sede |
| Ger | = Pr1 | = Pr4 | = Pr1 | = Pr4 | = Pr4 | = Pr4 | = Pr4 | = Imp | = Ju4 | = Pr4 | = Pr4 | = Pr4 |
| Pps | = Inf | = Pr1 | kuvɛʁt | = Ps4 | = Ps4 | = Pr5 | = Inf | ete | = Ps4 | = Ps4 | = Inf | = Inf |

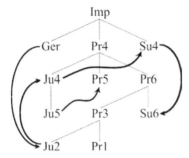

Figure 9.4 *Boyé's diagram of inheritance relations among French verb stems*

(10)    Inheritance relations in Figure 9.4
    a. **Hierarchical inheritance**. Where α immediately dominates β, the form
      of a lexeme's β-stem (if not lexically listed) is, by default, identical to
      that of its α-stem.
    b. **Non-hierarchical inheritance**. Where an arrow points from γ to β, the
      form of a lexeme's β-stem (if not lexically listed) is that of its γ-stem if
      this is lexically listed or induced by non-hierarchical inheritance.

These patterns make it possible to simplify a verb's lexical entry. For example, if the lexical entry of the verb FAIRE do' is assumed to include the nine
stems on the first row of Table 9.19, then its seven remaining stems may be
inferred by the inheritance principles in (10), as in the second and third rows of
Table 9.19.

    Boyé demonstrates that the inheritance relations represented in Figure 9.4
and defined in (10) yield a surprising prediction when they are combined with
the assumption that verbs may be defective because they lack particular stems:
The prediction is that if a lexeme lacks a particular stem *s*, then in the absence
of any overriding lexical stipulation, any stem that inherits its form from *s* in
accordance with the principles in (10) should be missing as well; that is, the
principles in (10) determine not merely relations of identity among existing
stem forms, but also dependencies among missing stems. Thus, if the lexical
entry of the defective verb FRIRE fry' specifies that it lacks the Imp and Ps4
stems, the inheritance principles entail that it likewise lacks the Pr4, Pr5, Pr6,
Su6, Su4, Ju4, Ju5 and Ger stems (Table 9.20).

### 9.4.2    *Modeling Boyé's analysis under the paradigm-linkage hypothesis*

Boyé's analysis affords a direct interpretation according to the paradigm-
linkage hypothesis. Stem labels can be used to define the ***Corr*** function in
a way which accounts for the distribution of stems within a paradigm, as in
Table 9.21. Defectiveness may be equated with the failure of ***Corr*** to supply a

Table 9.19 *Stem inheritance in the inflection of French* FAIRE *'do'*

| | Pr1 | Pr3 | Pr4 | Pr5 | Pr6 | Su6 | Su4 | Imp | Ju2 | Ju4 | Ju5 | Ger | Ps4 | Fut | Inf | Pps |
|---|---|---|---|---|---|---|---|---|---|---|---|---|---|---|---|---|
| Lexically listed stems | | fɛ | | | fɔ̃ | | fas | fəz | | | fɛtə | | fi | fə | fɛʁ | fɛ(t) |
| Non-hierarchical inheritance | | | fɔz | fɛtə | | fas | | | | | | | | | | |
| Hierarchical inheritance | fɛ | | | | | | | | fɛ | fɔz | | fɔz | | | | |

Table 9.20 *Stem inheritance in the inflection of French* FRIRE *'fry'*

| | Pr1 | Pr3 | Pr4 | Pr5 | Pr6 | Su6 | Su4 | Imp | Ju2 | Ju4 | Ju5 | Ger | Ps4 | Fut | Inf | Pps |
|---|---|---|---|---|---|---|---|---|---|---|---|---|---|---|---|---|
| Lexically listed stems | | fʁi | | | | | | ∅ | | | | | ∅ | fʁi | fʁiʁ | fʁi(t) |
| Non-hierarchical inheritance | | | ∅ | ∅ | ∅ | ∅ | ∅ | | | ∅ | ∅ | ∅ | | | | |
| Hierarchical inheritance | fʁi | | | | | | | | fʁi | | | | | | | |

Table 9.21 *Partial definition of Corr in French*

| If σ satisfies κ, then ***Corr***(⟨L, σ⟩) = ⟨X, σ⟩: | |
|---|---|
| κ | X |
| {s g pres ind} | L's Pr1 stem |
| { g pres ind} | L's Pr3 stem |
| {pl pre s ind} | L's Pr4 stem |
| {2pl pre s ind} | L's Pr5 stem |
| {3pl pre s ind} | L's Pr6 stem |
| [[{ g} ∨ { pl}] ∧ pre s sbjv} | L's Su6 stem |
| {pre s sbjv} | L's Su4 stem |
| {mpe rf} | L's Imp stem |
| [{mpe rf sbjv} ∨ {pre t} | L's Ps4 stem |
| [{fut} ∨ { ond} | L's Fut stem |
| { g impv} | L's Ju2 stem |
| {pl impv} | L's Ju4 stem |
| {pl impv} | L's Ju5 stem |
| {nf} | L's Inf stem |
| {pre s ptcp} | L's Ger stem |
| {ptc p} | L's Pps stem |

Table 9.22 *The stems of two French verbs*

| Stem | ALLER ǧo' | BRAIRE br ay' |
|---|---|---|
| Pr1 | vɛ | bʁɛ |
| Pr3 | va | bʁɛ |
| Pr4 | al | *undefined* |
| Pr5 | al | *undefined* |
| Pr6 | võ | bʁɛ |
| Su4 | al | *undefined* |
| Su6 | aj | bʁɛ |
| Imp | al | *undefined* |
| Ps4 | al | *undefined* |
| Fut | i | bʁɛ |
| Ju2 | va | bʁɛ |
| Ju4 | al | *undefined* |
| Ju5 | al | *undefined* |
| Inf | ale | bʁɛʁ |
| Ger | al | *undefined* |
| Pps | ale | bʁɛ |

form correspondent for a given content cell. Thus, ALLER is nondefective because for any relevant value of σ, the value of ***Corr*** (⟨ALLER, σ⟩) is defined as in Table 9.22. By contrast, Table 9.22 shows that ***Corr***(⟨BRAIRE, σ⟩) is undefined for several values of σ. The examples in (11) illustrate.

(11)    Some form correspondents in the inflection of ALLER 'go' and BRAIRE 'bray'

     a. ***Corr***(⟨ALLER, {s  g fut}⟩)        = ⟨Z, {1sg fut}⟩, where Z is ALLER's Fut stem
                                      = ⟨i, {1sg fut}⟩

     b. ***Corr***(⟨BRAIRE, {s  g fut}⟩)        = ⟨Z, {1sg fut}⟩, where Z is BRAIRE's Fut stem
                                        = ⟨bʁɛ, {1sg fut}⟩

     c. ***Corr***(⟨ALLER, {s  g impf ind}⟩)        = ⟨Z, {1sg impf ind}⟩, where Z is ALLER's Imp stem
                                        = ⟨al, {1sg impf ind}⟩

     d. ***Corr***(⟨BRAIRE, {s  g impf ind}⟩)        = ⟨Z, {1sg impf ind}⟩, where Z is BRAIRE's Imp stem
                                        = *undefined*

Boyé's inheritance principles may be formulated as the lexical redundancy rules in (12). These entail the patterns of inheritance exemplified above for FAIRE and FRIRE (Tables 9.18–9.19), accounting both for the default patterns of formal identity among stems and for the isomorphic patterns of defectiveness in verbs' form paradigms.

(12)    Lexical redundancy rules

| | | W | X | Y | Z |
|---|---|---|---|---|---|
| **a.** | **Non-hierarchical inheritance** | | | | |
| | If X is lexically unlisted but W is lexically listed (or is induced by a non-hierarchical inheritance), then X has the same form as W. | Ger | Ju2 | Ger, Pr4 or Su4 | Imp |
| | | Ju2 | Ju4 | Ju4, Pr5 or Pr6 | Pr4 |
| | | Ju5 | Pr5 | Ju5 | Ju4 |
| | Otherwise, | Ju4 | Su4 | Pr3 or Su6 | Pr6 |
| **b.** | **Hierarchical inheritance** By default, Y has the same form as Z. | Su4 | Su6 | Ju2 or Pr1 | Pr3 |

Boyé's inheritance principles strongly support the irreducibility hypothesis ("Some morphological regularities are, irreducibly, regularities in paradigm structure"; Section 1.3.1). In particular, they define regularities that are only observable through the comparison of distinct cells in a verbal lexeme's paradigm, and these regularities are restricted neither by the choice of lexeme nor by the specific morphology involved in the realization of the property sets with which it is paired.

## *9.5*    *Conclusion*

We have examined several deviations from two canonical symmetries, (a) between content cells and form cells in the inflection of an individual lexeme, and (b) between the paradigms of different lexemes belonging to the same syntactic category. Instances of overabundance are of two kinds, one involving one-to-many relations between a lexeme's content cells and form correspondents, the other involving one-to-many relations between a form paradigm's cells and their realizations. Instances of overdifferentiation are likewise of two kinds. One involves a lexeme of category C whose content paradigm expresses inflectional categories that are not usual for other members of C; the other involves a lexeme of category C whose morphology gives fuller expression to the inflectional categories usual for members of C. True defectiveness is the property of a lexeme some of whose content cells lack form correspondents, often as a matter of sheer morphological poverty, such as an incomplete stem inventory.

# 10 *Syncretism*

In the last chapter, I examined the phenomenon of form defectiveness, the existence of content paradigms some of whose cells unexpectedly lack any form correspondent (and hence any realization) – unexpectedly in the sense that there is no syntactic or semantic justification for this lacuna in their realization. Here, I examine another phenomenon in which cells in a lexeme's content paradigm outnumber the form cells through whose mediation they get their realization. This phenomenon – syncretism – is unlike defectiveness because it doesn't leave content cells unrealized; instead, it is the realization of two or more content cells through the mediation of a single form cell.

Instances of syncretism are of various kinds. In instances of natural-class syncretism, a morphosyntactically coherent set of content cells has a common realization (Section 10.1). Syncretisms that don't simply encompass a natural class of content cells are of two kinds. In cases of directional syncretism, the realization of one property set systematically patterns after that of some distinct property set (Section 10.2); in instances of morphomic syncretism, two or more property sets that do not form a natural class are nevertheless alike in their realization and neither set is associated with that realization independently of the other set (Section 10.3). Drawing on evidence from Bhojpuri, Turkish and Sanskrit, I discuss several examples embodying these distinctions. As I show, the paradigm-linkage hypothesis affords a simple way of understanding each of these kinds of syncretism. More generally, the phenomenon of syncretism provides clear motivation for both the irreducibility hypothesis and the interface hypothesis (Section 10.4).

## 10.1 *Natural-class syncretism*

In the simplest examples of syncretism, the syncretized cells in a lexeme's paradigm belong together in that their property sets constitute a natural class.

Table 10.1 *The inflection of Bhojpuri* DĒKH *'see'*

|  |  | Singular |  | Plural |  |
|---|---|---|---|---|---|
|  |  | masculine | feminine | masculine | feminine |
| Present | 1 | *dēkh-īl-ā* | *dēkh-īl-ā* | *dēkh-īl-ā* | *dēkh-īl-ā* |
| indicative | 2 | *dēkh-āl-ā* | *dēkh-æl-iu* | *dēkh-āl-ā* | *dēkh-æl-iu* |
|  | 3 | *dēkh-āl-ā* | *dēkh-ēl-ē* | *dēkh-æl-æ̃* | *dēkh-æl-ini* |
| Past | 1 | *dekh-al-ī̃* | *dekh-al-ī̃* | *dekh-al-ī̃* | *dekh-al-ī̃* |
| indicative | 2 | *dekh-al-ā* | *dekh-al-iu* | *dekh-al-ā* | *dekh-al-iu* |
|  | 3 | *dēkh-al* | *dēkh-al-i* | *dekh-al-æ̃* | *dekh-al-ini* |
| Future | 1 | *dēkh-ab* | *dēkh-ab* | *dekh-ab-æ̃* | *dekh-ab-æ̃* |
| indicative | 2 | *dekh-ab-ā* | *dekh-ab-iu* | *dekh-ab-ā* | *dekh-ab-iu* |
|  | 3 | *dēkh-ī* | *dēkh-ī* | *dekh-ih-æ̃* | *dekh-ih-æ̃* |
| Optative | 1 | *dēkh-ī̃* | *dēkh-ī̃* | *dēkh-ī̃* | *dēkh-ī̃* |
|  | 2 | *dēkh-ā* | *dēkh-ā* | *dēkh-ā* | *dēkh-ā* |
|  | 3 | *dēkh-æ* | *dēkh-æ* | *dēkh-æ̃* | *dēkh-æ̃* |

*Source:* Shukla 1981

Consider again the synthetic inflection of the Bhojpuri verb DĒKH Ŝ ee' in Table 10.1. These forms are built on two morphomic stems: The shaded forms exhibit the long stem *dēkh-* and the remaining forms, the short stem *dekh-*. As was seen in Section 3.7, the word forms arising from these stems present numerous instances of syncretism in which the syncretized forms all realize a natural class of morphosyntactic properties. The members of each syncretized set of forms share one of the suffixes in Table 10.2. For example, the forms realizing the property sets

      {1sg masc prs ind}     {1pl masc prs ind}
      {1sg fem prs ind}      {1pl fem prs ind}

share the suffix *-īlā*, and the fully specified property sets that they realize constitute a natural class defined by the shared subset {1 prs ind}.

    Under the paradigm-linkage hypothesis, there are at least three ways of analyzing the instances of natural-class syncretism exhibited by the inflection of DĒKH. The fundamental differences among these three analyses pertain to the status they assign to two candidate paradigms for Bhojpuri verb inflection – the

Table 10.2  *Affixal exponents of Bhojpuri verb inflection*

|  | Present indicative | | Past indicative | | Future indicative | | Optative | |
|---|---|---|---|---|---|---|---|---|
|  | sg | pl | sg | pl | sg | pl | sg | pl |
| 1m | -*īlā* | | -*alī̃* | | -*ab* | -*abæ̃* | -*ī̃* | |
| 1f | | | | | | | | |
| 2m | -*ālā* | | -*alā* | | -*abā* | | -*ā* | |
| 2f | -*æliu* | | -*aliu* | | -*abiu* | | | |
| 3m | -*ālā* | -*ælæ̃* | -*al* | -*alæ̃* | -*ī* | -*ihæ̃* | -*æ* | -*æ̃* |
| 3f | -*ēlē* | -*ælini* | -*ali* | -*alini* | | | | |

Table 10.3  *Candidate paradigm A for Bhojpuri verb inflection (forty-eight cells)*

|  |  | Present indicative | | Past indicative | | Future indicative | | Optative | |
|---|---|---|---|---|---|---|---|---|---|
|  |  | sg | pl | sg | pl | sg | pl | sg | pl |
| 1 | masc | | | | | | | | |
|  | fem | | | | | | | | |
| 2̇ | masc | | | | | | | | |
|  | fem | | | | | | | | |
| 3 | masc | | | | | | | | |
|  | fem | | | | | | | | |

forty-eight-celled paradigm A in Table 10.3 and the twenty-four-celled paradigm B in Table 10.4.

Under **Analysis 1**, both the content paradigm and the form paradigm of DĒKH have the twenty-four-celled paradigm B; on this analysis, the structure of DĒKH's content paradigm is restricted by the property coöccurrence restriction entertained earlier (Section 3.7), repeated in (1). In this analysis, there is no real syncretism in Table 10.1; instead, each apparent instance of syncretism involves a single, underspecified form; for example, the first-person present indicative form *dēkhīlā* is unspecified for either gender or number.

Table 10.4 *Candidate paradigm B for Bhojpuri verb inflection (twenty-four cells)*

|  |  | Present indicative | | Past indicative | | Future indicative | | Optative | |
|---|---|---|---|---|---|---|---|---|---|
|  |  | (sg) | (pl) | (sg) | (pl) | (sg) | (pl) | (sg) | (pl) |
| 1 |  |  |  |  |  |  |  |  |  |
| 2 | (masc) |  |  |  |  |  |  |  |  |
|   | (fem) |  |  |  |  |  |  |  |  |
| 3 | (masc) |  |  |  |  |  |  |  |  |
|   | (fem) |  |  |  |  |  |  |  |  |

(1)  Property coöccurrence restriction in Analysis 1
     A morphosyntactic property set σ is well-formed if and only if
     for some τ ∈ { $p, n, g, t, m$} $p ∈ S_{\text{PERSON}}$, $n ∈ S_{\text{NUMBER}}$, $g ∈ S_{\text{GENDER}}$,
     $t ∈ S_{\text{TENSE}}$, $m ∈ S_{\text{MOOD}}$  σ is the largest subset of τ that satisfies all of the
     following property constraints:
     a. {ind}    ∧ [{prs } ∨ {ps t} ∨ {ut}]]
     b. {opt}    ∧ [{prs } ∨ {ps t} ∨ {ut}]]
     c. {} ∧ [{ma sc} ∨ {e m}]
     d. {} ∧ [{prs } ∨ {ps t} ∨ {opt}  ∧ [{ g} ∨ { l}]]]
     e. {2}  ∧ [{ g} ∨ {pl}]]
     f. {2}  ∧ {opt} ∧ [{ma sc} ∨ {e m}]]
     g. {3}  ∧ [{ut} ∨ {opt}  ∧ [{ma sc} ∨ {e m}]] .

Under **Analysis 2**, both the content paradigm of DĒKH and the corresponding form paradigm have the forty-eight cells distinguished in paradigm A. On this analysis, the instances of syncretism in Table 10.1 reflect a kind of poverty in the system of rules of exponence by which the form paradigm of DĒKH is realized; in particular, these rules simply fail to realize the morphosyntactic distinctions among the members of each syncretized set of forms.

  In Section 3.7, I rejected Analysis 1 for two reasons. First, it is based on a premise that can't be generalized to all instances of syncretism – the assumption that apparently syncretized property sets invariably realize a natural class of properties. Second, given the assumption that content paradigms represent the interface of a language's inflectional morphology with its syntax, Analysis 3 unmotivatedly suggests that certain property coöccurrences (those excluded by (1)) are in fact excluded in the syntax.

As I showed earlier, Analysis 2 is subject to neither objection. Yet, Analysis 2 portrays certain inflectional regularities as pure coincidence. In Bhojpuri verb inflection, gender is never distinguished in either the first person or the optative, nor is number ever distinguished in the second person; but in Analysis 2, these facts emerge only as accidents of the formulation of independent rules realizing the properties of first person, second person and optative mood.

A refinement of Analysis 2 that overcomes this defect is **Analysis 3**, according to which the content paradigm of DĒKH has the forty-eight cells of paradigm A while the corresponding form paradigm only has the twenty-four cells of paradigm B. On this analysis, the morphosyntactic property sets associated with the content cells in paradigm A are mapped onto the reduced property sets associated with the form cells in paradigm B by means of the property mapping *pm* in (2).

(2)     The Bhojpuri property mapping *pm*
   a.  **Intensional definition.** If $p \in \{1, 2, 3\}$, $n \in \{sg, pl\}$, $g \in \{masc, fem\}$, $t \in \{prs, pst, fut\}$ and $m \in \{ind, opt\}$ then $\{p, t, m\} \subseteq \sigma$ if and only if $\{p, t, m\} \subseteq pm(\sigma)$. If $\{g, n\} \subseteq \sigma$, then by default, $\{g, n\} \subseteq pm(\sigma)$. But:
       i.   If $\{1\ g\} \subseteq \sigma$, then $\{g\} \not\subseteq pm(\sigma)$.
       ii.  If $\{2\ n\} \subseteq \sigma$, then $\{n\} \not\subseteq pm(\sigma)$.
       iii. If $\{opt\ g\} \subseteq \sigma$, then $\{g\} \not\subseteq pm(\sigma)$.
       iv.  If $\{3\ fut\ g\} \subseteq \sigma$, then $\{g\} \not\subseteq pm(\sigma)$.
       v.   If $\sigma$ satisfies $[\{1\ n\} \wedge fut]$, then $\{n\} \not\subseteq pm(\sigma)$.
   b.  **Extensional definition.** Where $\tau$ is any of the property sets in (c) and $\tau \subseteq \sigma$, $pm(\sigma) = \tau$; otherwise, $pm(\sigma) = \sigma$.
   c.  

| | | | |
|---|---|---|---|
| {1 prs ind} | {1 opt} | {2 fem pst ind} | {3sg fut ind} |
| {1 pst ind} | {2 masc prs ind} | {2 masc fut ind} | {3pl fut ind} |
| {1 sg fut ind} | {2 fem prs ind} | {2 fem fut ind} | {3sg opt} |
| {1 pl fut ind} | {2 masc pst ind} | {2 opt} | {3pl opt} |

In Analysis 3, the property mapping *pm* explicitly captures the fact that gender is never distinguished in either the first person (2a.i) or the optative (2a.iii) and that number is never distinguished in the second person (2a.ii). And like Analysis 2, Analysis 3 does not suggest that the property coöccurrence restriction (1) has any importance at the syntactic interface, nor does it entail that domains of syncretism correspond to natural classes of morphosyntactic property sets. I conclude that Analysis 3 is preferable to its alternatives. Figure 10.1 is a schematic representation of the kind of paradigm linkage assumed by Analysis 3.

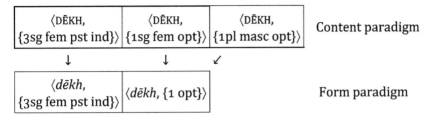

Figure 10.1 *An example of natural-class syncretism in Bhojpuri*

## 1⟨2 *Directional syncretism*

Some instances of syncretism are not simply the expression of a natural class of morphosyntactic properties (or equivalently, the expression of an underspecified set of morphosyntactic properties), but instead exhibit a kind of asymmetry in that the realization of one syncretized cell patterns after that of another. **Directional syncretisms**[1] of this sort have a "parasitic" quality, with one cell depending on another for its realization.

Turkish nominal inflection presents a striking example of directional syncretism. In Turkish, nouns inflect for case and number, but they may also inflect for the person and number of an associated possessor. Thus, Table 10.5 shows the possessor-inflected forms of the noun ADAM *fna* n.'

In general, the forms in Table 10.5 are very systematic in their realization. Consider, for example, the four realizations in Table 10.6. As these examples show, nominal inflection involves four suffixal positions. The first position is occupied by *-lar* (or its vowel-harmony alternant *-ler*) in forms denoting a plural possessum, and is unoccupied in forms denoting a singular possessum. The second and third positions are occupied by affixes expressing a possessor's person and number, respectively; for instance, *-im* signals a first-person possessor, and *-iz*, a plural possessor. (Position 3 is unoccupied if the possessor is singular.) Finally, position 4 is occupied by the relevant case suffix (but is unoccupied in the nominative case).

Although this systematic structure is embodied by most of the word forms in Table 10.5, there are certain forms that fail to conform to it: Thus, in all six cases, forms that are inflected for a third-person possessor and that entail either a plural possessum or a plural possessor (or both) are syncretized (Göksel and

---

1 For discussion of this phenomenon and its theoretical significance, see Stump 1993a, 2001: 213ff, Wunderlich 2004, Baerman, Brown and Corbett 2005: 133ff.

Table 10.5 *The possessive inflection of Turkish* ADAM *'man'*

|          | Possessor | Nominative | Accusative | Dative |
|----------|-----------|------------|------------|--------|
| Singular | 1sg | adam-ɪm | adam-ɪm-ɪ | adam-ɪm-a |
|          | 2sg | adam-ɪn | adam-ɪn-ɪ | adam-ɪn-a |
|          | 3sg | adam-ɪ | adam-ɪn-ɪ | adam-ɪn-a |
|          | 1pl | adam-ɪm-ɪz | adam-ɪm-ɪz-ɪ | adam-ɪm-ɪz-a |
|          | 2pl | adam-ɪn-ɪz | adam-ɪn-ɪz-ɪ | adam-ɪn-ɪz-a |
|          | 3pl | adam-lar-ɪ | adam-lar-ɪn-ɪ | adam-lar-ɪn-a |
| Plural   | 1sg | adam-lar-ɪm | adam-lar-ɪm-ɪ | adam-lar-ɪm-a |
|          | 2sg | adam-lar-ɪn | adam-lar-ɪn-ɪ | adam-lar-ɪn-a |
|          | 3sg | adam-lar-ɪ | adam-lar-ɪn-ɪ | adam-lar-ɪn-a |
|          | 1pl | adam-lar-ɪm-ɪz | adam-lar-ɪm-ɪz-ɪ | adam-lar-ɪm-ɪz-a |
|          | 2pl | adam-lar-ɪn-ɪz | adam-lar-ɪn-ɪz-ɪ | adam-lar-ɪn-ɪz-a |
|          | 3pl | adam-lar-ɪ | adam-lar-ɪn-ɪ | adam-lar-ɪn-a |

|          |     | Locative | Ablative | Genitive |
|----------|-----|----------|----------|----------|
| Singular | 1sg | adam-ɪm-da | adam-ɪm-dan | adam-ɪm-ɪn |
|          | 2sg | adam-ɪn-da | adam-ɪn-dan | adam-ɪn-ɪn |
|          | 3sg | adam-ɪn-da | adam-ɪn-dan | adam-ɪn-ɪn |
|          | 1pl | adam-ɪm-ɪz-da | adam-ɪm-ɪz-dan | adam-ɪm-ɪz-ɪn |
|          | 2pl | adam-ɪn-ɪz-da | adam-ɪn-ɪz-dan | adam-ɪn-ɪz-ɪn |
|          | 3pl | adam-lar-ɪn-da | adam-lar-ɪn-dan | adam-lar-ɪn-ɪn |
| Plural   | 1sg | adam-lar-ɪm-da | adam-lar-ɪm-dan | adam-lar-ɪm-ɪn |
|          | 2sg | adam-lar-ɪn-da | adam-lar-ɪn-dan | adam-lar-ɪn-ɪn |
|          | 3sg | adam-lar-ɪn-da | adam-lar-ɪn-dan | adam-lar-ɪn-ɪn |
|          | 1pl | adam-lar-ɪm-ɪz-da | adam-lar-ɪm-ɪz-dan | adam-lar-ɪm-ɪz-ɪn |
|          | 2pl | adam-lar-ɪn-ɪz-da | adam-lar-ɪn-ɪz-dan | adam-lar-ɪn-ɪz-ɪn |
|          | 3pl | adam-lar-ɪn-da | adam-lar-ɪn-dan | adam-lar-ɪn-ɪn |

Kerslake 2005: 152, Stump 2014a). For example, the form *adamlarından* has each of the three interpretations in (3). The relation among these three interpretations is asymmetrical, in the sense that (3a) is the "expected" interpretation for *adamlarından*. To judge from Table 10.6, the *-lar* in *adamlarından* should express the number of the possessum; and just as *-ɪn* expresses a singular possessor in *adamından* from your (sg)/her/his man,' it should do the same in *adamlarından*. But *adamlarından* serves to express a third-person possessor whether it is the possessum or the possessor that is plural.

Table 10.6 *Four inflectional suffix positions in Turkish nominal inflection*

| | Stem | Possessum number | Possessor | | Case | |
| | | | person | number | | |
|---|---|---|---|---|---|---|
| e.g. | *adam* | *-lar* | *-ım* | *-ız* | *-dan* | 'from our men' |
| | *adam* | – | *-ım* | *-ız* | *-dan* | 'from our man' |
| | *adam* | *-lar* | *-ım* | – | *-dan* | 'from my men' |
| | *adam* | *-lar* | *-ım* | *-ız* | – | 'our men (nominative)' |

(3)     *adam-lar-ın-dan*
      a. {NUMBER:plural, POSSESSOR:3s g} CASE:ablative}: 'from her/his men'
      b. {NUMBER:singular, POSSESSOR:3pl} CASE:ablative}: 'from their man'
      c. {NUMBER:plural, POSSESSOR:3pl} CASE:ablative}: 'from their men'

The paradigm-linkage hypothesis affords a straightforward account of this syncretism. In this account, a Turkish noun's form paradigm has fewer cells than its content paradigm: The content paradigm has seventy-two cells, the product of the six possessor properties, two number properties and six case properties in (4a); by contrast, the form paradigm has the sixty cells[2] defined in (4b), in which the third-person plural does not figure as a possessor property. The mismatch between a noun's content and form paradigms is mediated by the property mapping in (5). Given this property mapping, the definition (6) of the Turkish *Corr* function induces the many-to-one mapping of content cells to form cells in Table 10.7.

(4)     Content paradigms and form paradigms for Turkish nouns
      a. Content:     POSSESSOR:{s g, 2sg, 3sg, 1pl, 2pl, 3pl}
                    × NUMBER:{ g, pl}
                    × CASE:{nom, a cc, dat, loc, abl, gen}
      b. Form:        POSSESSOR:{s g, 2sg, 3sg, 1pl, 2pl}
                    × NUMBER:{ g, pl}
                    × CASE:{nom,   acc, dat, loc, abl, gen}

2 Given that forms specified for a second- or third-person singular possessor are identical except in the nominative, one might argue that there are fewer than sixty cells in the form paradigm of adam – that in every case but the nominative, the second- and third-person singular forms arise from the same form cell. The nominative case forms do, however, suggest a different analysis: As the expression of a third-person singular possessor, *-ın* has the alternant *-ı* in the nominative case; by contrast, *-ın* doesn't alternate as the expression of a second-person singular posses- sor. One might therefore suppose that there is a morphophonological distinction between the second-person singular suffix *-ın* and the third-person singular suffix *-ıN*, whose *N* drops word- finally but otherwise becomes *n*, neutralizing the morphophonological distinction between the two suffixes.

Table 10.7 *Schematic content and form paradigms for Turkish nouns*

**Content paradigm**

| | | N | Ac | D | L | Ab | G |
|---|---|---|---|---|---|---|---|
| Sg | 1sg | | | | | | |
| | 2sg | | | | | | |
| | 3sg | | | | | | |
| | 1pl | | | | | | |
| | 2pl | | | | | | |
| | 3pl | | | | | | |
| Pl | 1sg | | | | | | |
| | 2sg | | | | | | |
| | 3sg | | | | | | |
| | 1pl | | | | | | |
| | 2pl | | | | | | |
| | 3pl | | | | | | |

**Form paradigm**
(Each form cell is annotated with the affixal exponence by which it is realized.)

| | | N | Ac | D | L | Ab | G |
|---|---|---|---|---|---|---|---|
| Sg | 1sg | -ım | -ım-ı | -ım-a | -ım-da | -ım-dan | -ım-ın |
| | 2sg | -ın | -ın-ı | -ın-a | -ın-da | -ın-dan | -ın-ın |
| | 3sg | -ı | -ın-ı | -ın-a | -ın-da | -ın-dan | -ın-ın |
| | 1pl | -ım-ız | -ım-ız-ı | -ım-ız-a | -ım-ız-da | -ım-ız-dan | -ım-ız-ın |
| | 2pl | -ın-ız | -ın-ız-ı | -ın-ız-a | -ın-ız-da | -ın-ız-dan | -ın-ız-ın |
| | 3pl | | | | | | |
| Pl | 1sg | -lar-ım | -lar-ım-ı | -lar-ım-a | -lar-ım-da | -lar-ım-dan | -lar-ım-ın |
| | 2sg | -lar-ın | -lar-ın-ı | -lar-ın-a | -lar-ın-da | -lar-ın-dan | -lar-ın-ın |
| | 3sg | -lar-ı | -lar-ın-ı | -lar-ın-a | -lar-ın-da | -lar-ın-dan | -lar-ın-ın |
| | 1pl | -lar-ım-ız | -lar-ım-ız-ı | -lar-ım-ız-a | -lar-ım-ız-da | -lar-ım-ız-dan | -lar-ım-ız-ın |
| | 2pl | -lar-ın-ız | -lar-ın-ız-ı | -lar-ın-ız-a | -lar-ın-ız-da | -lar-ın-ız-dan | -lar-ın-ız-ın |
| | 3pl | | | | | | |

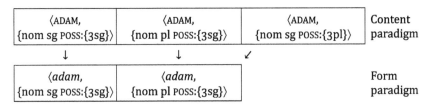

| ⟨ADAM,<br>{nom sg POSS:{3sg}}⟩ | ⟨ADAM,<br>{nom pl POSS:{3sg}}⟩ | ⟨ADAM,<br>{nom sg POSS:{3pl}}⟩ | Content<br>paradigm |
|---|---|---|---|
| ↓ | ↓ | ✓ | |
| ⟨adam,<br>{nom sg POSS:{3sg}}⟩ | ⟨adam,<br>{nom pl POSS:{3sg}}⟩ | | Form<br>paradigm |

Figure 10.2 *An example of directional syncretism in Turkish*

(5)    Definition of the Turkish property mapping ***pm***
       ***pm***({NUM:{α}  CASE:{β}  POSS:{3pl}}
       ={ NUM:{pl} , CASE:{β} POSS:{3s g}}
       otherwise, ***pm***(σ) = σ
(6)    ***Corr***(⟨L, σ⟩) = ⟨*Stem*(⟨L, σ⟩), ***pm***(σ)⟩

As this example shows, one way in which economy is achieved in a language's inflectional system is to extend the use of one content cell's form correspondent in the realization of other content cells (Figure 10.2).

In some inferential-realizational approaches to inflection, directional syncretisms are modeled by means of rules of referral – realization rules that cause the rules of exponence for one property set to be pressed into service in the realization of a contrasting property set (Zwicky 1985, Stump 1993a, 2001: 218ff). Whereas rules of referral have been postulated primarily to account for directional syncretism, property mappings can be used in modeling a variety of deviations from canonical inflection, including inflection-class distinctions (Section 7.3), morphomic properties (Section 8), deponency (Section 12) and polyfunctionality (Section 13) as well as syncretism. The use of property mappings is perhaps to be preferred, since it allows syncretism to be assimilated to a wider category of deviations.

## 1⍵  Morphomic syncretism

A syncretic form that does not express a coherent class of morphosyntactic properties may or may not exhibit the sort of directionality observed in the expression of Turkish possessor inflection (Section 10.2). In some instances, the relation between the alternative property sets expressed by a syncretic form may be symmetrical, in that neither set must be seen as deriving its exponence from that of the other set.

Consider, for example, the inflection of the Sanskrit noun KARTṚ ḥna ker,' whose paradigm (Table 10.8) presents six groups of syncretized forms. In each group, none of the syncretized property sets has a stronger claim to the shared morphology than the other property set(s). **Morphomic** (or **symmetrical**)

Table 10.8  *The declension of Sanskrit* KARTṚ
'*maker*' *(m.)*

|        | Singular  | Dual        | Plural      |
|--------|-----------|-------------|-------------|
| Nom    | *kartā*   | *kartārau*  | *kartāras*  |
| Voc    | *kartar*  | *kartārau*  | *kartāras*  |
| Acc    | *kartāram*| *kartārau*  | *kartr̄n*   |
| Ins    | *kartrā*  | *kartṛbhyām*| *kartṛbhis* |
| Dat    | *kartre*  | *kartṛbhyām*| *kartṛbhyas*|
| Abl    | *kartur*  | *kartṛbhyām*| *kartṛbhyas*|
| Gen    | *kartur*  | *kartros*   | *kartr̄ṇām* |
| Loc    | *kartari* | *kartros*   | *kartṛṣu*   |

**syncretisms**[3] of this sort suggest that in form cells, stems are paired with property sets in which certain morphosyntactic distinctions are neutralized by a morphomic property. Under this assumption, the form paradigm associated with KARTṚ contains the cells in (7); this entails that the inflection of Sanskrit nouns is subject to the property mapping defined in (8), in which **AbG**, **NVA**, **IDAb**, **GL**, **NV** and **DAb** are morphomic properties.

(7)    The form paradigm associated with the Sanskrit noun KARTṚ 'maker' (m.)
       $\langle kartṛ,$ {na sc nom sg r}$\rangle\langle kartṛ,$ {na sc **NVA** du r}$\rangle$  $\langle kartṛ,$ {masc **NV** pl r}$\rangle$
       $\langle kartṛ,$ {na sc voc sg r}$\rangle$  $\langle kartṛ,$ {masc **IDAb** du r}$\rangle$  $\langle kartṛ,$ {masc acc pl r}$\rangle$
       $\langle kartṛ,$ {na sc acc sg r}$\rangle$  $\langle kartṛ,$ {na sc **GL** du r}$\rangle$  $\langle kartṛ,$ {masc ins pl r}$\rangle$
       $\langle kartṛ,$ {na sc ins sg r}$\rangle$
       $\langle kartṛ,$ {na sc dat sg r}$\rangle$                              $\langle kartṛ,$ {masc **DAb** pl r}$\rangle$
       $\langle kartṛ,$ {na sc **AbG** sg r}$\rangle$                          $\langle kartṛ,$ {masc gen pl r}$\rangle$
       $\langle kartr.,$ {na sc loc sg r}$\rangle$                            $\langle kartṛ,$ {masc loc pl r}$\rangle$

(8)    Definition of the Sanskrit property mapping $pm_c$
       Where γ is any gender and c is the inflection-class index associated with any declension,
       a. $pm_c(\{γ \text{ abl sg}\})$       $= pm_c(\{γ \text{ gen sg}\})$       $= \{γ \textbf{ AbG} \text{ sg c}\}$,
          provided that c is not the index of the *a*-stem declension;[4]
       b. $pm_c(\{γ \text{ nom du}\})$       $= pm_c(\{γ \text{ voc du}\})$       $= pm_c(\{γ \text{ acc du}\})$
                                                                               $= \{γ \textbf{ NVA} \text{ du c}\};$
       c. $pm_c(\{γ \text{ ins du}\})$       $= pm_c(\{γ \text{ dat du}\})$       $= pm_c(\{γ \text{ abl du}\})$
                                                                               $= \{γ \textbf{ IDAb} \text{ du c}\};$
       d. $pm_c(\{γ \text{ gen du}\})$       $= pm_c(\{γ \text{ loc du}\})$       $= \{γ \textbf{ GL} \text{ du c}\};$

---

3  For detailed discussion of this phenomenon, see Stump 1993a, 2001: 222f and Baerman, Brown and Corbett 2005: 133ff.

4  The qualification on clause (8a) accommodates the fact that the *a*-stem declension actually distinguishes ablative singular and genitive singular forms, e.g. *aśvāt* from a horse,' *aśvasya* of a horse.' By contrast, the patterns of neutralization in (8b–f) hold for all declensions.

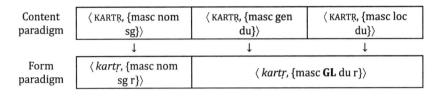

| Content paradigm | ⟨ KARTṚ, {masc nom sg}⟩ | ⟨ KARTṚ, {masc gen du}⟩ | ⟨ KARTṚ, {masc loc du}⟩ |
|---|---|---|---|
| | ↓ | ↓ | ↓ |
| Form paradigm | ⟨ kartṛ, {masc nom sg r}⟩ | ⟨ kartṛ, {masc **GL** du r}⟩ | |

Figure 10.3 *An example of morphomic syncretism in Sanskrit*

e. $pm_c(\{\gamma \text{ nom pl}\})$      $= pm_c(\{\gamma \text{ voc pl}\})$      ={ $\gamma$ **NV** pl c};

f. $pm_c(\{\gamma \text{ dat pl}\}$      $= pm_c(\{\gamma \text{ abl pl}\}$      ={ $\gamma$ **DAb** pl c}.

g. Otherwise, $pm_c(\sigma) = \sigma \cup \{$  }

The many-to-one property mapping defined in (8) produces a third kind of many-to-one relation between content cells and the form cells through whose mediation they are realized (Figure 10.3).

The phenomenon of syncretism raises a technical question concerning the paradigm-linkage model: Can rules of exponence always be used in place of property mappings in accounting for syncretism? Consider, for example, the inflection of the Latin second-declension nouns DOMINUS ṁa ster' (masculine) and DŌNUM ġift' (neuter) in Table 10.9. Typically of masculine nouns, DOMINUS exhibits distinct morphology in the nominative and accusative singular; typically of neuter nouns, DŌNUM exhibits the same morphology in the nominative and accusative singular, in both cases employing the same morphology as the accusative singular form *dominum*.

One approach to analyzing this syncretism is to formulate a property mapping that maps both ṫe ut nom sg} and ṫe ut acc sg} onto ṫe ut acc sg}, a directional syncretism. The effect of this property mapping is to produce form paradigms for neuter nouns that have fewer cells than the form paradigms of masculine nouns. Under this analysis, the content cells ⟨DŌNUM, ṫe ut nom sg}⟩ and ⟨DŌNUM, ṫe ut acc sg}⟩ share the form correspondent ⟨dōn, ṫe ut acc sg}⟩, which is realized by means of the rule of exponence in (13); this rule also serves to realize ⟨domin, ṁa sc acc sg}⟩, but ⟨domin, ṁa sc nom sg}⟩ is instead realized by means of (14).

(13)    X, N, ḁ cc sg} → X*um*

(14)    X, N, ṁ asc nom sg} → X*us*

An alternative approach is to assume that in the inflection of DŌNUM, the nominative singular and accusative singular content cells correspond to the distinct form cells in (15), but that both of these are realized by the rule of exponence in (16). This rule also serves to realize the form cell (17a), but (17b)

Table 10.9  *Singular forms of two
second-declension nouns in Latin*

|  | DOMINUS<br>ˈma ster'<br>(masculine) | DŌNUM<br>ˈgift'<br>(neuter) |
|---|---|---|
| Nom | *dominus* | *dōnum* |
| Voc | *domine* | *dōnum* |
| Gen | *dominī* | *dōnī* |
| Dat | *dominō* | *dōnō* |
| Acc | *dominum* | *dōnum* |
| Abl | *dominō* | *dōnō* |

is instead realized by means of rule (14), which overrides (16) as an effect of
Pāṇini's principle (Baerman, Brown and Corbett 2005: 134ff).

(15)   a. ⟨*dōn*, {e ut nom sg}⟩
       b. ⟨*dōn*, {e ut acc sg}⟩
(16)   X, N, [{ g} ∧ [{nom} ∨ { cc]]  → X*um*
(17)   a. ⟨*domin*, {ma sc acc sg}⟩
       b. ⟨*domin*, {ma sc nom sg}⟩

Although these two analyses might seem to be equally workable, the former,
property-mapping analysis is superior, since it entails that in the inflection of
neuter nouns, the syncretism of nominative and accusative is not simply a local
characteristic of rules such as (16), but is a general pattern that holds true of
neuter nouns having any sort of accusative morphology. The rule of exponence
analysis misses this generalization.

## *10.4   Conclusion*

Syncretism invariably involves a pattern of paradigm linkage in which two or
more content cells share a single form correspondent. As I have shown, patterns of this kind can arise in more than one way. They can arise through a kind
of "impoverishment" (Bonet 1991), by which morphosyntactic distinctions
that are relevant for syntax and semantics are simply unavailable for realization
by a language's inflectional morphology.[5] They can also arise as the effect of a

5  In his model of Kayardild inflection, Round (2013: 72f) characterizes certain pairs of morphosyntactic feature values as "antagonistic"; where the feature values F and G are antagonistic,
   a word's syntax may depend on its association with both F and G, but F and G cannot both be
   overtly realized in that word's inflection. This phenomenon can be seen as involving a property
   mapping that systematically reduces a property set containing F and G to one containing either
   F or G but not both.

property mapping that causes a morphosyntactic property set relevant for syntax and semantics to be realized by means of the morphology that is usual for realizing a contrasting property set. And they can arise through the introduction of a morpheme whose realization neutralizes a distinction that is relevant for syntax and semantics and therefore expresses a kind of disjunctive content.

The phenomenon of syncretism is an important kind of evidence for both the irreducibility hypothesis ("Some morphological regularities are, irreducibly, regularities in paradigm structure"; Section 1.3.1) and the interface hypothesis ("Paradigms are the interfaces of inflectional morphology with syntax and semantics"; Section 1.3.2). Because the same syncretic pattern may be embodied by different morphology in different paradigms or in different cells of the same paradigm, syncretism is, irreducibly, a characteristic of inflectional paradigms: One realized cell $\langle w, \sigma \rangle$ is syncretized with another realized cell $\langle w, \tau \rangle$ by virtue of (i) the identity of their forms, (ii) the distinctness of their property sets, and (iii) the fact that (i) and (ii) recurrently coincide independently of the particular shared morphology involved. And syncretism is clearly an interface phenomenon: Paradigm cells that are associated with different syntactic contexts and with different semantic interpretations may nevertheless be treated identically by a language's inflectional morphology.

# 11 *Suppletion and heteroclisis*

In a realized paradigm of the canonical sort, all word forms share the same stem. It is nevertheless extremely common for a realized paradigm to exhibit two or more stems in alternation. In Section 5.2, we saw that when stem Y alternates with stem Z in a realized paradigm, the relation between Y and Z may be of three different kinds.

- Y and Z are **sandhi alternants** if principles of automatic phonology determine the choice between Y and Z. Distinctions between sandhi alternants needn't be represented at all in form paradigms, since they may be assumed to be introduced by the phonological component.
- Y and Z are **class-determined** (or **kindred**) **stems** if they form part of the inflectional pattern of a single inflection class. Within a form paradigm, different cells may have different stems provided that they are kindred stems.
- Y and Z are **independent stems** if their difference in form does not follow from their membership in a particular inflection class. Stems that are independent of each other but which realize the same lexeme may belong to the same inflection class or to different inflection classes. In either case, their alternation is **suppletive**; in the latter case, their alternation is additionally **heteroclitic**.

In this chapter, I examine paradigms exhibiting two or more independent stems in alternation. I begin with an overview of suppletive and heteroclitic alternations and of the ways in which such alternations may be conditioned (Section 11.1). In Section 11.2, I show how the paradigm-linkage hypothesis elucidates the properties of suppletion and heteroclisis, then focus attention on the implications of suppletion for morphological theory (Section 11.3).

Table 11.1  *The heteroclite declension of Latin* ARX *'citadel' (f.)*

(Arrows indicate cells in which the declension of TUSSIS and that of PRĪNCEPS
are indistinguishable.)

|  |  | TUSSIS (f.) ċ ough' | ARX (f.) ċ itadel' | | PRĪNCEPS (m.) 'chief' |
|---|---|---|---|---|---|
| Declension: | | 3ʳᵈ, i-stem | | 3ʳᵈ, C-stem | |
| Singular | Nom | *tussis* | | ⠇ *ar*[ks] | *prīnceps* |
| | Gen | *tussis* | ← *arcis*→ | | *prīncipis* |
| | Dat | *tussī* | ← *arcī*→ | | *prīncipī* |
| | Acc | *tussim* | | ⠇ *arcem* | *prīncipem* |
| | Voc | *tussis* | | ⠇ *ar*[ks] | *prīnceps* |
| | Abl | *tussī* | | ⠇ *arce* | *prīncipe* |
| Plural | Nom | *tussēs* | ← *arcēs*→ | | *prīncipēs* |
| | Gen | *tussium* | *arcium* ⠇ | | *prīncipum* |
| | Dat | *tussibus* | ← *arcibus*→ | | *prīncipibus* |
| | Ac | *tussīs, ēs* | *arcīs, ēs* ⠇ | | *prīncipēs* |
| | Voc | *tussēs* | ← *arcēs*→ | | *prīncipēs* |
| | Abl | *tussibus* | ← *arcibus*→ | | *prīncipibus* |

## 11.1  Suppletive and heteroclitic alternations

Suppletion is an alternation between independent stems in a lexeme's paradigm. In the clearest cases, the alternating stems lack any phonological similarity; thus, *go ~ went*, *bad ~ worse* and *be ~ am ~ are ~ is ~ was* are textbook
examples of suppletion. But suppletion may also be assumed to include stems
which, though independent, nevertheless exhibit a partial similarity in form;
thus, *can ~ could*, *was ~ were* and *better ~ best* are also examples of suppletion,
though of a slightly more subtle sort.

Heteroclisis is the property of a suppletive paradigm whose independent
stems belong to distinct inflection classes. An example is the inflection of Latin
ARX ċ itadel,' in which some forms are based on a stem *arc* belonging to the
same subclass of the third declension as PRĪNCEPS ċ hief,' while other forms
are based on a stem *arci* belonging to the same subclass of the third declension
as TUSSIS ċ ough.' (See Table 11.1.) The stems *arc* and *arci* deviate from the
clearest cases of suppletion by virtue of their similarity in form; even so, they
are independent stems belonging to distinct declensions.

Certain forms in the paradigm of ARX are ambiguous with respect to their
conjugation-class affiliation; for instance, the morphology of the genitive

Table 11.2 *The heteroclite declension of Sanskrit* AHAN *'day' (n.)*

| | | NĀMAN (n.) ħa me' | | AHAN (n.) 'day' | MANAS (n.) 'mind' |
|---|---|---|---|---|---|
| Declension: | | neuter *an*-stem | | | neuter *as*-stem |
| Singular | Nom, Voc, Acc | *nāma* | | *ahas* | *manas* |
| | Instr | *nāmnā* | *ahnā* | | *manasā* |
| | Dat | *nāmne* | *ahne* | | *manase* |
| | Abl, Gen | *nāmnas* | *ahnas* | | *manasas* |
| | Loc | *nāmni* | *ahni* | | *manasi* |
| Dual | Nom, Voc, Acc | *nāmnī* | *ahnī* | | *manasī* |
| | Instr, Dat, Abl | *nāmabhyām* | | *ahobhyām* | *manobhyām* |
| | Gen, Loc | *nāmnos* | *ahnos* | | *manasos* |
| Plural | Nom, Voc, Acc | *nāmāni* | *ahāni* | | *manāṃsi* |
| | Instr | *nāmabhis* | | *ahobhis* | *manobhis* |
| | Dat, Abl | *nāmabhyas* | | *ahobhyas* | *manobhyas* |
| | Gen | *nāmnām* | *ahnām* | | *manasām* |
| | Loc | *nāmasu* | | *ahaḥsu* | *manaḥsu* |

singular form *arcis* could be like that of *prīncip-is* or instead like that of *tussi-s*. But not all heteroclite paradigms exhibit such points of overlap between their component inflection classes; for instance, there is no overlap in the inflection of Sanskrit AHAN ɗa y' (Table 11.2).

Notwithstanding the points of overlap between the two declensions in the inflection of Latin ARX, the obvious generalization is that ARX inflects like TUSSIS in the singular but like PRĪNCEPS in the plural. Thus, in the inflection of ARX, the alternation between declensional patterns is morphosyntactically conditioned.

Heteroclisis has a close kinship with the phenomenon of segregated inflection classes (Section 6.2): Both involve the coexistence, within a single realized paradigm, of stems belonging to distinct inflection classes. The only essential difference between the two phenomena is a rather trivial one: Heteroclitic paradigms are exceptions set against a backdrop of nonheteroclitic paradigms, while segregated inflection classes are a systemic property of a language's inflectional morphology. Heteroclisis may be a characteristic of some members of a given syntactic category, but if the inflection classes of some syntactic category are segregated, that separation is observable in the inflection of all members of that category.

Table 11.3 *The declension of two Vedic Sanskrit nominals*

|  |  | Singular | Dual | Plural |
|---|---|---|---|---|
| DEVÍ (f.) | Nom | *devī́* | *devī́* | *devī́-s* |
| 'godde ss' | Voc | *dévi* | *dévī* | *dévī-s* |
|  | Acc | *devī́-m* | *devī́* | *devī́-s* |
|  | Ins | *devy-ā́* | *devī́-bhyām* | *devī́-bhis* |
|  | Dat | *devy-ái* | *devī́-bhyām* | *devī́-bhyas* |
|  | Abl | *devy-ā́s* | *devī́-bhyām* | *devī́-bhyas* |
|  | Gen | *devy-ā́s* | *devy-ós* | *devī́-n-ām* |
|  | Loc | *devy-ā́m* | *devy-ós* | *devī́-ṣu* |
| śÚCI bright' | Nom | *śúci-s* | *śúcī* | *śúcay-as* |
| (feminine forms) | Voc | *śúce* | *śúcī* | *śúcay-as* |
|  | Acc | *śúci-m* | *śúcī* | *śúcī-s* |
|  | Ins | *śúcy-ā ~ śúcī ~ śúci* | *śúci-bhyām* | *śúci-bhis* |
|  | Dat | *śúcay-e* | *śúci-bhyām* | *śúci-bhyas* |
|  | Abl | *śúce-s* | *śúci-bhyām* | *śúci-bhyas* |
|  | Gen | *śúce-s* | *śúcy-os* | *śúcī-n-ām* |
|  | Loc | *śúcā ~ śúcau* | *śúcy-os* | *śúci-ṣu* |

Heteroclisis always involves some kind of partial similarity between realized paradigms, but not all instances of such partial similarity should be
attributed to heteroclisis. Consider, for example, the forms of the feminine
noun DEVÍ 'goddess' and the feminine forms of the adjective śÚCI 'bright' in
Vedic Sanskrit (Table 11.3). These two realized paradigms are in some respects alike and in other respects different; the similarities are in the shaded
cells. While one might suppose that this partial similarity is a sign that one
of the paradigms is heteroclite, there is, in fact, a better explanation for it.
Very often, systems of inflection classes have default exponents that surface
as part of the pattern of more than one class. In the realized paradigms of
DEVÍ and śÚCI, the points of inflectional similarity are precisely those cells
in which their inflection classes share the default exponence. Moreover, the
inflection classes to which DEVÍ and śÚCI belong each have a large number
of members; that is, their inflectional patterns do not have the exceptional
character typical of heteroclitic paradigms.

Suppletive alternations (including heteroclitic alternations) may be conditioned
in three ways. Some alternations are phonologically conditioned: The choice between suppletive alternants is determined by the phonological context created by
their inflection. Thus, the inflection of Sanskrit AHAN 'day' (Table 11.2) follows

the *an*-stem declension (with the kindred stems *ahn-/ahān-*) in the presence of a suffix-initial vowel; otherwise, it follows the *as*-stem declension (with the stem *ahas-*, whose sandhi forms include *aho-* and *ahaḥ-*).

In instances of morphosyntactically conditioned suppletion, the choice of inflection class in the realization of a paradigm's individual cells is directly determined by the morphosyntactic property sets expressed by those cells; as noted above, the alternation exhibited by Latin ARX is morphosyntactically conditioned.

Cases of morphologically conditioned suppletion are those in which a choice between independent stems is determined by an independently observable pattern of alternation among kindred stems. In Sanskrit, for example, we have seen that masculine nominals exhibit a distinctive pattern of stem alternation in many declensions (Section 6.4). In this pattern, the strong stem appears in the nominative, vocative and accusative singular and dual as well as in the nominative and vocative plural; elsewhere, the weak stem appears.[1] This pattern of stem alternation is exhibited by the paradigm of PAD foot, ' in which the strong stem is *pād-*, and the weak stem, *pad-* (Table 11.4). The heteroclitic paradigm of MĀS month ' exhibits a pattern of suppletive stem alternation that is subject to this same morphological conditioning: Its strong stem is *māsa-*, which inflects according to the *a*-stem declension, and its weak stem is *mās-* (sandhi variant *mād-*), which inflects according to the C-stem declension (Table 11.5). As with the *pād-* ~ *pad-* alternation in Table 11.4, the *māsa-* ~ *mās-*alternation in Table 11.5 conforms to a pattern that is morphosyntactically incoherent (in other words, a morphomic pattern).

## *11.2 Suppletion and the paradigm-linkage hypothesis*

A suppletive paradigm often has the appearance of a group of defective paradigms that complement each other to form a nondefective, patchwork paradigm. In Latin, for example, the verb FERRE ċ arry' exhibits a stem *tul-* in finite perfect forms (e.g. *tulī* I have carried'), another stem *lā-* in the future active participle, the perfect passive participle and the supine (*lātus* ċ arried'), and a third stem *fer-* in the remaining forms (*ferō* I carry'). Such cases might be regarded as involving a single content paradigm, different parts of which draw their form correspondents from different form paradigms (Figure 11.1), in accordance with the Latin ***Stem*** function, partially defined in (1).

---

1 In the inflection of many nominals, the weak stem itself has two forms: a weakest stem appearing prevocalically and a middle stem appearing elsewhere; see Section 6.4.

Table 11.4 *The declension of Sanskrit* PAD *'foot' (m.)*

|        | Singular | Dual      | Plural   |
|--------|----------|-----------|----------|
| Nom    | *pād*    | *pādau*   | *pādas*  |
| Voc    | *pād*    | *pādau*   | *pādas*  |
| Acc    | *pādam*  | *pādau*   | *padas*  |
| Instr  | *padā*   | *padbhyām*| *padbhis*|
| Dat    | *pade*   | *padbhyām*| *padbhyas*|
| Abl    | *padas*  | *padbhyām*| *padbhyas*|
| Gen    | *padas*  | *pados*   | *padām*  |
| Loc    | *padi*   | *pados*   | *patsu*  |

Table 11.5 *The heteroclite inflection of Sanskrit* MĀS *'month' (m.)*

| Declension: | | AŚVA (m.) hors e' | | MĀS (m.) mont h' | | MARUT (m.) 'wind' |
|---|---|---|---|---|---|---|
| | | *a*-stem | | | C-stem | |
| Singular | Nom | *aśvas* | *māsas* | | | *marut* |
| | Voc | *aśva* | *māsa* | | | *marut* |
| | Acc | *aśvam* | | ← *māsam* → | | *marutam* |
| | Instr | *aśvena* | | | *māsā* | *marutā* |
| | Dat | *aśvāya* | | | *māse* | *marute* |
| | Abl | *aśvāt* | | | *māsas* | *marutas* |
| | Gen | *aśvasya* | | | *māsas* | *marutas* |
| | Loc | *aśve* | | | *māsi* | *maruti* |
| Dual | Nom,Voc, Acc | *aśvau* | | ← *māsau* → | | *marutau* |
| | Instr, Dat, Abl | *aśvābhyām* | | | *mādbhyām* | *marudbhyām* |
| | Gen, Loc | *aśvayos* | | | *māsos* | *marutos* |
| Plural | Nom, Voc | *aśvās* | *māsās* | | | *marutas* |
| | Acc | *aśvān* | | | *māsas* | *marutas* |
| | Instr | *aśvais* | | | *mādbhis* | *marudbhis* |
| | Dat, Abl | *aśvebhyas* | | | *mādbhyas* | *marudbhyas* |
| | Gen | *aśvānām* | | | *māsām* | *marutām* |
| | Loc | *aśveṣu* | | | *māssu* | *marutsu* |

(1)    Partial definition of the Latin **Stem** function

   **Stem**(⟨FERRE, σ:{ nite perf}⟩) = *tul*

   **Stem**(⟨FERRE, σ⟩) = *lā* if σ satisfies [{pa rticiple} ∧ [{future} ∨ {past}]]

   **Stem**(⟨FERRE, σ⟩) = *fer* otherwise.

I assume that in general, the property set σ of a form cell ⟨Z, σ⟩ includes the specification of stem Z's inflection-class membership. Thus, if a lexeme has

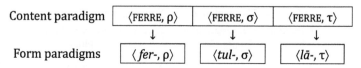

Figure 11.1 *The suppletion of Latin* FERRE *'carry'*

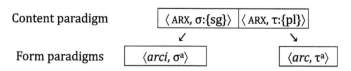

Figure 11.2 *The heteroclisis of Latin* ARX *'citadel'*

the suppletive stem alternants $Z_1$, $Z_2$ and these belong to the distinct inflection classes A, B, then for any form cells $\langle Z_1, \sigma \rangle$, $\langle Z_2, \tau \rangle$, it must be the case that $A \in \sigma$ and $B \in \tau$. To make this explicit, suppose that the inflection class C to which stem Z belongs is the value of a function *ic* applied to Z: $ic(Z) = C$. We can then introduce the simplifying notation in (2); with this notation, the heteroclisis of Latin ARX may be represented schematically as in Figure 11.2. This representation presupposes the (partial) definitions in (3) and (4) for the Latin *Corr* and *Stem* functions.

(2)    Augmented MPS notation. Given a stem Z and a property set $\sigma$, $\langle Z, \sigma^a \rangle$
       represents $\langle Z, \sigma \cup ic(Z) \rangle$.

(3)    Partial definition of the Latin *Corr* function:
       $Corr(\langle L, \sigma \rangle) = \langle Stem(\langle L, \sigma \rangle), \sigma^a \rangle$

(4)    More clauses in the definition of the Latin *Stem* function
       $Stem(\langle ARX, \sigma:\{ g\} \rangle) = arci(\in 3^{rd}$ Declension/*i*-stem)
       $Stem(\langle ARX, \sigma:pl\} \rangle) = arc(\in 3^{rd}$ Declension/C-stem)

The clauses in the definition of the Latin *Stem* function given in (1) and (4) entail that the alternation of suppletive stems in the paradigms of FERRE and ARX is morphosyntactically conditioned. By contrast, the *SC* operation (Section 5.5.2) serves to account for phonologically conditioned suppletion. For example, the Sanskrit *Stem* function applies to cells in the content paradigm of AHAN *da y'* to yield the values defined in (5), in which *SC* has the deferred interpretation in (6).

(5)    $Stem(\langle AHAN, \{$e  ut acc pl$\} \rangle)$  $= ah\bar{a}n$
       Otherwise, $Stem(\langle AHAN, \sigma \rangle)$  $= SC(ahas)$

(6)    $SC(ahas)$  $= ahn$ prevocalically
                    $ahas$ otherwise

The morphologically conditioned alternation of the suppletive stems of Sanskrit MĀS 'month' is ultimately a matter of lexical listing: The lexical entry of MĀS specifies that it has *māsa-* (∈ *a*-stem declension) as its Strong stem and *mās-* (∈ C-stem declension) as its Weak stem. The distribution of these stems (with their declensional characteristics) in the form paradigm associated with MĀS is determined by the **Stem** function, in accordance with the default stipulations in (7) (from Section 6.4).

(7)    a. Where σ satisfies property constraint (8), **Stem**($\langle$L, σ$\rangle$) = L's Strong stem
       b. Otherwise, **Stem**($\langle$L, σ$\rangle$) = **SC**(Z), where Z is L's Middle[2] stem

(8)    [[{nom} ∨ {voc} ∨ {cc} ∧ [{he ut pl} ∨ [[{na sc} ∨ {fem}] ∧ ¬{acc pl}]]]

## *11.3  Generalizations abut  suppletion*

Suppletive inflectional paradigms vary in the complexity of the conditions that determine the alternation of their stems. In the simplest cases, the alternation of stems in a suppletive paradigm depends on a single inflectional category. In the heteroclitic paradigm of Latin ARX 'itadel,' the alternation between the *i*-stem *arci-* and the C-stem *arc-* depends only on number: *arci-* is the basis for every singular case-form and *arc-* is invariably the basis for the corresponding plural form. Stump (2006) refers to suppletive paradigms of this type – in which the choice of stem correlates with properties belonging to a single inflectional category – as "cloven" paradigms.[3] Not all suppletive paradigms are cloven; in the heteroclitic paradigm of Latin DOMUS 'hous e,' the choice between the second-declension and fourth-declension stems does not correlate with properties in a single inflectional category, but rather with combinations of number properties with case properties (Table 11.6). The paradigm of DOMUS is therefore "fractured" rather than cloven.

If cloven paradigms are thought of as a canonical extreme, then fractured paradigms are deviations from this extreme. Stump (2006) proposes a measure of "A-correlation" as a way of comparing degrees of such deviation. Where P is a realized paradigm that is suppletive and A is an inflectional category having $v_1, \dots, v_m$ as its possible values, the degree of A-correlation in P is defined as in (9).

---

2  For a nominal L that does not have distinct Middle and Weakest forms, I equate L's Weak stem with its Middle and Weakest stems. Given that equation, (7b) entails that **Stem**($\langle$MĀS, σ$\rangle$) = *mās-* (∈ C-stem declension) when σ doesn't satisfy (8).

3  Stump's discussion focuses strictly on heteroclitic paradigms, but the distinction at issue extends naturally to suppletive stem alternations of any kind.

Table 11.6 *The heteroclite declension of Classical Latin* DOMUS *'house' (f.)*

| | | DOMINUS (m.) fna ster' | DOMUS (f.) 'house' | | PORTUS (m.) 'port' |
|---|---|---|---|---|---|
| Declension: | | 2nd | | 4th | |
| Singular | Nom | *dominus* | ← *domus* → | | *portus* |
| | Gen | *dominī* | | *domūs* | *portūs* |
| | Dat | *dominō* | | *domuī* | *portuī* |
| | Acc | *dominum* | ← *domum* → | | *portum* |
| | Abl | *dominō* | *domō* | | *portū* |
| | Voc | *domine* | | *domus* | *portus* |
| | Loc | ( = gen) | *domī* | | ( = abl) |
| Plural | Nom | *dominī* | | *domūs* | *portūs* |
| | Gen | *dominōrum* | *domōrum* | | *portuum* |
| | Dat | *dominīs* | | *domibus* | *portibus* |
| | Acc | *dominōs* | *domōs* | *domūs* | *portūs* |
| | Abl | *dominīs* | | *domibus* | *portibus* |
| | Voc | *dominī* | | *domūs* | *portūs* |
| | Loc | ( = abl) | *domīs* | | ( = abl) |

(9)     Let y be the number of cells in P and for each value $v_i$ in $\{v_1, .., v_m\}$, let $n_i$ be the largest number of cells in P that carry the specification $v_i$ and are based on the same stem. In that case, the **degree of A-correlation in P** is x/y, where x is the sum of $n_1, .., n_m$.

By definition, every cloven paradigm P has an inflectional category A such that the degree of A-correlation in P is 1.0; in that case, we can say that A is the **absolute correlate** of P's suppletion. Thus, because the degree of number correlation in the paradigm of Latin ARX is 1.0, number is the absolute correlate of suppletion in this paradigm. By contrast, the degree of case correlation in the paradigm of ARX is only 0.5 (= 6/12). In the fractured paradigm of DOMUS hous e,' there is no absolute correlate of suppletion: The degree of number correlation is 0.7 (10/14), while the degree of case correlation is 0.9 (12/14).

Languages vary with respect to the inflectional categories that serve as their absolute correlates of suppletion. In Latin, number is the absolute correlate of suppletion in nominal paradigms, as in the inflection of ARX 'citadel'; case is not. In Sanskrit, by contrast, the reverse is true. In the cloven paradigm of Sanskrit HṚDAYA 'heart' (Table 11.7), case is the absolute correlate of suppletion: The *a*-stem alternant *hṛdaya-* appears in the nominative, vocative and accusative cases of all three numbers; in the remaining cases, the C-stem

Table 11.7 *The heteroclite declension of Sanskrit* HṚDAYA *'heart'*

|  |  | ĀSYA (n.)<br>ṁouth' | HṚDAYA (n.)<br>he art' | | TRIVṚT<br>'threefold'<br>(neuter forms) |
|---|---|---|---|---|---|
|  | Declension: | neuter *a*-stem | | | neuter C-stem |
| Singular | Nom | *āsyam* | *hṛdayam* |  | *trivṛt* |
|  | Voc | *āsya* | *hṛdaya* |  | *trivṛt* |
|  | Acc | *āsyam* | *hṛdayam* |  | *trivṛt* |
|  | Instr | *āsyena* |  | *hṛdā* | *trivṛtā* |
|  | Dat | *āsyāya* |  | *hṛde* | *trivṛte* |
|  | Abl | *āsyāt* |  | *hṛdas* | *trivṛtas* |
|  | Gen | *āsyasya* |  | *hṛdas* | *trivṛtas* |
|  | Loc | *āsye* |  | *hṛdi* | *trivṛti* |
| Dual | Nom,Voc, Acc | *āsye* | *hṛdaye* |  | *trivṛtī* |
|  | Instr, Dat, Abl | *āsyābhyām* |  | *hṛdbhyām* | *trivṛdbhyām* |
|  | Gen, Loc | *āsyayos* |  | *hṛdos* | *trivṛtos* |
| Plural | Nom, Voc, Acc | *āsyāni* | *hṛdayāni* |  | *trivṛnti* |
|  | Instr | *āsyāis* |  | *hṛdbhis* | *trivṛdbhis* |
|  | Dat, Abl | *āsyebhyas* |  | *hṛdbhyas* | *trivṛdbhyas* |
|  | Gen | *āsyānām* |  | *hṛdām* | *trivṛtām* |
|  | Loc | *āsyeṣu* |  | *hṛtsu* | *trivṛtsu* |

alternant *hṛd-* instead appears. By contrast, number is not an absolute correlate of suppletion in Sanskrit. This typological generalization is irreducibly a generalization about paradigms; as such, it favors the irreducibility hypothesis (Section 1.3.1).

Let an inflectional category A be the **maximal correlate** of a paradigm P's suppletion if and only if the degree of A-correlation is higher than any other inflectional category's degree of correlation in P; in that case, the maximal correlate of suppletion is number in the paradigm of ARX and case in the paradigm of DOMUS. Stump (2006) presents evidence that in a given language, the inflectional categories appearing as maximal correlates in fractured paradigms tend to be the same as those appearing as absolute correlates in cloven paradigms belonging to the same syntactic category; he notes, however, that this is no more than a tendency (as the examples of ARX and DOMUS suggest). At the same time, a weaker correspondence does seem to exist between cloven paradigms and their fractured counterparts.

Where P is a fractured paradigm and $A_1, \ldots, A_n$ are inflectional categories, the intersective correlates of P's suppletion are defined as in (10).

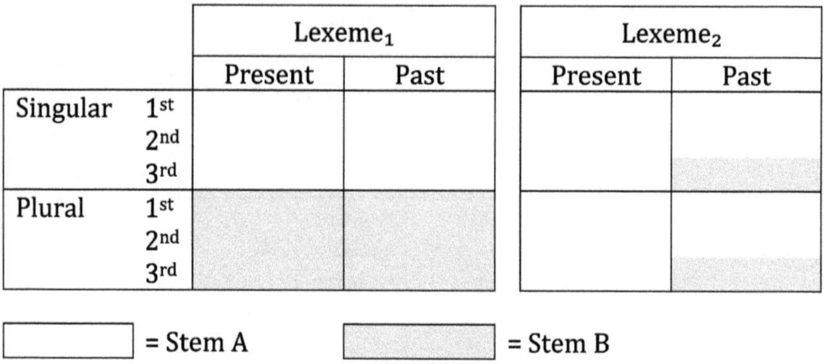
Lexeme₁
Present
Past
Lexeme₂
Present
Past
Singular
1st
2nd
3rd
Plural
1st
2nd
3rd
= Stem A
= Stem B

Figure 11.3 *Coöccurrence of cloven and fractured paradigms incompatible with the MIC hypothesis*

(10) If for each well-formed property set $\tau$ that is specified for exactly the categories $A_1$, ,.. $A_n$ there is a single stem Z such that every cell in P that realizes $\tau$ is based on Z, then $A_1$, ,.. $A_n$ are **intersective correlates** of P's suppletion. In addition, the inflectional categories $A_1$, ,.. $A_n$ are **minimal intersective correlates** of P's suppletion if and only if there is no proper subset of {$A_1$, ,.. $A_n$}w hose members are intersective correlates of P's suppletion.

Given this definition, suppose now that S is the set of inflectional categories each of whose members serves as the absolute correlate of suppletion in a cloven paradigm of a lexeme belonging to syntactic category C in language $\ell$. In that case, a plausible hypothesis is that every fractured paradigm of category C in $\ell$ has a member of S as one of its minimal intersective correlates (= the minimal intersective correlate [MIC] hypothesis).

Consider an example. As Table 11.8 shows, the paradigm of the West Armenian verb GAL 'come' is cloven, and that of LAL 'cry' is fractured. Tense is the absolute correlate of suppletion in the paradigm of GAL, and tense, person and number are the minimal intersective correlates of suppletion in the paradigm of LAL; thus, the paradigms in Table 11.8 are compatible with the MIC hypothesis. What this hypothesis excludes is the possibility exemplified by the hypothetical case in Figure 11.3: In this example, number is the absolute correlate of $\text{Lexeme}_1$'s suppletion, but contrary to the MIC hypothesis, it is person and tense (and not number) that are the minimal intersective correlates of $\text{Lexeme}_2$'s suppletion.

The MIC hypothesis is irreducibly a hypothesis about paradigms; should this hypothesis be borne out, it provides additional support for the irreducibility hypothesis (Section 1.3.1), strengthening the case against the viability of paradigm-free approaches to inflectional morphology.

Table 11.8 *The heteroclite inflection of West Armenian* GAL *'come' and* LAL *'cry' (indicative forms)*

| | | TESNEL 'see' | GAL 'come' | KARDAL 'read' | LAL 'cry' | XŌSIL 'speak' |
|---|---|---|---|---|---|---|
| | | 1st Conjugation of secondary verbs | 3rd Conjugation of primary verbs | | | 2nd Conjugation of primary verbs |
| Present | 1sg | kə tesnem | kū gam | kə kardam | kū lam | kə xōsim |
| | 2sg | kə tesnes | kū gas | kə kardas | kū las | kə xōsis |
| | 3sg | kə tesnē | kū gay | kə karday | kū lay | kə xōsi |
| | 1pl | kə tesnenk' | kū gank' | kə kardank' | kū lank' | kə xōsink' |
| | 2pl | kə tesnēk' | kū gak' | kə kardak' | kū lak' | kə xōsik' |
| | 3pl | kə tesnen | kū gan | kə kardan | kū lan | kə xōsin |
| Impfect | 1sg | kə tesnēi | kū gayi | kə kardayi | kū layi | kə xōsēi |
| | 2sg | kə tesnēir | kū gayir | kə kardayir | kū layir | kə xōsēir |
| | 3sg | kə tesnēr | kū gar | kə kardar | kū lar | kə xōsēr |
| | 1pl | kə tesnēink' | kū gayink' | kə kardayink' | kū layink' | kə xōsēink' |
| | 2pl | kə tesnēik' | kū gayik' | kə kardayik' | kū layik' | kə xōsēik' |
| | 3pl | kə tesnēin | kū gayin | kə kardayin | kū layin | kə xōsēin |
| Aorist | 1sg | tesay | yekay | kardaċi | laċi | xōseċay |
| | 2sg | tesar | yekar | kardaċir | laċir | xōseċar |
| | 3sg | tesav | yekav | kardaċ | laċav | xōseċav |
| | 1pl | tesank' | yekank' | kardaċink' | laċink' | xōseċank' |
| | 2pl | tesak' | yekak' | kardaċik' | laċik' | xōseċak' |
| | 3pl | tesan | yekan | kardaċin | laċin | xōseċan |

*Source:* Kogian 1949

More generally, the phenomenon of suppletion (which properly includes the phenomenon of heteroclisis) provides strong motivation for the paradigm-linkage hypothesis: It shows that what is homogeneous at the level of content – the regular pairing of a lexeme with the morphosyntactic property sets with which it may be associated in syntax – may be heterogeneous in its formal expression, which may involve stems that are phonologically unrelated and belong to distinct inflection classes.

# 12 *Deponency and metaconjugation*

Among the most striking kinds of evidence supporting the paradigm-linkage hypothesis is the phenomenon of deponency.[1] The classic instance of this phenomenon is that of Latin deponent verbs, whose defining feature is that their active forms inflect by means of the morphology that ordinarily serves to express a verb's passive forms; thus, a deponent verb's passive forms have "laid aside" (Latin *deponere* ʻa y aside') their passive function in favor of an active function. Although Latin deponent verbs present a content–form mismatch with respect to voice, deponency in the general sense may, in principle, involve mismatches with respect to any inflectional category. Mismatches of this kind must often be seen as interface phenomena, and in the case of deponency and related marvels, the dimensions of this interface are those of the paradigm.

In this chapter, I discuss the properties of Latin deponency as canonical characteristics of the phenomenon (Section 12.1), then contrast some phenomena from Sanskrit (Section 12.2) and Kashmiri (Section 12.3) that deviate in certain respects from the example of Latin verbs. I examine a complex case from Old Norse in which deponency interacts with heteroclisis (Section 12.4), concluding in Section 12.5.

## 12.1 *Latin deponent verb*

Latin verbs exhibit segregated conjugation classes (Section 6.2), but are traditionally classified by their imperfective conjugation, according to which there

---

1 The focus in this chapter is on **form deponency** – the use of the same inflectional morphology to realize distinct morphosyntactic content in distinct paradigms. This may be distinguished from **property deponency** – the use of the same morphosyntactic properties to represent distinct content in distinct paradigms; see Stump 2007, Müller 2013.

Table 12.1 *The imperfective present indicative inflection of five Latin verbs*

|  |  | I<br>PARĀRE<br>þre pare' | II<br>MONĒRE<br>te mind' | III<br>REGERE<br>tul e' | III (-iō)<br>CAPERE<br>'take' | IV<br>AUDĪRE<br>'hear' |
|---|---|---|---|---|---|---|
| Active | 1sg | parō | moneō | regō | capiō | audiō |
|  | 2sg | parās | monēs | regis | capis | audīs |
|  | 3sg | parat | monet | regit | capit | audit |
|  | 1pl | parāmus | monēmus | regimus | capimus | audīmus |
|  | 2pl | parātis | monētis | regitis | capitis | audītis |
|  | 3pl | parant | monent | regunt | capiunt | audiunt |
| Passive | 1sg | paror | moneor | regor | capior | audior |
|  | 2sg | parāris | monēris | regeris | caperis | audīris |
|  | 3sg | parātur | monētur | regitur | capitur | audītur |
|  | 1pl | parāmur | monēmur | regimur | capimur | audīmur |
|  | 2pl | parāminī | monēminī | regiminī | capiminī | audīminī |
|  | 3pl | parantur | monentur | reguntur | capiuntur | audiuntur |

Table 12.2 *The imperfective present indicative inflection of five deponent verbs in Latin*

|  |  | I<br>CŌNĀRĪ<br>try' | II<br>VERĒRĪ<br>fe ar, respect' | III<br>LĀBĪ<br>š lip, fall' | III (-iō)<br>PATĪ<br>'allow, suffer' | IV<br>INGREDĪ<br>'enter' |
|---|---|---|---|---|---|---|
| Active | 1sg | cōnor | vereor | lābor | patior | ingredior |
|  | 2sg | cōnāris | verēris | lāberis | pateris | ingrederis |
|  | 3sg | cōnātur | verētur | lābitur | patitur | ingreditur |
|  | 1pl | cōnāmur | verēmur | lābimur | patimur | ingredimur |
|  | 2pl | cōnāminī | verēminī | lābiminī | patiminī | ingrediminī |
|  | 3pl | cōnantur | verentur | lābuntur | patiuntur | ingrediuntur |
| Passive |  | (none) | (none) | (none) | (none) | (none) |

are four main conjugations, with Conjugation III subdivided into the REGERE-type conjugation on the one hand and the CAPERE-type conjugation – sometimes labeled the "III (-iō) conjugation" – on the other. Transitive verbs in each conjugation inflect for both active and passive voices, as in Table 12.1. What is striking is that Latin has certain verbs – the deponent verbs – that lack synthetic forms expressing a passive meaning, but whose active forms employ the morphology that is ordinarily reserved for expressing a passive meaning. As Table 12.2 shows, deponent verbs exist in all of the imperfective conjugations;

Table 12.3 *The perfective present indicative inflection of five Latin verbs*

|        |     | I<br>PARĀRE<br>þre pare' | II<br>MONĒRE<br>te mind' | III<br>REGERE<br>tule ' | III (-*iō*)<br>CAPERE<br>'take' | IV<br>AUDĪRE<br>'hear' |
|--------|-----|------------|------------|------------|------------|------------|
| Active | 1sg | parāvī | monuī | rēxī | cēpī | audīvī |
|        | 2sg | parāvistī | monuistī | rēxistī | cēpistī | audīvistī |
|        | 3sg | parāvit | monuit | rēxit | cēpit | audīvit |
|        | 1pl | parāvimus | monuimus | rēximus | cēpimus | audīvimus |
|        | 2pl | parāvistis | monuistis | rēxistis | cēpistis | audīvistis |
|        | 3pl | parāvērunt | monuērunt | rēxērunt | cēpērunt | audīvērunt |
| Passive | 1sg | parātus sum | monitus sum | rēctus sum | captus sum | audītus sum |
|        | 2sg | parātus es | monitus es | rēctus es | captus es | audītus es |
|        | 3sg | parātus est | monitus est | rēctus est | captus est | audītus est |
|        | 1pl | parātī sumus | monitī sumus | rēctī sumus | captī sumus | audītī sumus |
|        | 2pl | parātī estis | monitī estis | rēctī estis | captī estis | audītī estis |
|        | 3pl | parātī sunt | monitī sunt | rēctī sunt | captī sunt | audītī sunt |

Table 12.4 *The perfective present indicative inflection of five deponent verbs in Latin*

|        |     | I<br>CŌNĀRĪ<br>try' | II<br>VERĒRĪ<br>fe ar,<br>respect' | III<br>LĀBĪ<br>ś lip, fall' | III (-*iō*)<br>PATĪ<br>à llow,<br>suffer' | IV<br>INGREDĪ<br>'enter' |
|--------|-----|------------|------------|------------|------------|------------|
| Active | 1sg | cōnātus sum | veritus sum | lapsus sum | passus sum | ingressus sum |
|        | 2sg | cōnātus es | veritus es | lapsus es | passus es | ingressus es |
|        | 3sg | cōnātus est | veritus est | lapsus est | passus est | ingressus est |
|        | 1pl | cōnātī sumus | veritī sumus | lapsī sumus | passī sumus | ingressī sumus |
|        | 2pl | cōnātī estis | veritī estis | lapsī estis | passī estis | ingressī estis |
|        | 3pl | cōnātī sunt | veritī sunt | lapsī sunt | passī sunt | ingressī sunt |
| Passive | | (none) | (none) | (none) | (none) | (none) |

but deponency is not restricted to imperfective forms. As Tables 12.3 and 12.4 show, the perfective forms of these same verbs exhibit the same phenomenon of deponency; these forms are especially striking, because they demonstrate that the periphrastic formation typical of perfect passive forms is precisely the formation that is used in the perfect active of deponent verbs.

Table 12.5 *The present indicative and perfect indicative inflection of three second-conjugation verbs in Latin*

|  |  | MONĒRE å dvise' | | FATĒRĪ 'confess' (deponent) | AUDĒRE 'dare' (semideponent) |
|  |  | Active | Passive | Active | Active |
|---|---|---|---|---|---|
| Present indicative | 1sg | *moneō* | *moneor* | *fateor* | *audeō* |
|  | 2sg | *monēs* | *monēris* | *fatēris* | *audēs* |
|  | 3sg | *monet* | *monētur* | *fatētur* | *audet* |
|  | 1pl | *monēmus* | *monēmur* | *fatēmur* | *audēmus* |
|  | 2pl | *monētis* | *monēminī* | *fatēminī* | *audētis* |
|  | 3pl | *monent* | *monentur* | *fatentur* | *audent* |
| Perfect indicative | 1sg | *monuī* | *monitus sum* | *fassus sum* | *ausus sum* |
|  | 2sg | *monuistī* | *monitus es* | *fassus es* | *ausus es* |
|  | 3sg | *monuit* | *monitus est* | *fassus est* | *ausus est* |
|  | 1pl | *monuimus* | *monitī sumus* | *fassī sumus* | *ausī sumus* |
|  | 2pl | *monuistis* | *monitī estis* | *fassī estis* | *ausī estis* |
|  | 3pl | *monuērunt* | *monitī sunt* | *fassī sunt* | *ausī sunt* |

One might try to argue that deponent verbs are not actually problematic – that their passive morphology actually has some kind of passive significance. For example, one might suppose that VERĒRĪ fe ar, respect' should actually have a passive gloss, perhaps something like be awed by.' To be sure, the deponent verbs do exhibit some semantic similarities (Xu, Aronoff and Anshen 2007), but their interpretation cannot in general be construed as passive; moreover, there are semideponent verbs such as AUDĒRE ɗa re' whose active forms exhibit ordinary active morphology in the imperfective but passive morphology in the perfective (Table 12.5).

Deponency provides especially compelling motivation for the paradigm-linkage hypothesis. We have already seen that content–form mismatches may be attributed to a property mapping (or property-mapping schema) effecting impoverishment (the elimination of a morphosyntactic property; Section 10.4) or the introduction of morphomic properties (either supplementing or supplanting morphosyntactic properties; Sections 7.2, 8, 10.3) or the mapping of one morphosyntactic property set onto a contrasting morphosyntactic property set (Section 10.2). Deponency, however, shows that the relation of content cells to their form correspondents may involve different property-mapping schemata from one paradigm to another. Ordinarily, Latin verbs are only subject to

Content paradigms

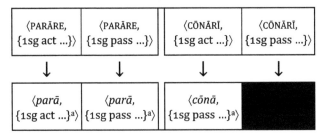

Form paradigms

Figure 12.1 *Deponency in Latin verbs*

the property-mapping schema $pm_c$ in (1a), whose effect on a morphosyntactic property set σ is simply to add to σ the inflection-class index c (Section 7.3). Deponent verbs, however, are instead subject to the property-mapping schema $pm2_c$ in (1b), which adds the morphomic property c but additionally changes σ's "active" property to "passive."

(1)     Property-mapping schemata for Latin:
        a. $pm_c(σ) = σ ∪ \{c\}$
        b. $pm2_c(σ:\{active\}) = σ[active/passive] ∪ \{c\}$
           $pm2_c(σ:\{passive\})$ is undefined.
        (N. B.: σ[x/y] represents the result of replacing x with y in σ.)

The definition of the Latin **Corr** function in (2) causes $pm2_c$ to apply in determining the form correspondent for a content cell ⟨L, σ⟩ such that L is a deponent or semideponent verb; otherwise, the form correspondent of a content cell ⟨L, σ⟩ is determined simply by means of $pm_c$. In this way, paradigms serve as the interface of inflectional morphology with syntax and semantics (= the interface hypothesis, Section 1.3.2): Syntax and semantics are sensitive to a lexeme's content paradigm, so that a deponent verb's finite forms are treated as syntactically and semantically active; but morphology is sensitive to a stem's form paradigm, so that a deponent verb's finite forms exhibit the morphology of passives (Figure 12.1).

(2)     Partial definition of **Corr** in Latin
        a. Where ⟨**Stem**(⟨L, σ⟩)⟩ belongs to the conjugation associated with the inflection-class index c, **Corr**(⟨L, σ⟩)
           = ⟨**Stem**(⟨L, σ⟩), $pm2_c(σ)$⟩ if L is deponent;
        b. = ⟨**Stem**(⟨L, σ⟩), $pm2_c(σ)$⟩ if L is semideponent and {perfective} ⊆ σ;
        c. = ⟨**Stem**(⟨L, σ⟩), $pm_c(σ)$⟩ otherwise.

Table 12.6 *The four tense systems in Classical Sanskrit*

| Present system | Aorist system | Perfect system | Future system |
|---|---|---|---|
| present indicative | aorist indicative | perfect indicative | future indicative |
| imperfect indicative | precative | | conditional |
| optative | | | |
| imperative | | | |

*Source:* Whitney 1889: Sections 527ff.

## 12.2 Sanskrit metaconjugation

In the case of Latin verbs, the phenomenon of deponency is logically independent of a verb's inflection-class membership; each of the principal conjugations has deponent as well as (mostly) nondeponent verbs as members. But there are content–form mismatches that resemble deponency but that are nevertheless directly tied to particular inflection classes. A phenomenon of this sort is that of metaconjugation. Before characterizing metaconjugation in a precise way, it will be helpful to examine an example of the phenomenon.

In Sanskrit, verb inflection is traditionally divided into four tense systems. In Classical Sanskrit, the present system comprises the present indicative, the imperfect (indicative), the optative and the imperative; the aorist system encompasses the aorist indicative and the precative (essentially an aorist optative); the perfect system contains only perfect indicative forms; and the future includes both the future indicative and the conditional (Table 12.6).[2] In general, a verbal lexeme has a different stem (or set of kindred stems; Section 5.2) for each tense system. The indicative forms of RUDH ɓb struct' illustrate; please refer to Table 8.3 above (p. 125).

The inflection-class distinctions to which the definition of Sanskrit verb inflection is sensitive are segregated (Section 6.2); in particular, the present and aorist systems each have their own inventory of conjugations, and a verb's conjugation in the present system cannot generally be inferred from its aorist-system conjugation, nor can the latter conjugation generally be inferred from the former. Traditionally, the present system is regarded as having ten conjugation classes, and the aorist system, seven (Table 12.7). The independence of a verb's present-system and aorist-system conjugations can be appreciated by considering the thirty-six verbal lexemes (chosen more or less at random) in Table 12.8;

---

2 The earliest, Vedic variety of Sanskrit exhibits a much larger array of morphosyntactic contrasts, with mood distinctions more fully and evenly distributed among the four tense systems.

Table 12.7 *Conjugation classes in the Classical Sanskrit present and aorist systems*

| a. | Present-system conjugations | | b. | Aorist-system conjugations | |
|---|---|---|---|---|---|
| | Thematic (stem in -*a*) | Athematic (stem not in -*a*) | | Asigmatic (stem lacks *s* suffix) | Sigmatic (stem has *s* suffix) |
| | 1st | 2nd | | root aorist | *s*-aorist |
| | 4th | 3rd | | thematic aorist | *iṣ*-aorist |
| | 6th | 5th | | reduplicated aorist | *siṣ*-aorist |
| | 10th | 7th | | | *sa*-aorist |
| | | 8th | | | |
| | | 9th | | | |

*Source:* Whitney 1889: Sections 527ff.

as this table shows, the present-system and aorist-system conjugations crosscut each other in ways which afford few predictions of one from the other.[3]

The conjugations of the aorist system are complicated in two ways. First, some verbs have aorist paradigms in which the active forms and the middle forms are based on distinct stems, belonging to distinct conjugations. In particular, if a verbal lexeme L's aorist active forms are based on a stem belonging to the root-, *siṣ*-, or *a*-aorist conjugation, then its aorist middle forms are based on a stem belonging to the *iṣ*-aorist conjugation if L's root is a *seṭ* root,[4] and otherwise to the *s*-aorist conjugation; the aorist paradigm of DĀ ǵi ve' (Table 12.9) illustrates.

Second, a verb's precative forms are generally based on a root-aorist stem in the active and on an *s*-aorist or *iṣ*-aorist stem in the middle, regardless of which conjugation that verb follows in the aorist indicative (Whitney 1889: Section 837f).

In both the present and aorist systems, the conjugations are distinguished largely by the manner in which their stems are formed; the usual patterns for each conjugation are schematized in Table 12.10. The ten present-system

3 In attested Sanskrit, the distinction between the active and middle voices is becoming bleached of its earlier significance. Many verbs inflect in both the active and middle voices. Some of these, however, inflect as members of distinct conjugations in the active and middle voices. Other verbs inflect only in the active, or only in the middle. In Table 12.8, "P" marks the active (*parasmaipada*) voice, and "Ā" the middle (*ātmanepada*) voice.

4 Sanskrit verb roots are traditionally classified as *seṭ* (= *sa-i-ṭ* "with *i*") or *aniṭ* (= *an-i-ṭ* "without *i*") according to whether or not they exhibit a linking vowel *i* in certain combinations; thus, the *i* in a lexeme's *iṣ*-aorist stem (e.g. *pāviṣ*-, lexeme PŪ ċ leanse') is the linking vowel associated with the lexeme's root, a *seṭ* root.

Table 12.8 *Thirty-six sanskrit verbs and their present-system and aorist-system conjugations*

| | Root | Thematic | Reduplicated | s | is | sis | sa |
|---|---|---|---|---|---|---|---|
| | | | | **AORIST CONJUGATIONS** | | | |
| 1st | BHŪ (P) 'become' | GAM (P) 'go' | KḶP (Ā) 'be ordered', PAT (P) 'fall' | NĪ (P) 'lead', SMṚ (P) 'remember' | BĀDH (Ā) 'repel', BUDH (P) 'wake', HAS (P) 'laugh' | GAI (P) 'sing' | KRUŚ (P) 'shriek' |
| 2nd | | VAC (P) 'speak' | | | VAS (Ā) 'clothe' | YĀ (P) 'go' | DVIṢ (P, Ā) 'hate' |
| 3rd | DĀ (P, Ā) 'give' | | | BHṚ (P, Ā) 'support', HĀ (Ā) 'abandon' | | HĀ (P) 'abandon' | |
| 4th | | TUṢ (P) 'be pleased' | | | | | |
| 5th | | ĀP (P) 'obtain', ŚAK (P) 'be able' | | SU (Ā) 'press out' | AŚ (Ā) 'pervade', SU (P) 'press out' | | |
| 6th | | | | | | | DIŚ (P) 'point' |
| 7th | | BHID (P) 'split', PIṢ (P) 'crush', YUJ (P) 'join' | RIC (P, Ā) 'evacuate' | BHID (Ā) 'split', BHUJ (Ā) 'eat, enjoy', RUDH (P, Ā) 'obstruct', YUJ (Ā) 'join' | HIṂS (P) 'injure' | | |
| 8th | | | | KṚ (P, Ā) 'make', TAN (P, Ā) 'stretch' | | | |
| 9th | | PUṢ (P) 'strengthen' | | KRĪ (P, Ā) 'buy' | KLIŚ (P) 'torment', MUṢ (P) 'rob', PŪ (P, Ā) 'cleanse' | | |
| 10th | | | CUR (P, Ā) 'steal' | | | | |

(Left margin vertical label spanning the rows: PRESENT CONJUGATIONS)

Table 12.9 *The aorist inflection of Sanskrit* DĀ *'give'*

|  |  | DĀ ği ve' | | | NĪ 'lead' | | |
|---|---|---|---|---|---|---|---|
| Conjugation: | | Root-aorist | | | *s*-aorist | | |
|  |  | Singular | Dual | Plural | Singular | Dual | Plural |
| Active | 1st | adām | adāva | adāma | anaiṣam | anaiṣva | anaiṣma |
|  | 2nd | adās | adātam | adāta | anaiṣīs | anaiṣṭam | anaiṣṭa |
|  | 3rd | adāt | adātām | adus | anaiṣīt | anaiṣṭām | anaiṣus |
| Middle | 1st | adiṣi | adiṣvahi | adiṣmahi | aneṣi | aneṣvahi | aneṣmahi |
|  | 2nd | adithās* | adiṣāthām | adidhvam | aneṣṭhās | aneṣāthām | anedhvam |
|  | 3rd | adita* | adiṣātām | adiṣata | aneṣṭa | aneṣātām | aneṣata |

\* Regarding the absence of stem-final *s* in the second- and third-person singular aorist middle forms of DĀ, see Whitney 1889: Sections 881c, 884.
Shaded word forms inflect as members of the *s*-aorist conjugation.

conjugations are exemplified in Table 12.11 by the imperfect active forms of ten verbs; the seven aorist-system conjugations are exemplified in Table 12.12 by aorist indicative forms.

Scrutiny of Tables 12.11 and 12.12 reveal three striking similarities between the present-system and aorist-system conjugations.

- The second present-system conjugation forms its stem in the same way as the root-aorist conjugation.
- The sixth present-system conjugation forms its stem in the same way as the thematic aorist conjugation.
- The prefixal inflections and terminations of the imperfect and those of the aorist indicative are alike.

In view of these similarities, there is no morphological distinction between the imperfect forms of PĀ þrote ct' and TUD ŝ trike' and the respective aorist indicative forms of DĀ ği ve' and TUṢ be happy' (Tables 12.13, 14). That is, from the point of view of form, the second present-system conjugation may be equated with the root-aorist conjugation, and the sixth present-system conjugation, with the thematic aorist conjugation (Figure 12.2).

Moreover, from the point of view of form, the only difference between a verb's imperfect forms and its aorist indicative forms is a difference of conjugation-class membership (expressed as a difference in stem formation). That is, the inflectional realization of a Sanskrit verb's form paradigm is not clearly conditioned by the distinction between the morphosyntactic properties "imperfect" and "aorist"; rather, it is conditioned by the conjugation-class

Table 12.10 *Morphological marks of the conjugation classes of the Sanskrit present and aorist systems*

|  |  | Conjugation | Stem-forming affix | Vocalism of root/stem |
|---|---|---|---|---|
| Present system | Thematic | 1 | suffix -*a* | root strong if possible |
|  |  | 4 | suffix -*ya* | root unchanged |
|  |  | 6 | suffix -*a* | root weak |
|  |  | 10 | suffix -*aya* | root strong if possible |
|  | Athematic | 2 | none | stem shows gradation* if possible |
|  |  | 3 | reduplicative prefix |  |
|  |  | 5 | suffix -*no*/-*nu* |  |
|  |  | 7 | infix -*na*-/-*n*- |  |
|  |  | 8 | suffix -*o*/-*u* |  |
|  |  | 9 | suffix -*nā*/-*nī* |  |
| Aorist system | Asigmatic | root | none | stem shows gradation* if possible |
|  |  | thematic | suffix -*a* | root weak |
|  |  | reduplicated | redup. prefix -s̩ uffix -*a* | root weak |
|  | Sigmatic | *s* | suffix -*s* | stem shows gradation* if possible |
|  |  | *iṣ* | suffix -*iṣ* | stem shows gradation* if possible |
|  |  | *siṣ* | suffix -*siṣ* | root strong if possible |
|  |  | *sa* | suffix -*sa* | root unchanged |

* Gradation is conditioned by the morphosyntactic property set being realized.
*Source:* Whitney 1889: Sections 527ff.

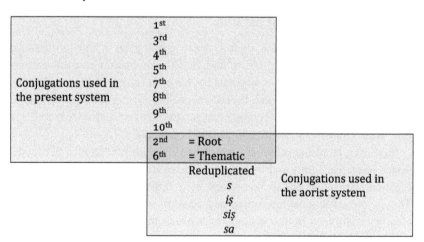

Figure 12.2 *The overlap of conjugations used in the present and aorist systems in Sanskrit*

Table 12.11 *Present-system conjugations in Sanskrit (imperfect active forms)*

## Thematic conjugations

| Conj. | SG | DU | PL |
|---|---|---|---|
| 1st | BHŪ 'become'; stem *bhava-* | | |
| | *a-bhava-m* | *a-bhavā-va* | *a-bhavā-ma* |
| | *a-bhava-s* | *a-bhava-tam* | *a-bhava-ta* |
| | *a-bhava-t* | *a-bhava-tām* | *a-bhava-n* |
| 4th | DIV 'play'; stem *dīvya-* | | |
| | *a-dīvya-m* | *a-dīvyā-va* | *a-dīvyā-ma* |
| | *a-dīvya-s* | *a-dīvya-tam* | *a-dīvya-ta* |
| | *a-dīvya-t* | *a-dīvya-tām* | *a-dīvya-n* |
| 6th | TUD 'strike'; stem *tuda-* | | |
| | *a-tuda-m* | *a-tudā-va* | *a-tudā-ma* |
| | *a-tuda-s* | *a-tuda-tam* | *a-tuda-ta* |
| | *a-tuda-t* | *a-tuda-tām* | *a-tuda-n* |
| 10th | CUR 'steal'; stem *coraya-* | | |
| | *a-coraya-m* | *a-corayā-va* | *a-corayā-ma* |
| | *a-coraya-s* | *a-coraya-tam* | *a-coraya-ta* |
| | *a-coraya-t* | *a-coraya-tām* | *a-coraya-n* |

## Athematic conjugations

| Conj. | SG | DU | PL |
|---|---|---|---|
| 2nd | PĀ 'protect'; stem *pā-* | | |
| | *a-pā-m* | *a-pā-va* | *a-pā-ma* |
| | *a-pā-s* | *a-pā-tam* | *a-pā-ta* |
| | *a-pā-t* | *a-pā-tām* | *a-p-us* |
| 3rd | HU 'sacrifice'; stems *juho-/juhu-* | | |
| | *a-juhav-am* | *a-juhu-va* | *a-juhu-ma* |
| | *a-juho-s* | *a-juhu-tam* | *a-juhu-ta* |
| | *a-juho-t* | *a-juhu-tām* | *a-juhav-us* |
| 5th | SU 'press out'; stems *suno-/sunu-* | | |
| | *a-sunav-am* | *a-sun-va* | *a-sun-ma* |
| | *a-suno-s* | *a-sunu-tam* | *a-sunu-ta* |
| | *a-suno-t* | *a-sunu-tām* | *a-sunv-an* |
| 7th | RUDH 'obstruct'; stems *ruṇadh-/rundh-* | | |
| | *a-ruṇadh-am* | *a-rundh-va* | *a-rundh-ma* |
| | *a-ruṇas* | *a-rund-dham* | *a-rund-dha* |
| | *a-ruṇat* | *a-rund-dhām* | *a-rundh-an* |
| 8th | TAN 'stretch'; stems *tano-/tanu-* | | |
| | *a-tanav-am* | *a-tan-va* | *a-tan-ma* |
| | *a-tano-s* | *a-tanu-tam* | *a-tanu-ta* |
| | *a-tano-t* | *a-tanu-tām* | *a-tanv-an* |
| 9th | KRĪ 'buy'; stems *krīṇā-/krīṇī-* | | |
| | *a-krīṇā-m* | *a-krīṇī-va* | *a-krīṇī-ma* |
| | *a-krīṇā-s* | *a-krīṇī-tama-* | *a-krīṇī-ta* |
| | *a-krīṇā-t* | *krīṇī-tām* | *a-krīṇ-an* |

Table 12.12 Aorist-system conjugations in Sanskrit (aorist indicative active forms)

| Conjugation | | Exemplar | Stem | Person | Singular | Dual | Plural |
|---|---|---|---|---|---|---|---|
| Asigmatic | root aorist | DĀ 'give' | dā- | 1 | a-dā-m | a-dā-va | a-dā-ma |
| | | | | 2 | a-dā-s | a-dā-tam | a-dā-ta |
| | | | | 3 | a-dā-t | a-dā-tām | a-d-us |
| | thematic aorist | TUS 'be happy' | tuṣa- | 1 | a-tuṣa-m | a-tuṣā-va | a-tuṣā-ma |
| | | | | 2 | a-tuṣa-s | a-tuṣa-tam | a-tuṣa-ta |
| | | | | 3 | a-tuṣa-t | a-tuṣa-tām | a-tuṣa-n |
| | reduplicated aorist | JAN 'give birth' | jījana- | 1 | a-jījana-m | a-jījanā-va | a-jījanā-ma |
| | | | | 2 | a-jījana-s | a-jījana-tam | a-jījana-ta |
| | | | | 3 | a-jījana-t | a-jījana-tām | a-jījana-n |
| Sigmatic | s-aorist | NĪ 'lead' | naiṣ- | 1 | a-naiṣ-am | a-naiṣ-va | a-naiṣ-ma |
| | | | | 2 | a-naiṣ-īs | a-naiṣ-ṭam | a-naiṣ-ṭa |
| | | | | 3 | a-naiṣ-īt | a-naiṣ-ṭām | a-naiṣ-us |
| | iṣ-aorist | PŪ 'cleanse' | pāviṣ- | 1 | a-pāviṣ-am | a-pāviṣ-va | a-pāviṣ-ma |
| | | | | 2 | a-pāvī-s | a-pāviṣ-ṭam | a-pāviṣ-ṭa |
| | | | | 3 | a-pāvī-t | a-pāviṣ-ṭām | a-pāviṣ-us |
| | siṣ-aorist | YĀ 'go' | yāsiṣ- | 1 | a-yāsiṣ-am | a-yāsiṣ-va | a-yāsiṣ-ma |
| | | | | 2 | a-yāsī-s | a-yāsiṣ-tam | a-yāsiṣ-ṭa |
| | | | | 3 | a-yāsī-t | a-yāsiṣ-ṭām | a-yāsiṣ-us |
| | sa-aorist | DIŚ 'point' | dikṣa- | 1 | a-dikṣā-m | a-dikṣā-va | a-dikṣā-ma |
| | | | | 2 | a-dikṣa-s | a-dikṣa-tam | a-dikṣa-ta |
| | | | | 3 | a-dikṣa-t | a-dikṣa-tām | a-dikṣa-n |

Source: Whitney 1889: Sections 824ff.

Table 12.13  *The imperfect and aorist indicative active inflection of two Sanskrit verbs*

| Present system | Conjugation: | | TUD 'strike' 6th | | | TUṢ 'be happy' 4th | | |
|---|---|---|---|---|---|---|---|---|
| | | | sg | du | pl | sg | du | pl |
| Imperfect active forms | 1st | | atudam | atudāva | atudāma | atuṣyam | atuṣyāva | atuṣyāma |
| | 2nd | | atudas | atudatam | atudata | atuṣyas | atuṣyatam | atuṣyata |
| | 3rd | | atudat | atudatām | atudan | atuṣyat | atuṣyatām | atuṣyan |
| Aorist system | Conjugation: | | s-aorist | | | thematic ( = 6th pres.) | | |
| Indicative active forms | 1st | | atautsam | atautsva | atautsma | atuṣam | atuṣāva | atuṣāma |
| | 2nd | | atautsīs | atauttam | atautta | atuṣas | atuṣatam | atuṣata |
| | 3rd | | atautsīt | atauttām | atautsus | atuṣat | atuṣatām | atuṣan |

Table 12.14 *The imperfect and aorist indicative active inflection of two Sanskrit verbs*

| Present system | Conjugation: | | PĀ 'protect' 2nd | | | DĀ 'give' 3rd | | |
|---|---|---|---|---|---|---|---|---|
| | | | Singular | Dual | Plural | Singular | Dual | Plural |
| Imperfect active forms | | 1st | apām | apāva | apāma | adadām | adadāva | adadāma |
| | | 2nd | apās | apātam | apāta | adadās | adadātam | adadāta |
| | | 3rd | apāt | apātām | apus | adadāt | adadātām | adadus |
| Aorist system | Conjugation: | | s-aorist | | | root aorist ( = 2nd present) | | |
| Indicative active forms | | 1st | apāsam | apāsva | apāsma | adām | adāva | adāma |
| | | 2nd | apāsīs | apāstam | apāsta | adās | adātam | adāta |
| | | 3rd | apāsīt | apāstām | apāsus | adāt | adātām | adus |

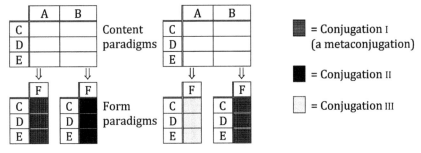

Figure 12.3 *Metaconjugation*

distinction between the verb's present-system stem and its aorist-system stem. The proof of this is the fact that in some cases, the conjugation class containing one verb's present-system stem contains another verb's aorist-system stem; in such cases, imperfect forms and aorist forms are not distinct in their morphology.

Stump (to appear A) refers to the pattern instantiated by the second present-system conjugation and the root-aorist conjugation and to the pattern instantiated by the sixth present-system conjugation and the thematic aorist conjugation as metaconjugations. A metaconjugation may be characterized in theoretical terms as in (3) and represented schematically as in Figure 12.3.

(3)     Given two distinct morphosyntactic property sets $\sigma$, $\tau$ and two distinct lexemes $L_1, L_2$,

If     a) $\textbf{\textit{pm}}_c(\sigma) = \textbf{\textit{pm}}_c(\tau)$ and
       b) $\textbf{\textit{Stem}}(\langle L_1, \sigma \rangle)$ and $\textbf{\textit{Stem}}(\langle L_2, \tau \rangle)$ both belong to inflection class c but neither $\textbf{\textit{Stem}}(\langle L_1, \tau \rangle)$ nor $\textbf{\textit{Stem}}(\langle L_2, \sigma \rangle)$ does,

then   c is a **metaconjugation**. In that case, the morphology of c indirectly expresses $\sigma$ in the realization of $\langle L_1, \sigma \rangle$ and $\tau$ in the realization of $\langle L_2, \tau \rangle$. That is, the content cells $\langle L_1, \sigma \rangle$ and $\langle L_2, \tau \rangle$ are realized by the same morphology.

In modeling Sanskrit metaconjugation, it is crucial to recognize that the morphological differences distinguishing forms in the present, future and aorist systems are fundamentally differences in stem formation; that is, these systems share the same inflectional prefixes and terminations.[5] Thus, if one leaves aside the differences of stem formation, the present, future and aorist systems can each be seen as instantiating all or part of the schematic form paradigm in Table 12.15. Each column in this schema is associated with the inventory of prefixes and terminations in the corresponding column of Table 12.16. In

---

5 The perfect system, however, employs a partially different inventory of terminations; see Whitney 1889: Section 553.

212 Deponency and metaconjugation

Table 12.15 *Schematic form paradigm for present-, future- and aorist-system verbs in Sanskrit*

|  | Nonpreterite indicative | | Preterite indicative | | Optative | | Imperative | |
|---|---|---|---|---|---|---|---|---|
|  | Active | Middle | Active | Middle | Active | Middle | Active | Middle |
| 1sg |  |  |  |  |  |  |  |  |
| 2sg |  |  |  |  |  |  |  |  |
| 3sg |  |  |  |  |  |  |  |  |
| 1du |  |  |  |  |  |  |  |  |
| 2du |  |  |  |  |  |  |  |  |
| 3du |  |  |  |  |  |  |  |  |
| 1pl |  |  |  |  |  |  |  |  |
| 2pl |  |  |  |  |  |  |  |  |
| 3pl |  |  |  |  |  |  |  |  |

the present system, the present indicative draws its affixes from the nonpreterite indicative part of the schema; the imperfect from the preterite indicative part; and the optative and imperative from the optative and imperative parts. In the future system, the future indicative draws its affixes from the nonpreterite indicative part, and the conditional, from the preterite indicative part. In the aorist system, the aorist indicative draws its affixes from the preterite indicative part, and the precative, from the optative part.

Under the paradigm-linkage hypothesis, this parallelism among a verb's present-, future- and aorist-system forms can be seen as a relation between a verb's present-, future- and aorist-system content paradigms to the single type of form paradigm in Table 12.15; this relation can be effected by means of the property mapping $pm_c$ defined in (4) and exemplified in (5). Together with the **Stem** function exemplified in (6)–(9), the property mapping $pm_c$ enters into the definition of the **Corr** function in (10), examples of whose application are given in (11).

(4)     Property mapping $pm_c$
     a. $pm_c$({prs ind Y})        = {nonpre t Y c}
        $pm_c$({fut ind Y})        = {nonpre t Y c}
     b. $pm_c$({impf ind Y})      = {pre t Y c}
        $pm_c$({a or ind Y})       = {pre t Y c}
        $pm_c$({c onditional Y})   = {pre t Y c}
     c. $pm_c(\sigma)$ is otherwise undefined.

Table 12.16 *Inflectional affixes used in the present, aorist and future systems in Classical Sanskrit*

| | | Nonpreterite indicative (= present, future indicative) | | Preterite indicative (= imperfect, aorist indicative); conditional | | Optative | | Imperative | |
|---|---|---|---|---|---|---|---|---|---|
| | | Thematic | Athematic | Thematic | Athematic | Thematic | Athematic | Thematic | Athematic |
| **Active** | | | | | | | | | |
| sg | 1st | | -mi | a-___-m | a-___-am | -īyam | -yām | -āni | |
| | 2nd | -si | | a-___-s | | -īs | -yās | — | -dhi/-hi[3] |
| | 3rd | -ti | | a-___-t | | -īt | -yāt | -tu | |
| du | 1st | -vas | | a-___-va | | -īva | -yāva | -āva | |
| | 2nd | -thas | | a-___-tam | | -ītam | -yātam | -tam | |
| | 3rd | -tas | | a-___-tām | | -ītām | -yātām | -tām | |
| pl | 1st | -mas | | a-___-ma | | -īma | -yāma | -āma | |
| | 2nd | -tha | | a-___-ta | | -īta | -yāta | -ta | |
| | 3rd | -nti | -anti[1] | a-___-n | a-___-an,/-us[2] | -īyus | -yus | -ntu | -antu[1] |

(cont.)

Table 12.16 (cont.)

| | | Nonpreterite indicative (= present, future indicative) | | Preterite indicative (= imperfect, aorist indicative); conditional | | Optative | | Imperative | |
|---|---|---|---|---|---|---|---|---|---|
| | | Thematic | Athematic | Thematic | Athematic | Thematic | Athematic | Thematic | Athematic |
| Middle | | | | | | | | | |
| sg | 1st | -e | -e | a-___-i | a-___-i | -īya | -īya | -ai | -ai |
| | 2nd | -se | -se | a-___-thās | a-___-thās | -īthās | -īthās | -sva | -sva |
| | 3rd | -te | -te | a-___-ta | a-___-ta | -īta | -īta | -tām | -tām |
| du | 1st | -vahe | -vahe | a-___-vahi | a-___-vahi | -īvahi | -īvahi | -āvahai | -āvahai |
| | 2nd | -ethe | -āthe | a-___-ethām | a-___-āthām | -īyāthām | -īyāthām | -ethām | -āthām |
| | 3rd | -ete | -āte | a-___-etām | a-___-ātām | -īyātām | -īyātām | -etām | -ātām |
| pl | 1st | -mahe | -mahe | a-___-mahi | a-___-mahi | -īmahi | -īmahi | -āmahai | -āmahai |
| | 2nd | -dhve | -dhve | a-___-dhvam | a-___-dhvam | -īdhvam | -īdhvam | -dhvam | -dhvam |
| | 3rd | -nte | -ate | a-___-nta | a-___-ata | -īran | -īran | -ntām | -atām |

[1] In the 3rd conjugation, the *n* in *-anti* and *-antu* is dropped.

[2] The suffix *-us* is used in the 3rd conjugation and with 2nd-conjugation verbs that have roots in *ā*; it is also used in the athematic sigmatic aorist conjugations.

[3] After a consonant, *-dhi*; after a vowel, *-hi*. This suffix is omitted in the 5th and 8th conjugations unless the root ends in a consonant; in the 9th conjugation, *-āna* replaces this suffix together with the conjugation-class suffix if the root ends in a consonant.

(5)    a. $pm_c$({s g impf ind act}) = {s g pret act c}
        $pm_c$({s g aor ind act}) = {s g pret act c}
    b. $pm_c$({s g prs ind act}) = {s g nonpret act c}
        $pm_c$({s g fut ind act}) = {s g nonpret act c}

(6)    Stems of Sanskrit RUDH òbs truct'
    a. Present stem:    *Stem*(⟨RUDH, σ:prs ⟩)    = *runadh* (∈ 7th)
    b. Aorist stem:    *Stem*(⟨RUDH, σ:{ or⟩)    = *rauts*   (∈ s-aorist)
    c. Perfect stem:    *Stem*(⟨RUDH, σ:pe rf⟩)    = *rurodh* (default)
    d. Future stem:    *Stem*(⟨RUDH, σ:fut⟩ ⟩)    = *rotsya* (default)

(7)    Some stems of Sanskrit TUD ś trike' and TUṢ be happy'
    a. Present stem:    *Stem*(⟨TUD, σ:prs ⟩)    = *tuda*    (∈ 6th)
    b. Aorist stem:    *Stem*(⟨TUD, σ:{ or⟩)    = *tauts*    (∈ s-aorist)
    c. Present stem:    *Stem*(⟨TUṢ, σ:prs ⟩)    = *tuṣya*    (∈ 4th)
    d. Aorist stem:    *Stem*(⟨TUṢ, σ:{ or⟩)    = *tuṣa*    (∈ 6th)

(8)    Some stems of Sanskrit PĀ prote ct' and DĀ ġi ve'
    a. Present stem:    *Stem*(⟨PĀ, σ:prs ⟩)    = *pā*    (∈ 2nd)
    b. Aorist stem:    *Stem*(⟨PĀ, σ:{ or⟩)    = *pās*    (∈ s-aorist)
    c. Present stem:    *Stem*(⟨DĀ, σ:prs ⟩)    = *dadā*    (∈ 3rd)
    d. Aorist stem:    *Stem*(⟨DĀ, σ:{ or⟩)    = *dā*    (∈ 2nd)

(9)    Lexical generalization:
    For every verbal lexeme L, *Stem*(⟨L, σ:prs ⟩) = *Stem*(⟨L, σ[prs/impf]⟩).

(10)    The Sanskrit *Corr* function: Where *Stem*(⟨L, σ⟩) belongs to inflection class c,
    *Corr*(⟨L, σ⟩) = ⟨*Stem*(⟨L, σ⟩), $pm_c$(σ)⟩

(11)    a. *Corr*(⟨RUDH, prs ind X⟩)    = ⟨*Stem*(⟨RUDH, σ⟩), {nonpret X 7th}⟩
    b. *Corr*(⟨RUDH, impf ind X ⟩)    = ⟨*Stem*(⟨RUDH, σ⟩), {pret X 7th}⟩
    c. *Corr*(⟨RUDH, { or ind X⟩)    = ⟨*Stem*(⟨RUDH, σ⟩), {pret X s-aor}⟩
    d. *Corr*(⟨RUDH, {fut ind X}⟩)    = ⟨*Stem*(⟨RUDH, σ⟩), {nonpret X default}⟩

In accordance with (3), the sixth present-system conjugation and the thematic aorist conjugation constitute a metaconjugation, because (for example)

    (a)    $pm_{6th}$(σ:{s g impf ind act} = $pm_{6th}$(τ:{s g aor ind act}) = {1sg pret act 6th} and
    (b)    *Stem*(⟨TUD, σ⟩) and *Stem*(⟨TUṢ, τ⟩) both belong to inflection class 6th( = sixth present/thematic aorist) but neither *Stem*(⟨TUD, τ⟩) nor *Stem*(⟨TUṢ, σ⟩) does.

For analogous reasons, the second present-system conjugation and the root-aorist conjugation constitute a metaconjugation. Given the values of *Stem* in (7) and (8), the imperfect realizations of TUD ś trike' and PĀ prote ct' are morphologically just like the aorist realizations of TUṢ be happy' and DĀ ġi ve,' as in the examples in Table 12.17.

Table 12.17 *Examples of paradigm linkage and realization for four Sanskrit verbs*

where $\rho$ = {3sg prs ind act}, $\sigma$ = {3sg impf ind act}, $\tau$ = {3sg aor ind act}:

| | Content cell | Form correspondent | | Realization |
|---|---|---|---|---|
| TUD 'strike' | $\langle \text{TUD}, \rho \rangle$ | $\langle \textbf{\textit{Stem}}(\text{TUD}, \rho) \rangle, \textbf{\textit{pm}}_{6\text{th}}(\rho) \rangle$ | $= \langle tuda, \{\text{3sg nonpret act } \textbf{6}^{\textbf{th}}\} \rangle$ | *tudati* |
| | $\langle \text{TUD}, \sigma \rangle$ | $\langle \textbf{\textit{Stem}}(\text{TUD}, \sigma) \rangle, \textbf{\textit{pm}}_{6\text{th}}(\sigma) \rangle$ | $= \langle tuda, \{\text{3sg pret act } \textbf{6}^{\textbf{th}}\} \rangle$ | *atudat* |
| | $\langle \text{TUD}, \tau \rangle$ | $\langle \textbf{\textit{Stem}}(\langle \text{TUD}, \tau \rangle), \textbf{\textit{pm}}_{\text{s-aor}}(\tau) \rangle$ | $= \langle tauts, \{\text{3sg pret act } \textbf{s-aor}\} \rangle$ | *atautsīt* |
| TUṢ 'be happy' | $\langle \text{TUṢ}, \rho \rangle$ | $\langle \textbf{\textit{Stem}}(\langle \text{TUṢ}, \rho \rangle), \textbf{\textit{pm}}_{4\text{th}}(\rho) \rangle$ | $= \langle tuṣya, \{\text{3sg nonpret act } \textbf{4}^{\textbf{th}}\} \rangle$ | *tuṣyati* |
| | $\langle \text{TUṢ}, \sigma \rangle$ | $\langle \textbf{\textit{Stem}}(\langle \text{TUṢ}, \sigma \rangle), \textbf{\textit{pm}}_{4\text{th}}(\sigma) \rangle$ | $= \langle tuṣya, \{\text{3sg pret act } \textbf{4}^{\textbf{th}}\} \rangle$ | *atuṣyat* |
| | $\langle \text{TUṢ}, \tau \rangle$ | $\langle \textbf{\textit{Stem}}(\langle \text{TUṢ}, \tau \rangle), \textbf{\textit{pm}}_{6\text{th}}(\tau) \rangle$ | $= \langle tuṣa, \{\text{3sg pret act } \textbf{6}^{\textbf{th}}\} \rangle$ | *atuṣat* |
| PĀ 'protect' | $\langle \text{PĀ}, \rho \rangle$ | $\langle \textbf{\textit{Stem}}(\langle \text{PĀ}, \rho \rangle), \textbf{\textit{pm}}_{2\text{nd}}(\rho) \rangle$ | $= \langle pā, \{\text{3sg nonpret act } \textbf{2}^{\textbf{nd}}\} \rangle$ | *pāti* |
| | $\langle \text{PĀ}, \sigma \rangle$ | $\langle \textbf{\textit{Stem}}(\langle \text{PĀ}, \sigma \rangle), \textbf{\textit{pm}}_{2\text{nd}}(\sigma) \rangle$ | $= \langle pā, \{\text{3sg pret act } \textbf{2}^{\textbf{nd}}\} \rangle$ | *apāt* |
| | $\langle \text{PĀ}, \tau \rangle$ | $\langle \textbf{\textit{Stem}}(\langle \text{PĀ}, \tau \rangle), \textbf{\textit{pm}}_{\text{s-aor}}(\tau) \rangle$ | $= \langle pās, \{\text{3sg pret act } \textbf{s-aor}\} \rangle$ | *apāsīt* |
| DĀ 'give' | $\langle \text{DĀ}, \rho \rangle$ | $\langle \textbf{\textit{Stem}}(\langle \text{DĀ}, \rho \rangle), \textbf{\textit{pm}}_{3\text{rd}}(\rho) \rangle$ | $= \langle dadā, \{\text{3sg nonpret act } \textbf{3}^{\textbf{rd}}\} \rangle$ | *dadāti* |
| | $\langle \text{DĀ}, \sigma \rangle$ | $\langle \textbf{\textit{Stem}}(\langle \text{DĀ}, \sigma \rangle), \textbf{\textit{pm}}_{3\text{rd}}(\sigma) \rangle$ | $= \langle dadā, \{\text{3sg pret act } \textbf{3}^{\textbf{rd}}\} \rangle$ | *adadāt* |
| | $\langle \text{DĀ}, \tau \rangle$ | $\langle \textbf{\textit{Stem}}(\langle \text{DĀ}, \tau \rangle), \textbf{\textit{pm}}_{2\text{nd}}(\tau) \rangle$ | $= \langle dā, \{\text{3sg pret act } \textbf{2}^{\textbf{nd}}\} \rangle$ | *adāt* |

Although metaconjugation and deponency both involve mismatches between content and form, metaconjugation is not the same thing as deponency. Deponency is not dependent on a language's inflection classes; indeed, deponency could arise in a language without inflection-class distinctions. Deponent lexemes are exceptional in that their inflection involves the realization of one morphosyntactic property set $\sigma$ by means of morphology whose usual function is to realize a contrasting property set $\tau$ – which simply goes unrealized (i.e. is a locus of defectiveness) in canonical instances of deponency.

By contrast, metaconjugation is by definition dependent on inflection-class distinctions; it is manifested as, in effect, the replacement of morphosyntactic properties with inflection-class indices, but in such a way that inflection-class distinctions cannot simply be equated with morphosyntactic distinctions. While deponency is an asymmetrical phenomenon in which the deponent pattern is exceptional with respect to the canonical pattern exhibited by nondeponents, metaconjugation is a symmetrical phenomenon in which neither of the mismatched patterns is clearly more canonical than the other.[6] While defectiveness is a symptom of canonical deponency, it does not seem to play any such role in instances of metaconjugation; for instance, the Sanskrit verbs TUD ś trike' and TUṢ 'be happy' exhibit metaconjugation (the former follows the sixth conjugation in the imperfect, while the latter follows this same conjugation in the aorist), but both verbs have both imperfect and aorist forms.

## 12.3 Verb inflection in Kashmiri

Kashmiri verb inflection presents a phenomenon which resembles both deponency and metaconjugation but must ultimately be distinguished from both. The Kashmiri system of verb inflection is quite complex, and existing descriptions suggest that this system is the locus of rather considerable dialect variation. Here, I focus specifically on the system described by Grierson (1899, 1911) and Stump (2015).

In this system, there are three basic conjugations, though (morpho)phonological effects engender a number of variant forms of each conjugation. The first conjugation is usual for transitive verbs. The incidence of both subject and object agreement in the inflection of first-conjugation verbs presents

---

6 It is relevant that according to Whitney1885, there are 142 verbs that follow the sixth conjugation in the imperfect and 86 that follow it in the aorist. (Whitney's figures do not count a verb's compounds separately from the verb itself, so that in both categories, the number of verbal lexemes is actually much higher than the number he cites.)

Table 12.18 *The past-tense inflection of two Kashmiri verbs*

|  |  |  | wup ɓ urn inside,' Conj. II | | wuph 'fly,' Conj. III | |
|---|---|---|---|---|---|---|
|  |  |  | Masc | Fem | Masc | Fem |
| Recent past | Sg | 1 | *wupus* | *wupÜs* | *wuphyōs* | *wuphyēyɛs* |
|  |  | 2 | *wupukh* | *wupÜkh* | *wuphyōkh* | *wuphyēyɛkh* |
|  |  | 3 | *wupU* | *wupÜ* | *wuphyōv* | *wuphyēyɛ* |
|  | Pl | 1 | *wupI* | *wupɛ* | *wuphyēy* | *wuphyēyɛ* |
|  |  | 2 | *wupIwa* | *wupɛwa* | *wuphyēwa* | *wuphyēyɛwa* |
|  |  | 3 | *wupI* | *wupɛ* | *wuphyēy* | *wuphyēyɛ* |
| Indefinite past | Sg | 1 | *wupyōs* | *wupyēyɛs* | *wuphyās* | *wuphyēyɛs* |
|  |  | 2 | *wupyōkh* | *wupyēyɛkh* | *wuphyākh* | *wuphyēyɛkh* |
|  |  | 3 | *wupyōv* | *wupyēyɛ* | *wuphyāv* | *wuphyēyɛ* |
|  | Pl | 1 | *wupyēy* | *wupyēyɛ* | *wuphyāy* | *wuphyēyɛ* |
|  |  | 2 | *wupyēwa* | *wupyēyɛwa* | *wuphyāwa* | *wuphyēyɛwa* |
|  |  | 3 | *wupyēy* | *wupyēyɛ* | *wuphyāy* | *wuphyēyɛ* |
| Remote past | Sg | 1 | *wupyās* | *wupyēyɛs* | *wuphiyās* | *wuphiyēyɛs* |
|  |  | 2 | *wupyākh* | *wupyēyɛkh* | *wuphiyākh* | *wuphiyēyɛkh* |
|  |  | 3 | *wupyāv* | *wupyēyɛ* | *wuphiyāv* | *wuphiyēyɛ* |
|  | Pl | 1 | *wupyāy* | *wupyēyɛ* | *wuphiyāy* | *wuphiyēyɛ* |
|  |  | 2 | *wupyāwa* | *wupyēyɛwa* | *wuphiyāwa* | *wuphiyēyɛwa* |
|  |  | 3 | *wupyāy* | *wupyēyɛ* | *wuphiyāy* | *wuphiyēyɛ* |

complications that are orthogonal to those at issue here; I shall therefore restrict my attention to the second and third conjugations, whose members are in general intransitive. These two conjugations are alike in the present tense, but they exhibit a striking difference in the three past tenses. Table 12.18 exemplifies this difference with the past-tense paradigms of the second-conjugation verb wup 'burn inside' and the third-conjugation verb wuph fl y.'

In these past-tense paradigms, both verbs inflect for tense, person, number and gender. On first consideration, the two conjugations seem quite different, but closer inspection turns up some shared patterns. Throughout, the first- and third-person plural forms for a given tense and gender are alike. Moreover, the feminine forms exhibit significant tense neutralization: In the second conjugation, the feminine forms of the indefinite past are identical to those of the remote past, and in the third conjugation, the feminine forms of the recent past are exactly those of the indefinite past.

These distinct patterns of tense neutralization exhibited by the two conjugations are, in fact, one manifestation of a more general difference: The morphology

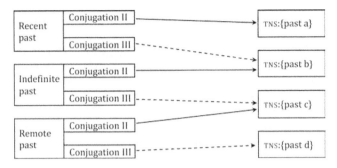

Figure 12.4 *Paradigm linkage in the realization of Kashmiri verbs*

of indefinite past-tense forms in the second conjugation is exactly that of recent past-tense forms in the third conjugation; and the morphology of remote past-tense forms in the second conjugation is exactly that of the indefinite past-tense forms in the third conjugation. By contrast, the morphology of recent past-tense forms in the second conjugation has no parallel in the third conjugation, nor does the morphology of the remote past in the third conjugation correspond directly to any of the second-conjugation morphology.

The generalization is that while Kashmiri has three past tenses from the point of view of content, it has four past tenses from the point of view of form; the correspondence between contentive distinctions and formal distinctions in the past tense is schematized in Figure 12.4, where a, b, c and d are tense morphomes (cf. Section 8.4).

The solid arrows in Figure 12.4 indicate the effects of a property mapping *pm2* in the realization of second-conjugation verbs; the dashed arrows indicate the effects of a distinct property mapping *pm3* in the realization of third-conjugation verbs. These property mappings are defined in (12).

(12)     Definition of the Kashmiri property mappings *pm2*, *pm3*
         (where σ[*x*/*y*] represents the result of replacing *x* with *y* in σ)
        *pm2*(σ:{TNS:{e cent})       = σ[recent/a]
        *pm2*(σ:{TNS:{nde finite})   = σ[indefinite/b]
        *pm2*(σ:{TNS:{e mote})    = σ[remote/c]
        *pm3*(σ:{TNS:{e cent})       = σ[recent/b]
        *pm3*(σ:{TNS:{nde finite})   = σ[indefinite/c]
        *pm3*(σ:{TNS:{e mote})    = σ[remote/d]

These property mappings enter into the definition of the Kashmiri **Corr** function, and thus into the definition of the Kashmiri paradigm function, as in (13) and (14).

(13)    Partial definition of the Kashmiri **Corr** function
a. Where **Stem**(⟨L, σ⟩) = X ∈ 2nd conjugation, **Corr**(⟨L, σ⟩) = ⟨X, **pm2**(σ)⟩
b. Where **Stem**(⟨L, σ⟩) = X ∈ 3rd conjugation, **Corr**(⟨L, σ⟩) = ⟨X, **pm3**(σ)⟩

(14)    Partial definition of the Kashmiri paradigm function
a. PF(⟨L, σ⟩) = PF(**Corr**(⟨L, σ⟩))
b. PF(⟨L, σ:{AGR:{pl} ⟩⟩) = PF(⟨L, σ[AGR:{1}/AGR:{3}]⟩)
c. PF(⟨X, σ⟩) = [ iv : [ iii : [ ii : [ i : ⟨X, σ⟩]]]]

Definition (14) presupposes that the rules of exponence for Kashmiri verb inflection fall into four blocks. These blocks correspond to the four affix position classes embodied by the partial paradigms in Table 12.18; these classes are isolated in the exploded representation of these paradigms in Table 12.19.

The four blocks of rules of exponence are defined in (15). None of these rules refers to any of the three contentive properties "recent past," "indefinite past" and "remote past"; instead, they realize the morphomic tense specifications "pst a," "pst b," "pst c" and "pst d."

(15)    Rules of exponence for a fragment of Kashmiri verb morphology

| | | |
|---|---|---|
| **Block i** | X, V, {TNS:ps t d} | → *Xi* |
| **Block ii** | X, V, {TNS:ps t a} AGR:{ g masc}} | → *Xu* |
| | X, V, {TNS:ps t a} AGR:{s g masc}} | → *XU* |
| | X, V, {TNS:ps t a} AGR:{na sc}} | → *XI* |
| | X, V, {TNS:ps t a} AGR:{ g fem}} | → *XÜ* |
| | X, V, {TNS:ps t a} AGR:{e m}} | → *Xε* |
| | X, V, {TNS:ps t} | → *Xy* |
| | X, V, {TNS:ps t a} | → *X* |
| **Block iii** | X, V, {TNS:ps t b} AGR:{na sc sg}} | → *Xō* |
| | X, V, {TNS:ps t b} AGR:{na sc}} | → *Xē* |
| | X, V, {TNS:ps t} AGR:{na sc} | → *Xā* |
| | X, V, {TNS:ps t} AGR:{e m} | → *Xēyε* |
| | X, V, [{TNS:ps t a} ∧ [{AGR:{masc}} | |
| | ∨ {AGR:{e m}]] | → *X* |
| **Block iv** | X, V, {AGR:{s g} | → *Xs* |
| | X, V, {AGR:{s g} | → *Xkh* |
| | X, V, {AGR:{} | → *Xwa* |
| | X, V, {AGR:{s g masc} | → *Xv* |
| | X, V, {AGR:{ masc} | → *Xy* |
| | X, V, [{TNS:ps t a} AGR:{ masc}} | |
| | ∧ [{AGR:{ g} ∨ {AGR:{pl} }]] | → *X* |

This analysis entails that while the content cells in (16a, b) receive similar semantic interpretations (involving an indefinite past-tense operator), they

Table 12.19 *The past-tense inflection of two Kashmiri verbs (exploded view)*

| | | WUP 'burn inside,' Conj. II | | | | | | | WUPH 'fly,' Conj. III | | | | | | | | | |
|---|---|---|---|---|---|---|---|---|---|---|---|---|---|---|---|---|---|---|---|
| | | Masculine | | | | Feminine | | | | Masculine | | | | | Feminine | | | | |
| | | | ii | iii | iv | | ii | iii | iv | | i | ii | iii | iv | | i | ii | iii | iv |
| Rec. past | Sg 1 | wup | -u | -ō | -s | wup | -Ü | | -s | wuph | | -y | -ō | -s | wuph | | -y | -ēyɛ | -s |
| | Sg 2 | wup | -u | -ō | -kh | wup | -Ü | | -kh | wuph | | -y | -ō | -kh | wuph | | -y | -ēyɛ | -kh |
| | Sg 3 | wup | -U | -ō | | wup | -Ü | | | wuph | | -y | -ō | -v | wuph | | -y | -ēyɛ | |
| | Pl 1 | wup | -I | | | wup | -ɛ | | | wuph | | -y | -ē | -y | wuph | | -y | -ēyɛ | |
| | Pl 2 | wup | -I | | -wa | wup | -ɛ | | -wa | wuph | | -y | -ē | -wa | wuph | | -y | -ēyɛ | -wa |
| | Pl 3 | wup | -I | | | wup | -ɛ | | | wuph | | -y | -ē | -y | wuph | | -y | -ēyɛ | |
| Indef. past | Sg 1 | wup | -y | -ō | -s | wup | -y | -ēyɛ | -s | wuph | | -y | -ā | -s | wuph | | -y | -ēyɛ | -s |
| | Sg 2 | wup | -y | -ō | -kh | wup | -y | -ēyɛ | -kh | wuph | | -y | -ā | -kh | wuph | | -y | -ēyɛ | -kh |
| | Sg 3 | wup | -y | -ō | -v | wup | -y | -ēyɛ | | wuph | | -y | -ā | -v | wuph | | -y | -ēyɛ | |
| | Pl 1 | wup | -y | -ē | -y | wup | -y | -ēyɛ | | wuph | | -y | -ā | -y | wuph | | -y | -ēyɛ | |
| | Pl 2 | wup | -y | -ē | -wa | wup | -y | -ēyɛ | -wa | wuph | | -y | -ā | -wa | wuph | | -y | -ēyɛ | -wa |
| | Pl 3 | wup | -y | -ē | -y | wup | -y | -ēyɛ | | wuph | | -y | -ā | -y | wuph | | -y | -ēyɛ | |
| Rem. past | Sg 1 | wup | -y | -ā | -s | wup | -y | -ēyɛ | -s | wuph | -i | -y | -ā | -s | wuph | -i | -y | -ēyɛ | -s |
| | Sg 2 | wup | -y | -ā | -kh | wup | -y | -ēyɛ | -kh | wuph | -i | -y | -ā | -kh | wuph | -i | -y | -ēyɛ | -kh |
| | Sg 3 | wup | -y | -ā | -v | wup | -y | -ēyɛ | | wuph | -i | -y | -ā | -v | wuph | -i | -y | -ēyɛ | |
| | Pl 1 | wup | -y | -ā | -y | wup | -y | -ēyɛ | | wuph | -i | -y | -ā | -y | wuph | -i | -y | -ēyɛ | |
| | Pl 2 | wup | -y | -ā | -wa | wup | -y | -ēyɛ | -wa | wuph | -i | -y | -ā | -wa | wuph | -i | -y | -ēyɛ | -wa |
| | Pl 3 | wup | -y | -ā | -y | wup | -y | -ēyɛ | | wuph | -i | -y | -ā | -y | wuph | -i | -y | -ēyɛ | |

222   *Deponency and metaconjugation*

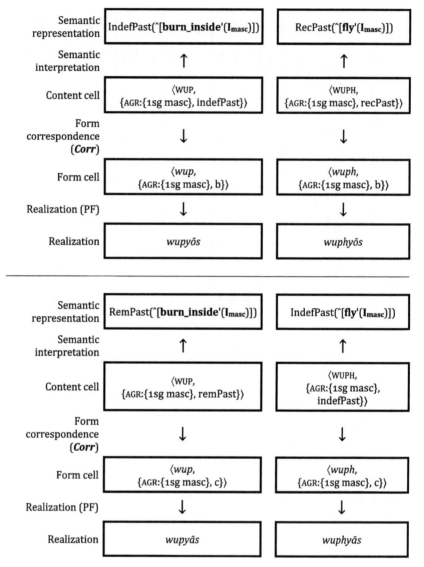

Figure 12.5 *Mismatches of content and form in the inflection of the Kashmiri verbs* wup *'burn inside' (Conj. II) and* wuph *'fly' (Conj. III)*

differ in their inflectional realization. By contrast, the content cells in (16a, c) differ in their semantics, but are alike in their morphology; and the same is true of the content cells in (16b, d). These mismatches of content and form are schematized in Figure 12.5.

(16)    a. ⟨WUP, {AGR:{s g masc} TNS:indefPast}⟩
      I (ma le) burned inside (indefinite past)'
    b. ⟨WUPH, {AGR:{s g masc} TNS:indefPast}⟩
      I (ma le) flew (indefinite past)'
    c. ⟨WUPH, {AGR:{s g masc} TNS:recPast}⟩
      I (ma le) flew (recent past)'
    d. ⟨WUP, {AGR:{s g masc} TNS:remPast}⟩
      I (male) burned inside (remote past)'

The content–form mismatches that Kashmiri verbs exhibit in the past tenses resemble Latin deponency, but differ from it in certain important respects. First, Latin deponency is accompanied by defectiveness (in that deponent verbs lack forms with passive content); by contrast, the Kashmiri mismatch does not entail any analogous defectiveness. Moreover, Latin deponent verbs deviate from a canonical pattern in that they appropriate morphology that ordinarily expresses one sort of morphosyntactic content (passive voice) in order to express contrasting content (active voice). But in the Kashmiri case, it is not clear that either Conjugation II or Conjugation III embodies a canonical pattern from which the other conjugation deviates; thus, while the Latin property mapping (1) causes active content to be exceptionally realized by morphology that is ordinarily reserved for the passive, the Kashmiri property mappings in (12) cause contentive tense properties ("recent past," "indefinite past," "remote past") to be realized by means of morphomic tense specifications ("pst a," "pst b," "pst c," "pst d") in both Conjugation II and Conjugation III.

The Kashmiri mismatches are also only partially similar to Sanskrit meta-conjugation. In Sanskrit, the property mapping (4) replaces tense/mood properties with the morphomic properties "preterite" and "nonpreterite"; comparably, the Kashmiri property mappings in (12) replace contentive tense properties with the morphomic tense properties "a," "b," "c" and "d." But in Sanskrit, there is stem-forming morphology that identifies the two meta-conjugations (namely the stem-forming morphology of the second and sixth present-system conjugations). In Kashmiri, by contrast, there is no morphology that distinguishes Conjugation II from Conjugation III; rather, the two conjugations exhibit essentially the same morphology, differing only with respect to the way in which they associate morphomic tense properties with contentive tense properties. (This would be as if two Sanskrit conjugations contrasted only according to whether they associated "imperfect" with "preterite" or "nonpreterite.")

Together, the evidence from Sanskrit and Kashmiri reveals that content–form mismatches resembling deponency may deviate from the canonical properties

Table 12.20  *Indicative forms of three Old Norse verbs*

|         |      | Strong class 3 | Preterite-present | Weak class 1 |
|---------|------|----------------|-------------------|--------------|
|         |      | BRENNA ƀ urn' | SKULU 'shall' | FELLA 'fell (tr.)' |
| Present | 1sg  | *brenn* | *skal* | *fell-i* |
|         | 2sg  | *brenn-r* | *skal-t* | *fell-ir* |
|         | 3sg  | *brenn-r* | *skal* | *fell-ir* |
|         | 1pl  | *brenn-um* | *skul-um* | *fell-um* |
|         | 2pl  | *brenn-ið* | *skul-uð* | *fell-ið* |
|         | 3pl  | *brenn-a* | *skul-u* | *fell-a* |
| Past    | 1sg  | *brann* | *skyld-a* | *felld-a* |
|         | 2sg  | *brann-t* | *skyld-ir* | *felld-ir* |
|         | 3sg  | *brann* | *skyld-i* | *felld-i* |
|         | 1pl  | *brunn-um* | *skyld-um* | *felld-um* |
|         | 2pl  | *brunn-uð* | *skyld-uð* | *felld-uð* |
|         | 3pl  | *brunn-u* | *skyld-u* | *felld-u* |

manifested by Latin deponent verbs in a variety of ways. In the following section, another sort of deviation is examined, in which deponency coincides with
heteroclisis.

### 12.4  *Ħ teroclisis and deponency in Old Norse*

Typically of the Germanic languages, Old Norse verb inflection exhibits a distinction between strong and weak conjugations (Faarlund 2004: 41ff): Verbs
belonging to the strong conjugations form their past-tense stem by ablaut (e.g.
BRENNA ƀ urn': *brenn* I burn,' *brann* I burned'), while verbs belonging to the
weak conjugations form their past-tense stem not by means of ablaut, but with
a dental suffix (FELLA fe ll (tr.)': *felli* I fell (a tree),' *fellda* I felled'). Also like
other Germanic languages, Old Norse has a closed class of preterite-present
verbs, whose inflectional peculiarity is that their present-tense forms have the
morphology usual for strong past-tense forms, and their past-tense forms have
the morphology usual for weak past-tense forms (Faarlund 2004: 47f). An example is the verb SKULU š hall,' whose present-tense forms parallel the past-
tense forms of BRENNA and whose past-tense forms parallel those of FELLA
(Table 12.20). Preterite-present verbs such as SKULU therefore exhibit both
deponency (e.g. with *skal* "setting aside" its past-tense function for a present-
tense function) and heteroclisis (with strong and weak conjugations determining the realization of different parts of SKULU's paradigm).

Table 12.21 *Stems of three Old Norse verbal lexemes*

| | | L's stems | | | | Conjugation |
|---|---|---|---|---|---|---|
| L | | Pres | SgPast | PlPast | WkPast | |
| BRENNA | 'burn' | *brenn* | *brann* | *brunn* | – | S3 |
| FELLA | fe ll (tr.)' | *fell* | = WkPast | = WkPast | *felld* | W1 |
| SKULU | ś hall' | – | *skal* | *skul* | *skyld* | *skyld* ∈ W1; otherwise S3 |

The paradigm-linkage hypothesis affords a straightforward account of these facts. We can postulate four main stems relevant for the inflection of Old Norse verbs.

- The Pres stem serves in the realization of ordinary present-tense forms.
- The SgPast stem serves in realizing singular past-tense forms.
- The PlPast stem serves in realizing plural past-tense forms.
- The WkPast stem is a weak verb's usual past-tense stem.

Given this four-way distinction, the stem profiles of Old Norse verbs may be distinguished as in Table 12.21. (For simplicity, let's assume that a verb's stems are listed in its lexical entry; redundant listings could, of course, be eliminated through the postulation of stem-formation rules; cf. Section 5.5.1.) A strong verb lacks any WkPast stem, and its Pres, SgPast and PlPast stems are distinguished by ablaut; a weak verb has a WkPast stem, to which its SgPast and PlPast stems are identical; and a preterite-present verb has a WkPast stem but lacks any Pres stem, and has SgPast and PlPast stems that are distinguished by ablaut and are distinct from its WkPast stem. The distribution of these stems within a lexeme's form paradigm is determined by the partial definition of the Old Norse **Stem** function in (17), which entails the equations in (18).

(17)   Partial definition of the Old Norse **Stem** function
    a. **Stem**(⟨L, σ:þrs ⟩))          = L's Pres stem
    b. **Stem**(⟨L, σ:þs t weak}))    = L's WkPast stem
      Otherwise,
    c. **Stem**(⟨L, σ:þs t sg}))       = L's SgPast stem
    d. **Stem**(⟨L, σ:þs t pl}))        = L's PlPast stem

(18)   Theorems of definition (17)
    a. **Stem**(⟨BRENNA, σ:þrs ⟩))    = *brenn*
    b. **Stem**(⟨BRENNA, σ:þs t sg}))  = *brann*

c. *Stem*(⟨BRENNA, σ:þs t pl}⟩)               = *brunn*
d. *Stem*(⟨FELLA, σ:þrs }⟩)                    = *fell*
e. *Stem*(⟨FELLA, σ:þs t sg}⟩)                 = *felld*
f. *Stem*(⟨FELLA, σ:þs t pl}⟩)                 = *felld*
g. *Stem*(⟨SKULU, σ:þs t weak}⟩)              = *skyld*
   Otherwise,
h. *Stem*(⟨SKULU, σ:þs t sg}⟩)                = *skal*
i. *Stem*(⟨SKULU, σ:þs t pl}⟩)                = *skul*

If σ is the property set associated with a cell ⟨L, σ⟩ in the content of a verbal lexeme L, then for most verbs, the form correspondent of ⟨L, σ⟩ is ⟨X, *pm*$_c$(σ)⟩, where X = *Stem*(⟨L, σ⟩), X belongs to conjugation c, and the property mapping *pm*$_c$ is as in (19a) (cf. Section 7.3). The realization of a preterite-present verb, however, depends on the additional property mapping defined in (19b). In particular, the Old Norse *Corr* function has the partial definition in (20), examples of whose application are given in (21)–(23).

(19)   Old Norse property mappings
       a. *pm*$_c$(σ)              = σ ∪ ¢ }
       b. *pm2*$_c$(þrs α}          = þs t α c}
          *pm2*$_c$(þs t α}         = þs t weak α c}

(20)   Partial definition of the Old Norse *Corr* function
       If L is a preterite-present verb, τ = *pm2*$_c$(σ) and *Stem*(⟨L, τ⟩) belongs to
          Conjugation c,
       then *Corr*(⟨L, σ⟩) = ⟨*Stem*(⟨L, τ⟩), τ⟩.
       Otherwise, if *Stem*(⟨L, σ⟩) belongs to Conjugation c,
       then *Corr*(⟨L, σ⟩) = ⟨*Stem*(⟨L, σ⟩), *pm*$_c$(σ)⟩.

(21)   a. *Corr*(⟨BRENNA, σ:þrs }⟩)       = ⟨*brenn*, *pm*$_{S3}$(σ)⟩
       b. *Corr*(⟨BRENNA, σ:þs t sg}⟩)    = ⟨*brann*, *pm*$_{S3}$(σ)⟩
       c. *Corr*(⟨BRENNA, σ:þs t pl}⟩)    = ⟨*brunn*, *pm*$_{S3}$(σ)⟩

(22)   a. *Corr*(⟨FELLA, σ:þrs }⟩)        = ⟨*fell*, *pm*$_{W1}$(σ)⟩
       b. *Corr*(⟨FELLA, σ:þs t sg}⟩)     = ⟨*felld*, *pm*$_{W1}$(σ)⟩
       c. *Corr*(⟨FELLA, σ:þs t pl}⟩)     = ⟨*felld*, *pm*$_{W1}$(σ)⟩

(23)   a. *Corr*(⟨SKULU, σ:þrs sg X}⟩)    = ⟨*Stem*(⟨SKULU, *pm2*$_{S3}$(σ)⟩), *pm2*$_{S3}$(σ)⟩
                                           = ⟨*skal*, {pst sg X **S3**}⟩
       b. *Corr*(⟨SKULU, σ:þrs pl X}⟩)    = ⟨*Stem*(⟨SKULU, *pm2*$_{S3}$(σ)⟩), *pm2*$_{S3}$(σ)⟩
                                           = ⟨*skul*, {pst pl X **S3**}⟩
       c. *Corr*(⟨SKULU, σ:{pst X}⟩)      = ⟨*Stem*(⟨SKULU, *pm2*$_{W1}$(σ)⟩), *pm2*$_{W1}$(σ)⟩
                                           = ⟨*skyld*, {pst weak X **W1**}⟩

In accordance with this analysis, the paradigm of SKULU is heteroclitic: Its present-tense forms inflect like strong past-tense forms, while its past-tense forms inflect as weak past-tense forms. By virtue of this heteroclisis, the content–form

Table 12.22 *Similarities and differences between syncretism, deponency and metaconjugation*

|  | Within or across paradigms? | Defectiveness? | Restricted by inflection class? | Within or across parts of speech? |
|---|---|---|---|---|
| Syncretism | within | no | possibly | within |
| Deponency | across | canonically | not canonically | within |
| Metaconjugation | across | no | yes | within |

mismatch exhibited by the Old Norse preterite-present verbs deviates from the canonical deponency of Latin deponent verbs: Their mismatch is partly an effect of their "strong present, weak past" pattern of inflection-class membership, and the fact that their present-tense forms have "set aside" their past-tense function does not entail the absence of any forms serving that function.

## 12.5  Same morphology, different function

In Chapter 10 and in this chapter, we have examined the phenomena of syncretism, deponency and metaconjugation. Instances of these phenomena are alike in that they exhibit the same morphology exhibiting different functions in different contexts. Notwithstanding this similarity, the three phenomena differ in more subtle ways (Table 12.22). While syncretism is ordinarily a property of individual paradigms, deponency and metaconjugation are phenomena that can only be identified by comparing distinct paradigms. While canonical instances of deponency involve defectiveness, neither syncretism nor metaconjugation has any logical connection to the incidence of defectiveness. And while metaconjugation is by definition sensitive to inflection-class distinctions, neither deponency nor syncretism has any necessary sensitivity to inflection-class distinctions (though this possibility is not strictly excluded in either case).

   An overarching generalization about patterns of syncretism, deponency and metaconjugation is that a given pattern is typically associated with a single part of speech. Nevertheless, instances in which the same morphology is systematically employed for more than one function do include cases in which the distinct functions may be associated with distinct parts of speech. Such polyfunctionality is yet another kind of mismatch between content and form; we examine its characteristics in the next chapter.

# 13 *Polyfunctionality*

In Section 7.2, I proposed that the canonical relation between inflected words' content and their form possesses the five characteristics in (1). We have subsequently seen deviations from characteristics (1a–d). While a content cell's morphosyntactic property set is canonically identical with that of its form correspondent (= (1a)), instances of morphomic properties, syncretism and deponency deviate from this canonical identity. Although the form correspondents of a content paradigm's cells canonically contain the same stem (= (1b)), some instances of overabundance (those engendered by the definition of ***Corr***) deviate from this uniformity, as do instances of true defectiveness and suppletion (including heteroclisis). Though it is canonical for cells in the content paradigms of distinct lexemes to have distinct form correspondents and hence distinct realizations (= (1c)), instances of homomorphy are deviations from this regularity. And while it is canonical for lexemes belonging to the same syntactic category to have isomorphic content paradigms (= (1d)), the phenomenon of overdifferentiation deviates from this canonical pattern.

(1)      The canonical relation between content paradigms and form paradigms possesses characteristics (a)–(e).

        a.  **Property-set preservation.** Content cells and their form correspondents have the same property set; that is, for any property set $\sigma$, $pm(\sigma) = \sigma$.
             *Deviations:* morphomic properties (Chapter 8), syncretism (Chapter 10), deponency (Chapter 12)

        b.  **Stem invariance.** All of a lexeme's inflected forms are based on the same stem; that is, each lexeme L has a single stem Z such that for each cell $\langle L, \sigma \rangle$ in L's content paradigm, ***Corr***$(\langle L, \sigma \rangle) = \langle Z, \sigma \rangle$.
             *Deviations:* overabundance engendered by ***Corr*** (Section 9.1), form defectiveness (Section 9.4), suppletion and heteroclisis (Chapter 11)

        c.  **Unambiguity.** Distinct lexemes do not have identical realizations; that is, there are no two lexemes $L_1$, $L_2$ such that for some morphosyntactic property set $\sigma$, ***Corr***$(\langle L_1, \sigma \rangle) = $ ***Corr***$(\langle L_2, \sigma \rangle)$.
             *Deviation:* homomorphy (Section 4.3)

    d. **Isomorphism of paradigms belonging to the same part of speech.**
Lexemes belonging to the same syntactic category have isomorphic
paradigms; that is, if two lexemes $L_1$, $L_2$ belong to the same syntactic
category, then $\langle L_1, \sigma \rangle$ is a cell in $L_1$'s content paradigm if and only if $\langle L_2, \sigma \rangle$ is a cell in $L_2$'s content paradigm.
      *Deviation:* overdifferentiation (Section 9.3)
    e. **Non-isomorphism of paradigms belonging to the distinct parts of
speech.** Lexemes belonging to distinct syntactic categories inflect for
distinct property sets; that is, if two lexemes $L_1$, $L_2$ belong to the distinct
syntactic categories, then there is no morphosyntactic property set $\sigma$ such
that $\langle L_1, \sigma \rangle$ is a cell in $L_1$'s content paradigm and $\langle L_2, \sigma \rangle$ is a cell in $L_2$'s
content paradigm.

In this chapter, I consider a final sort of deviation from the canonical relation
between content and form in morphology. This is the phenomenon of polyfunctionality, the systematic use of the same morphology for more than one
purpose. Instances of polyfunctionality vary widely in their characteristics. In
some cases, the same morphology has more than one use in the inflection of the
same class of lexemes. In Section 8.3, we observed that in Noon, the verb suffix *-uunun* expresses the perfect passive in some cases (e.g. (2)) and the perfect
plural in other cases (e.g. (3)); in some instances, it is ambiguous between these
two uses (Maria Soukka, personal communication), as in (4). But the phenomenon of polyfunctionality also comprises cases in which the same morphology
expresses one kind of content in the inflection of one category of lexemes and a
distinct kind of content in the inflection of a distinct category of lexemes.

(2)      *Jën-aa*     *tóoh*    *ñam-uunun.*
        fish-DEF    all      eat-PASS.PERF
        The  whole fish has been eaten.'
(3)      *Oomaa-caa*    *fool-uunun*    *bes-ii*     *tóoh.*
        children-DEF    run-PL.PERF    day-DEF    all
        The  children have run all day.'
(4)      *Pe'-caa*     *ñam-uunun.*
        goats-DEF   eat-PL.PERF   OR           eat-PASS.PERF
        Ambiguous: The  goats have eaten.'       The  goats have been eaten.'

Canonically, lexemes in different syntactic categories exhibit different morphology. This is because, canonically, they inflect for different morphosyntactic property sets, and canonically, different morphosyntactic property sets
have different exponents. In English, for example, the inflectional exponents of
plural number in nouns are generally distinct from those of past tense in verbs
(Table 13.1). Occasionally distinct content is expressed by the same morphology in different syntactic categories; in the simplest cases (e.g. *Pat like-s dog-s*),
this is apparently nothing more than simple homophony. But there are also

Table 13.1 *Examples of number marking in English nouns and tense marking in English verbs*

| Noun plurals | | Past-tense verb forms | |
|---|---|---|---|
| -s | *dogs* | -d | *walked* |
| -en | *oxen* | /i/ → /ɛ/ + *t* | *meant* |
| /æ/ → /ɛ/ | *men* | /ɪ/ → /æ/ | *sang* |
| /ʊ/ → /ɪ/ | *women* | /ɪ/ → /ʌ/ | *dug* |
| /u/ → /i/ | *teeth* | /ʌ/ → /e/ | *came* |
| /aw/ → /aj/ | *mice* | /aj/ → /o/ | *wrote* |
| | | /aj/ → /ɪ/ | *bit* |
| | | rime → /ɔt/ | *taught, sought* |

Table 13.2 *Three series of person/number suffixes in Noon*

| | | Relational | Object | Possessor |
|---|---|---|---|---|
| 1SG | | -roo | -roo | -goo |
| 2SG | | -fu | -raa | -garaa |
| 3SG | | -ci | -ri | -gari |
| 1PL | EXCL | -ríi | -ríi | -gёríi |
| | INCL | -ruu | -ruu | -garuu |
| 2PL | | -rúu | -rúu | -gёrúu |
| 3PL | | -ɓa | -ɓa | -gaɓa |

cases in which distinct but related content is systematically expressed by the same morphology in different syntactic categories. Such cases are instances of **transcategorial polyfunctionality**.

I consider three examples of transcategorial polyfunctionality and demonstrate the interpretation of their characteristics under the paradigm-linkage hypothesis. All three examples involve polyfunctional person/number marking: The first is from Noon (Section 13.1), the second from Baure (Section 13.2), and the third from Hungarian (Section 13.3).

## 13.1   *Polyfunctional person/number marking in Noon (Niger-Congo:Senegal)*

The Noon language has three series of person/number markers (Table 13.2). The three series exhibit a number of similarities; indeed, in the expression of certain

Table 13.3 *Noun-class markers in Noon*

| Class | sg | pl |
|-------|-----|-----|
| cl1 | ∅ | *c-* |
| cl2 | *f-* | *c-* |
| cl3 | *m-* | *c-* |
| cl4 | *k-* | *t-* |
| cl5 | *p-* | *t-* |
| cl6 | *j-* | *t-* |

Table 13.4 *Noon location markers*

| | | |
|------|-------|---------------------|
| loc1 | *-ii* | (near the speaker) |
| loc2 | *-um* | (near the addressee) |
| loc3 | *-aa* | (distant) |

person/number combinations, the relational suffix is identical to the corresponding object suffix. Moreover, as I now show, the three series are not each simply reserved for the expression of its own distinct kind of person/number inflection.

### 13.1.1 Person/number markers in Noon

In analyzing the Noon noun-class system, Soukka (2000) distinguishes six classes (essentially genders) whose characteristic singular and plural prefixes are as in Table 13.3. In indefinite uses, a noun's noun-class membership is either marked prefixally or is not overtly marked. In particular, indefinite forms of nouns in classes 4–6 carry the prefixal noun-class marker of the appropriate number; indefinite forms in class 3, by contrast, carry the noun-class marker *m-* in both the singular and the plural (so it may instead be seen as a stem-initial consonant that happens to coincide with the noun's singular noun-class prefix); and indefinites in classes 1 and 2 lack any noun-class prefix. In definite uses, prefixal marking is as in indefinite forms; but here, a noun's class marker also appears suffixally (no matter which class the noun belongs to) and is in turn obligatorily followed by one of the three location markers in Table 13.4. The examples in Table 13.5 illustrate.

Ordinary possession is expressed by means of a person/number suffix attached at the end of a definite form; example (5) illustrates. (See again Table 13.2 for the full inventory of these possessor suffixes.) Because the use of these suffixes crosscuts that of the location markers, a given noun has a wide range of possessor-marked definite forms; for example, the noun K-EDIK tre e' has the forty-two possessor-marked forms in Table 13.6.

Table 13.5 *Indefinite and definite forms of nouns in the six Noon noun classes*

| | Class | Gloss | Indefinite | Definite | | |
|---|---|---|---|---|---|---|
| | | | | loc1 | loc2 | loc3 |
| SG | cl1 | door' | *hal* | *hal-ii* | *hal-um* | *hal-aa* |
| | cl2 | hous e' | *kaan* | *kaan-fii* | *kaan-fum* | *kaan-faa* |
| | cl3 | s̆ auce' | *mesip* | *mesip-mii* | *mesip-mum* | *mesip-maa* |
| | cl4 | tre e' | *k-edik* | *k-edik-kii* | *k-edik-kum* | *k-edik-kaa* |
| | cl5 | thre ad' | *p-ëlkít* | *p-ëlkít-pii* | *p-ëlkít-pum* | *p-ëlkít-paa* |
| | cl6 | fi nger' | *j-okon* | *j-okon-jii* | *j-okon-jum* | *j-okon-jaa* |
| PL | cl1 | doors ' | *hal* | *hal-cii* | *hal-cum* | *hal-caa* |
| | cl2 | hous es' | *kaan* | *kaan-cii* | *kaan-cum* | *kaan-caa* |
| | cl3 | s̆ auces' | *mesip* | *mesip-cii* | *mesip-cum* | *mesip-caa* |
| | cl4 | tre es' | *t-edik* | *t-edik-tii* | *t-edik-tum* | *t-edik-taa* |
| | cl5 | thre ads' | *t-ëlkít* | *t-ëlkít-tii* | *t-ëlkít-tum* | *t-ëlkít-taa* |
| | cl6 | fi ngers' | *t-okon* | *t-okon-tii* | *t-okon-tum* | *t-okon-taa* |

*ë* = [ə].

Table 13.6 *Possessed forms of the Noon noun к-ЕDIK 'tree' (Class 4, Type A)*

| | Possessor | Definite | | |
|---|---|---|---|---|
| | | LOC1 | LOC2 | LOC3 |
| SG | 1SG | *k-edik-kii-goo* | *k-edik-kum-goo* | *k-edik-kaa-goo* |
| | 2SG | *k-edik-kii-garaa* | *k-edik-kum-garaa* | *k-edik-kaa-garaa* |
| | 3SG | *k-edik-kii-gari* | *k-edik-kum-gari* | *k-edik-kaa-gari* |
| | 1PL EXCL | *k-edik-kii-gëríi* | *k-edik-kum-gëríi* | *k-edik-kaa-gëríi* |
| | 1PL INCL | *k-edik-kii-garuu* | *k-edik-kum-garuu* | *k-edik-kaa-garuu* |
| | 2PL | *k-edik-kii-gërúu* | *k-edik-kum-gërúu* | *k-edik-kaa-gërúu* |
| | 3PL | *k-edik-kii-gaɓa* | *k-edik-kum-gaɓa* | *k-edik-kaa-gaɓa* |
| PL | 1SG | *t-edik-tii-goo* | *t-edik-tum-goo* | *t-edik-taa-goo* |
| | 2SG | *t-edik-tii-garaa* | *t-edik-tum-garaa* | *t-edik-taa-garaa* |
| | 3SG | *t-edik-tii-gari* | *t-edik-tum-gari* | *t-edik-taa-gari* |
| | 1PL EXCL | *t-edik-tii-gëríi* | *t-edik-tum-gëríi* | *t-edik-taa-gëríi* |
| | 1PL INCL | *t-edik-tii-garuu* | *t-edik-tum-garuu* | *t-edik-taa-garuu* |
| | 2PL | *t-edik-tii-gërúu* | *t-edik-tum-gërúu* | *t-edik-taa-gërúu* |
| | 3PL | *t-edik-tii-gaɓa* | *t-edik-tum-gaɓa* | *t-edik-taa-gaɓa* |

(5)   *k-edik-kii-gëríi*
      CL4-tree-CL4.DEF.LOC1-1PL.EXCL.POSS
      this  tree of ours (excl.) near me'

The possessor suffixes in Table 13.2 are used to express ordinary kinds of possession. Many nouns, however, have referents that stand in some kind of intrinsic relation to a particular individual or individuals; inalienable possession is one such relation, genetic or legal relationships are another. I shall call nouns of this kind "Type R" nouns. With Type R nouns, the person and number of the related individual(s) is expressed not by a possessive suffix, but by one of the relational suffixes in Table 13.2. For example, 'your (sg) wife/woman' is expressed by means of the relational suffix *-fu*, as in (6b).

(6)    a. *ɓeti*              c. *\*ɓeti-fii-fu*
          woman
          (CL2)
       b. *ɓeti-fu*           d. *ɓeti-fii*
          woman-2SG.REL          woman-CL2.DEF.LOC1
          ʲour  wife'            'this woman near me'

The relational suffixes in Table 13.2 have some distinctive distributional characteristics. Even though a noun bearing a relational suffix is definite in reference, it does not exhibit the kind of definiteness marking exemplified in Table 13.5; (6c) is ungrammatical, notwithstanding its parallelism to the well-formed examples in Table 13.6. This does not, however, mean that Type R nouns cannot carry definite marking; for instance, (6d) is perfectly grammatical, because its definite marking does not coincide with relational marking. Finally, the relational suffixes in Table 13.2 are only used with singular Type R nouns; in the plural, a Type R noun instead exhibits the ordinary pattern of possessor marking observed in Table 13.6. Thus, the Type R noun KAAN 'hous e' has relational person/number marking in the singular but possessive person/number marking in the plural, as in Table 13.7.

The possessive and relational suffixes are person/number markers that are used with nouns, but Noon verbs also inflect for the person and number of a pronominal object, as in (7). (See again Table 13.2 for the full inventory of these object suffixes.)

(7)    *Kodu lóm-í'-tii-ri*              *dara.*
       Kodu buy-TRANS-ASP.NEG-3SG.OBJ   nothing
       K odu hasn't bought her anything.'

There is, again, a considerable overlap in form among the three series of person/number suffixes. The relational and object suffixes differ only in the second and third persons of the singular, and the possessor suffixes are, in general, combinations of a formative *gA* with the object suffixes, where *A* is realized as *ë* ([ə]) before a long tense syllable, and as *a* otherwise. The three series of suffixes also overlap in their function. In particular, Noon prepositions

Table 13.7 *Relational and possessed forms of the Noon noun* KAAN *'house'*
*(Class 2, Type R)*

| SG: Relation PL: Possessor | Location unspecified | Definite | | |
|---|---|---|---|---|
| | | LOC1 | LOC2 | LOC3 |
| SG 1SG | *kaan-doo* (← *-roo*) | | | |
| 2SG | *kaan-fu* | | | |
| 3SG | *kaan-ci* | | | |
| 1PL EXCL | *kaan-díí*( ← *-ríí*) | | | |
| 1PL INCL | *kaan-duu* (← *-ruu*) | | | |
| 2PL | *kaan-dúu* (← *-rúu*) | | | |
| 3PL | *kaan-ɓa* | | | |
| PL 1SG | | *kaan-cii-goo* | *kaan-cum-goo* | *kaan-caa-goo* |
| 2SG | | *kaan-cii-garaa* | *kaan-cum-garaa* | *kaan-caa-garaa* |
| 3SG | | *kaan-cii-gari* | *kaan-cum-gari* | *kaan-caa-gari* |
| 1PL EXCL | | *kaan-cii-gëríi* | *kaan-cum-gëríi* | *kaan-caa-gëríi* |
| 1PL INCL | | *kaan-cii-garuu* | *kaan-cum-garuu* | *kaan-caa-garuu* |
| 2PL | | *kaan-cii-gërúu* | *kaan-cum-gërúu* | *kaan-caa-gërúu* |
| 3PL | | *kaan-cii-gaɓa* | *kaan-cum-gaɓa* | *kaan-caa-gaɓa* |

inflect for the person and number of a pronominal object, and prepositions fall into three groups according to which of the three series of suffixes they employ (Table 13.8). The preposition BALAA ̀be fore' employs the relational suffixes, as in (8); NA ̀w ith' employs the object suffixes, as in (9); and FODII ̀lik e, as' is distinguished from all other prepositions in employing the possessor suffixes, as in (10).[1]

(8)   *Mi le'-'a        kaan  balaa-fu.*
      I    reach-NARR home before-2SG.REL
      I came home before you.'

(9)   *Mi  hay      na-raa.*
      I    come  with-2SG.OBJ
      'I come with you.'

(10)  *Mi  tum  fodii-garaa.*
      I    do   like-2SG.POSS
      I do a s you do.'

---

1 One can imagine processes of grammaticalization by which BALAA and FODII might have developed from nouns (in the latter case, a Type R noun), and NA, from a verb. A historical account of these prepositions awaits further research; at issue here, however, are their synchronic characteristics.

Table 13.8 *Person/number inflections of three prepositions in Noon*

|  | BALAA be fore' | NA w ith' | FODII lik e, as' |
|---|---|---|---|
| 1SG | balaa-roo | na-roo | fodii-goo |
| 2SG | balaa-fu | na-raa | fodii-garaa |
| 3SG | balaa-ci | na-ri | fodii-gari |
| 1PL EXCL | balaa-ríi | na-ríi | fodii-gëríi |
| 1PL INCL | balaa-ruu | na-ruu | fodii-garuu |
| 2PL | balaa-rúu | na-rúu | fodii-gërúu |
| 3PL | balaa-ɓa | na-ɓa | fodii-gaɓa |

Thus, there are two kinds of polyfunctionality in Noon person/number inflections. First, most suffixes serve more than one function because they appear in more than one series, e.g. -*ríi* can code a relational target (as in (11a)), an object target (as in (11b, c)) or (as part of the combination -*gëríi*) a possessor target (as in (11d)). Second, the relational and possessor series each have more than one function, serving both to code a relational or possessor target (as in (12a, b)) and to code a preposition's pronominal object (as in (12c, d)).

(11)  a. *kaan-díi( ← -ríi)*      ɓur (excl) house'
      b. *feek-kíi( ← -ríi)*      'hit us (excl)'
      c. *balaa-ríi*      'before us (excl)'
      d. *k-edik-kii-gë-ríi*      ɓur (excl) tree near me'
(12)  a. *ɓeti-fu*      ẏour (sg) wife'
      b. *k-edik-kii-ga-raa*      ẏour (sg) tree near me'
      c. *balaa-fu*      ɓe fore you (sg)'
      d. *fodii-ga-raa*      'like you (sg)'

*13.1.2  Modeling Noon person/number marking*
Noon's person/number morphology involves the inflectional categories in Table 13.9, where the value of CTRL is a specification of a head's agreement controller.

The ***Corr*** and PF functions are defined as in (13) and (14). The rules of exponence for person/number agreement occupy the rule blocks V and VI and the portmanteau rule block [ VI, V];[2] these rules are formulated in (15). (The rules in blocks I through IV account for other aspects of nominal and verbal inflection; because these are not directly relevant to the polyfunctionality of person/ number agreement in Noon, they are omitted here.)

2 A portmanteau rule block [ A, B ] houses rules whose application overrides the successive application of rules from blocks A and B. See Stump 2001: 139ff for discussion.

Table 13.9 *Property sets for Noon nouns, verbs and prepositions (partial)*

| Syntactic category | Inflectional categories | Permissible values | |
|---|---|---|---|
| | | Atoms | Sets |
| all | PER | 1, 2, 3 | |
| | NUM | sg pl | |
| | INCL* | +− | |
| N | CTRL | poss, rel | |
| | AGR | | {PER:α NUM:β (INCL:γ) CTRL:poss} |
| | | | {PER:α NUM:β (INCL:γ) CTRL:rel} |
| V, P | CTRL | obj | |
| | AGR | | {PER:α NUM:β (INCL:γ) CTRL:obj} |

*permissible only with {pl}

(13)   Definition of the Noon ***Corr*** function

| | ***Corr***(⟨L, σ⟩) = | ***pm***₁(σ) = | ***pm***₂(σ) = |
|---|---|---|---|
| If L = FODII, | ⟨***Stem***(⟨L, σ⟩), ***pm***₁(σ)⟩ | σ[obj/poss] | |
| If L ∈ [BALAA type], | ⟨***Stem***(⟨L, σ⟩), ***pm***₂(σ)⟩ | | σ[obj/rel] |
| Otherwise, | ⟨***Stem***(⟨L, σ⟩), σ⟩ | | |

(14)   Paradigm function for Noon:
a. PF(⟨L, σ⟩) =PF( ***Corr***(⟨L, σ⟩))
b. PF(⟨X, σ⟩) =[ VI, V] : [IV : [III : [II : [I : ⟨X, σ⟩ ]]]]]

(15)   Rules of exponence for person/number inflection in Noon

| | | | Realizes person and number of | | |
|---|---|---|---|---|---|
| | | | Relation | Object | Possessor |
| **Block [vi, v]** | X, U, {AGR:{s g poss} | → X*goo* | | | ✓ |
| **Block v** | X, U, {AGR:{pos s} | → X*gA* | | | ✓ |
| **Block vi** | X, U, {AGR:{s g} | → X*roo* | ✓ | ✓ | |
| | X, U, {AGR:2s g} | → X*raa* | | ✓ | ✓ |
| | X, U, {AGR:2s g rel} | → X*fu* | ✓ | | |
| | X, U, {AGR:3s g} | → X*ri* | | ✓ | ✓ |
| | X, U, {AGR:3s g rel} | → X*ci* | ✓ | | |
| | X, U, {AGR:{pl excl}} | → X*rıí* | ✓ | ✓ | ✓ |
| | X, U, {AGR:{pl incl} | → X*ruu* | ✓ | ✓ | ✓ |
| | X, U, {AGR:2pl} | → X*rúu* | ✓ | ✓ | ✓ |
| | X, U, {AGR:3pl} | → X*6a* | ✓ | ✓ | ✓ |

Morphophonology: A → ë ([ə]) before a long tense syllable, → a otherwise.

The -*goo* rule in the portmanteau Block [ VI, V] expresses agreement with a first-person singular possessor; the application of this rule excludes that of any rule from Blocks V and VI. All other instances of possessor agreement require the application of the -*gA* rule in Block V, and all other instances of agreement of any sort require the application of a rule from Block VI. Most of the rules of exponence in Block VI are underspecified with respect to the kind of agreement relation they realize. For example, the -*rfí* rule is applicable in the realization of ρ:{AGR:{pl excl rel} σ:{AGR:{pl excl obj} or τ:{AGR:{pl excl poss} Examples (16)–(18) show how these rules define the realization of *kaanfu* 'your (sg) house,' *balaafu* 'be fore you (sg)' and *feekkaa* 'hit you (sg).'[3]

(16) Proof for *kaanfu* 'your (s g) house'
 a. PF(⟨KAAN, σ:{AGR:{2s g rel} ⟩)
 b.   = PF(**Corr**(⟨KAAN, σ⟩))              [by (14a)]
 c.   = PF(⟨*kaan*, σ⟩)                   [by (13)]
 d.   = [ [ VI, V] : [ IV : [ III : [ II : [ I : ⟨*kaan*, σ⟩]]]]]  [by (14b)]
 e.   = [ VI : ⟨*kaan*, σ⟩]              [IFD, FCD]
 f.   = ⟨*kaan-fu*, σ⟩                 [by (15)]

(17) Proof for *balaafu* 'be fore you (sg)'
 a. PF(⟨BALAA, σ:{AGR:{2s g obj} ⟩)
 b.   = PF(**Corr**(⟨BALAA, σ⟩))           [by (14a)]
 c.   = PF(⟨*balaa*, τ:{AGR:{2s g rel} ⟩)     [by (13)]
 d.   = [ [ VI, V] : [ IV : [ III : [ II : [ I : ⟨*balaa*, τ⟩]]]]]  [by (14b)]
 e.   = [ VI : ⟨*balaa*, τ⟩]           [IFD, FCD]
 f.   = ⟨*balaa-fu*, τ⟩             [by (15)]

(18) Proof for *feekkaa* 'hit you (s g)'
 a. PF(⟨FEEK, σ:{AGR:{2s g obj} ⟩)
 b.   = PF(**Corr**(⟨FEEK, σ⟩))            [by (14a)]
 c.   = PF(⟨ *feek*, σ⟩)               [by (13)]
 d.   = [ [ VI, V] : [ IV : [ III : [ II : [ I : ⟨ *feek*, σ⟩]]]]]  [by (14b)]
 e.   = [ VI : ⟨ *feek*, σ⟩]           [IFD, FCD]
 f.   = ⟨ *feek-raa*, σ⟩            [by (15)]
 g.   = ⟨ *feekkaa*, σ⟩           [by sandhi]

Consider again the two types of polyfunctionality seen above in (11) and (12). In the analysis proposed here, the polyfunctionality in (11) might be characterized as **polyfunctionality by underspecification**: The -*rfí* rule in Block VI is not specific about the kind of agreement controller whose person and number it expresses. By contrast, the polyfunctionality in (12) is not an effect

---

3 According to the Identity Function Default (IFD), [ A : ⟨X, σ⟩ ] = ⟨X, σ⟩ if there is no rule in Block A that is applicable to ⟨X, σ⟩. According to the Function Composition Default (FCD), the absence of any applicable rule in a portmanteau rule block [ A, B ] causes [ [ A, B ] : ⟨L, σ⟩ ] to default to [ A : [ B : ⟨L, σ⟩ ]]. See Stump 2001: 139ff for discussion.

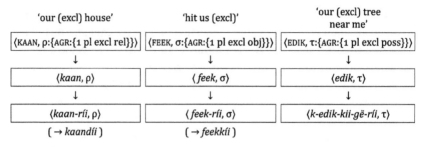

Figure 13.1 *Polyfunctionality by underspecification in Noon*

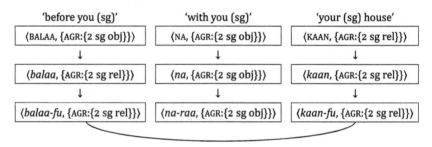

Figure 13.2 *Polyfunctionality by stipulation in Noon*

of underspecification, but depends on the definition of ***Corr*** in (13) – specifically, on the definition of its property mappings ***pm***$_1$ and ***pm***$_2$. Thus, this might be described as **stipulated polyfunctionality**. These distinct kinds of polyfunctionality are represented schematically in Figures 13.1 and 13.2.

### 13.2    *Second example : Polyfunctional person/number marking in Baure (Maipurean:Bolivia)*

In the Noon example, the polyfunctional morphology has the same morphotactics throughout. On the other hand, the possessor, relational and object suffixes are sometimes distinguished in form: The relational suffixes are distinguished in the second and third persons singular; and while the possessor suffixes can usually be analyzed as the combination of a formative *gA* with an object suffix, this is not the case in the first person singular. The following example of polyfunctionality from Baure is therefore quite different from the Noon example. In Baure, the person/number clitics in Table 13.10 are used to encode different kinds of agreement relations. Unlike the Noon affixes, these clitics do not fall into different series with different privileges of occurrence; but, again unlike

Table 13.10 *Baure person/*
*number clitics*

|   |   | SG | PL |
|---|---|----|----|
| I |   | *ni* | *vi* |
| 2 |   | *pi* | *yi* |
| 3 | MASC | *ro* | *no* |
|   | FEM | *ri* |  |

the Noon affixes, they do vary in their morphotactics, appearing sometimes
proclitically and sometimes enclitically.

### 13.2.1 The Baure person/number clitics

The person/number clitics in Table 13.10 serve to express five kinds of agreement relations. As verbal proclitics, they express (i) **subject agreement**, as in
(19)–(21).[4] As verbal enclitics, they express (ii) **direct object agreement**, as in
(20a, b) and (21), and (iii) **indirect object agreement** (as in (21)); when both
are present, the indirect-object clitic precedes the direct-object clitic. Unlike
subject agreement, object agreement is optional; thus, there is no object agreement in (20c). As nominal proclitics, they express (iv) **the person and number
of a possessor**, as in (22) and (24). And as enclitics, they express (v) **agreement with the subject of a nonverbal predicate**, appearing after its copula-
tive morphology, as in (23) and (24). The full range of agreement patterns
realized by the Baure person/number clitics may be summarized as in (25).

(19)   Intransitive verbs
    a. *ro= šim    teč    aren.*
       3SG.M =arrive  DEM2.M  bird
       'A bird arrived.'
    b. *piti'  pi = kotoreko-wo  maiyok.*
       2SG    2SG = work-COP  much
       'You work a lot.'

(20)   Transitive verbs
    a. *ver   ni=ikomorik=ro.*
       PERF  1SG=kill= 3SG.M
       'I already killed it.'
    b. *te      simori  no=ikomorik=ro.*
       DEM1.M  pig    3PL=kill=3SG.M
       'They killed the pig.'

4  All Baure examples are taken from Danielsen 2007, Danielsen and Granadillo 2008, and Keine
   2012.

c. *nti'   ni=komorik  p-a-š       simori.*
1SG  1SG=kill    one-CLF-one  pig
I killed one pig.'

(21)   Ditransitive verbs

a. *pi = pa = ni= ro.*
2SG = give = 1SG = 3SG.M
You give it to me.'

c. *pi = ihek-ino= ni= ro.*
2SG = comb-BEN = 1SG = 3SG.M
You comb him for me.'

b. *ni= pa = pi = ro.*
1SG = give = 2SG = 3SG.M
I give it to you.'

(22)   Possessors

a. *vi = tovian*
1PL =ne ighbor
our neighbor'

b. *to    ni= ašok*
ART  1SG =gra ndpa
my grandfather'

c. *to    ro= wer       to    ni= tovian*
ART  3SG.M = house  ART  1SG = neighbor
my neighbor's house'

(23)   Nonverbal predicates

a. *nka    pero-no-wo= ni.*
NEG  be.lazy-NMLZ1-COP = 1SG
I am not a lazybones.'

b. *ver    ane-wapa= ni.*
PERF  old-COS = 1SG
I am already old.'

(24)   Nominal predicates with possessor

a. *ni= tobiano-wo= ro.*
1SG = neighbor-COP = 3SG.M
He is my neighbor.'

b. *tič      eton    ni= torie-wo= ri.*
DEM2.F  woman  1SG = friend-COP = 3SG.F
That woman is my friend.'

c. *tič      ti        ro= eto-wo= ri              to    ni= avinon.*
DEM2.F  DEM1.F  3SG.M = sister-COP = 3SG.F  ART  1SG = husband
This (she) is the sister of my husband.'

(25)   Morphotactics of the Baure person/number clitics

a. *Intransitives:*
SUBJ-Stem

d. *Nominal possessors:*
POSS-Stem

b. *Transitives:*
SUBJ-Stem-DIRObj

e. *Non-verbal predication:*
Stem-COP-SUBJ

c. *Ditransitives:*
SUBJ-Stem-INDObj-DIRObj

f. *Possessed nominal predicates:*
POSS-Stem-COP-SUBJ

### 13.2.2 Modeling Baure person/number clitics

Stump (1993b) floats the idea that a rule of affixal exponence should be divided into two independent parts, one specifying the affix's form and morphosyntactic content, and the other specifying its morphotactics; this idea is motivated by the fact that an affix may have constant form and content yet exhibit variable morphotactics. Pursuing this idea, Stump (2014c) proposes a morphological framework distinguishing exponence declarations from sequencing rules: An **exponence declaration** [[Z, τ]] simply specifies that an affix Z has the property set τ as its content; a **sequencing rule** specifies how an affix with declaration [[ Z, τ ]] combines with a stem in realizing some property set σ such that τ ⊆ σ. This conception of inflectional morphology affords a satisfactory account of the Baure person/number clitics.

I assume that where ⟨L, σ⟩ is a cell in the content paradigm of a Baure noun or verb L, σ contains zero to three agreement sets. An **agreement set** is an instantiation of {CTRL PER NUM (GEND)} based on the values in (26a) and the property coöccurrence restriction in (26b). For example, (27a) is the cell in the content paradigm of IKOMORIK ʼkillʼ that is specified for first-person singular subject agreement and third-person singular masculine object agreement; and (27b) is the cell in the content paradigm of TOVIAN 'neighbor' that is specified for a first-person plural possessor.

(26)  a.  Agreement properties in Baure

| Inflectional category | Permissible values |
|---|---|
| CTRL | sbj, iobj, dobj, copsbj, poss |
| PER | 1, 2, 3 |
| NUM | sg, pl |
| GEND | masc, fem |

     b.  Property coöccurrence restriction:

[{GEND:masc} ∨ {GEND:fem}] ↔ {PER:3, NUM:sg}

(27)  Two content cells
    a.  ⟨IKOMORIK, { bj 1sg }{obj 3s g masc} ⟩
    b.  ⟨TOVIAN, {pos s 1pl} ⟩

Content cells such as those in (27) are assigned their form correspondents by the *Corr* function defined in (28), whose property mapping *pm* is defined in (29); in accordance with (29), a content cell's controller properties are replaced with the morphomic properties "i," "ii" and "iii," whose significance will emerge presently. Given these definitions, the content cells in (27) have the form correspondents in (30).

(28)  Definition of *Corr* for Baure: *Corr*(⟨L, σ⟩) = ⟨*Stem*(⟨L, σ⟩), *pm*(σ)⟩

'You give it to me.'

| 2SG= give | | =1SG | =3SG.M |
|---|---|---|---|
| pi= | pa | =ni | =ro |

| ↑ | ↑ | ↑ | ↑ |
|---|---|---|---|
| Block III | Stem | Block I | Block II |

Figure 13.3 *Blocks of sequencing rules for Baure pronominal clitics*

(29)   Definition of the Baure property mapping **pm**
a. $pm(\{\alpha_1, \ldots \alpha_n\}) = \{ pm(\alpha_1), \ldots pm(\alpha_n)\}$
b. $pm(\text{iobj}) = pm(\text{copsbj}) = \text{i}$
c. $pm(\text{dobj}) = \text{ii}$
d. $pm(\text{sbj}) = pm(\text{poss}) = \text{iii}$
e. Otherwise, $pm(\alpha) = \alpha$

(30)   Form correspondents of the content cells in (27)
a. ⟨*ikomorik*, {ii 1s   g}{i 3s   g masc} ⟩
b. ⟨*tovian*, {ii 1pl}   ⟩

In accordance with the assumptions of Stump 2014c, form cells such as those in (30) are realized not by simple rules of exponence, but by exponence declarations together with sequencing rules. The Baure pronominal clitics have the exponence declarations in (31). The sequencing rules for these clitics are organized into three blocks such that Block I sequences inner enclitics, Block II outer enclitics and Block III proclitics, as in Figure 13.3. The five agreement patterns exemplified above can thus be defined by the paradigm function in (32) and the sequencing rules in (33). These rules cause agreement sets bearing the morphemes "i" and "ii" to be realized by suffixal exponents in Blocks I and II (respectively) and cause agreement sets bearing the morpheme "iii" to be realized by prefixal exponents in Block III. The proof of *ni= ikomorik= ro* 'I kill it' in (34) exemplifies the workings of the analysis.

(31)   Exponence declarations for the Baure pronominal clitics
⟦*ni*, {s g} ⟧          ⟦*vi*, {pl}⟧  ⟧
⟦*pi*, {2s g} ⟧        ⟦*yi*, {2pl}⟧  ⟧
⟦*ro*, {3 sg masc} ⟧   ⟦*no*, {3pl}⟧  ⟧
⟦*ri*, {3 sg fem} ⟧

(32)   Partial definition of the Baure paradigm function:
a. $\text{PF}(\langle L, \sigma \rangle) = \text{PF}( \textbf{\textit{Corr}}(\langle L, \sigma \rangle))$
b. $\text{PF}(\langle X, \sigma \rangle) = [ \text{III} : [ \text{II} : [ \text{I} : \langle X, \sigma \rangle ]]]$

(33)   Sequencing rules for Baure person/number clitics
Where ⟦ C, τ ⟧ is a pronominal clitic such that $\tau \subseteq \sigma$,

| Block I. | X, V, {σ:i} | → XC |
|---|---|---|
| Block II. | X, V, {σ:ii} | → XC |
| Block III. | X, V, {σ:iii} | → CX |

(34)    Proof of *ni= ikomorik= ro* I kill it'
        Where σ = {{sbj 1sg} {dobj 3sg masc}} and ***Stem***(⟨IKOMORIK, σ⟩) = *ikomorik*:

    a.  PF(⟨IKOMORIK, σ⟩)

    b.  = PF(***Corr***(⟨IKOMORIK, σ⟩))    [by (32a)]

    c.  = PF(⟨*ikomorik*, ***pm***(σ)⟩)    [by (28)]

    d.  = PF(⟨*ikomorik*, τ:{i 1s  g}i 3s  g masc} ⟩)    [by (29)]

    e.  = [III : [II : [ I : ⟨*ikomorik*, τ⟩]]]    [by (32b)]

    f.  = [III : [II : ⟨*ikomorik*, τ⟩]]    [IFD][5]

    g.  = [III : ⟨*ikomorik=ro*, τ⟩]    [by (31), (33)]

    h.  = ⟨*ni=ikomorik=ro*, τ⟩    [by (31), (33)]

According to this analysis, the polyfunctionality of Baure person/number clitics involves both underspecification and stipulation. The exponence declarations in (31) cause possessor agreement, direct- and indirect-object agreement, verbal subject agreement and copular subject agreement to be assigned the same exponence; on the other hand, the property mapping (29) and the sequencing rules in (30) cause the agreement clitics to follow three different morphotactic patterns, with indirect-object and copular subject agreement expressed by an inner enclitic, direct-object agreement expressed by an outer enclitic, and possessor and verbal subject agreement expressed by a proclitic. The realizations schematized in Figure 13.4 exemplify the polyfunctionality of the third-person singular masculine proclitic *ro=* .

## 13.3    Third example : Polyfunctional person⁄number marking in Hungarian

In the analyses proposed for person/number marking in Noon and Baure, polyfunctionality arises in two ways: Stipulated polyfunctionality arises from property mappings (whose effect is to cause distinct kinds of content to be realized the same way); and polyfunctionality by underspecification arises from rules of exponence that realize an underspecified property set (Noon) or from a set of underspecified exponence declarations (Baure). Hungarian presents a very different source of polyfunctionality.

### 13.3.1    Person/number suffixes in Hungarian

In Hungarian, there is a single system of person/number suffixes that has three functions. In the inflection of nouns, these suffixes express the person and number of a possessor; in the inflection of ordinary postpositions, they express

---

5  According to the Identity Function Default (IFD), [ A : ⟨X, σ⟩ ] = ⟨X, σ⟩ if there is no rule in Block A that is applicable to ⟨X, σ⟩.

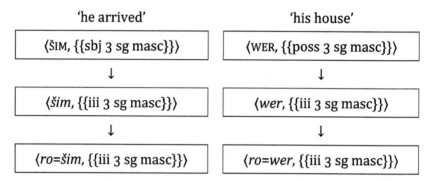

Figure 13.4 *Polyfunctionality in Baure person/number marking*

Table 13.11 *Comparison of (a) a noun's possessor marking, (b) a postposition's pronominal object marking and (c) the ablative case forms of personal pronouns in Hungarian*

| KÖNYV'book' (singular possessee) | | MÖGÖTT'be hind' | | Ablative case forms of personal pronouns | |
|---|---|---|---|---|---|
| *könyv-e-m* | ḟny book' | *mögött-e-m* | be hind me' | *től-e-m* | 'from me' |
| *könyv-e-d* | ỳour (s g) book' | *mögött-e-d* | be hind you (sg)' | *től-e-d* | 'from you (sg)' |
| *könyv-e* | he r/his book' | *mögött-e* | be hind her/him' | *től-e* | 'from her/him' |
| *könyv-ünk* | ȯur book' | *mögött-ünk* | be hind us' | *től-ünk* | 'from us' |
| *könyv-e-tek* | ỳour (pl) book' | *mögött-e-tek* | be hind you (pl)' | *től-e-tek* | 'from you (pl)' |
| *könyv-ük* | the ir book' | *mögött-ük* | be hind them' | *től-ük* | 'from them' |

the person and number of the postposition's pronominal object; and these suffixes serve in expressing a personal pronoun's oblique case forms by inflecting a postposition-like case marker for the pronoun's person and number. Table 13.11 exemplifies these three functions: In the first column, the noun "book" inflects for the person and number of its possessor(s); in the second, the postposition "behind" inflects for the person and number of its pronominal object; and in the third, the ablative case stem *től-* gives rise to the ablative form of each personal pronoun by inflecting for that pronoun's person and number. (For fuller exemplification of these three functions, including all pronominal case forms, see Spencer and Stump 2013.)

### 13.3.2 *Modeling Hungarian person/number marking*
Spencer and Stump (2013) propose an analysis of Hungarian person/number inflections that is based on the paradigm-linkage hypothesis; here, I briefly

Table 13.12 *The content paradigm of Hungarian* ÉN '*I*'

| | |
|---|---|
| ⟨ÉN, nomina tive INFL:{s g} ⟩ | ⟨ÉN, de lative INFL:{1sg}}⟩ |
| ⟨ÉN, a ccusative INFL:{s g} ⟩ | ⟨ÉN, a llative INFL:{1sg}}⟩ |
| ⟨ÉN, illa tive INFL:{ sg}}⟩ | ⟨ÉN, a dessive INFL:{1sg}}⟩ |
| ⟨ÉN, ine ssive INFL:{ sg}}⟩ | ⟨ÉN, a blative INFL:{1sg}}⟩ |
| ⟨ÉN, e lative INFL:{s g}}⟩ | ⟨ÉN, da tive INFL:{1sg}}⟩ |
| ⟨ÉN, s ublative INFL:{s g} ⟩ | ⟨ÉN, ins trumental INFL:{1sg}}⟩ |
| ⟨ÉN, s uperessive INFL:{s g} ⟩ | ⟨ÉN, c ausal-final INFL:{1sg}}⟩ |

summarize the key characteristics of this analysis, highlighting the contrasts between the Hungarian person/number inflections and those of Noon and Baure.

In their analysis, Spencer and Stump assume that postpositions have content cells that are specified for an inflectional category INFL having seven possible values: (i) "no," and (ii) {PER:$\alpha$, NUM:$\beta$} where $\alpha \in \{1, 2, 3\}$ and $\beta \in \{$ g, pl$\}$ A postposition's INFL specification relates to the person and number of its object, in case this is pronominal. Nouns also have content cells that are specified for INFL; this specification relates to the person and number of the possessor(s) of the noun's referent (or to the absence of any possessor). Nouns are additionally specified for case and number; see Spencer and Stump for a full account of nominal case and number and their morphological realization. Finally, a personal pronoun has content cells that are specified for INFL (the pronoun's person and number) and for case; the pronoun ÉN I, ' for example, has the content cells in Table 13.12.

Given any cell ⟨L, $\sigma$⟩ in the content paradigm of a noun, postposition or personal pronoun L, the form correspondent of ⟨L, $\sigma$⟩ is determined by the definition of ***Corr*** in Table 13.13. When L is a noun or postposition, ***Corr***(⟨L, $\sigma$⟩) = ⟨***Stem***(⟨L, $\sigma$⟩), $\sigma$⟩; the same is true for the direct cases of personal pronouns. But where L is a personal pronoun and $\sigma$ is specified for an oblique case, ***Corr***(⟨L, $\sigma$⟩) = ⟨***ab t***($\sigma$), $\sigma$⟩, where ***ab t*** is a function that applies to a morphosyntactic property set that is specified for an oblique case to yield the absolute stem[6] of the corresponding case marker; Table 13.14 gives an extensional definition of the ***ab t*** function.

6  Spencer and Stump assume that each of the postposition-like case markers has both an "absolute" stem and a "conjunct" stem. For each oblique case $\alpha$, the absolute stem of the $\alpha$-case marker inflects with person/number suffixes in order to produce the $\alpha$-case forms of the personal pronouns; the conjunct stem of the $\alpha$-case marker is compounded with a noun's singular or plural stem in order to produce the noun's $\alpha$-case forms. Some case markers have absolute and conjunct stems that are similar or identical, e.g. *től-e* 'from him,' *Ferenc-től* 'from Ferenc' [ablatives]. But for some case markers, the two stems are dissimilar, e.g. *rajt-a* 'on it,' *könyv-ön* 'on a book' [superessives].

Table 13.13 *The value of **Corr** for nominal, postpositional and pronominal content cells in Hungarian*

| Lexeme L | Content cell $\langle$L, σ$\rangle$ | ***Stem***($\langle$L, σ$\rangle$) | Form correspondent ( = ***Corr***($\langle$L, σ$\rangle$)) |
|---|---|---|---|
| Noun N | $\langle$N, σ$\rangle$ | n | $\langle$n, σ$\rangle$ |
| Postposition P | $\langle$P, σ$\rangle$ | p | $\langle$p, σ$\rangle$ |
| Personal pronoun R <br> • if σ is nom or acc: <br> • otherwise: | $\langle$R, σ$\rangle$ | <br> r <br> – | <br> $\langle$r, σ$\rangle$ <br> $\langle$***ab** t*(σ), σ$\rangle$ <br> = $\langle$c, σ$\rangle$* |

**ʻc** is the absolute stem of the case marker corresponding to σ.

Table 13.14 *Extensional definition of the Hungarian **ab** t function*

| Morphosyntactic property set σ | Absolute stem ***ab** t*(σ) |
|---|---|
| σ:{illa tive} | *bel* |
| σ:{ine ssive} | *benn* |
| σ:{ lative} | *belől* |
| σ:{ ublative} | *rá* |
| σ:{ uperessive} | *rajt* |
| σ:{de lative} | *ról* |
| σ:{ llative} | *hozz* |
| σ:{ dessive} | *nál* |
| σ:{ blative} | *től* |
| σ:{da tive} | *nek* |
| σ:{ins trumental} | *vel* |
| σ:{ ausal-final} | *ért* |

By virtue of this definition, the form correspondent of the pronominal content cell $\langle$ÉN, {ablative INFL:{1sg}}$\rangle$ is $\langle$*től*, {ablative INFL:{1sg}}$\rangle$ – a cell in the form paradigm of a case marker. That is, a pronominal lexeme has a content paradigm but not a form paradigm, a case marker has a form paradigm but not a content paradigm, and the relation between the content paradigms of personal pronouns and the form paradigms of case markers is complex: Each of a pronoun's content cells has its form correspondent in the form paradigm of

| | | Personal pronouns, each with its own content paradigm | | | | | |
|---|---|---|---|---|---|---|---|
| | | 1sg | 2sg | 3sg | 1pl | 2pl | 3pl |
| Oblique case markers, each with its own form paradigm | illative | | | | | | |
| | inessive | | | | | | |
| | elative | | | | | | |
| | sublative | | | | | | |
| | superessive | | | | | | |
| | delative | | | | | | |
| | allative | | | | | | |
| | adessive | | | | | | |
| | ablative | | | | | | |
| | dative | | | | | | |
| | instrumental | | | | | | |
| | causal-final | | | | | | |

Figure 13.5 *The relationship between pronominal lexemes and oblique case markers in Hungarian*

a different case marker. Thus, in Figure 13.5, there are six pronominal content paradigms, each with twelve oblique-case cells, and the form correspondents of these content cells are drawn from the six-celled form paradigms of the twelve oblique case markers; oblique cells from the same content paradigm never draw their form correspondents from the same form paradigm. For illustration, the content, form and realized paradigms of the postposition MÖGÖTT 'behind' and the noun KÖNYV 'book' (nominative singular cells only) are given in Tables 13.15 and 13.16, and the content, form and realized cells of the first-person singular pronominal lexeme are given in Table 13.17.

These results follow from the assumption that Hungarian nouns, postpositions and pronouns inflect in accordance with the paradigm function in (35) and the rules of exponence in (36). The formulation of the rules in Block II accounts for the polyfunctionality of Hungarian person/number inflections: these rules apply to nouns in the realization of properties of possessor agreement; to postpositions to realize the properties of a pronominal object; and to oblique case markers to realize the oblique case forms of pronouns. This polyfunctionality is represented schematically in Figure 13.6.

(35) Paradigm function for Hungarian
Where L is noun, postposition or pronoun,
a. PF($\langle$L, σ$\rangle$) =PF( *Corr*($\langle$L, σ$\rangle$))
b. PF($\langle$X, σ$\rangle$) = III: [II: [I : $\langle$X, σ$\rangle$]]]

Table 13.15　*The content, form and realized paradigms of Hungarian* MÖGÖTT *'behind'*

| Content | Form | Realized |
|---|---|---|
| $\langle$MÖGÖTT, $\sigma_1$:{INFL:no}$\rangle$ | $\langle$mögött, $\sigma_1\rangle$ | $\langle$mögött, $\sigma_1\rangle$ |
| $\langle$MÖGÖTT, $\sigma_2$:{INFL:{1sg}}$\rangle$ | $\langle$mögött, $\sigma_2\rangle$ | $\langle$mögöttem, $\sigma_2\rangle$ |
| $\langle$MÖGÖTT, $\sigma_3$:{INFL:{2sg}}$\rangle$ | $\langle$mögött, $\sigma_3\rangle$ | $\langle$mögötted, $\sigma_3\rangle$ |
| $\langle$MÖGÖTT, $\sigma_4$:{INFL:{3sg}}$\rangle$ | $\langle$mögött, $\sigma_4\rangle$ | $\langle$mögötte, $\sigma_4\rangle$ |
| $\langle$MÖGÖTT, $\sigma_5$:{INFL:{1pl}}$\rangle$ | $\langle$mögött, $\sigma_5\rangle$ | $\langle$mögöttünk, $\sigma_5\rangle$ |
| $\langle$MÖGÖTT, $\sigma_6$:{INFL:{2pl}}$\rangle$ | $\langle$mögött, $\sigma_6\rangle$ | $\langle$mögöttetek, $\sigma_6\rangle$ |
| $\langle$MÖGÖTT, $\sigma_7$:{INFL:{3pl}}$\rangle$ | $\langle$mögött, $\sigma_7\rangle$ | $\langle$mögöttük, $\sigma_7\rangle$ |

Table 13.16　*The content, form and realized paradigms of Hungarian* KÖNYV *'book' (nominative singular cells only)*

| Content | Form | Realized |
|---|---|---|
| $\langle$ KÖNYV, $\sigma_1$:{INFL:no}$\rangle$ | $\langle$könyv, $\sigma_1\rangle$ | $\langle$könyv, $\sigma_1\rangle$ |
| $\langle$ KÖNYV, $\sigma_2$:{INFL:{1sg}}$\rangle$ | $\langle$könyv, $\sigma_2\rangle$ | $\langle$könyvem, $\sigma_2\rangle$ |
| $\langle$ KÖNYV, $\sigma_3$:{INFL:{2sg}}$\rangle$ | $\langle$könyv, $\sigma_3\rangle$ | $\langle$könyved, $\sigma_3\rangle$ |
| $\langle$ KÖNYV, $\sigma_4$:{INFL:{3sg}}$\rangle$ | $\langle$könyv, $\sigma_4\rangle$ | $\langle$könyve, $\sigma_4\rangle$ |
| $\langle$ KÖNYV, $\sigma_5$:{INFL:{1pl}}$\rangle$ | $\langle$könyv, $\sigma_5\rangle$ | $\langle$könyvünk, $\sigma_5\rangle$ |
| $\langle$ KÖNYV, $\sigma_6$:{INFL:{2pl}}$\rangle$ | $\langle$könyv, $\sigma_6\rangle$ | $\langle$könyvetek, $\sigma_6\rangle$ |
| $\langle$ KÖNYV, $\sigma_7$:{INFL:{3pl}}$\rangle$ | $\langle$könyv, $\sigma_7\rangle$ | $\langle$könyvük, $\sigma_7\rangle$ |

Table 13.17　*The content, form and realized cells of Hungarian* ÉN *'I'*

| Content | Form | Realized |
|---|---|---|
| $\langle$ÉN, $\sigma_1$:nomina tive INFL:{s g}$\rangle$ | $\langle$én, $\sigma_1\rangle$ | $\langle$én, $\sigma_1\rangle$ |
| $\langle$ÉN, $\sigma_2$:a ccusative INFL:{s g}$\rangle$ | $\langle$én, $\sigma_2\rangle$ | $\langle$engem(et), $\sigma_2\rangle$ |
| $\langle$ÉN, $\sigma_3$:illa tive INFL:{s g}$\rangle$ | $\langle$bel, $\sigma_3\rangle$ | $\langle$belém, $\sigma_3\rangle$ |
| $\langle$ÉN, $\sigma_4$:ine ssive INFL:{s g}$\rangle$ | $\langle$benn, $\sigma_4\rangle$ | $\langle$bennem, $\sigma_4\rangle$ |
| $\langle$ÉN, $\sigma_5$:e lative INFL:{s g}$\rangle$ | $\langle$belől, $\sigma_5\rangle$ | $\langle$belőlem, $\sigma_5\rangle$ |
| $\langle$ÉN, $\sigma_6$:s ublative INFL:{s g}$\rangle$ | $\langle$rá, $\sigma_6\rangle$ | $\langle$rám, $\sigma_6\rangle$ |
| $\langle$ÉN, $\sigma_7$:s uperessive INFL:{s g}$\rangle$ | $\langle$rajt, $\sigma_7\rangle$ | $\langle$rajtam, $\sigma_7\rangle$ |
| $\langle$ÉN, $\sigma_8$:de lative INFL:{s g}$\rangle$ | $\langle$ról, $\sigma_8\rangle$ | $\langle$rólam, $\sigma_8\rangle$ |
| $\langle$ÉN, $\sigma_9$:a llative INFL:{s g}$\rangle$ | $\langle$hozz, $\sigma_9\rangle$ | $\langle$hozzám, $\sigma_9\rangle$ |
| $\langle$ÉN, $\sigma_{10}$:a dessive INFL:{s g}$\rangle$ | $\langle$nál, $\sigma_{10}\rangle$ | $\langle$nálam, $\sigma_{10}\rangle$ |
| $\langle$ÉN, $\sigma_{11}$:a blative INFL:{s g}$\rangle$ | $\langle$től, $\sigma_{11}\rangle$ | $\langle$tőlem, $\sigma_{11}\rangle$ |
| $\langle$ÉN, $\sigma_{12}$:da tive INFL:{s g}$\rangle$ | $\langle$nek, $\sigma_{12}\rangle$ | $\langle$nekem, $\sigma_{12}\rangle$ |
| $\langle$ÉN, $\sigma_{13}$:ins trumental INFL:{s g}$\rangle$ | $\langle$vel, $\sigma_{13}\rangle$ | $\langle$velem, $\sigma_{13}\rangle$ |
| $\langle$ÉN, $\sigma_{14}$:c ausal-final INFL:{s g}$\rangle$ | $\langle$ért, $\sigma_{14}\rangle$ | $\langle$értem, $\sigma_{14}\rangle$ |

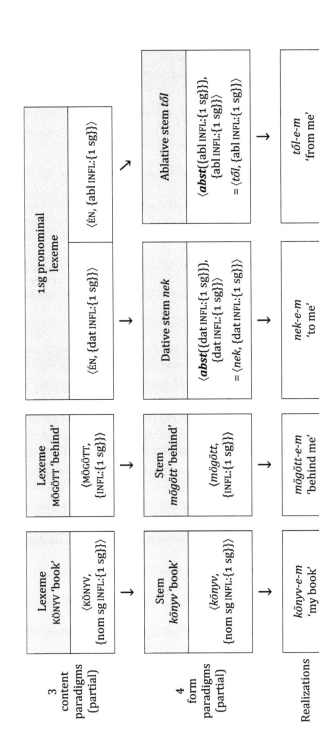

Figure 13.6 *Polyfunctionality in Hungarian person/number inflection*

(36)    Rules of exponence for Hungarian
        Block I. Where X′ is the thematized[7] stem of X,
        a.  X, [–V], {INFL:{PER:α, NUM:β}  → X′
        b.  X, N, ₱l}  → X′ k
        c.  X, N, {pl, INFL:{PER:α, NUM:β}  → X′ i
        d.  X, {nek} {INFL:₿}   → Xi                          (nek : dative case postposition)
        e.  X, {nek} {INFL:₿pl}   → X
        Block II
        f.  X, [–V], {INFL:{s g}   → Xm
        g.  X, [–V], {INFL:₿s g}   → Xd
        h.  X, {belé, rá, hozzá} {INFL:₿s g}   → X(jA)
                        (belé, rá, hozzá : illative, sublative, allative postpositions)
        i.  X, [–V], {INFL:{pl}   → XUnk
        j.  X, [–V], {INFL:₿pl}   → XtOk
        k.  X, [–V], {INFL:₿pl}   → XUk
        Block III. Where γ is an oblique case and X′ is the thematized stem of X,
        l.  X, N, {CASE:γ} → the compound of X with the conjunct stem of the
            γ-case marker
        m. X, N, ₳ ccusative} → X′t

In the analyses proposed for person/number marking in Noon and Baure,
polyfunctionality arises from property mappings and from underspecification.
Underspecification is also relevant for Hungarian: Although a noun's person/
number properties are interpreted as possessor properties and a postposition's
person/number properties are interpreted as pronominal object properties, the
rules that realize these properties are unspecified for the possessor/object distinction. On the other hand, property mappings play no role in the polyfunctionality of Hungarian person/number morphology; instead, the **Corr** and **ab t**
functions cause a personal pronoun's intrinsic properties of person and number
to be expressed morphologically in the same way as a noun's possessor properties or a postposition's pronominal object properties. As this evidence shows,
polyfunctionality is a multifaceted phenomenon, arising in a variety of ways
(Stump 2014b).

## 13.4   Conclusion

The incidence of polyfunctional morphology provides exceptionally strong support for the paradigm-linkage hypothesis. In the instances of polyfunctionality
examined here, lexemes belonging to different syntactic categories employ the
same morphology in the expression of different (though related) content. This

---

7 See Spencer and Stump 2013 for discussion of theme vowels and thematized stems in
  Hungarian.

evidence shows that in inflectional paradigms, form does not mirror content. Rather, form and content each have their own logic, and it is one of the main jobs of a language's inflectional morphology to translate from one logic to the other. The principles governing this translation make essential reference to paradigmatic organization at both the level of content and that of form. The precise definition of these principles varies considerably from one inflectional system to another, but invariably draws upon certain fundamental relations – specifically, the relations formalized as the functions *Corr*, *Stem*, *pm* and PF in the paradigm-linkage theory.

# 14 A theoretical synopsis and two further issues

My objective in this book has been to elucidate the importance of inflectional paradigms as the interface of a language's inflectional morphology with its syntax and semantics, drawing particular attention to their role in accounting for mismatches between inflectional morphology and the content that it expresses. In this concluding chapter, I present a synopsis of the paradigm-linkage theory developed in Chapters 7 through 13 (Section 14.1) and discuss two issues pertaining to its formulation and application: the prospect of a purely abstractive approach to defining realized paradigms (Section 14.2) and the relevance of the paradigm linkage to understanding morphological change (Section 14.3). I end with a very brief general conclusion (Section 14.4).

## 14.1 A synopsis of the paradigm-linkage theory

The paradigm-linkage theory presented here is an inferential-realizational theory of inflectional morphology, but it possesses several features that set it apart from other such theories (including that of Anderson 1992, Stump 2001 and Brown and Hippisley 2012). It will therefore be useful to synopsize the characteristics of this theory.

The paradigm-linkage theory is built on the assumption that a language's inflectional morphology involves three kinds of paradigms and the relations among them. A lexeme L's content paradigm contains only content, in the form of cells pairing L with different morphosyntactic property sets with which L may be associated in syntax. Where $\langle L, \sigma \rangle$ is such a cell and L belongs to category C, the realization $w$ of $\langle L, \sigma \rangle$ may be inserted as the representative of L into any C node bearing the property set $\sigma$; in addition, the semantic content of $w$ is fully determined by $\langle L, \sigma \rangle$. A lexeme's content paradigm is therefore the interface of its word forms with syntax and semantics.

A stem Z's form paradigm contains cells pairing Z (or a kindred stem Z′; Section 5.2) with each property set for which Z (or Z′) may be inflected. Each form cell in a stem's form paradigm is linked to a content cell in some lexeme's content paradigm; the form cell is in that case the content cell's form correspondent. Where $\langle$Z, $\tau\rangle$ is the form correspondent of $\langle$L, $\sigma\rangle$, the realization of $\langle$Z, $\tau\rangle$ is that of $\langle$L, $\sigma\rangle$.

Each form cell $\langle$Z, $\tau\rangle$ is realized by a word form $w$ inflected for $\tau$; in that case, the pairing $\langle w, \tau\rangle$ is the realized cell for $\langle$Z, $\tau\rangle$. For each form paradigm $P$, the full set of realized cells for $P$'s form cells constitutes a realized paradigm.

The relation between content paradigms and form paradigms is the form-correspondence relation; this is formalized as the function **Corr**. The relation between form paradigms and realized paradigms is the realization relation; this is formalized by means of the paradigm function PF. For any content cell $\langle$L, $\sigma\rangle$, any form cell $\langle$Z, $\tau\rangle$ and any realized cell $\langle w, \tau\rangle$,

if **Corr**($\langle$L, $\sigma\rangle$) = $\langle$Z, $\tau\rangle$    [i.e. $\langle$Z, $\tau\rangle$ is the form correspondent of $\langle$L, $\sigma\rangle$]
and PF($\langle$Z, $\tau\rangle$) = $\langle w, \tau\rangle$,    [i.e. $w$ realizes $\langle$Z, $\tau\rangle$]
then PF($\langle$L, $\sigma\rangle$) = $\langle w, \tau\rangle$.    [i.e. $w$ realizes $\langle$L, $\sigma\rangle$]

A language's inflectional morphology is therefore a definition of the form-correspondence and realization relations in that language.

Functions and operations play a central role in the paradigm-linkage theory; chief among these are those summarized in Table 14.1. A language's form-correspondence function **Corr** is defined in terms of the **Stem** function and one or more property mappings. A language's realization relation is defined by means of rules of exponence whose interaction is determined by the definition of the language's paradigm function PF.

The canonical property mapping $pm$ is such that $pm(\sigma) = \sigma$; a form-correspondence function **Corr** is canonical if each lexeme L has a single stem Z such that for any cell $\langle$L, $\sigma\rangle$ in L's content paradigm, **Corr**($\langle$L, $\sigma\rangle$) = $\langle$Z, $\sigma\rangle$. These canonical idealizations are both overridden in a variety of ways, each of which produces a different pattern of mismatch between content and form. Various types of property mappings are classified in Table 14.2, and various types of form correspondence, in Table 14.3.

The paradigm-linkage theory has the desirable structural properties inherent in inferential-realizational inflectional architecture (Stump 2001: Ch. 1); in addition, it is fully compatible with the irreducibility and interface hypotheses.

I have discussed several varieties of evidence supporting the irreducibility hypothesis (according to which some morphological regularities are, irreducibly, regularities in paradigm structure; Section 1.3.1). Patterns of systematic

Table 14.1 *Functions and operations in the paradigm-linkage theory*

| Function/operation | Domain | Range | Interpretation |
|---|---|---|---|
| Paradigm function **PF** | content cells, form cells | realized cells | For any cell c, if PF(c) = $\langle w, \tau \rangle$, then $w$ is the realization of c. |
| Form-correspondence function **Corr** | content cells | form cells | For any content cell c, **Corr**(c) is the form correspondent of c. |
| Property mapping ***pm*** | morphosyntactic property sets | property sets | For any content cell $\langle L, \sigma \rangle$ having $\langle Z, \tau \rangle$ as its form correspondent, the definition of **Corr**($\langle L, \sigma \rangle$) depends on a property mapping ***pm*** such that ***pm***$(\sigma) = \tau$. |
| ***Stem*** function | lexeme/property set pairings | stems | For any content cell $\langle L, \sigma \rangle$, ***Stem***($\langle L, \sigma \rangle$) is the stem employed in realizing $\langle L, \sigma \rangle$. |
| ***SC*** operation | stems | stems | For any stem Z, the value of ***SC***(Z) in a particular syntagmatic context is the form of Z appropriate to that context. |
| ***ic*** function | stems | morphomic properties | For any stem Z, ***ic***(Z) is the morphomic property indexing Z's inflection class. |

syncretism are regularities in paradigm structure (Chapter 10); the distribution of morphomic properties (and that of the stems or inflectional exponents that express them) is a regularity in paradigm structure (Chapter 8), as are patterns of defectiveness that reflect gaps in a lexeme's morphomic stem inventory (Section 9.4); and the generalization that languages may differ with respect to which inflectional categories serve as absolute correlates of suppletion is a typological generalization about paradigm structure, as is the minimal intersective correlate hypothesis, according to which every fractured paradigm in a language has a minimal intersective correlate of suppletion that also serves as an absolute correlate of suppletion in that language (Section 11.3).

I have discussed a range of grammatical evidence supporting the interface hypothesis (according to which paradigms are the interfaces of inflectional morphology with syntax and semantics; Section 1.3.2). In general, any mismatch between a word form's morphosyntactic property set and the property set that its morphology realizes is evidence for the interface hypothesis. Such mismatches may therefore take a variety of forms: (a) a word form's syntax and semantics

Table 14.2 *Kinds of property mappings*

| Morphosyntactic property sets in content cells | Property sets in form cells | Examples |
|---|---|---|
| $\sigma$ | $\sigma$ | canonical (Section 7.2) |
| | $pm(\sigma) \subseteq \sigma$ | Bhojpuri verb inflection (Section 10.1) |
| | $pm(\sigma)$ contains $\geq 1$ morphomic property | Hua verb agreement (Sections 8.2–8.3), Twi tense marking (Section 8.5), Nepali verb agreement (Section 8.6), Kashmiri tense marking (Section 12.3), Baure person/number marking (Section 13.2) |
| $\sigma, \tau$ (where $\sigma$ and $\tau$ contrast) | $pm(\sigma) = pm(\tau)$ and $\sigma \subseteq pm(\sigma)$ but $\tau \not\subseteq pm(\sigma)$ (directional syncretism of $\sigma$ and $\tau$) | Turkish possessor inflection (Section 10.2) |
| | $pm(\sigma) = pm(\tau)$ but $\sigma, \tau \not\subseteq pm(\sigma)$ (morphomic syncretism of $\sigma$ and $\tau$) | Sanskrit oblique cases (Section 10.3) |
| | $\tau \subseteq pm(\sigma)$ but $pm(\tau)$ is undefined (deponency) | Latin voice (Section 12.1), Old Norse tense (Section 12.4) |

may depend on a distinction that is not overtly expressed by its morphology; (b) a word form's morphology may express a distinction to which its syntax and semantics are insensitive; or (c) a word form's syntax and semantics may depend on one distinction while its morphology expresses a different distinction. Cross-cutting (a)–(c) is the criterion of whether the content–form mismatch exhibited by *w* is observable (i) within its paradigm or (ii) only across paradigms. There are therefore six logically possible kinds of grammatical evidence supporting the interface hypothesis, and as Table 14.4 shows, each type is instantiated by one or another deviation from canonical paradigm linkage.

There is also lexical evidence supporting the interface hypothesis. Any mismatch between a word form's lexical content and the stem that its morphology realizes is evidence for the interface hypothesis. Logically, it is possible that

Table 14.3 *Kinds of form correspondence*

| Content cells | Form correspondents | Examples |
|---|---|---|
| $\langle L, \sigma \rangle$ | $\langle X, \sigma \rangle$, where X is L's only stem | canonical (Section 7.1) |
| $\langle L, \sigma \rangle$ | no form correspondent (defectiveness) | French FRIRE 'fry' (Section 9.4) |
| $\langle L, \sigma \rangle$ | $\langle X, \textit{pm}(\sigma) \rangle$, $\langle Y, \textit{pm}(\sigma) \rangle$ (overabundance engendered by ***Corr***) | English DREAM (Section 9.1) |
| $\langle L_1, \sigma \rangle$, $\langle L_2, \sigma \rangle$ | $\langle X, \textit{pm}(\sigma) \rangle$ (homomorphy) | English WEAR (Section 4.3) |
| $\langle L, \sigma \rangle$, $\langle L, \tau \rangle$ | $\langle X, \textit{pm}(\sigma) \rangle$, $\langle Y, \textit{pm}(\tau) \rangle$, where X and Y are independent stems (suppletion; also heteroclisis if X, Y belong to distinct inflection classes) | Sanskrit KROṢṬAR 'jackal' (Section 5.6) |
| $\langle L, \sigma \rangle$ | $\langle f(\sigma), \textit{pm}(\sigma) \rangle$ (functor-argument reversal) | Hungarian pronominal case (Section 13.3) |

Table 14.4 *Grammatical evidence supporting the interface hypothesis*

| | Content–form mismatch is observable … | |
|---|---|---|
| | .(i) w  ithin paradigms | .(.  ii) only across paradigms |
| (a) A word form's syntax and semantics depend on a distinction that is not overtly expressed by its morphology. | Syncretism (Chapter 10) | Polyfunctionality (Chapter 13) |
| (b) A word form's morphology expresses a distinction to which its syntax and semantics are insensitive. | Overabundance (Chapter 9) | inflection classes (Section 7.3) |
| (c) A word form's syntax and semantics depend on one distinction while its morphology expresses a different distinction. | morphomic property (Chapter 8) | deponency, metaconjugation (Chapter 12) |

lexemes may be distinct without any corresponding distinction among their stems; it is likewise possible that a single lexeme may have two or more distinct stems – not merely kindred stems or sandhi variants, but independent stems (Section 5.2). The former possibility is realized by the phenomenon of homomorphy (Section 4.3); the latter possibility, by the phenomenon of suppletion (Chapter 11).

While the grammatical architecture entailed by the paradigm-linkage theory may seem innovative, the motivation for this architecture is, in fact, of a kind that is very familiar in linguistics. The awareness that language exhibits systematic patterns both of an abstract nature and of a concrete nature is the basis for a good many distinctions in linguistic theory – the distinction between phonetics and phonology, the distinction between c-structure and f-structure, even the distinction between allomorphs and morphemes. If speech sounds, sentences and word forms are all seen as exhibiting an abstract/concrete dichotomy, the realization that inflectional paradigms exhibit this same sort of dichotomy should not, in the end, be too surprising.

## *14.2 The implicative structure of inflectional paradigms*

In pedagogical descriptions of languages with complex inflection-class systems, it is customary to identify a lexeme's principal parts as an aid to learning that lexeme's full paradigm of word forms. Principal parts are, in effect, cells in a lexeme's realized paradigm from which all of the other cells in that paradigm can be logically deduced, given a language's patterns of inflection. In Latin pedagogy, for example, it is usual to cite nouns by their nominative singular and genitive singular forms, since together, these two forms reveal a noun's declension. Principal parts "work" because realized paradigms generally exhibit networks of implicative relations: While one can construct hypothetical paradigms none of whose realized cells is deducible from any other cell or cells,[1] realized paradigms in natural languages are rarely – if ever – this impenetrable.

The implicative relations among a realized paradigm's cells make it possible to define the realization of a content cell $\langle L, \sigma \rangle$ in more than one way. On one hand, one can formulate an **exponence-based** definition: According to such a definition, the realization of $\langle L, \sigma \rangle$ is the systematic result of adding the inflectional exponents of $\sigma$ to the appropriate stem of L. On the other hand, one can formulate an **implicative** definition, by which the realization of the content cell $\langle L, \sigma \rangle$ is inferred from the realization of some contrasting content cell $\langle L, \tau \rangle$. (Inferences of this sort are sometimes referred to as "Priscianic rules," since they are extensively employed by the ancient grammarian Priscian in his description of Latin morphology; Matthews 1991: 193f.) In French, for example, the realization of the content cell

$\langle$CHANTER, {pl fut ind} $\rangle$ 'w e will sing'

---

1 See Stump and Finkel 2013: 317ff for an example of a hypothetical paradigm of this sort.

can be defined as the result of applying two rules to CHANTER's stem /ʃɑt/: a rule realizing {ut ind} through the suffixation of /ʁ/ and a rule realizing {pl} through the suffixation of /ɔ̃/. By contrast, the realization of ⟨CHANTER, {pl fut ind}⟩ can also be determined from that of ⟨CHANTER, {2pl fut ind}⟩, in accordance with the fact that a second-person plural future indicative form /Xʁe/ (such as /ʃɑtʁe/) implies a first-person plural future indicative form /Xʁɔ̃/ (such as /ʃɑtʁɔ̃/).

Blevins (2006) refers to these two approaches to defining a language's inflectional morphology as the **constructive** and the **abstractive** approaches (respectively).[2] Although he portrays it as a dichotomous choice (cf. also O'Neill 2014, Pirrelli et al. 2015), the need to choose between constructive and abstractive approaches to modeling inflectional morphology is a false dilemma. There is no logical reason why an inferential-realizational theory of inflection couldn't simultaneously incorporate exponence-based and implicative principles. Rules of referral express implicative generalizations and are widely assumed in exponence-based approaches to inflection (Zwicky 1985, Stump 1993a, 2001); in the paradigm-linkage theory, rules of referral in the strict sense are dispensed with,[3] but a *Corr* function may be defined as mapping two or more content cells to the same form cell (whether directionally or not; Sections 10.2–10.3) and this likewise has

---

2 The label "constructive" is intended to subsume morphological theories that postulate morphological units that are smaller than a word form; any such theory is described as one in which "surface word forms are b uilt' from sub-word units" (Blevins 2006: 531). But however apt this metaphor might be for morpheme-based theories of morphology, it is, technically, inaccurate in the case of inferential-realizational theories of inflection such as the paradigm-linkage theory. In the paradigm-linkage theory, a word form *w* is abstractly represented as a content cell ⟨L, σ⟩, the pairing of a lexeme L with a morphosyntactic property set σ. No part of this paradigm cell is "built" from sub-word units – nor, indeed, is the concrete word form *w* itself "built" from sub-word units, since it is directly defined as a phonological interpretation of ⟨L, σ⟩. In particular, the language's paradigm function PF applies to ⟨L, σ⟩ to yield the phonological representation of the full word form *w* as its value. To be sure, the definition of the function PF involves more specific rules of exponence that are intended to capture generalizations about particular aspects of the morphology of whole classes of cells by the corresponding word forms, but these rules are simply part of the definition of PF; as such, they themselves express generalizations about whole word forms. They make it possible to account for French speakers' confident intuition that the word forms *gisez* (ẏou lie') and *ferez* (ẏou will do') are partially alike in their morphology. Given that the verb GÉSIR łie ' lacks future-tense forms and that the verb FAIRE đo' has *faites* as its second-person plural present indicative form, this intuition inevitably remains inexplicable in any purely abstractive theory of inflectional morphology.

3 Following Zwicky 1985, Stump 2001 treats rules of referral together with rules of exponence as realization rules projecting fully inflected word forms from their stem. In the paradigm-linkage theory, rules realizing word forms from their stems are in general rules of exponence; instances of systematic syncretism are instead defined as part of the mapping from content cells to their form correspondents.

the effect of expressing an implicative generalization. Moreover, exponence-based theories have rules inducing one stem from another (Section 5.5.1), e.g. a rule inducing the zero-grade stem *pitṛ-* of Sanskrit PITAR 'father' (dat sg *pitṛ-e*) from its full-grade stem *pitar-* (acc sg *pitar-am*); given that these stems are associated with different realized cells, this, too, is implicative morphology – below the word level.

Although it is logically possible to combine exponence-based and implicative approaches to morphology, one might try to argue that Occam's razor makes it preferable to choose one or the other exclusively. In that vein, one might argue that a purely implicative approach is preferable because it avoids the need to segment words into smaller parts – that while exponence-based morphology trades in roots, stems, affixes and nonconcatenative processes, implicative morphology simply involves phonological similarities and differences among whole word forms. If one could credibly restrict oneself to a purely implicative approach, one could seemingly abandon any reference to form paradigms and to the mapping by which they are expressed as realized paradigms. Instead, a purely implicative approach could seemingly involve a direct mapping from content cells to a realized paradigm's predictive cells (its "principal parts"), from which its predictable cells could then be logically deduced. This goal of reducing all inflectional morphology to implicative morphology is, however, unrealistic.

An implicative description cannot avoid segmentation in languages with certain kinds of sandhi phenomena. Consider, for example, the Sanskrit nouns MARUT 'w ind' and AŚVA 'hors e.' The vocative singular form of MARUT is *marut*, and its locative singular form has an additional *i*: *maruti*. Superficially, AŚVA is different: Its vocative singular form is *aśva*, but its locative singular form is *aśve*. It seems like MARUT and AŚVA exhibit different patterns in these examples, but in fact, they do not: It is a regular part of Sanskrit automatic phonology that *a* combines with *i* to form *e*, as when the syntactic sequence of *atha* he re' and *idam* this ' regularly becomes *athedam*. The locative singular form *aśve* can therefore be resolved into *aśva-i*, making it parallel to *maruti* after all. But what are the parts into which *aśva-i* has been resolved? Not every *e* can be split in this way; here, the splitting is licensed precisely by the fact that *aśva-* is a noun stem and *-i*, a suffixal exponent of the locative singular. Thus, in order to account for the fact that MARUT and AŚVA both participate in the implicative pattern relating a vocative singular word form X to a locative singular word form X*i*, a segmentation of *aśve* must be taken into account; otherwise, a generalization is missed.

The notion that a purely implicative approach to modeling inflectional paradigms excludes the need for morphological segmentation is, in any event, a non sequitur, because there are implicative relations below the level of whole word forms (Stump and Finkel 2013: 270, 292). On one hand, one word form's morphology may allow one to determine another word form's stem without allowing one to determine the rest of its morphology. In Sanskrit, a nominal whose genitive singular has the form X*sya* has a nominative singular form based on the same stem X; genitive singular X*sya* does not, however, uniquely determine the nominative singular form's case suffix. For example, the genitive singular forms *aśva-sya* 'horse's' and *āsya-sya* 'mouth's' have the corresponding nominative singular forms *aśva-s* and *āsya-m*. On the other hand, one word form's morphology may allow one to determine another word form's suffix without allowing one to determine its stem. Sanskrit locative singulars having the form X*au* have -*s* as their affixal exponent in the genitive singular; but locative singular X*au* does not uniquely determine the genitive singular form's stem. For example, the locative singular forms *agnau* 'in a fire' and *śatrau* 'at an enemy' have the corresponding genitive singular forms *agne-s* and *śatro-s*.

If one assumes an exponence-based approach to modeling inflectional morphology, one in effect gets implicative generalizations for free, since given ordinary principles of logical inference, implicative rules are derivable as theorems of exponence-based descriptions. Consider, for example, the hypothetical system of six two-celled realized paradigms in (1). One possible exponence-based analysis for this system is (2a); one possible implicative analysis is (2b). Every stipulation and rule in the implicative analysis is logically derivable from the exponence-based analysis; that is, the exponence-based analysis itself indirectly defines an implicative analysis.

(1)    A hypothetical system of six realized paradigms
       ⟨Pg, {a}⟩ ⟨Qg, ∯ ⟩ ⟨Rh, ∯ ⟩ ⟨Sh, ∯ ⟩ ⟨Th, {a}⟩ ⟨Uh, {a}⟩
       ⟨Pi, ♭⟩ ⟩ ⟨Qi, ♭⟩ ⟩ ⟨Rj, ♭⟩ ⟩ ⟨Sj, ♭⟩ ⟩ ⟨Tk, {b}⟩ ⟨Uk, {b}⟩

(2)    Analyses of the hypothetical system in (1)
       a. Exponence-based analysis

| Inflection classes | | | Rules of exponence |
|---|---|---|---|
| Class 1 | Class 2 | Class 3 | X, [Class 1], {a}   → X*g* |
| P , Q} | {R, S} | Ţ , U} | X, [any], {a} → X*h* (default) |
| | | | X, [Class 1], {b}   → X*i* |
| Where X ∈ Class 1 ∪ Class 2 ∪ Class 3, | | | X, [Class 2], {b}   → X*j* |
| X has the form paradigm {⟨X, ∯ ⟩, ⟨X, ♭⟩ ⟩}. | | | X, [Class 3], {b}   → X*k* |

       b. Implicative analysis

| Lexical stipulations | Implicative rules |
|---|---|
| ⟨Pi, {b}⟩ ⟨Qi, ♭⟩ ⟩ ⟨Rj, ♭⟩ ⟩ | ⟨X*i*, {b}⟩ → ⟨X*g*, {a}⟩ |
| ⟨Sj, {b}⟩ ⟨Tk, ♭⟩ ⟩ ⟨Uk, ♭⟩ ⟩ | [⟨X*j*, {b}⟩ ∨ ⟨X*k*, {b}⟩] → ⟨X*h*, {a}⟩ |

Still, there are generalizations that can be stated more compactly if they are directly stated as implicative rules rather than as sets of exponence-based rules having those implicative rules as theorems. For example, a rule of referral stating that by default, a verb's past participial form is the same as its past-tense form is a simple generalization instantiated by forms whose past-tense exponence varies (*spied, meant, dug, told, cut*, and so on).

These facts point to the conclusion that the exponence-based approach and the implicative approach have strengths that make them good for different things. The implicative approach is good at expressing generalizations that are not tied to any specific exponent, but involve paradigm-based patterns that may be instantiated with different morphology in the inflection of different lexemes (e.g. the "past participle = past tense" default).

The implicative approach also sheds valuable light on analogical phenomena in language learning and language change (e.g. overregularizations such as *goed* or shifts of inflection-class membership such as that of *sneaked* to *snuck*). The widespread incidence of these phenomena clearly shows how heavily language learners rely on the implicative relations among a realized paradigm's cells in deducing word forms that they haven't heard from those that they have. This reliance is obvious when it results in innovative forms such as *goed* and *snuck*, but there can be little doubt that, much more frequently, it results in established forms that call no attention to themselves because they are indistinguishable from forms that the learner might actually have heard.

Finally, the implicative approach provides a new basis for the typological comparison of inflectional systems, focusing not on the inner structure of individual word forms (Schlegel 1808, Humboldt 1836, Sapir 1921, Greenberg 1960) or on individual word forms' syntactic dependencies (Juola 1998), but on the complexity of entire paradigms (Moscoso del Prado Martín et al. 2004, Bane 2008, Milin et al. 2009, Ackerman, Blevins and Malouf 2009, Bonami et al. 2011, Stump and Finkel 2013).

Unlike the implicative approach, the exponence-based approach is good at capturing generalizations tied to specific exponents. For this reason, it allows many kinds of patterns to be defined very compactly. Consider, for example, the partial paradigm of Sanskrit BHID 'split' in Table 14.5. The implicative approach portrays as accidental the fact that many imperfect/optative pairs (e.g. *abhindma* ẁ e split'/*bhindyāma* ẁ e should split') use the same agreement morphology. In such an approach, the implicative relation between *abhindma* and *bhindyāma* –

⟨*aXma*, {pl impf ind a ct}⟩ ↔ ⟨*Xyāma*, {pl op t act}⟩

Table 14.5 *A fragment of the inflectional paradigm of Sanskrit* BHID *'split'*
*(7th conjugation)*

|  |  | Active | | | Middle | | |
|---|---|---|---|---|---|---|---|
|  |  | Singular | Dual | Plural | Singular | Dual | Plural |
| Imperfect indicative | 1st | *abhinadam* | *abhindva* | *abhindma* | *abhindi* | *abhindvahi* | *abhindmahi* |
|  | 2nd | *abhinat* | *abhinttam* | *abhintta* | *abhintthās* | *abhindāthām* | *abhinddhvam* |
|  | 3rd | *abhinat* | *abhinttām* | *abhindan* | *abhintta* | *abhindātām* | *abhindata* |
| Optative | 1st | *bhindyām* | *bhindyāva* | *bhindyāāma* | *bhindīya* | *bhindīvahi* | *bhindīmahi* |
|  | 2nd | *bhindyās* | *bhindyātam* | *bhindyāta* | *bhindīthās* | *bhindīyāthām* | *bhindīdhvam* |
|  | 3rd | *bhindyāt* | *bhindyātām* | *bhindyur* | *bhindīta* | *bhindīyātām* | *bhindīran* |

Shaded cells exhibit the strong stem; unshaded cells, the weak stem.

– is no simpler than the implicative relation between *abhindan* the y split' and *bhindyur* the y should split,' which share no agreement morphology:

$$\langle aXan, \text{3pl impf ind a ct}\} \rangle \leftrightarrow \langle Xyur, \text{3pl opt act}\} \rangle.$$

In an exponence-based approach, by contrast, the definitions of *abhindma* and *bhindyāma* are more alike than those of *abhindan* and *bhindyur*, since *abhindma* and *bhindyāma* both associate the suffixation of *-ma* with the realization of the properties "first person," "plural" and "active."[4] Ultimately, an implicative definition of the forms in Table 14.5 must relate thirty-six independent patterns (corresponding to the thirty-six word forms in the table), but the exponence-based definition in (3) specifies only thirty inflectional patterns (marked (i)–(xxx)), nearly all of which are pertinent to the morphology of more than one cell.

(3)    An exponence-based analysis of the subparadigm of BHID 'split' in Table 14.4

a. Paradigm function:    (i) $PF(\langle L, \sigma \rangle) = [\text{Block 2} : [\text{Block 1} : \langle \textbf{\textit{Stem}}(\langle L, \sigma \rangle), \sigma \rangle]]$

b. Stem:    (ii) $\textbf{\textit{Stem}}(\langle L, \sigma: \{\text{sg impf act}\} \rangle) = $ L's Strong Stem
   (iii) otherwise, $\textbf{\textit{Stem}}(\langle L, \sigma \rangle) = $ L's Weak Stem

c. BHID's Stem Forms:    (iv) Strong Stem *bhi-na-d* ⎤
   (v) Weak Stem *bhi-n-d*    ⎥ (7th conjugation)

d. Block 1    (vi) X, V, $\sigma:\{$ mpf$\} \to aX$
   (vii) X, V, $\sigma:\{$opt act$\} \to Xy\bar{a}$
   (viii) X, V, $\sigma:\{$opt mid$\} \to X\bar{i}(y)$ [$y$ prevocalic]

4 Matthews (1972: 27f) makes the same point with examples from Latin.

e. Block 2

| | | |
|---|---|---|
| (ix) | X, V, σ:{1s g act} | → X(a)m [a postconsonantal] |
| (x) | X, V, σ:{2s g act} | → Xs |
| (xi) | X, V, σ:{3s g act | → Xt |
| (xii) | X, V, σ:{1 du a ct} | → Xva |
| (xiii) | X, V, σ:{2 du a ct} | → Xtam |
| (xiv) | X, V, σ:{3 du a ct} | → Xtām |
| (xv) | X, V, σ:{1pl act} | → Xma |
| (xvi) | X, V, σ:{2pl act} | → Xta |
| (xvii) | X, V, σ:{3pl impf a ct} | → Xan |
| (xviii) | Xā, V, σ:{3pl act} | → Xur |
| (xix) | X, V, σ:{1s g impf mid} | → Xi |
| (xx) | X, V, σ:{1s g mid} | → Xa |
| (xxi) | X, V, σ:{2s g mid} | → Xthās |
| (xxii) | X, V, σ:{3s g mid} | → Xta |
| (xxiii) | X, V, σ:{1 du mid} | → Xvahi |
| (xxiv) | X, V, σ:{2 du mid} | → Xāthām |
| (xxv) | X, V, σ:{3 du mid} | → Xātām |
| (xxvi) | X, V, σ:{1pl mid} | → Xmahi |
| (xxvii) | X, V, σ:{2pl mid} | → Xdhvam |
| (xxviii) | X, V, σ:{3pl impf mid} | → Xata |
| (xxix) | X, V, σ:{3pl mid} | → Xran |
| (xxx) | X, V, σ:{ | → X |

Because of the ways in which their parts interact, exponence-based definitions make it possible to distinguish very general patterns from restricted patterns. Consider, for example, the dative plural forms of the three Sanskrit nominals MARUT 'wind,' VIDVAT 'knowing'and AŚVA 'horse': *marudbhyas, vidvadbhyas* and *aśvebhyas*. These forms are alike in that they all end in the suffix *-bhyas*, a fact expressible by means of the simple rule of exponence in (4). On the other hand, the three word forms differ in their choice of stem. On one hand, *marut-* (sandhi form *marud-*) is the default stem of MARUT; this is a nonalternating stem, appearing throughout the realized paradigm of MARUT. On the other hand, *vidvat-* (sandhi form *vidvad-*) is the default stem of the perfect active participle VIDVAT, but as a Middle stem, it alternates with the Weakest stem *viduṣ-*; and *aśve-* is the *e*-stem of AŚVA.Thus, the **Stem** function must enforce the three patterns in (5). This means that in an implicative approach, the generalization captured by (4) cannot be captured, and the forms *marudbhyas, vidvadbhyas* and *aśvebhyas* must be seen as instantiating three independent patterns.

(4)     X, Nominal, {da t pl} → X*bhyas*

(5)     Where X is L's default stem,

**Stem**(⟨L, {da t pl}⟩))     = **SC**(X) if L is a perfect active participle [where the syntagmatic context operation **SC** is defined so that

*SC*(*vidvat*) = *viduṣ* before a vowel, otherwise *vidvat*]
= L's *e*-stem if X belongs to the *a*-stem declension;
= X by default.

Another shortcoming of purely implicative models is that they necessitate arbitrary choices in lexical representations. In an implicative model, a lexeme's inflection-class membership could be represented lexically in either of two ways: by means of a set of principal parts or by means of an inflection-class label together with a citation form.

The use of principal parts to represent a lexeme's inflection-class membership entails arbitrary choices. As Stump and Finkel (2013) have shown, inflection-class systems are nearly always subject to more than one optimal principal-part analysis – and very often, to a surprisingly large number of equally good alternative analyses. In Latin, for example, one might identify the declension-class membership of the neuter noun CORPUS body' in the traditional way, by means of its singular nominative and genitive forms *corpus* and *corporis*. But one could just as easily have used the nominative singular and plural forms *corpus* and *corpora*, among several other possibilities. The choice is fundamentally arbitrary (Matthews 1972: 28f).

Representing a lexeme's inflection-class membership by means of an inflection-class label and a citation form likewise engenders an arbitrary choice. For instance, if the lexeme AQUA ẁ ater' is labeled as a first-declension noun, then any one of its forms suffices as a citation form.

Exponence-based models do not force one to make these arbitrary choices; in particular, the practice of listing a lexeme with an inflection-class and a subset of its stems (those that are not predictable, often simply a single stem) does not give rise to arbitrary choices of these kinds.

Moreover, the notion that a lexeme L's inflection-class membership is lexically specified by a set of principal parts gives a kind of lexical priority to those members of L's paradigm that are most clearly diagnostic of its inflection-class membership. But if the most diagnostic members of a lexeme's paradigm were invariably specified in its lexical entry, one would expect maximally diagnostic forms to be more rapidly recognized than unstored, nondiagnostic forms; to my knowledge, there is no psycholinguistic evidence confirming this expectation.

## *14.3 Paradigm linkage and inflectional change*

The grammatical architecture assumed by the paradigm-linkage hypothesis accords well with the fact that some inflectional changes are essentially changes of content and others, primarily changes of form. Changes of inflectional content can be situated at the level of content paradigms, at the interface of morphology with syntax and semantics. Consider, for example, the loss of the dual number in the prehistory of the Pāli language (Geiger 1994, Perniola 1997): The Vedic ancestor of Pāli distinguishes dual number in all three persons in both declension and conjugation, but Pāli inflection only distinguishes singular from plural. This development in Pāli is manifested as a simplification in the rules of semantic interpretation, as a reduction in the number of morphosyntactic properties available for syntactic agreement relations, and as a simplification in the morphological expression of number; all three of these manifestations can be seen as a reduction in the size of content paradigms whereby cells are no longer distinguished by the property "dual."

Changes of inflectional form that do not involve any concomitant change in content can be situated at the level of form paradigms. As in Vedic, Pāli nominal paradigms have a genitive singular cell, but the morphological expression of this cell is simplified in Pāli. Consider, for example, the four nouns in Table 14.6. In Vedic, these nouns exhibit three distinct exponents of the genitive singular: The *a*-stem has *-sya*, the *i*- and *u*-stems have *-s* (with the Guṇa-grade stem alternant), and the *in*-stem has *-as*; the principles of Vedic phonology do not support the hypothesis that either of *-s* and *-as* comes from the other as an effect of sandhi. The Pāli reflexes of these nouns have the same syntax and semantics, but their morphology has simplified: All four now exhibit *-ssa* (the expected phonological development for *-sya*). Thus, the realization of the property set {gen sg} is no longer sensitive to the declensional distinction between *a*-stem, *i*- or *u*-stem, and *in*-stem form paradigms.

In the paradigm-linkage architecture, the morphosyntactic property sets associated with a content paradigm's cells may fail to match those of their form correspondents. Logically, two kinds of diachronic developments may ensue from this kind of mismatch. Because they presumably contribute to an inflectional system's complexity, such mismatches may be leveled away through time, in such a way as to approximate more closely the canonical relation of isomorphism between content cells and their form correspondents (Section 7.2). On the other hand, a particular pattern of mismatch may, by virtue of its sheer frequency, actually spread to new contexts, notwithstanding its presumed contribution to system complexity. Consider a case of each sort from the history of Pāli.

As we have already seen (Sections 5.1, 6.4), several nominal declensions in Sanskrit are sensitive to a morphomic distinction between Strong, Middle and Weakest stems: In these declensions, forms realizing morphosyntactic property

Table 14.6 *Genitive singular forms of four masculine nouns in Vedic and Pāli*
(Shaded forms are innovative.)

|  | DEVA ġod' *a*-stem | BHIKṢU monk' *u*-stem | AGNI fi re' *i*-stem | HASTIN 'elephant' *in*-stem |
|---|---|---|---|---|
| Vedic | *deva-sya* | *bhikṣo-s* | *agne-s* | *hastin-as* |
| Pāli | *deva-ssa* | *bhikkhu-ssa* | *aggi-ssa* | *hatthi-ssa* |

sets that satisfy the property constraint in (6) are based on the Strong stem, and
other forms are based on either the Weakest stem (before a vowel-initial suffix)
or the Middle stem (otherwise). This pattern is typical not only of Sanskrit, but
also of Vedic (the predecessor of both Sanskrit and the Middle Indic languages,
including Pāli).

(6)    [[{nom} ∨ {ᵥ oc} ∨ {ₐ cc} ∧ [{ᵦe ut pl} ∨ [[{masc} ∨ {fem}] ∧ ꝥ acc pl}]]]

In the analysis proposed in Section 6.4, the default distribution of a nominal's Strong, Middle and Weakest stems is determined by the clauses (7a, b) in
the definition of the *Stem* function and by the definition (8) of the syntagmatic
context operation *SC*; the default patterns in (7a,b) are sometimes overridden,
as by the vocative singular rule (9a) and, in certain declensions, the locative
singular rule (9b).

(7)    Default clauses in the definition of the Sanskrit *Stem* function
       a. Where σ satisfies property constraint (6), *Stem*(⟨L, σ⟩) = L's Strong stem.
       b. Otherwise, *Stem*(⟨L, σ⟩) = *SC*(Z), where Z is L's Middle stem.
(8)    Where L has Z as its Middle stem,
       *SC*(Z)    = L's Weakest stem before a vowel-initial suffix
                  = Z otherwise.
(9)    Some overrides of the default clauses in (7)
       a. *Stem*(⟨L, {na sc voc sg}⟩) = L's Guṇa-grade stem
       b. Where L's Strong stem belongs to the RĀJAN, KARTAR or PITAR declen-
          sion, *Stem*(⟨L, σ:{oc sg}⟩) = L's Guṇa-grade stem.

The property constraint in (6) defines a fundamentally morphomic distributional pattern for a nominal's Strong stem. Neuter nominals exhibit their
Strong stem in the realization of plural direct-case property sets (a natural
class); but non-neuter nominals exhibit their Strong stem in the realization
of all direct-case property sets except those that are accusative plural – an
exception that keeps the conditioning property sets from constituting a natural class.

Table 14.7 *The distribution of the Strong stem of 'king' in Old Indic and in Pāli*
(Shaded forms are based on the Strong stem.)

|  |  | Old Indic | Pāli |
|---|---|---|---|
| Singular | Nominative | *rājā* | *rājā* |
|  | Vocative | *rājan* | *rājā* ~ *rāja* |
|  | Accusative | *rājānam* | *rājānā* |
|  | Instrumental | *rājñā* | *raññā* ~ *rājinā* |
|  | Dative | *rājñe* | *rañño* ~ *rājino* |
|  | Ablative | *rājñas* | *raññā* ~ *rājinā* |
|  | Genitive | *rājñas* | *rañño* ~ *rājino* |
|  | Locative | *rājñi* ~ *rājani* | *rājini* |
| Plural | Nominative/Vocative | *rājānas* | *rājāno* |
|  | Accusative | *rājñas* | *rājāno* |
|  | Instrumental | *rājabhis* | *rājūhi* |
|  | Dative | *rājabhyas* | *rājūnaṃ* ~ *raññaṃ* |
|  | Ablative | *rājabhyas* | *rājūhi* |
|  | Genitive | *rājñām* | *rājūnaṃ* ~ *raññaṃ* |
|  | Locative | *rājasu* | *rājūsu* |

Although this pattern of morphomic conditioning is observable in Old Indic, it disappears in Pāli, where it is reanalyzed as an instance of morphosyntactic conditioning, with the Strong stem appearing in all direct-case property sets and the Weak stems elsewhere. Table 14.7 exemplifies this change with the inflection of the noun 'king.'[5] The Pāli forms in this table are generally the expected phonological development of the corresponding Old Indic forms, but with some differences. First, the patterns of ablative syncretism in Old Indic (ablative/genitive syncretism in the singular and dative/ablative syncretism in the plural) are supplanted by distinct patterns in Pāli (dative/genitive and instrumental/ablative syncretism in both numbers). But in addition, the pattern of stem alternation formalized in (6)–(9) is simplified: The accusative plural forms such as *rājāno* exhibit a Strong stem instead of inheriting the Weak stem from their Old Indic predecessor;[6] and the Guṇa-grade stem dictated by

---

5 Because the dual number disappears in Pāli, the Old Indic dual forms are omitted from Table 14.6.

6 This change cannot be seen as the effect of a regular phonological pattern of epenthesis, because the Old Indic genitive singular form *rājñas*, which is homophonous with the accusative plural form, develops as *rañño* in Pāli, paralleling (for example) the development from *rājñā* to *raññā* in the instrumental singular.

Table 14.8 *Singular forms of the demonstrative pronoun* TA *'that' in Old Indic and Pāli*

(Shaded forms are based on the *sm*-stem.)

| | Old Indic | | | Pāli | | |
|---|---|---|---|---|---|---|
| | Masculine | Neuter | Feminine | Masculine | Neuter | Feminine |
| Nom | sas | tat | sā | so | tam | sā |
| Voc | – | – | – | – | – | – |
| Acc | tam | tat | tām | tam | tam | tam |
| Ins | tena | | tayā | tena | | tāya |
| Dat | tasmai | | tasyai | tassa | | tassā, tissā |
| Abl | tasmāt | | tasyās | tasmā | | tāya |
| Gen | tasya | | tasyās | tassa | | tassā, tissā |
| Loc | tasmin | | tasyām | tasmim | | tassam, tissam |

the vocative singular rule (9a) begins to be abandoned in favor of the Strong stem. Thus, while the distribution of a nominal's Strong stem constitutes one kind of mismatch between content and form in Old Indic (where the Strong stem's distribution is not morphosyntactically coherent), this mismatch is re- solved in Pāli, where the use of the Strong stem becomes an exponent of the di- rect ( = nominative, vocative and accusative) cases. This example suggests that in some instances, the morphological complexity engendered by a mismatch between a content paradigm and the corresponding form paradigm motivates a change in the direction of greater isomorphism; see Stump 2002, Brown and Hippisley 2012: Ch. 6 and Gardani 2014 for other evidence to this effect.

Notwithstanding this observation, it is also clear that the impulse toward greater isomorphism is not an irresistible one; indeed, under the right circum- stances, patterns of content–form mismatch in inflectional paradigms may actually spread through time (Maiden 2005). In the inflection of Old Indic demonstrative, interrogative and relative pronouns (and of certain adjectives following the pronominal declension), masculine/neuter singular forms of the dative, ablative and locative cases are based on a morphomic stem in *sm* (Whitney 1889: Section 496a); in Table 14.8, for example, the masculine/neu- ter singular forms of the demonstrative pronoun TA 'that' exhibit the stem *tasm*- in the dative, ablative and locative. In Pāli, this stem is preserved in the abla- tive and locative cases. (The dative singular form of TA, like that of RĀJAN in Table 14.7, becomes syncretized with the genitive singular form.)

In Old Indic, the *sm*-stem pattern is restricted to pronominal declensions. In Pāli, however, it begins to spread to the ablative and locative singular of

Table 14.9 *The spread of the morphomic sm-stem pattern in Pāli* (All forms are masculine and singular.)

|          |     | DEVA 'god' *a*-stem | BHIKṢU 'monk' *u*-stem | AGNI 'fire' *i*-stem | HASTIN 'elephant' *in*-stem |
|----------|-----|---------------------|------------------------|----------------------|-----------------------------|
| Sanskrit | abl | *devāt*             | *bhikṣos*              | *agnes*              | *hastinas*                  |
|          | loc | *deve*              | *bhikṣau*              | *agnau*              | *hastini*                   |
| Pāli     | abl | *devasmā*           | *bhikkhusmā*           | *aggismā*            | *hatthismā*                 |
|          | loc | *devasmiṃ*          | *bhikkhusmiṃ*          | *aggismiṃ*           | *hatthismiṃ*                |

nonpronominal masculine and neuter nominals belonging to the *a*-stem, *u*-stem, *i*-stem and *in*-stem declensions; the examples in Table 14.9 illustrate.[7] Superficially, this seems like an unexpected development, since the pronominal declensions are the most irregular declensions in Old Indic. Why, then, should one of their irregularities – the morphomic *sm*-stem pattern in certain oblique cases – spread so widely?

The answer is surely tied to the high frequency of the demonstrative, interrogative and relative pronouns. Indeed, the spread of the genitive singular suffix *-ssa* in Table 14.6 is at least partly attributable to the fact that *-sya* is a feature of the pronominal declension (e.g. masc./neut. *tasya* 'of that'), though it is also a feature of ordinary *a*-stem nouns, which are themselves extremely frequent. It is plausible to assume that in the prehistory of Pāli, the similarity between the pronominal declensions and the nonpronominal *a*-stem declension caused the analogical extension of the morphomic *sm*-stem pattern from the former to the latter, which then lent its added weight to an even wider extension of the *sm*-stem pattern to the *u*-, *i*- and *in*-stem declensions.

As the Pāli cases suggest, the paradigm-linkage hypothesis affords a natural framework for identifying the pressures that guide morphological change, including the impulse toward content–form isomorphism and the (possibly conflicting) promotion of highly frequent patterns.

---

7 Pāli does, however, exhibit some dialect variation in the genitive singular. In some varieties, the *in*-stem expression of the genitive singular (the suffixation of *-as* to a stem in *n*) spreads to the *i*- and *u*-stem declensions; such varieties preserve *hatthino* (the expected phonological development of the genitive singular form *hastinas* è lephant' in Pāli) and exhibit such innovative genitive singulars as *bhikkhuno* ɦonk' and *aggino* ɦ re.'

### *14.4  General conclusion*

Inflectional paradigms are real. A word's inflectional paradigm differs according to whether it is structured according to content or according to form. While
canonically isomorphic, the relation between content paradigms and form paradigms may exhibit any of a wide variety of mismatches. A lexeme's content
paradigm is the interface of its inflection with its syntax and semantics; the
realization of a lexeme's word forms is mediated by the form paradigms of its
stems. The definition of a language's inflectional morphology must therefore
define both its patterns of inflectional exponence (modeled in the paradigm-
linkage theory as a mapping from form cells to realized cells) and its patterns
of content–form correspondence (modeled in the paradigm-linkage theory as a
mapping from content cells to their form correspondents, the form cells whose
realization they share).

# References

Ackerman, Farrell, James P. Blevins and Robert Malouf. 2009. Parts and wholes: Implicative patterns in inflectional paradigms. In James P. Blevins and Juliette Blevins (eds.), *Analogy in grammar: Form and acquisition*, 54–82. Oxford University Press.

Ackerman, Farrell and Gregory Stump. 2004. Paradigms and periphrastic expression: A study in realization-based lexicalism. In Louisa Sadler and Andrew Spencer (eds.), *Projecting Morphology*, 111–57. Stanford: CSLI Publications.

Ackerman, Farrell, Gregory Stump and Gert Webelhuth. 2011. Lexicalism, periphrasis and implicative morphology. In B. Borsley and K. Börjars (eds.), *Non-transformational theories of grammar*, 325–58. Oxford: Blackwell.

Alcoba, Santiago. 1999. La flexión verbal. In Ignacio Bosque Muñoz and Violeta Demonte Barreto (eds.), *Gramática descriptiva de la lengua española: Entre la oración y el discurso*, vol. III: *Morfología*, 4915–91. Madrid: Editorial Espasa Calpe.

Anderson, Stephen R. 1985. Inflectional morphology. In Timothy Shopen (ed.), *Language typology and syntactic description*, vol. III, 150–201. Cambridge University Press.

1992. *A-morphous morphology*. Cambridge University Press.

2005. *Aspects of the theory of clitics*. Oxford University Press.

2008. Phonologically conditioned allomorphy in Surmiran (Rumantsch). *Word Structure* 1: 109–34.

Aronoff, Mark. 1994. *Morphology by itself: Stems and inflectional classes*. Cambridge, MA, and London: MIT Press.

Ashton, E. O. 1944. *Swahili grammar*. Essex: Longman.

Asudeh, Ash, and Ewan Klein. 2002. Shape conditions and phonological context. In Frank van Eynde, Lars Hellan and Dorothee Beermann (eds.), *Proceedings of the 8th International HPSG Conference, Norwegian University of Science and Technology (August 3–5, 2001)*, 20–30. Stanford: CSLI Publications.

Baayen, R. Harald and Robert Schreuder (eds.). 2003. *Morphological structure in language processing*. Berlin: Mouton de Gruyter.

Baerman, Matthew. 2007. Morphological reversals. *Journal of Linguistics* 43: 33–61.

Baerman, Matthew, Dunstan Brown and Greville G. Corbett. 2005. *The syntax–morphology interface: A study of syncretism*. Cambridge University Press.

Baerman, Matthew, Greville G. Corbett and Dunstan Brown (eds.). 2010. *Defective paradigms: Missing forms and what they tell us.* Proceedings of the British Academy 163. Oxford University Press.

Baerman, Matthew, Greville G. Corbett, Dunstan Brown, and Andrew Hippisley (eds.). 2007. *Deponency and morphological mismatches.* Proceedings of the British Academy 145. Oxford University Press.

Bane, Max. 2008. Quantifying and measuring morphological complexity. In Charles B. Chang and Hannah J. Haynie (eds.), *Proceedings of the 26th West Coast Conference on Formal Linguistics*, 69–76. Somerville, MA: Cascadilla Proceedings Project.

Bauer, Laurie. 2000. Word. In Booij et al. (eds.), *Morphologie*, 247–57.

Beesley, Kenneth R. and Lauri Karttunen. 2003. *Finite state morphology.* Stanford: CSLI Publications.

Bittner, Dagmar, Wolfgang U. Dressler and Marianne Kilani-Schoch (eds.). 2003. *Development of verb inflection in first language acquisition.* Studies on Language Acquisition. Berlin: Mouton de Gruyter.

Blevins, James. 2000. Stems and paradigms. Manuscript.

   2006. Word-based morphology. *Journal of Linguistics* 42: 531–73.

Bloch, Bernard. 1947. English verb inflection. *Language* 23: 399–418.

Bloomfield, Leonard. 1933. *Language.* New York: Henry Holt.

Bobaljik, Jonathan. 2002. Syncretism without paradigms: Remarks on Williams 1981, 1994. *Yearbook of Morphology 2001*, 53–85.

Bonami, Olivier and Gert Webelhuth. 2012. The phrase-structural diversity of periphrasis: A lexicalist account. In M. Chumakina et G. Corbett (eds.), *Periphrasis: The role of syntax and morphology in paradigms*, 141–67. London: British Academy; Oxford: Oxford University Press.

Bonami, Olivier and Gilles Boyé. 2007. French pronominal clitics and the design of Paradigm Function Morphology. In Geert Booij et al. (eds.), *On-line proceedings of the Fifth Mediterranean Morphology Meeting (MMM5)*, Fréjus, September 15–18, 2005. University of Bologna.

   2008. Paradigm shape is morphomic in Nepali. Paper presented at the 13th International Morphology Meeting, Vienna.

   2010. Opaque paradigms, transparent forms in Nepali conjugation. Paper presented at the Workshop on Theoretical Morphology 5, June 25–26, 2010, Lutherstadt Wittenberg, Germany.

Bonami, Olivier, Gilles Boyé and Fabiola Henri. 2011. Measuring inflectional complexity: French and Mauritian. Paper presented at the Workshop on Quantitative Measures in Morphology and Morphological Development, Center for Human Development, UC San Diego, January 15–16, 2011.

Bonet, Eulàlia. 1991. Morphology after syntax: Pronominal clitics in Romance. Ph.D. dissertation, MIT.

Booij, Geert. 1994. Against split morphology. *Yearbook of Morphology 1993*, 27–50.

   1996. Inherent versus contextual inflection and the Split Morphology Hypothesis. *Yearbook of Morphology 1995*, 1–16.

   2000. Inflection and derivation. In Booij et al. (eds.), *Morphologie*, 360–69.

Booij, Geert, Christian Lehmann and Joachim Mugdan (eds.) 2000. *Morphologie: Ein internationales Handbuch zur Flexion und Wortbildung / Morphology: An international handbook on inflection and word formation*, vol. I. Berlin and New York: Walter de Gruyter.

Börjars, Kersti, Nigel Vincent and Carol Chapman. 1997. Paradigms, periphrases and pronominal inflection: A feature-based account. *Yearbook of Morphology 1996*, 155–180.

Boyé, Gilles. 2000. Problèmes de morpho-phonologie verbale en français, en espagnol et en italien. Ph.D. dissertation, University of Paris VII.

Brown, Dunstan. 2007. Peripheral functions and overdifferentiation: The Russian second locative. *Russian Linguistics* 31/1: 61–76.

Brown, Dunstan, and Andrew Hippisley. 2012. *Network Morphology: A defaults-based theory of word structure*. Cambridge University Press.

Brown, Dunstan and Marina Chumakina. 2013. What there might be and what there is: An introduction to canonical typology. In Brown, Chumakina and Corbett (eds.), *Canonical morphology and syntax*, 1–19.

Brown, Dunstan, Marina Chumakina and Greville G. Corbett (eds.). 2013. *Canonical morphology and syntax*. Oxford University Press.

Bybee, Joan. 1985. *Morphology: A study of the relation between meaning and form*. Amsterdam: Benjamins.

Carstairs, Andrew. 1987. *Allomorphy in inflexion*. London: Croom Helm.

1988. Some implications of phonologically conditioned suppletion. *Yearbook of Morphology 1988*, 67–94.

Carstairs-McCarthy, Andrew. 2000. Inflection classes. In Booij et al. (eds.), *Morphologie*, 630–37.

Chumakina, Marina and Greville G. Corbett (eds.). 2013. *Periphrasis: The role of syntax and morphology in paradigms*. Oxford University Press.

Clahsen, H. 1999. Lexical entries and rules of language: A multidisciplinary study of German inflection. *Behavioral and Brain Sciences* 22: 991–1013.

Corbett, Greville G. 2005. The canonical approach in typology. In Zygmunt Frajzyngier, Adam Hodges and David S. Rood (eds.), *Linguistic diversity and language theories*, Studies in Language Companion Series 72, 25–49. Amsterdam: John Benjamins.

2007. Canonical typology, suppletion and possible words. *Language* 83/1: 8–42.

2009. Canonical inflectional classes. In Fabio Montermini, Gilles Boyé and Jesse Tseng (eds.), *Selected proceedings of the 6th Décembrettes*, 1–11. Somerville, MA: Cascadilla Proceedings Project.

2012. *Features*. Cambridge University Press.

Corbett, Greville G. and Matthew Baerman. 2006. Prolegomena to a typology of morphological features. *Morphology* 16/2: 231–46.

Cruschina, Silvio, Martin Maiden, and John Charles Smith (eds.). 2013. *The boundaries of pure morphology: Diachronic and synchronic perspectives*. Oxford University Press.

Danielsen, Swintha. 2007. *Baure: An Arawak language of Bolivia*. Leiden: CNWS Publications.

Danielsen, Swintha and Tania Granadillo. 2008. Agreement in two Arawak languages: Baure and Kurripako. In Mark Donohue and Søren Wichmann (eds.), *The typology of semantic alignment*, 396–411. Oxford and New York: Oxford University Press.

Di Sciullo, Anna Maria and Edwin Williams. 1987. *On the definition of word.* Cambridge, MA: MIT Press.

Faarlund, Jan Terje. 2004. *The syntax of Old Norse.* Oxford and New York: Oxford University Press.

Fertig, David L. 2013. *Analogy and morphological change.* Edinburgh University Press.

Fuß, Eric. 2005. *The rise of agreement: A formal approach to the syntax and grammaticalization of verbal inflection.* Amsterdam: Benjamins.

Gardani, Francesco. 2013. *Dynamics of morphological productivity: The evolution of noun classes from Latin to Italian.* Leiden: Brill.

2014. Emergence and decay of inflectional class systems – An evolutionary perspective. Paper presented at the 16th International Morphology Meeting, Budapest, Hungary.

Gazdar, Gerald, Ewan Klein, Geoffrey Pullum and Ivan Sag. 1985. *Generalized phrase structure grammar.* Cambridge, MA: Harvard University Press.

Gazdar, Gerald, Geoffrey K. Pullum and Ivan A. Sag. 1982. Auxiliaries and related phenomena in a restrictive theory of grammar. *Language* 58: 591–638.

Gazdar, Gerald, Geoffrey K. Pullum, Robert Carpenter, Ewan Klein, Thomas E. Hukari and Robert D. Levine. 1988. Category structures. *Computational Linguistics* 14: 1–19.

Geiger, Wilhelm. 1994. *A Pāli Grammar,* trans. Batakrishna Ghosh, rev. and ed. K. R. Norman. Oxford: Pali Text Society.

Gerner, Matthias. 2014. Noncompositional scopal morphology in Yi. *Morphology* 24: 1–24.

Göksel, A. and C. Kerslake. 2005. *Turkish: A comprehensive grammar.* London and New York: Routledge.

Greenberg, Joseph H. 1960. A quantitative approach to the morphological typology of language. *International Journal of American Linguistics* 26: 178–94.

1966. *Language universals, with special reference to feature hierarchies.* The Hague: Mouton.

Grierson, George A. 1899. On the Kāçmīrī verb. *Journal of the Asiatic Society of Bengal* 68/1: 1–92.

1911. *A manual of the Kāshmīrī language.* Oxford: Clarendon Press.

Haegeman, Liliane. 1992. *Theory and description in generative syntax: A case study in West Flemish.* Cambridge University Press.

Haiman, John. 1980. *Hua: A Papuan language of the eastern highlands of New Guinea.* Amsterdam: John Benjamins.

Halle, Morris and Alec Marantz. 1993. Distributed Morphology and the pieces of inflection. In Kenneth Hale and Samuel J. Keyser (eds.), *The view from Building 20: Linguistic essays in honor of Sylvain Bromberger,* 111–76. Cambridge, MA: MIT Press.

Halpern, Aaron. 1995. *On the placement and morphology of clitics.* Stanford: CSLI Publications.

Harley, Heidi and Rolf Noyer. 1999. State-of-the-article: Distributed Morphology. *GLOT International* 4/4: 3–9.

Harris, Zellig S. 1942. Morpheme alternants in linguistic analysis. *Language* 18: 169–80.

Hockett, Charles F. 1947. Problems of morphemic analysis. *Language* 23: 321–43.

Humboldt, Wilhelm von. 1836. *Über die Verschiedenheit des menschlichen Sprachbaues und ihren Einfluss auf die geistige Entwickelung des Menschengeschlechts.* Berlin: F. Dümmler.

Hyman, Larry. 2003. Suffix ordering in Bantu: A morphocentric approach. *Yearbook of morphology 2002*, 245–81.

Jakobson, Roman. 1984. Morphological observations on Slavic declension (the structure of Russian case forms). In Linda R. Waugh and Morris Halle (eds.), *Roman Jakobson: Russian and Slavic Grammar, Studies 1931–1981*, 105–33. Berlin: Mouton. [Translation of Roman Jakobson, Morfologičeskie nabljudenija nad slavjanskim skloneniem (sostav russkix padežnyx form). In *American contributions to the Fourth International Congress of Slavicists, Moscow, September 1958*, 127–56. The Hague: Mouton, 1958.]

Juola, Patrick. 1998. Measuring linguistic complexity: The morphological tier. *Journal of Quantitative Linguistics* 5/3: 206–13.

Kasper, Robert T. and William C. Rounds. 1986. A logical semantics for feature structures. In *Proceedings of the 24th annual meeting of the Association for Computational Linguistics*, 257–266. Stroudsburg, PA: Association for Computational Linguistics.

Keine, Stefan. 2012. How complex are complex words? Evidence from linearization. *Lingua* 122: 1268–81.

Kogian, S. L. 1949. *Armenian grammar (west dialect)*. Vienna: Mechitharist Press.

Lieber, Rochelle. 1992. *Deconstructing morphology*. University of Chicago Press.

Maiden, Martin. 2005. Morphological autonomy and diachrony. *Yearbook of Morphology 2004*, 137–75.

Maiden, Martin, John Charles Smith, Maria Goldbach and Marc-Olivier Hinzelin (eds.). 2011. *Morphological autonomy: Perspectives from romance inflectional morphology*. Oxford University Press.

Matthews, P. H. 1972. *Inflectional morphology: A theoretical study based on aspects of Latin verb conjugation*. Cambridge University Press.

1991. *Morphology*. 2nd edn. Cambridge University Press.

McCreight, Katherine and Catherine V. Chvany. 1991. Geometric representation of paradigms in a modular theory of grammar. In Plank (ed.), *Paradigms*, 91–111.

Milin, Petar, Victor Kuperman, Aleksandar Kostić and R. Harald Baayen. 2009. Words and paradigms bit by bit: An information-theoretic approach to the processing of paradigmatic structure in inflection and derivation. In James P. Blevins and Juliette Blevins (eds.), *Analogy in grammar: Form and acquisition*, 214–52. Oxford University Press.

Miller, Philip. 1992. *Clitics and constituents in phrase structure grammar*. New York: Garland.

Montague, Richard. 1973. The proper treatment of quantification in ordinary English. In Jaakko Hintikka, Julius Moravcsik and Patrick Suppes (eds.), *Approaches to natural language*, 221–42. Dordrecht: Reidel. [Repr. in Richmond Thomason (ed.), Formal philosophy: Selected papers by Richard Montague. New Haven, CT: Yale University Press, 1974.]

Moscoso del Prado Martín, Fermín, Aleksandar Kostic and R. Harald Baayen. 2004. Putting the bits together: An information-theoretical perspective on morphological processing. *Cognition* 94/1: 1–18.

Müller, Gereon. 2002. Remarks on nominal inflection in German. In Ingrid Kaufmann and Barbara Stiebels (eds.), *More than words: A Festschrift for Dieter Wunderlich*, 113–45. Berlin: AkademieVerlag.

2007. Extended exponence by enrichment: Argument encoding in German, Archi, and Timucua. *University of Pennsylvania Working Papers in Linguistics* 13/1: 253–66.

2013. Approaches to deponency. *Language and Linguistics Compass* 7/6: 351–69.

Nesset, Tore and Laura A. Janda. 2010. Paradigm structure: Evidence from Russian suffix shift. *Cognitive Linguistics* 21/4: 699–725.

Nikolaeva, Irina. 1999. *Ostyak*. Munich: LINCOM Europa.

Noyer, Robert Rolf. 1992. Features, positions and affixes in autonomous morphological structure. Ph.D. dissertation, MIT.

O'Neill, Paul. 2011. The notion of the morphome. In Maiden et al. (eds.), *Morphological Autonomy*, 70–94.

2013. The morphome and morphosyntactic/semantic features. In Cruschina et al. (eds.), *Boundaries of pure morphology*, 221–46.

2014. The morphome in constructive and abstractive theories of morphology. *Morphology* 24: 25–70.

Partee, Barbara. 1977. John is easy to please. In A. Zampolli (ed.), *Linguistic structures processing*, 281–312. Amsterdam: North-Holland Publishing.

Paster, Mary. 2006. Phonological conditions on affixation. Ph.D. dissertation, University of California, Berkeley.

2009. Explaining phonological conditions on affixation: Evidence from suppletive allomorphy and affix ordering.*Word Structure* 2/1: 18–37.

2010. The verbal morphology and phonology of Asante Twi. *Studies in African Linguistics* 39/1: 77–120.

2015. Phonologically conditioned suppletive allomorphy: Cross-linguistic results and theoretical consequences. In Eulàlia Bonet, Maria-Rosa Lloret and Joan Mascaro (eds.), *Understanding allomorphy: Perspectives from OT*. London: Equinox.

Perniola, Vito. 1997. *Pali grammar*. Oxford: Pali Text Society.

Pinker, Steven. 1999. *Words and rules*. New York: Basic Books.

Pirrelli, Vito, Marcello Ferro and Claudia Marzi. 2015. Computational complexity of abstractive morphology. In Matthew Baerman, Dunstan Brown and Greville G. Corbett (eds.), *Understanding and measuring morphological complexity*, 141–66. Oxford University Press.

Plank, Frans (ed.). 1990. *Paradigms: The economy of inflection*. Berlin and New York: Mouton de Gruyter.

Round, Erich R. 2009. Kayardild morphology, phonology and morphosyntax. Ph.D dissertation, Yale University.

2013. *Kayardild morphology and syntax*. Oxford University Press.

Sadler, Louisa and Andrew Spencer. 2001. Syntax as an exponent of morphological features. *Yearbook of Morphology 2000*, 71–96.

Sapir, Edward. 1921. *Language: An introduction to the study of speech*. New York: Harcourt, Brace and Co.

Schlegel, Friedrich von. 1808. *Über die Sprache und Weisheit der Indier: Ein Beitrag zur Begründung der Alterthumskunde*. Heidelberg: Mohr und Zimmer.

Selkirk, Elisabeth O. 1982. *The syntax of Words*. Cambridge, MA: MIT Press.

Shukla, Shaligram. 1981. *Bhojpuri grammar*. Washington, DC: Georgetown University Press.

Soukka, Maria. 2000. *A descriptive grammar of Noon: A Cangin language of Senegal*. Munich: LINCOM Europa.

Spencer, Andrew. 2003. Periphrastic paradigms in Bulgarian. In Uwe Junghanns and Luka Szucsich (eds.), *Syntactic structures and morphological information*, 249–82. Berlin and New York: Mouton de Gruyter.

2013. *Lexical relatedness*. Oxford University Press.

Spencer, Andrew and Ana R. Luís. 2012. *Clitics: An introduction*. Cambridge University Press.

Spencer, Andrew and Gregory Stump. 2013. Hungarian pronominal case and the dichotomy of content and form in inflectional morphology. *Natural Language and Linguistic Theory* 31: 1207–48.

Stemberger, Joseph Paul and Brian MacWhinney. 1988. Are inflected forms stored in the lexicon? In Michael T. Hammond and Michael P. Noonan (eds.), *Theoretical morphology: Approaches in modern linguistics*, 101–16. San Diego: Academic Press.

Stewart, Tom and Gregory Stump. 2007. Paradigm Function Morphology and the morphology/syntax interface. In Gillian Ramchand and Charles Reiss (eds.), *The Oxford handbook of linguistic interfaces*, 383–421. Oxford University Press.

Stump, Gregory. 1985. *The semantic variability of absolute constructions*. Dordrecht: Reidel.

1988. Nonlocal spirantization in Breton. *Journal of Linguistics* 24: 457–81.

1993a. On rules of referral. *Language* 69: 449–79. [Repr. in Francis Katamba (ed.), *Morphology: Critical concepts in linguistics*, vol. II: Primes, phenomena and processes, 94–129. London: Routledge, 2004.]

1993b. Position classes and morphological theory. *Yearbook of Morphology 1992*, 129–80.

1998. Inflection. In Andrew Spencer and Arnold M. Zwicky (eds.), *The handbook of morphology*, 13–43. Oxford and Malden, MA: Blackwell.

2001. *Inflectional morphology: A theory of paradigm structure*. Cambridge University Press.

2002. Morphological and syntactic paradigms: Arguments for a theory of paradigm linkage. *Yearbook of Morphology 2001*, 147–80.

2006. Heteroclisis and paradigm linkage. *Language* 82: 279–322.

2007. A noncanonical pattern of deponency and its theoretical implications. In Baerman et al. (eds.), *Deponency and morphological mismatches*, 71–95.

2009. Cells and paradigms in inflectional semantics. In Erhard Hinrichs and John Nerbonne (eds.), *Theory and evidence in semantics*, 215–33. Stanford: CSLI Publications.

2010. Interactions between defectiveness and syncretism. In Baerman et al. (eds.), *Defective paradigms*, 181–210.

2012. The formal and functional architecture of inflectional morphology. In Angela Ralli, Geert Booij, Sergio Scalise and Athanasios Karasimos (eds.), *Morphology and the Architecture of Grammar: On-line Proceedings of the Eighth Mediterranean Morphology Meeting (MMM8), Cagliari, Italy, 14–17 September 2011*, 254–70. https://geertbooij.files.wordpress.com/2014/02/mmm8_proceedings.pdf.

2014a. Morphosyntactic property sets at the interface of inflectional morphology, syntax and semantics. *Lingvisticæ Investigationes* 37/2 [special issue: *Morphology and its interfaces – Syntax, semantics and the lexicon*, ed. Dany Amiot, Delphine Tribout, Natalia Grabar, Cédric Patin and Fayssal Tayalati], 290–305.

2014b. Polyfunctionality and inflectional economy. *Linguistic Issues in Language Technology* 11/3 [special issue: *Theoretical and computational morphology: New trends and synergies*, ed. Bruno Cartoni, Delphine Bernhard and Delphine Tribout], 73–93. Stanford: CSLI Publications.

2014c. Polyfunctionality and the variety of inflectional exponence relations. Paper presented at the 16th International Morphology Meeting, May 29 – June 1, 2014, Budapest, Hungary.

2015. The interface of semantic interpretation and inflectional realization. In Laurie Bauer, Lívia Körtvélyessy and Pavol Štekauer (eds.), *Semantics of complex words*, 27–45. Dordrecht: Springer.

To appear A. Morphomic categories and the realization of morphosyntactic properties. Forthcoming in Ana Luís and Ricardo Bermudez-Otero (eds.), *The morphome debate*. Oxford University Press.

To appear B. Paradigms at the interface of a lexeme's syntax and semantics with its inflectional morphology. Forthcoming in Daniel Siddiqi and Heidi Harley (eds.), *Morphological metatheory*.

Stump, Gregory and Raphael A. Finkel. 2013. *Morphological typology: From word to paradigm*. Cambridge University Press.

Thornton, Anna M. 2012. Reduction and maintenance of overabundance: A case study on Italian verb paradigms. *Word Structure* 5/2: 183–207.

Trommer, Jochen. 2012. Introduction. In Jochen Trommer (ed.), *The morphology and phonology of exponence*, 1–7. Oxford University Press.

Tucker, A. N. 1940. *The Eastern Sudanic languages*. London, New York and Toronto: Oxford University Press, for the International Institute of African Languages and Cultures.

Walther, Géraldine. 2013. Sur la canonicité en morphologie: Perspective empirique, formelle et computationnelle. Ph.D. dissertation, Université Paris Diderot.

Weiss, Helmut. 2005. Inflected complementizers in continental West Germanic dialects. *Zeitschrift für Dialektologie und Linguistik*, 72/2: 148–66.

Whitney, William Dwight. 1885. *The roots, verb-forms, and primary derivatives of the Sanskrit language*. Leipzig: Breitkopf & Härtel.

1889. *Sanskrit grammar*. 2nd edn. Cambridge, MA: Harvard University Press.

Wolf, Matthew. 2013. Candidate chains, unfaithful spell-out, and outwards-looking phonologically-conditioned allomorphy. *Morphology* 23: 145–78.

Wunderlich, Dieter. 2004. Is there any need for the concept of directional syncretism? In Gereon Müller, Lutz Gunkel and Gisela Zifonun (eds.), *Explorations in nominal inflection*, 373–95. Berlin: Mouton de Gruyter.

Xu, Zheng, Mark Aronoff and Frank Anshen. 2007. Deponency in Latin. In Baerman et al. (eds.), *Deponency and morphological mismatches*, 127–43.

Zwicky, Arnold M. 1985. How to describe inflection. In Mary Niepokuj, Mary Van Clay, Vassiliki Nikiforidou and Deborah Feder (eds.), *Proceedings of the Eleventh*

*Annual Meeting of the Berkeley Linguistics Society*, 372–386. Berkeley Linguistics Society.

1987. Suppressing the Z's. *Journal of Linguistics* 23/1: 133–48.

1990. Syntactic representations and phonological shapes. In Sharon Inkelas and Draga Zec (eds.), *The phonology–syntax connection*, 379–97. University of Chicago Press.

1992. Some choices in the theory of morphology. In Robert Levine (ed.), *Formal grammar: Theory and implementation*, 327–71. Vancouver: University of British Columbia.

Zwicky, Arnold M. and Geoffrey K. Pullum. 1983. Cliticization vs. inflection: English *n't*. *Language* 59/3: 502–13.

# Index

For EU product safety concerns, contact us at Calle de José Abascal, 56–1°,
28003 Madrid, Spain or eugpsr@cambridge.org.